ASSASSINISTAS

ASSASSINISTAS

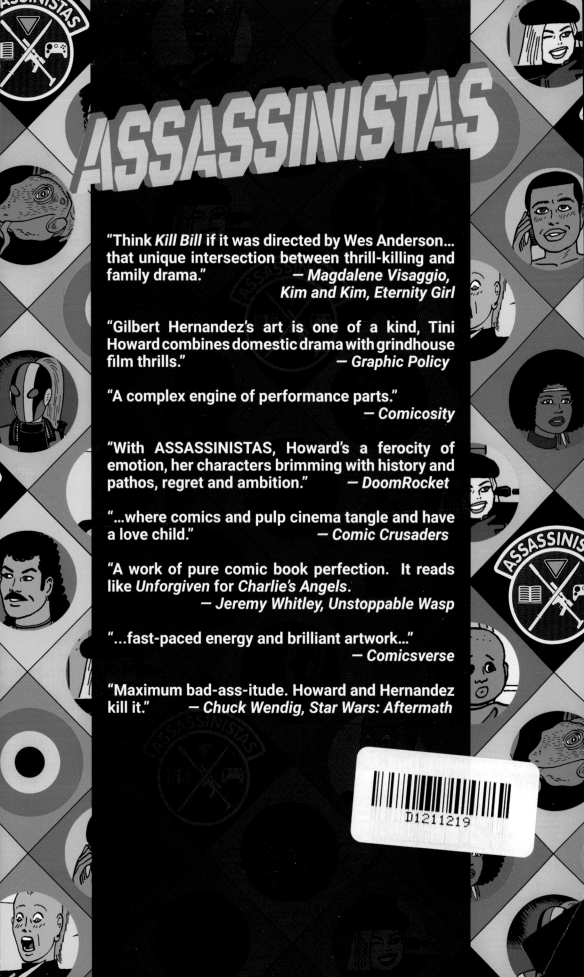

ASSASSINISTAS

"Think *Kill Bill* if it was directed by Wes Anderson... that unique intersection between thrill-killing and family drama."
— *Magdalene Visaggio, Kim and Kim, Eternity Girl*

"Gilbert Hernandez's art is one of a kind, Tini Howard combines domestic drama with grindhouse film thrills."
— *Graphic Policy*

"A complex engine of performance parts."
— *Comicosity*

"With ASSASSINISTAS, Howard's a ferocity of emotion, her characters brimming with history and pathos, regret and ambition."
— *DoomRocket*

"...where comics and pulp cinema tangle and have a love child."
— *Comic Crusaders*

"A work of pure comic book perfection. It reads like *Unforgiven* for *Charlie's Angels*.
— *Jeremy Whitley, Unstoppable Wasp*

"...fast-paced energy and brilliant artwork..."
— *Comicsverse*

"Maximum bad-ass-itude. Howard and Hernandez kill it."
— *Chuck Wendig, Star Wars: Aftermath*

Written by **Tini Howard**
Art by **Gilbert Hernandez**

Lettering by **Aditya Bidikar**
Color by **Rob Davis**
Flats by **Robin Henley**

Editorial Assistance by **Chase Marotz**
Edited by **Shelly Bond**
Logo and Publication Design by **Philip Bond**

ASSASSINISTAS is created by Howard & Hernandez

BLACK CROWN HQ
Shelly Bond, Editor • **Chase Marotz**, Editorial Assistant • **Aditya Bidikar**, Letterer
Arlene Lo, Proofreader • **Kahlil Schweitzer**, Marketing Maestro • **Keith Davidsen,** Publicity
Philip Bond, logo, publication design and general dogsbody • **Greg Goldstein,** President & Publisher

BLACK CROWN is a fully functioning curation operation based in Los Angeles by way of IDW Publishing.
Accept No Substitutes!

For international rights, contact licensing@idwpublishing.com

ISBN: 978-1-68405-271-4

21 20 19 18   1 2 3 4

Greg Goldstein, President & Publisher • **John Barber**, Editor-In-Chief • **Robbie Robbins**, EVP/Sr. Art Director • **Cara Morrison**, Chief Financial Officer • **Matthew Ruzicka,**
Chief Accounting Officer • **Anita Frazier**, SVP of Sales and Marketing • **David Hedgecock**, Associate Publisher • **Jerry Bennington**, VP of New Product Development •
Lorelei Bunjes, VP of Digital Services • **Justin Eisinger**, Editorial Director, Graphic Novels and Collections • **Eric Moss**, Sr. Director, Licensing & Business Development

Ted Adams, Founder & CEO of IDW Media Holdings

www.IDWPUBLISHING.com

Facebook: facebook.com/idwpublishing • Twitter: @idwpublishing • YouTube: youtube.com/idwpublishing
Tumblr: tumblr.idwpublishing.com • Instagram: instagram.com/idwpublishing

INISTAS

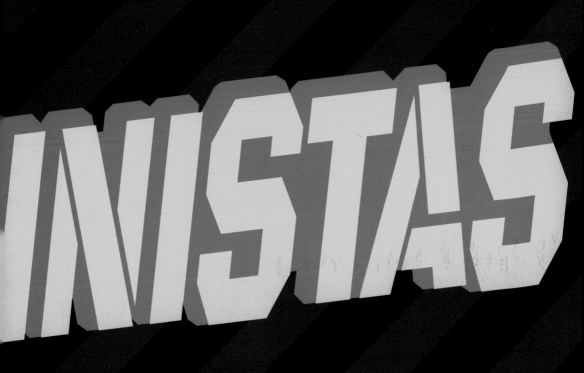

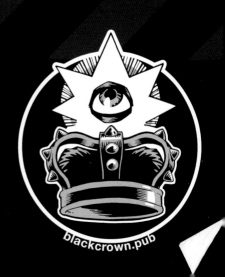

blackcrown.pub

"My mom is an assassin. Well, she used to be. And now she is again, apparently."

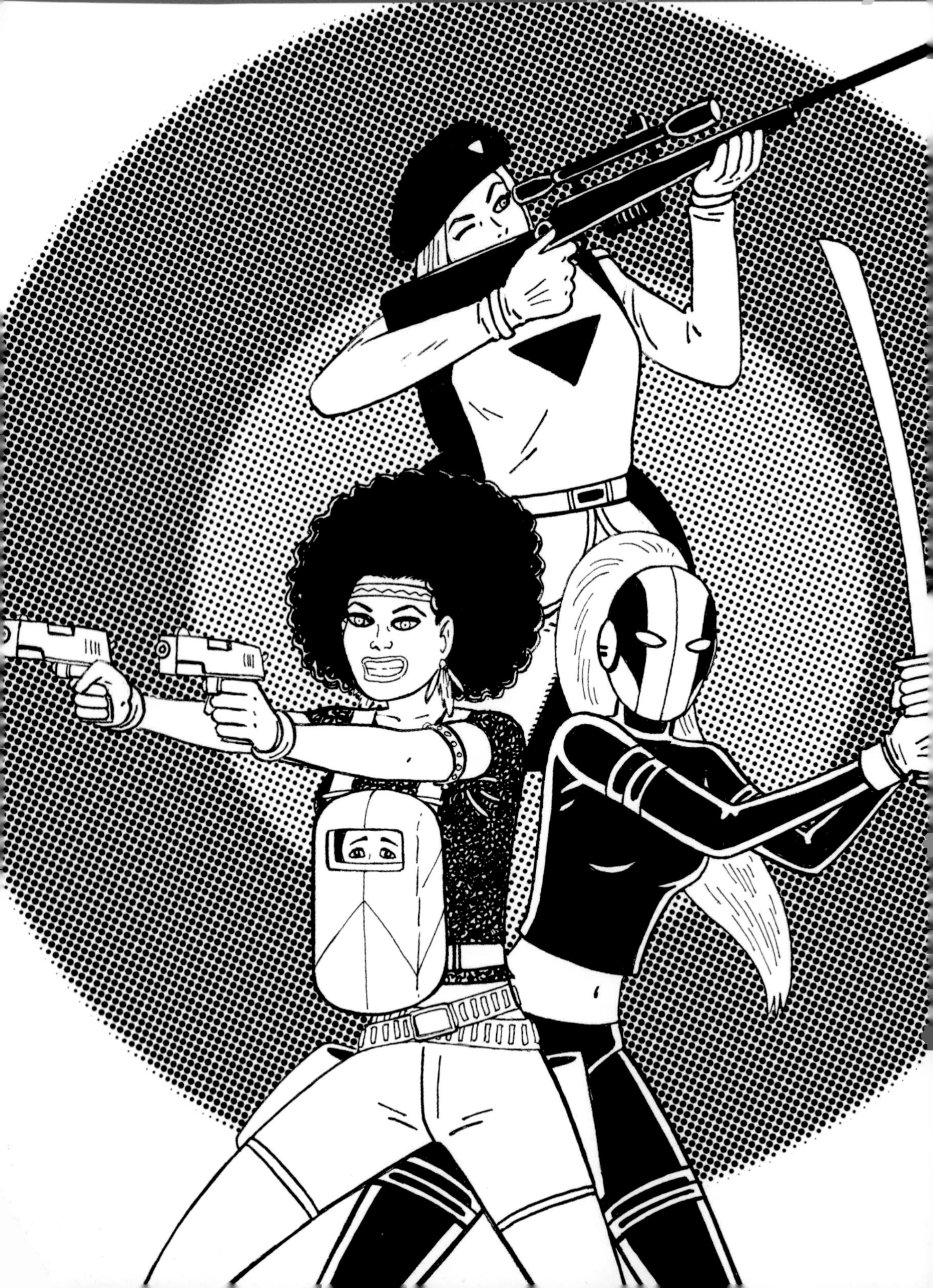

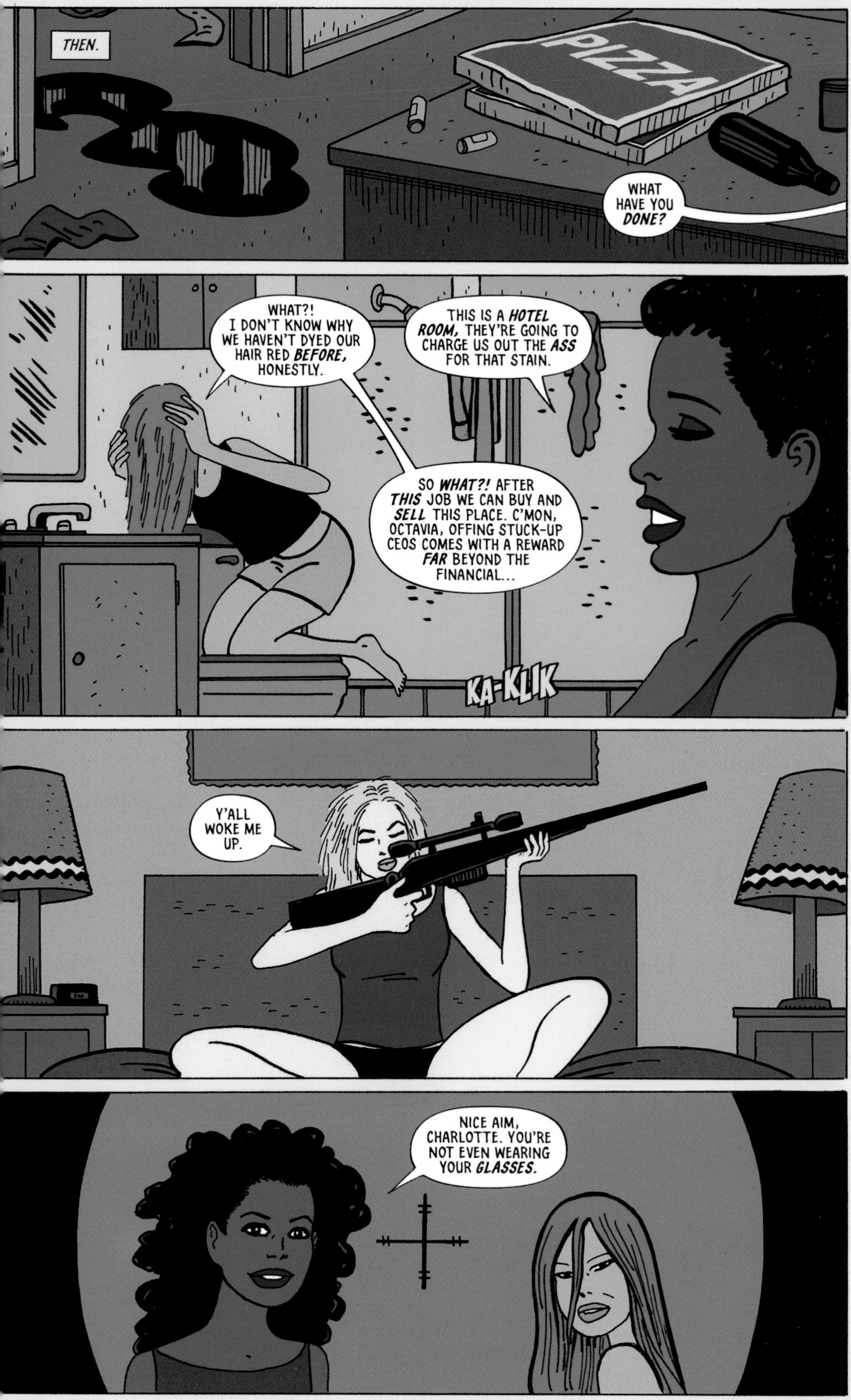
THEN.
WHAT HAVE YOU DONE?
WHAT?! I DON'T KNOW WHY WE HAVEN'T DYED OUR HAIR RED BEFORE, HONESTLY.
THIS IS A HOTEL ROOM, THEY'RE GOING TO CHARGE US OUT THE ASS FOR THAT STAIN.
SO WHAT?! AFTER THIS JOB WE CAN BUY AND SELL THIS PLACE. C'MON, OCTAVIA, OFFING STUCK-UP CEOS COMES WITH A REWARD FAR BEYOND THE FINANCIAL...
KA-KLIK
Y'ALL WOKE ME UP.
NICE AIM, CHARLOTTE. YOU'RE NOT EVEN WEARING YOUR GLASSES.

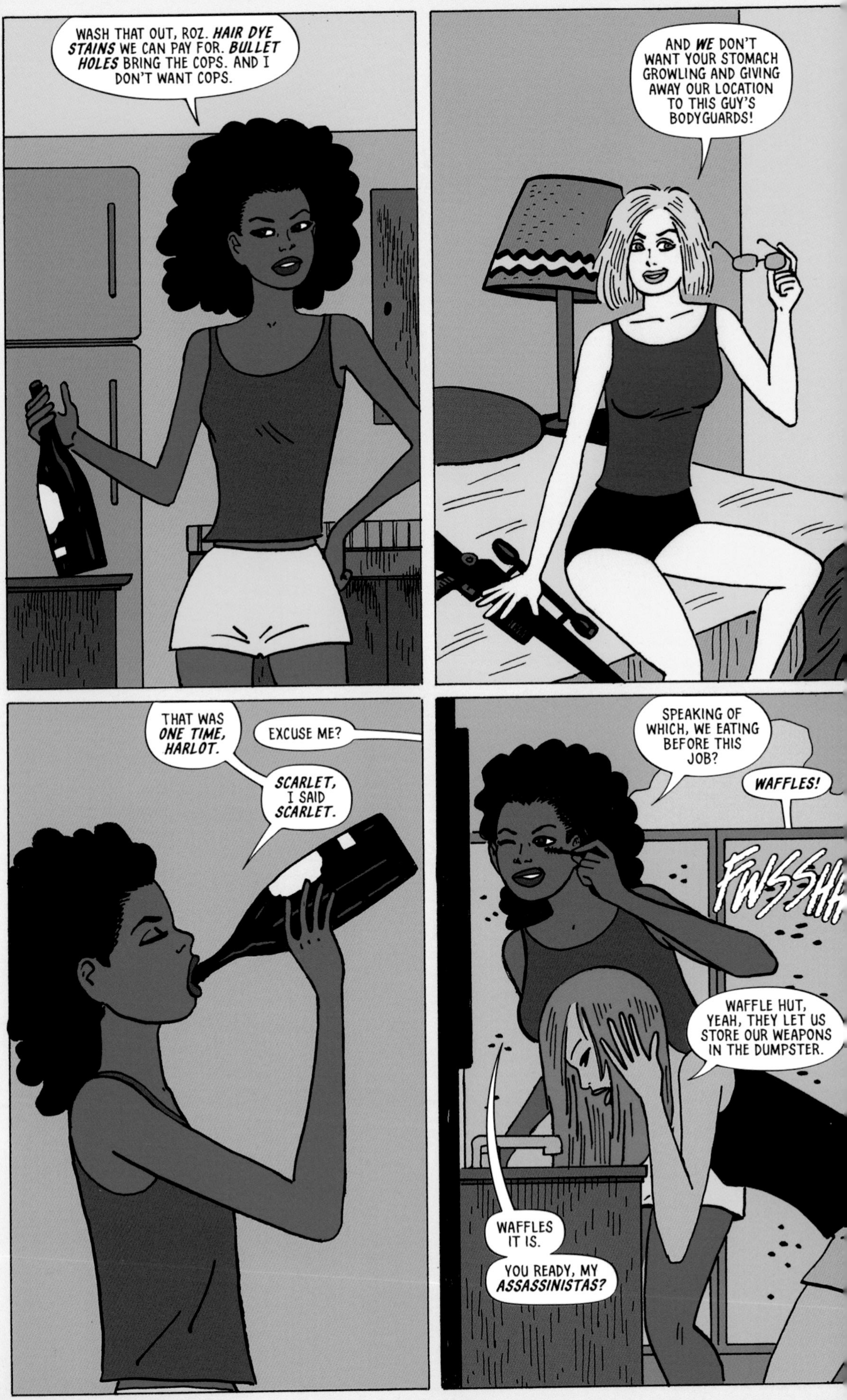
WASH THAT OUT, ROZ. HAIR DYE STAINS WE CAN PAY FOR. BULLET HOLES BRING THE COPS. AND I DON'T WANT COPS.
AND WE DON'T WANT YOUR STOMACH GROWLING AND GIVING AWAY OUR LOCATION TO THIS GUY'S BODYGUARDS!
THAT WAS ONE TIME, HARLOT.
EXCUSE ME?
SCARLET, I SAID SCARLET.
SPEAKING OF WHICH, WE EATING BEFORE THIS JOB?
WAFFLES!
FWSSHH
WAFFLE HUT, YEAH, THEY LET US STORE OUR WEAPONS IN THE DUMPSTER.
WAFFLES IT IS.
YOU READY, MY ASSASSINISTAS?

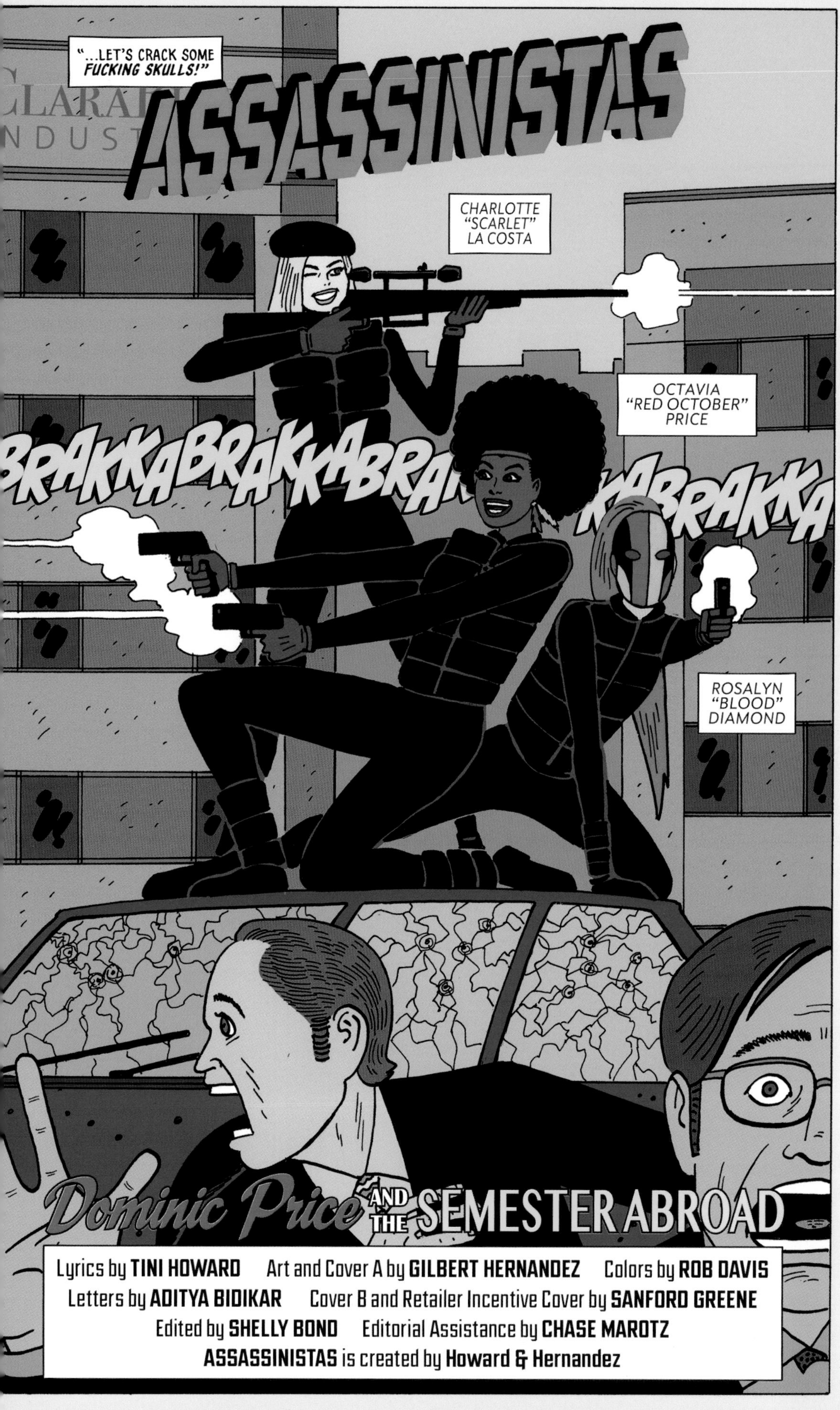
"...LET'S CRACK SOME FUCKING SKULLS!"
ASSASSINISTAS
CHARLOTTE "SCARLET" LA COSTA
OCTAVIA "RED OCTOBER" PRICE
BRAKKABRAKKABRAKKABRAKKA
ROSALYN "BLOOD" DIAMOND
Dominic Price AND THE SEMESTER ABROAD

Lyrics by **TINI HOWARD** Art and Cover A by **GILBERT HERNANDEZ** Colors by **ROB DAVIS**
Letters by **ADITYA BIDIKAR** Cover B and Retailer Incentive Cover by **SANFORD GREENE**
Edited by **SHELLY BOND** Editorial Assistance by **CHASE MAROTZ**
ASSASSINISTAS is created by **Howard & Hernandez**

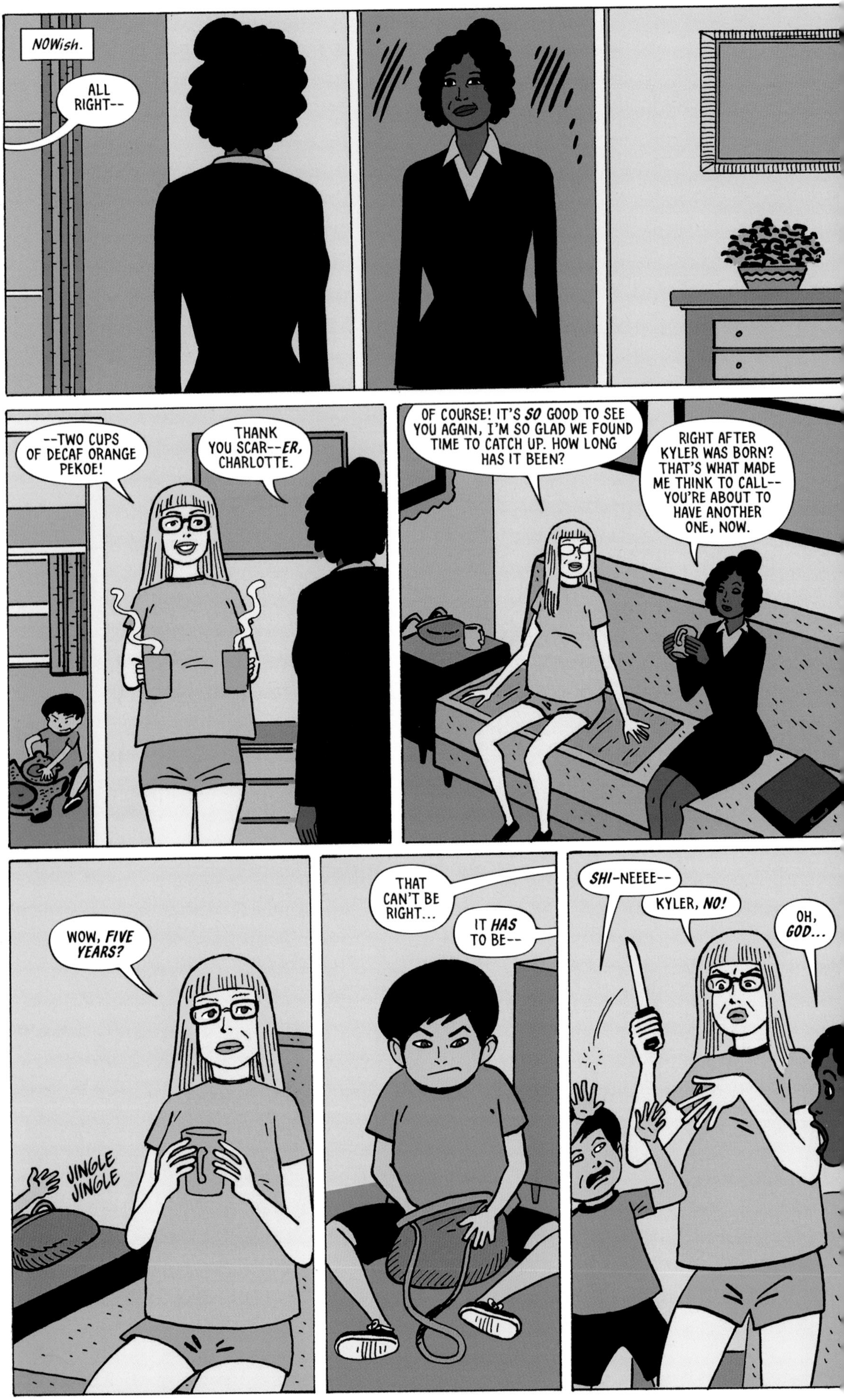
NOWish.
ALL RIGHT--
--TWO CUPS OF DECAF ORANGE PEKOE!
THANK YOU SCAR--ER, CHARLOTTE.
OF COURSE! IT'S SO GOOD TO SEE YOU AGAIN, I'M SO GLAD WE FOUND TIME TO CATCH UP. HOW LONG HAS IT BEEN?
RIGHT AFTER KYLER WAS BORN? THAT'S WHAT MADE ME THINK TO CALL-- YOU'RE ABOUT TO HAVE ANOTHER ONE, NOW.
WOW, FIVE YEARS?
JINGLE JINGLE
THAT CAN'T BE RIGHT...
IT HAS TO BE--
SHI-NEEEE--
KYLER, NO!
OH, GOD...

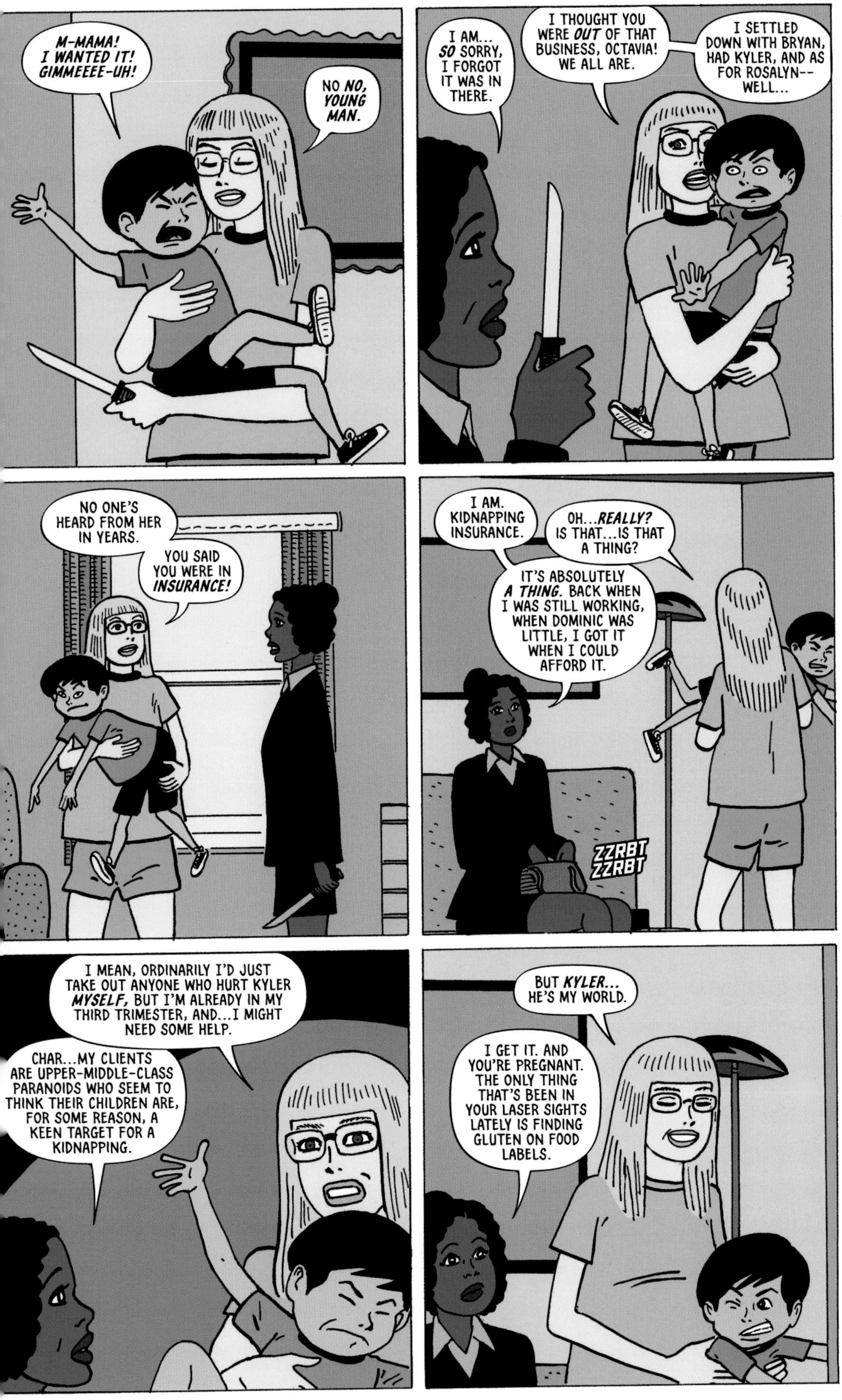
M-MAMA! I WANTED IT! GIMMEEEE-UH!
NO NO, YOUNG MAN.
I AM... SO SORRY, I FORGOT IT WAS IN THERE.
I THOUGHT YOU WERE OUT OF THAT BUSINESS, OCTAVIA! WE ALL ARE.
I SETTLED DOWN WITH BRYAN, HAD KYLER, AND AS FOR ROSALYN-- WELL...
NO ONE'S HEARD FROM HER IN YEARS.
YOU SAID YOU WERE IN INSURANCE!
I AM. KIDNAPPING INSURANCE.
OH...REALLY? IS THAT...IS THAT A THING?
IT'S ABSOLUTELY A THING. BACK WHEN I WAS STILL WORKING, WHEN DOMINIC WAS LITTLE, I GOT IT WHEN I COULD AFFORD IT.
ZZRBT ZZRBT
I MEAN, ORDINARILY I'D JUST TAKE OUT ANYONE WHO HURT KYLER MYSELF, BUT I'M ALREADY IN MY THIRD TRIMESTER, AND...I MIGHT NEED SOME HELP.
CHAR...MY CLIENTS ARE UPPER-MIDDLE-CLASS PARANOIDS WHO SEEM TO THINK THEIR CHILDREN ARE, FOR SOME REASON, A KEEN TARGET FOR A KIDNAPPING.
BUT KYLER... HE'S MY WORLD.
I GET IT. AND YOU'RE PREGNANT. THE ONLY THING THAT'S BEEN IN YOUR LASER SIGHTS LATELY IS FINDING GLUTEN ON FOOD LABELS.

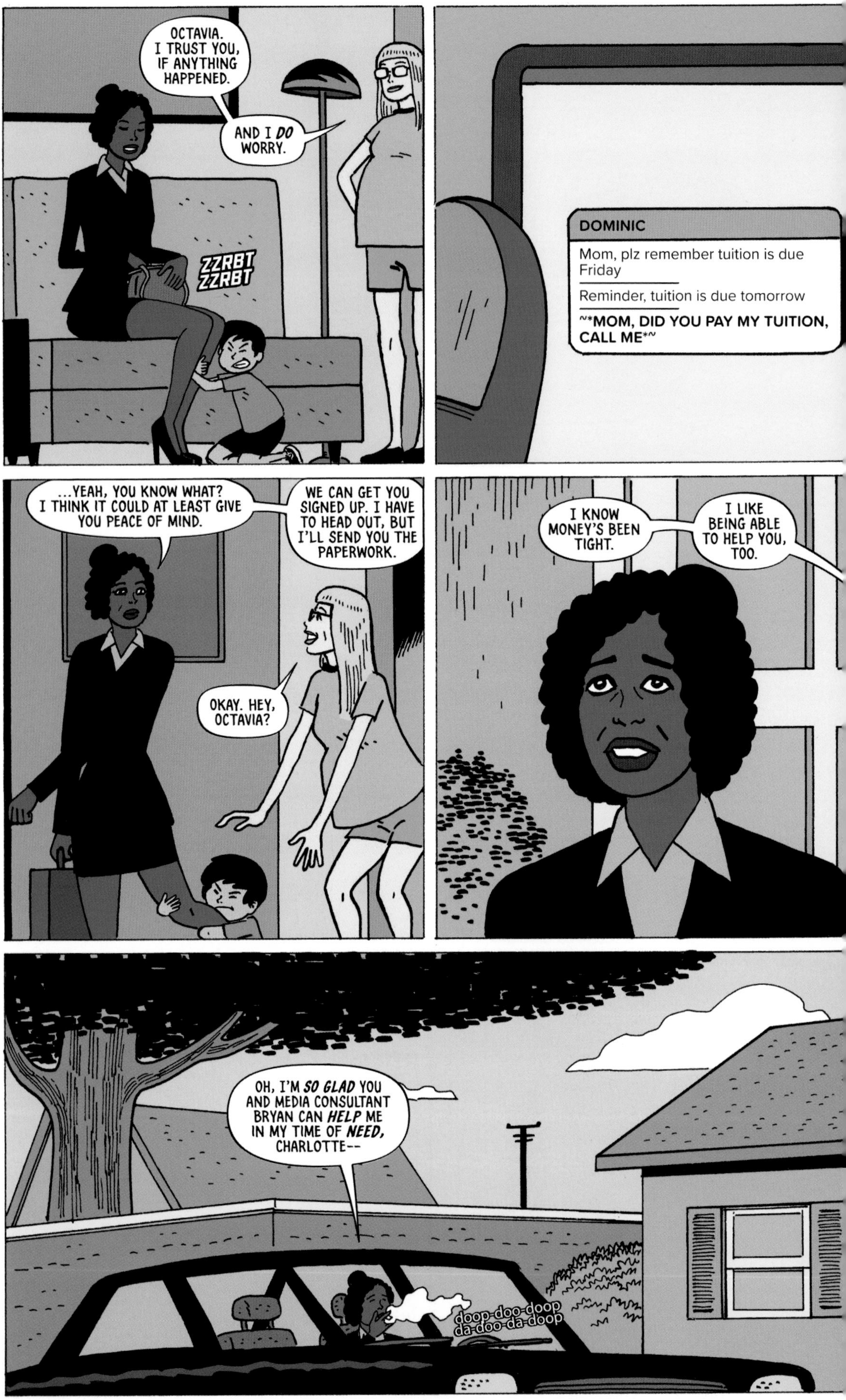

OCTAVIA. I TRUST YOU, IF ANYTHING HAPPENED.
AND I DO WORRY.
ZZRBT ZZRBT
DOMINIC
Mom, plz remember tuition is due Friday
Reminder, tuition is due tomorrow
~*MOM, DID YOU PAY MY TUITION, CALL ME*~
...YEAH, YOU KNOW WHAT? I THINK IT COULD AT LEAST GIVE YOU PEACE OF MIND.
WE CAN GET YOU SIGNED UP. I HAVE TO HEAD OUT, BUT I'LL SEND YOU THE PAPERWORK.
OKAY. HEY, OCTAVIA?
I KNOW MONEY'S BEEN TIGHT.
I LIKE BEING ABLE TO HELP YOU, TOO.
OH, I'M SO GLAD YOU AND MEDIA CONSULTANT BRYAN CAN HELP ME IN MY TIME OF NEED, CHARLOTTE--
doop-doo-doop
da-doo-da-doop

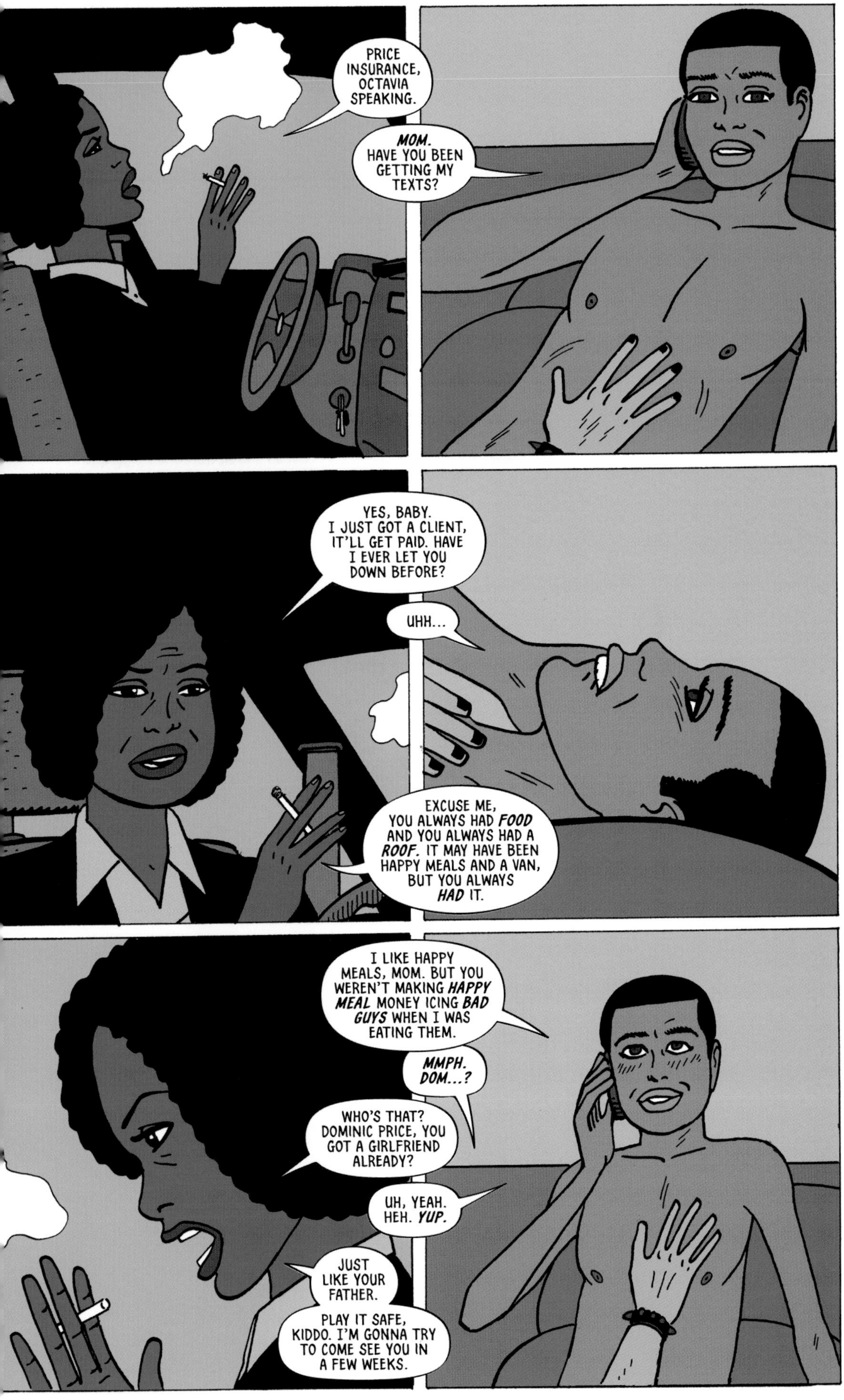

PRICE INSURANCE, OCTAVIA SPEAKING.
MOM. HAVE YOU BEEN GETTING MY TEXTS?
YES, BABY. I JUST GOT A CLIENT, IT'LL GET PAID. HAVE I EVER LET YOU DOWN BEFORE?
UHH...
EXCUSE ME, YOU ALWAYS HAD *FOOD* AND YOU ALWAYS HAD A *ROOF.* IT MAY HAVE BEEN HAPPY MEALS AND A VAN, BUT YOU ALWAYS *HAD* IT.
I LIKE HAPPY MEALS, MOM. BUT YOU WEREN'T MAKING *HAPPY MEAL* MONEY ICING *BAD GUYS* WHEN I WAS EATING THEM.
MMPH. DOM...?
WHO'S THAT? DOMINIC PRICE, YOU GOT A GIRLFRIEND ALREADY?
UH, YEAH. HEH. *YUP.*
JUST LIKE YOUR FATHER.
PLAY IT SAFE, KIDDO. I'M GONNA TRY TO COME SEE YOU IN A FEW WEEKS.

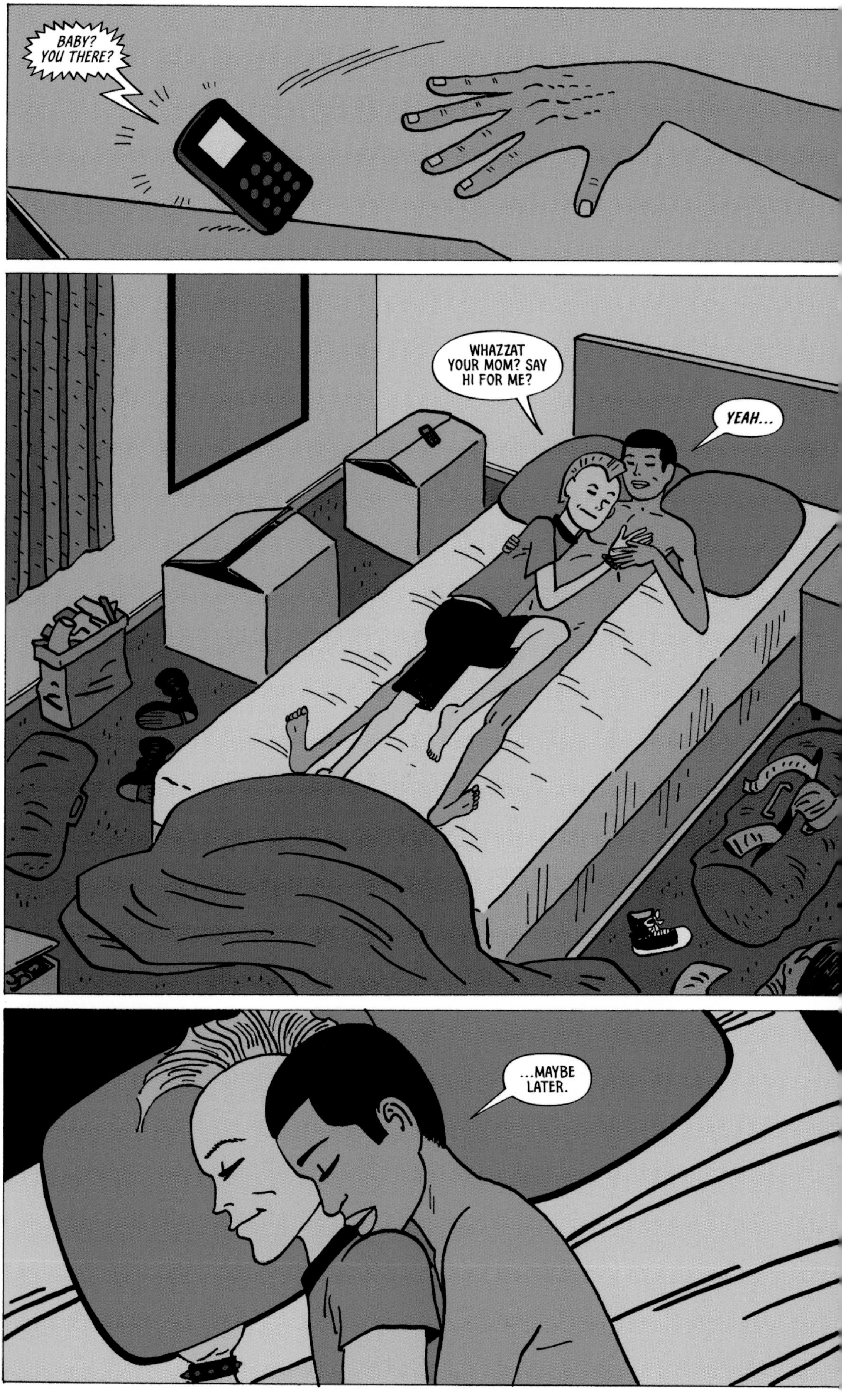
BABY? YOU THERE?
WHAZZAT YOUR MOM? SAY HI FOR ME?
YEAH...
...MAYBE LATER.

THAT NIGHT.

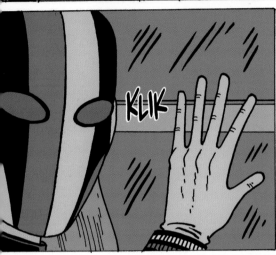

KLIK

SHHNK

BEEEP THE WINDOW IS AJAR. YOU HAVE THIRTY SECONDS TO CLOSE THE WINDOW.

BLOOD DIAMOND

FLIK

KYLER...?

RATTLE RATTLE

...KYLER?!

THUNK

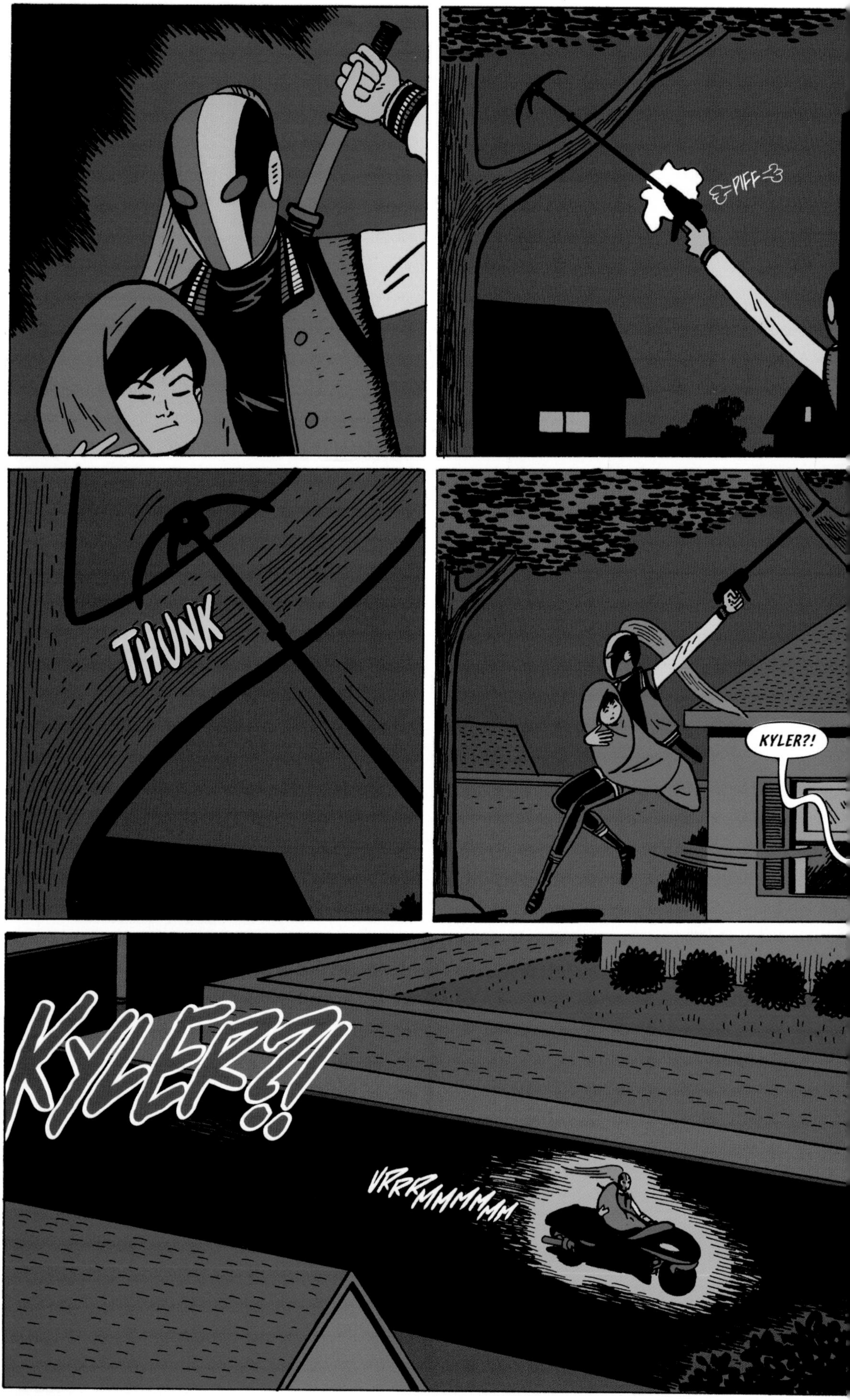
PIFF
THUNK
KYLER?!
KYLER?!
VRRRMMMMMM

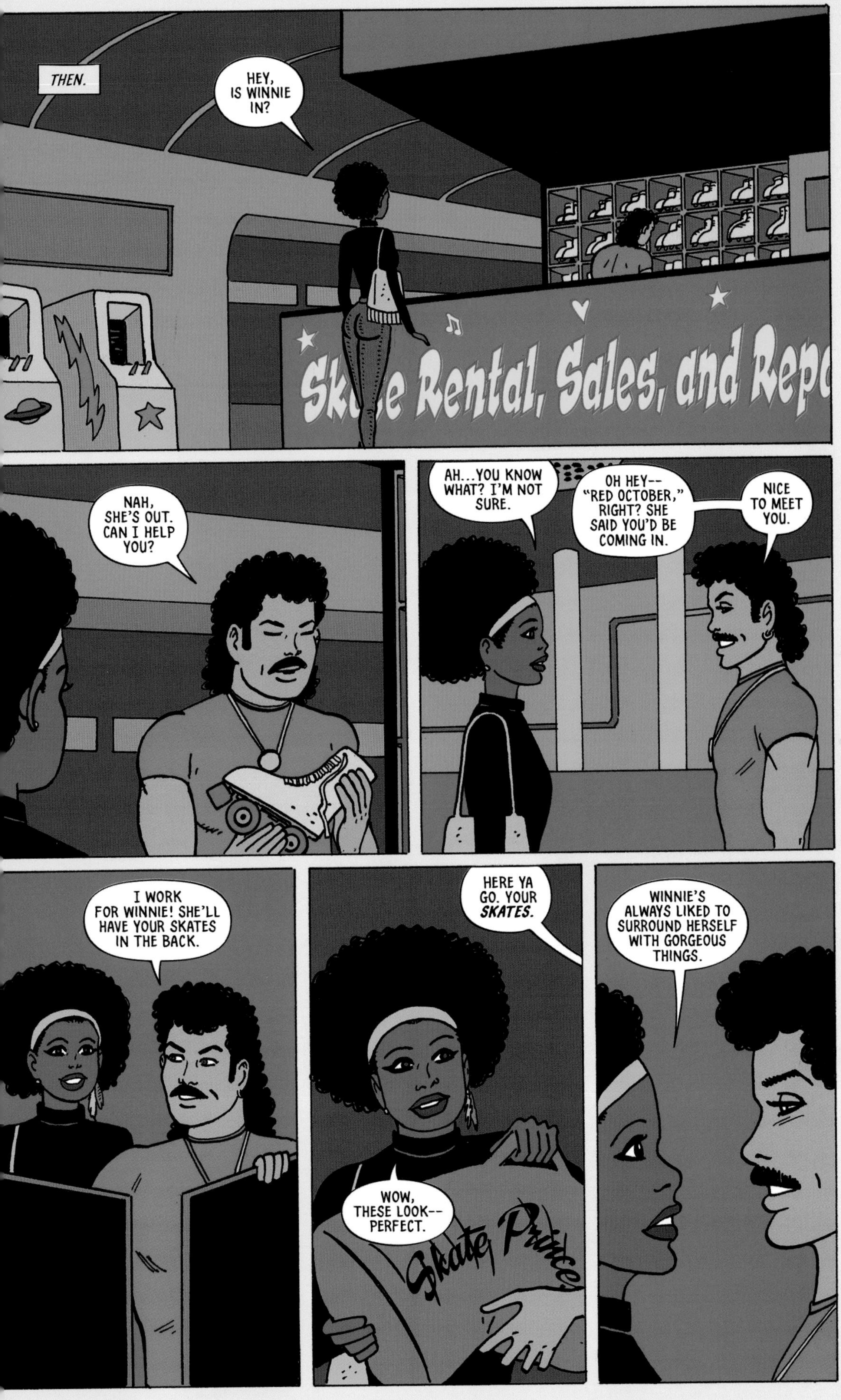
THEN.
HEY, IS WINNIE IN?
Skate Rental, Sales, and Repa
NAH, SHE'S OUT. CAN I HELP YOU?
AH...YOU KNOW WHAT? I'M NOT SURE.
OH HEY-- "RED OCTOBER," RIGHT? SHE SAID YOU'D BE COMING IN.
NICE TO MEET YOU.
I WORK FOR WINNIE! SHE'LL HAVE YOUR SKATES IN THE BACK.
HERE YA GO. YOUR SKATES.
WOW, THESE LOOK-- PERFECT.
Skate Prince
WINNIE'S ALWAYS LIKED TO SURROUND HERSELF WITH GORGEOUS THINGS.

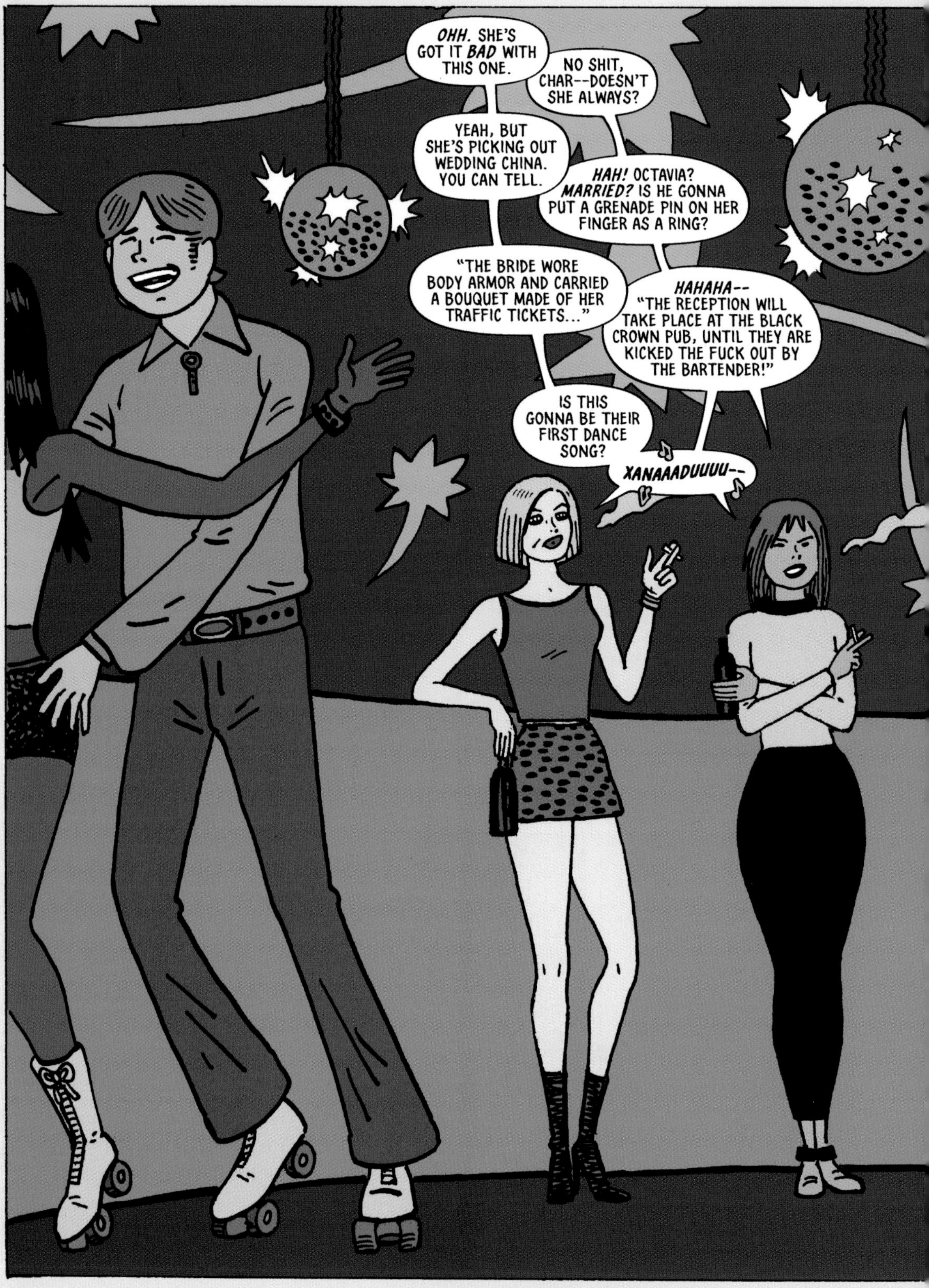
OHH. SHE'S GOT IT BAD WITH THIS ONE.
NO SHIT, CHAR--DOESN'T SHE ALWAYS?
YEAH, BUT SHE'S PICKING OUT WEDDING CHINA. YOU CAN TELL.
HAH! OCTAVIA? MARRIED? IS HE GONNA PUT A GRENADE PIN ON HER FINGER AS A RING?
"THE BRIDE WORE BODY ARMOR AND CARRIED A BOUQUET MADE OF HER TRAFFIC TICKETS..."
HAHAHA-- "THE RECEPTION WILL TAKE PLACE AT THE BLACK CROWN PUB, UNTIL THEY ARE KICKED THE FUCK OUT BY THE BARTENDER!"
IS THIS GONNA BE THEIR FIRST DANCE SONG?
XANAAADUUUU--

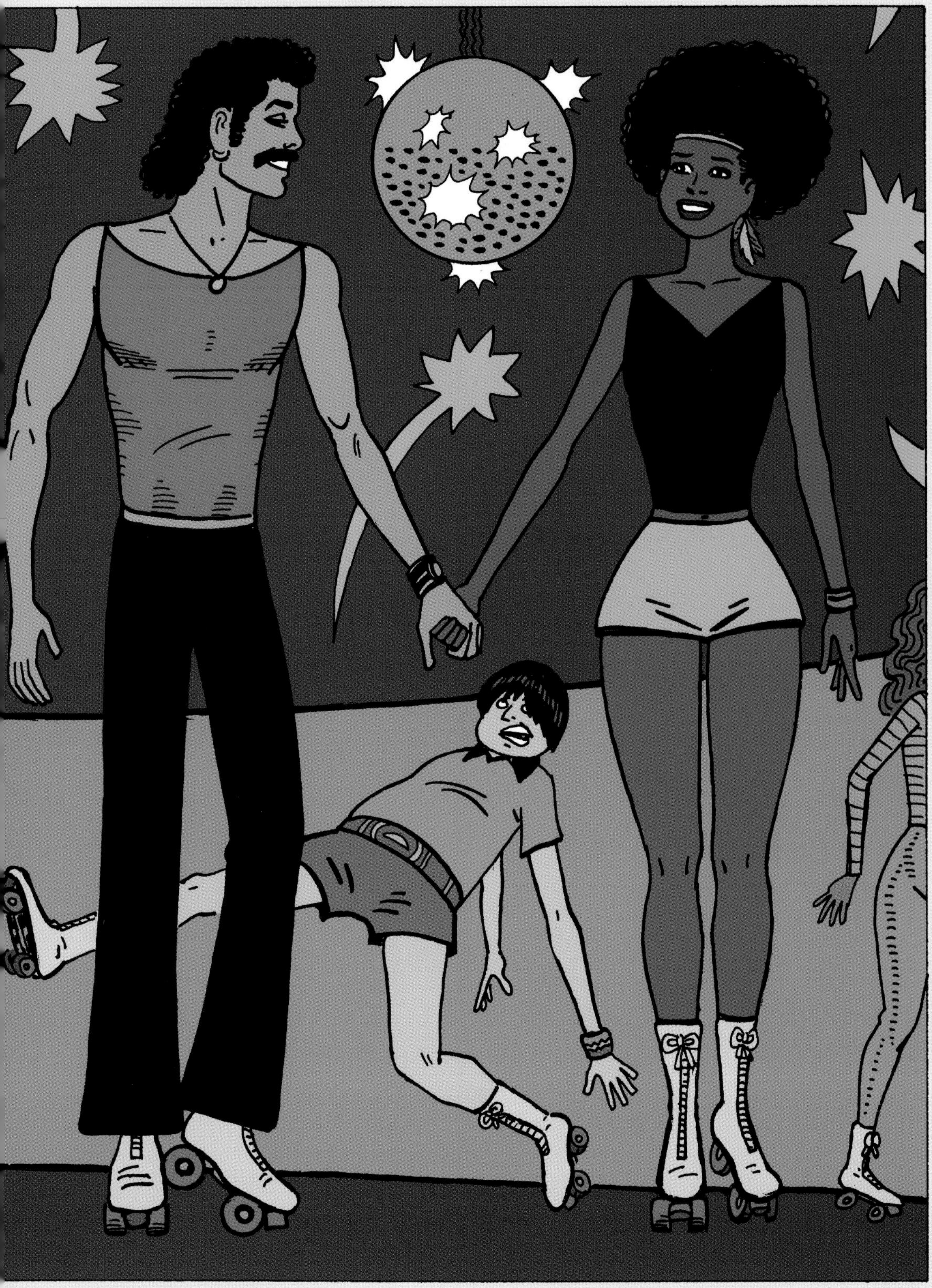

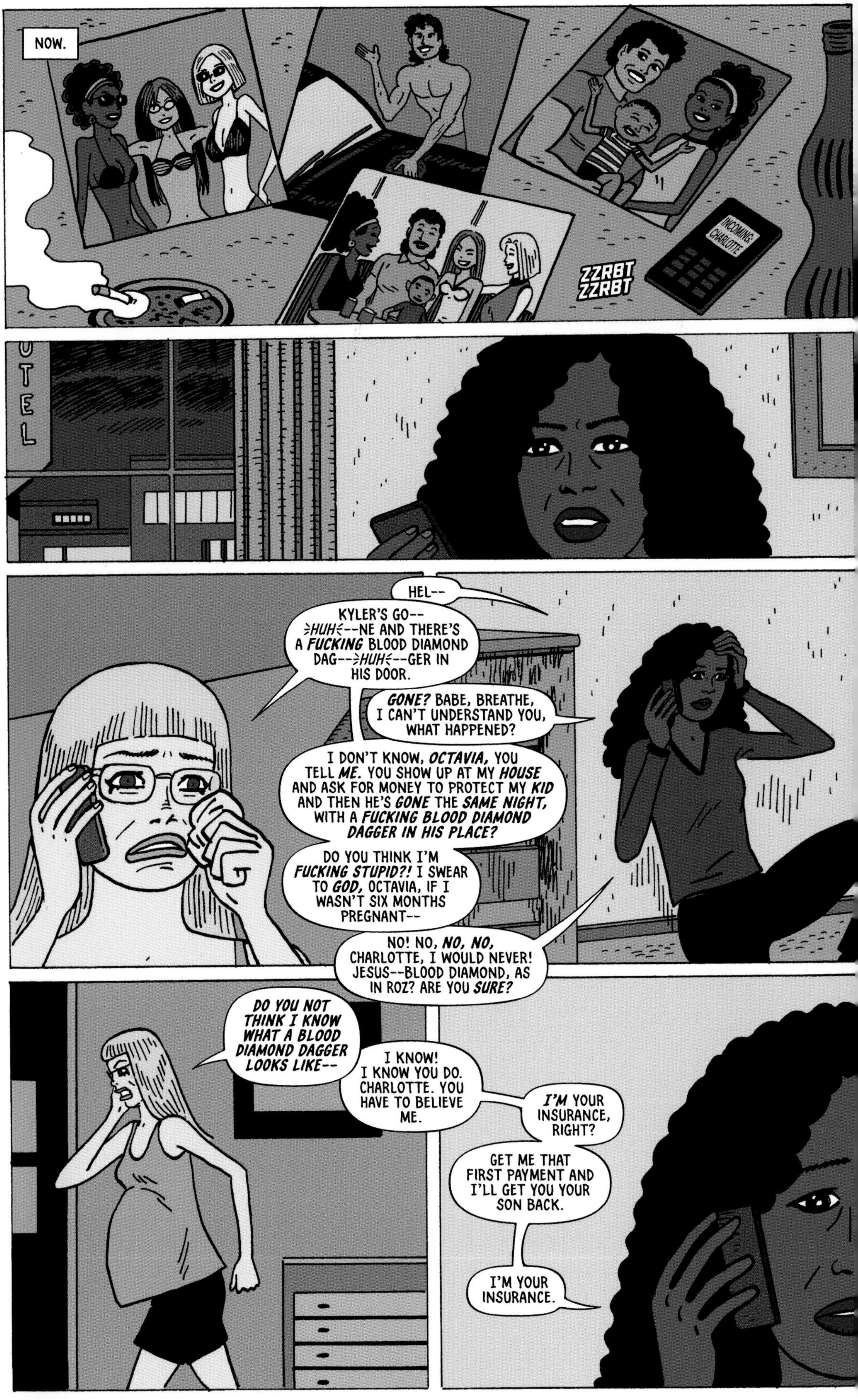
NOW.
INCOMING: CHARLOTTE
ZZRBT ZZRBT
UTEL
HEL--
KYLER'S GO-- *HUH* --NE AND THERE'S A *FUCKING* BLOOD DIAMOND DAG-- *HUH* --GER IN HIS DOOR.
GONE? BABE, BREATHE, I CAN'T UNDERSTAND YOU, WHAT HAPPENED?
I DON'T KNOW, *OCTAVIA*, YOU TELL *ME*. YOU SHOW UP AT MY *HOUSE* AND ASK FOR MONEY TO PROTECT MY *KID* AND THEN HE'S *GONE* THE *SAME NIGHT*, WITH A *FUCKING BLOOD DIAMOND DAGGER IN HIS PLACE?*
DO YOU THINK I'M *FUCKING STUPID?!* I SWEAR TO *GOD*, OCTAVIA, IF I WASN'T SIX MONTHS PREGNANT--
NO! NO, *NO, NO*, CHARLOTTE, I WOULD NEVER! JESUS--BLOOD DIAMOND, AS IN ROZ? ARE YOU *SURE?*
DO YOU NOT THINK I KNOW WHAT A BLOOD DIAMOND DAGGER LOOKS LIKE--
I KNOW! I KNOW YOU DO. CHARLOTTE. YOU HAVE TO BELIEVE ME.
I'M YOUR INSURANCE, RIGHT?
GET ME THAT FIRST PAYMENT AND I'LL GET YOU YOUR SON BACK.
I'M YOUR INSURANCE.

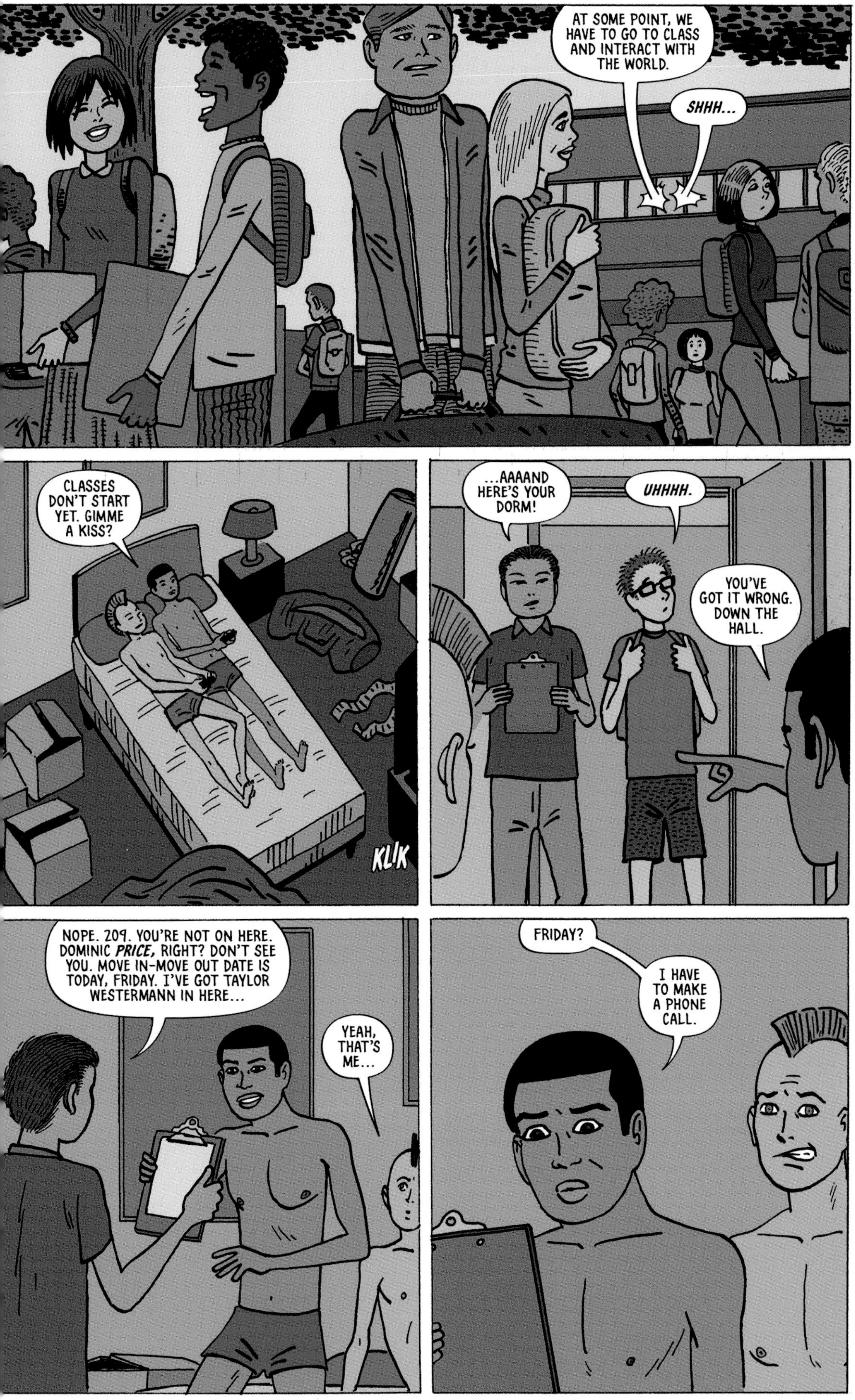

AT SOME POINT, WE HAVE TO GO TO CLASS AND INTERACT WITH THE WORLD.
SHHH...
CLASSES DON'T START YET. GIMME A KISS?
KLIK
...AAAAND HERE'S YOUR DORM!
UHHHH.
YOU'VE GOT IT WRONG. DOWN THE HALL.
NOPE. 209. YOU'RE NOT ON HERE. DOMINIC PRICE, RIGHT? DON'T SEE YOU. MOVE IN-MOVE OUT DATE IS TODAY, FRIDAY. I'VE GOT TAYLOR WESTERMANN IN HERE...
YEAH, THAT'S ME...
FRIDAY?
I HAVE TO MAKE A PHONE CALL.

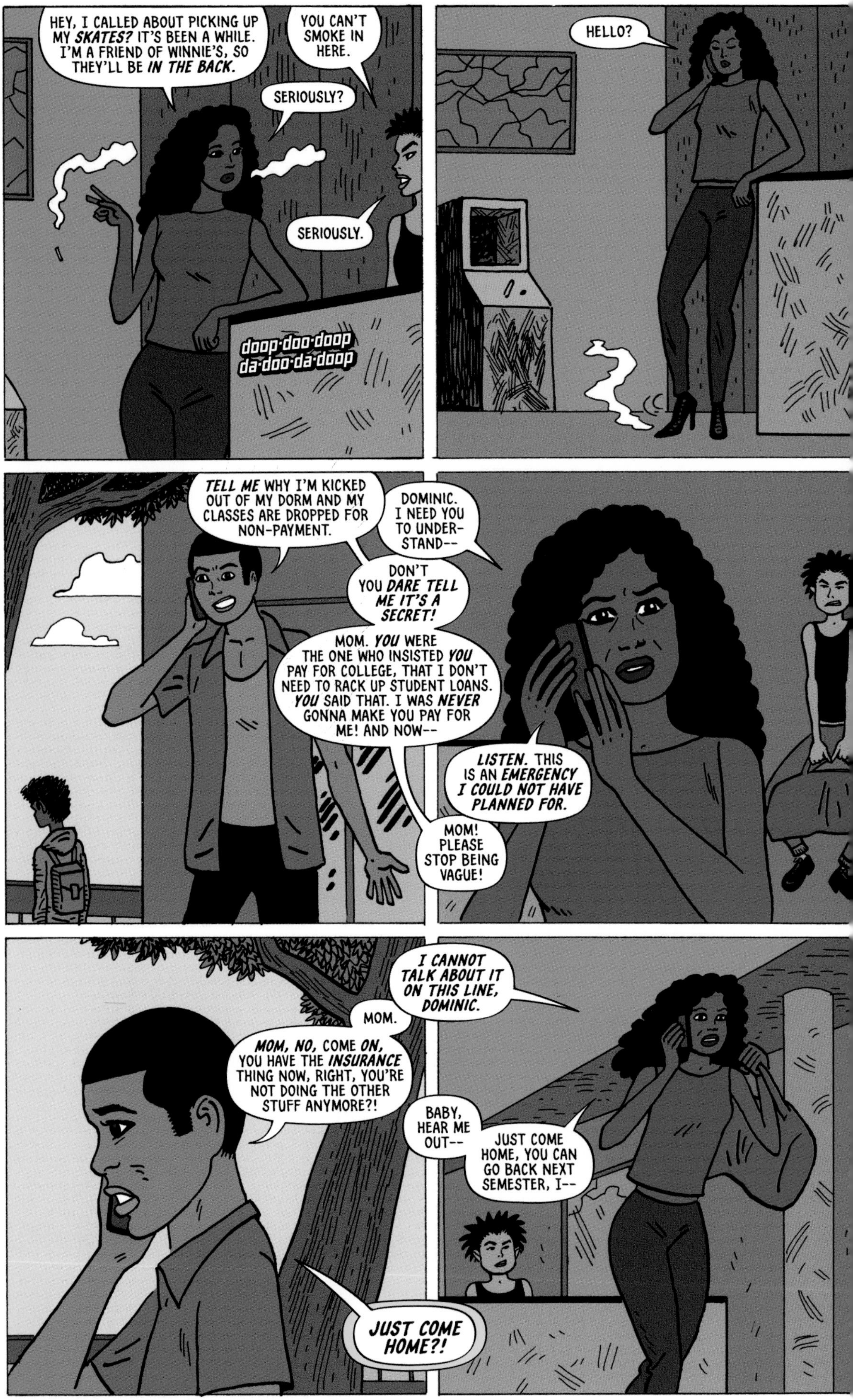
HEY, I CALLED ABOUT PICKING UP MY *SKATES?* IT'S BEEN A WHILE. I'M A FRIEND OF WINNIE'S, SO THEY'LL BE *IN THE BACK.*
YOU CAN'T SMOKE IN HERE.
SERIOUSLY?
SERIOUSLY.
doop·doo·doop da·doo·da·doop
HELLO?
TELL ME WHY I'M KICKED OUT OF MY DORM AND MY CLASSES ARE DROPPED FOR NON-PAYMENT.
DOMINIC. I NEED YOU TO UNDER-STAND--
DON'T YOU *DARE TELL ME IT'S A SECRET!*
MOM. *YOU* WERE THE ONE WHO INSISTED *YOU* PAY FOR COLLEGE, THAT I DON'T NEED TO RACK UP STUDENT LOANS. *YOU* SAID THAT. I WAS *NEVER* GONNA MAKE YOU PAY FOR ME! AND NOW--
LISTEN. THIS IS AN *EMERGENCY I COULD NOT HAVE PLANNED FOR.*
MOM! PLEASE STOP BEING VAGUE!
I CANNOT TALK ABOUT IT ON THIS LINE, DOMINIC.
MOM.
MOM, NO, COME *ON,* YOU HAVE THE *INSURANCE* THING NOW, RIGHT, YOU'RE NOT DOING THE OTHER STUFF ANYMORE?!
BABY, HEAR ME OUT--
JUST COME HOME, YOU CAN GO BACK NEXT SEMESTER, I--
JUST COME HOME?!

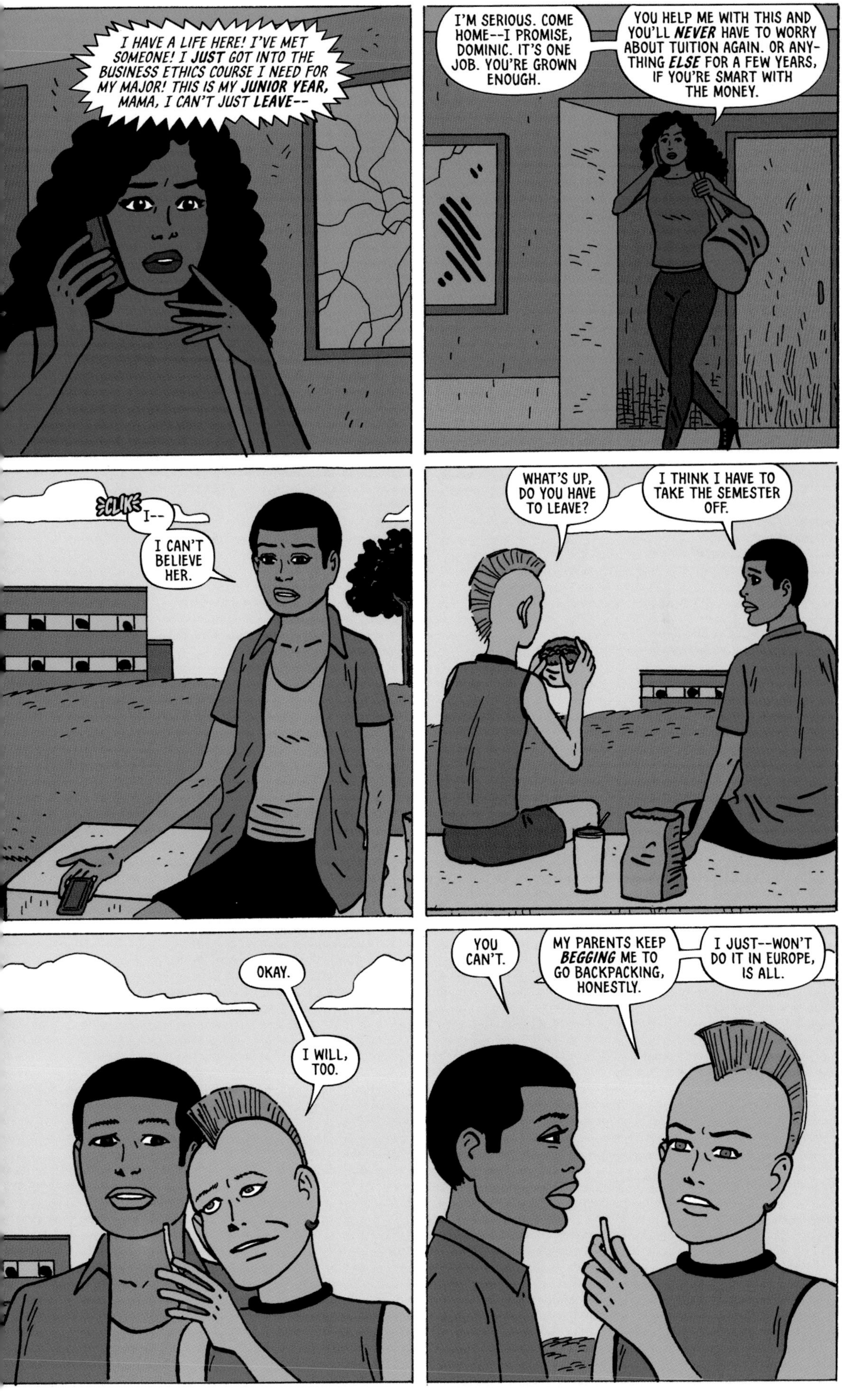
I HAVE A LIFE HERE! I'VE MET SOMEONE! I JUST GOT INTO THE BUSINESS ETHICS COURSE I NEED FOR MY MAJOR! THIS IS MY JUNIOR YEAR, MAMA, I CAN'T JUST LEAVE--
I'M SERIOUS. COME HOME--I PROMISE, DOMINIC. IT'S ONE JOB. YOU'RE GROWN ENOUGH.
YOU HELP ME WITH THIS AND YOU'LL NEVER HAVE TO WORRY ABOUT TUITION AGAIN. OR ANYTHING ELSE FOR A FEW YEARS, IF YOU'RE SMART WITH THE MONEY.
CLIK
I--
I CAN'T BELIEVE HER.
WHAT'S UP, DO YOU HAVE TO LEAVE?
I THINK I HAVE TO TAKE THE SEMESTER OFF.
OKAY.
I WILL, TOO.
YOU CAN'T.
MY PARENTS KEEP BEGGING ME TO GO BACKPACKING, HONESTLY.
I JUST--WON'T DO IT IN EUROPE, IS ALL.

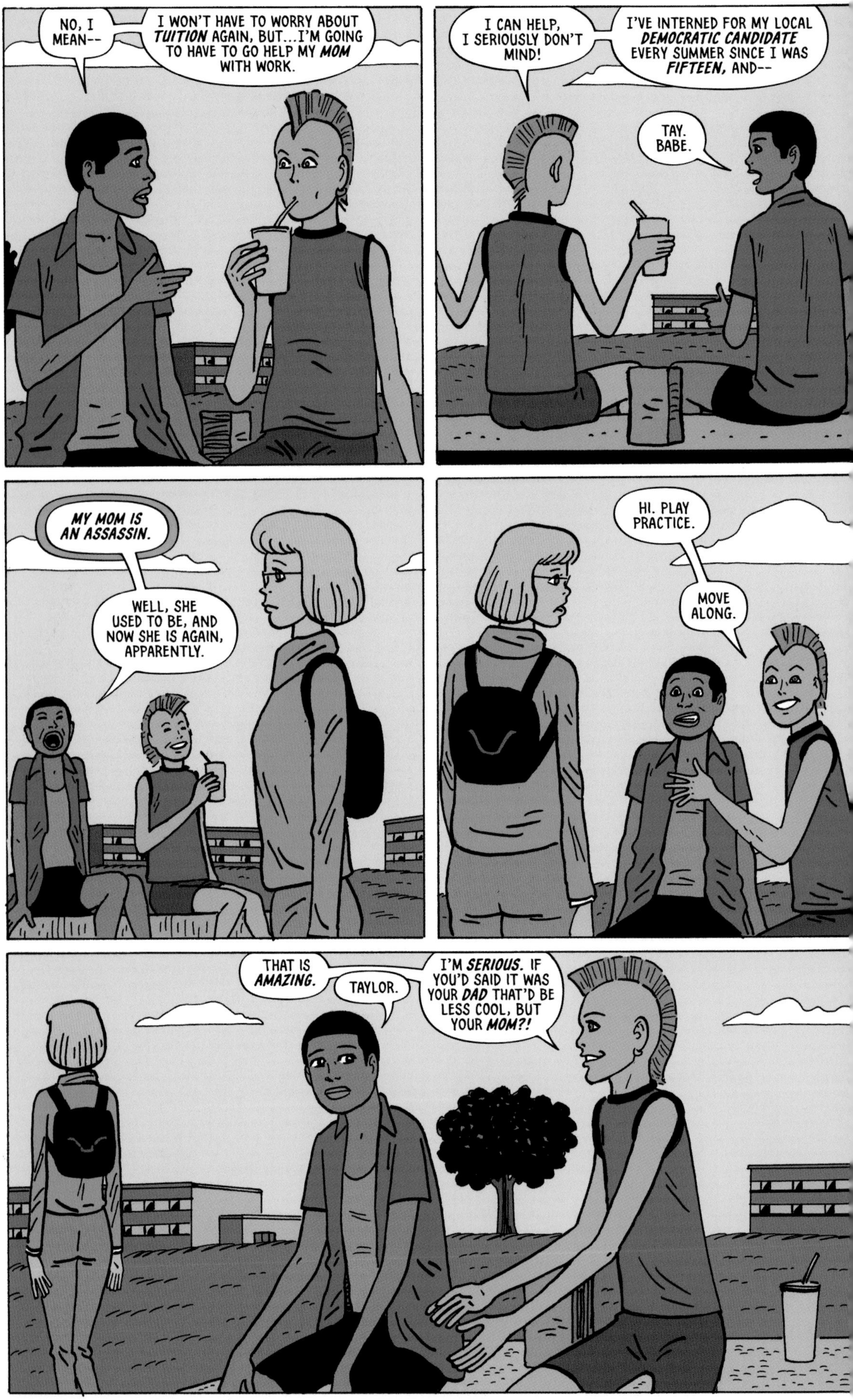
NO, I MEAN--
I WON'T HAVE TO WORRY ABOUT TUITION AGAIN, BUT...I'M GOING TO HAVE TO GO HELP MY MOM WITH WORK.
I CAN HELP, I SERIOUSLY DON'T MIND!
I'VE INTERNED FOR MY LOCAL DEMOCRATIC CANDIDATE EVERY SUMMER SINCE I WAS FIFTEEN, AND--
TAY. BABE.
MY MOM IS AN ASSASSIN.
WELL, SHE USED TO BE, AND NOW SHE IS AGAIN, APPARENTLY.
HI. PLAY PRACTICE.
MOVE ALONG.
THAT IS AMAZING.
TAYLOR.
I'M SERIOUS. IF YOU'D SAID IT WAS YOUR DAD THAT'D BE LESS COOL, BUT YOUR MOM?!

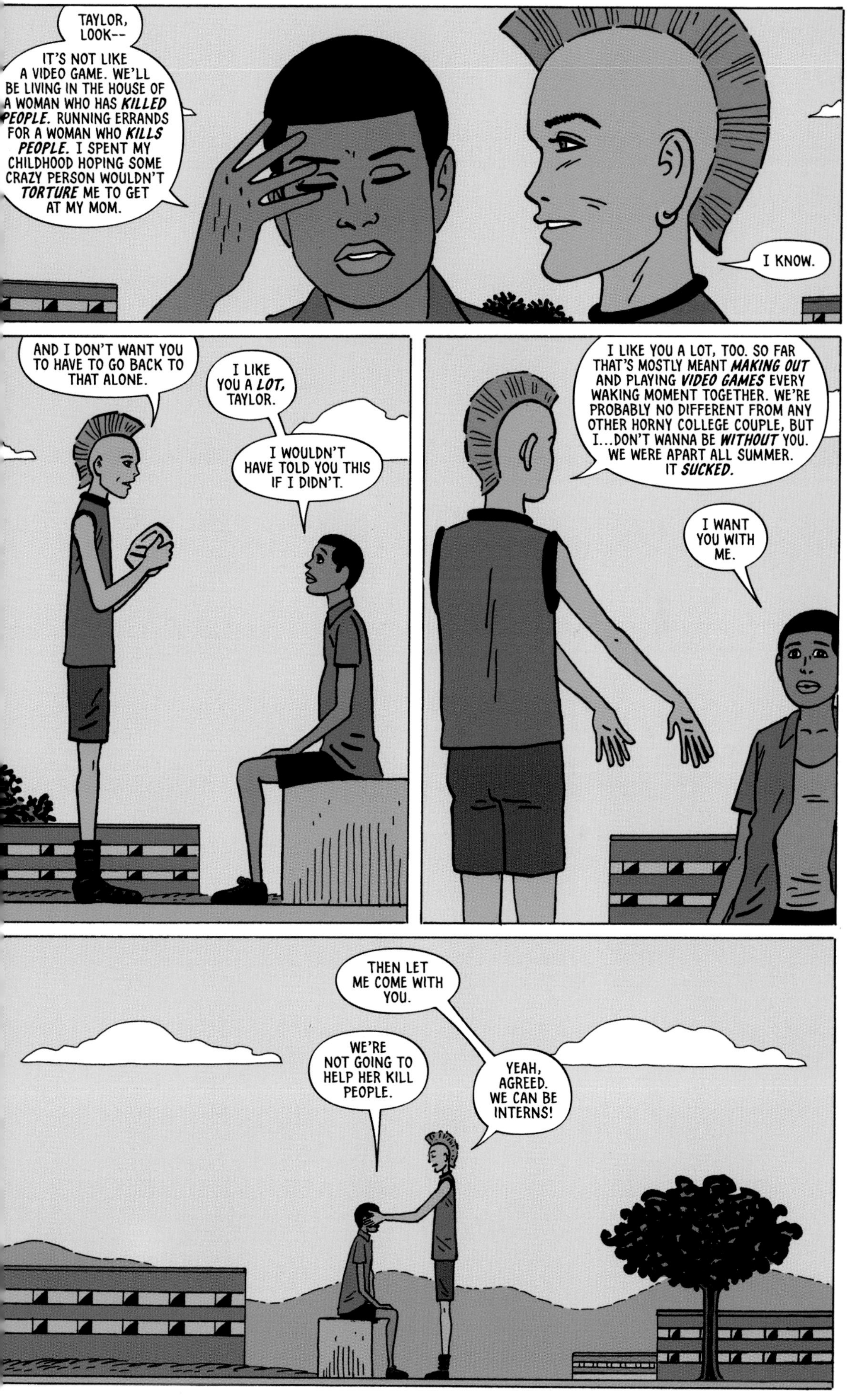

TAYLOR, LOOK--
IT'S NOT LIKE A VIDEO GAME. WE'LL BE LIVING IN THE HOUSE OF A WOMAN WHO HAS *KILLED PEOPLE.* RUNNING ERRANDS FOR A WOMAN WHO *KILLS PEOPLE.* I SPENT MY CHILDHOOD HOPING SOME CRAZY PERSON WOULDN'T *TORTURE* ME TO GET AT MY MOM.
I KNOW.
AND I DON'T WANT YOU TO HAVE TO GO BACK TO THAT ALONE.
I LIKE YOU A *LOT,* TAYLOR.
I WOULDN'T HAVE TOLD YOU THIS IF I DIDN'T.
I LIKE YOU A LOT, TOO. SO FAR THAT'S MOSTLY MEANT *MAKING OUT* AND PLAYING *VIDEO GAMES* EVERY WAKING MOMENT TOGETHER. WE'RE PROBABLY NO DIFFERENT FROM ANY OTHER HORNY COLLEGE COUPLE, BUT I...DON'T WANNA BE *WITHOUT* YOU. WE WERE APART ALL SUMMER. IT *SUCKED.*
I WANT YOU WITH ME.
THEN LET ME COME WITH YOU.
WE'RE NOT GOING TO HELP HER KILL PEOPLE.
YEAH, AGREED. WE CAN BE INTERNS!

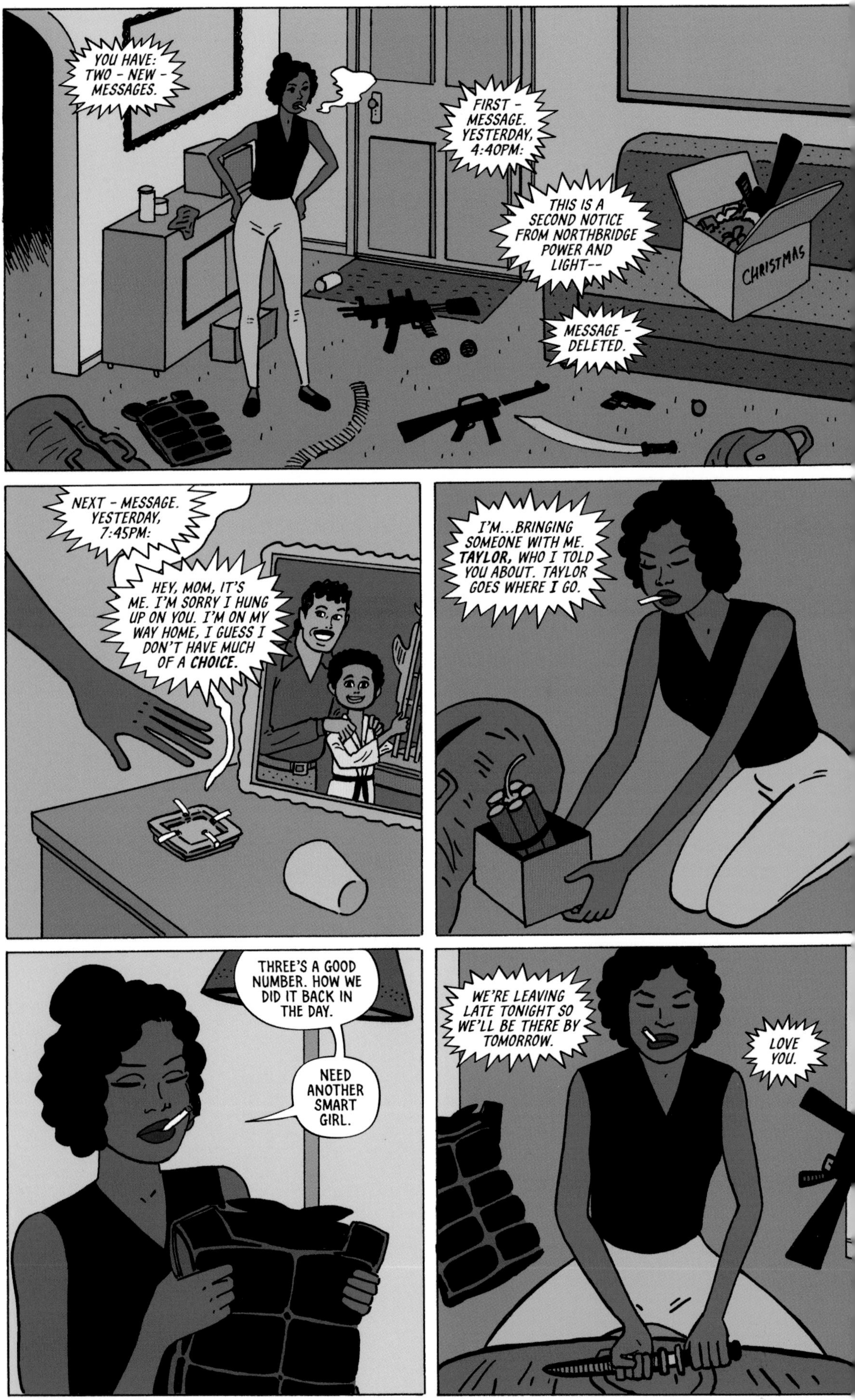
YOU HAVE: TWO - NEW - MESSAGES.
FIRST - MESSAGE. YESTERDAY, 4:40PM:
THIS IS A SECOND NOTICE FROM NORTHBRIDGE POWER AND LIGHT--
CHRISTMAS
MESSAGE - DELETED.
NEXT - MESSAGE. YESTERDAY, 7:45PM:
HEY, MOM, IT'S ME. I'M SORRY I HUNG UP ON YOU. I'M ON MY WAY HOME, I GUESS I DON'T HAVE MUCH OF A **CHOICE.**
I'M...BRINGING SOMEONE WITH ME. **TAYLOR,** WHO I TOLD YOU ABOUT. TAYLOR GOES WHERE **I** GO.
THREE'S A GOOD NUMBER. HOW WE DID IT BACK IN THE DAY.
NEED ANOTHER SMART GIRL.
WE'RE LEAVING LATE TONIGHT SO WE'LL BE THERE BY TOMORROW.
LOVE YOU.

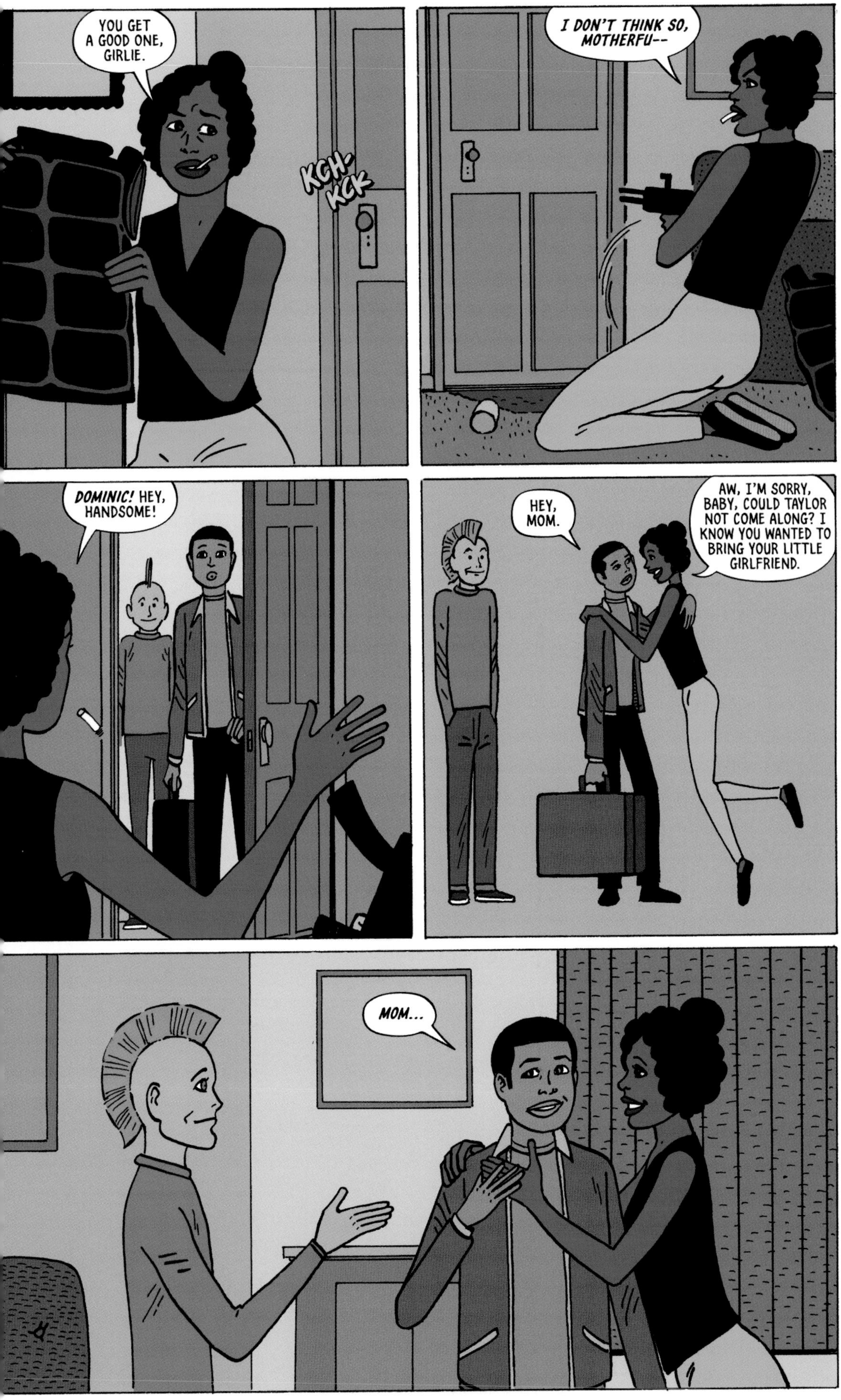
YOU GET A GOOD ONE, GIRLIE.
KCH-KCK
I DON'T THINK SO, MOTHERFU--
DOMINIC! HEY, HANDSOME!
HEY, MOM.
AW, I'M SORRY, BABY, COULD TAYLOR NOT COME ALONG? I KNOW YOU WANTED TO BRING YOUR LITTLE GIRLFRIEND.
MOM...

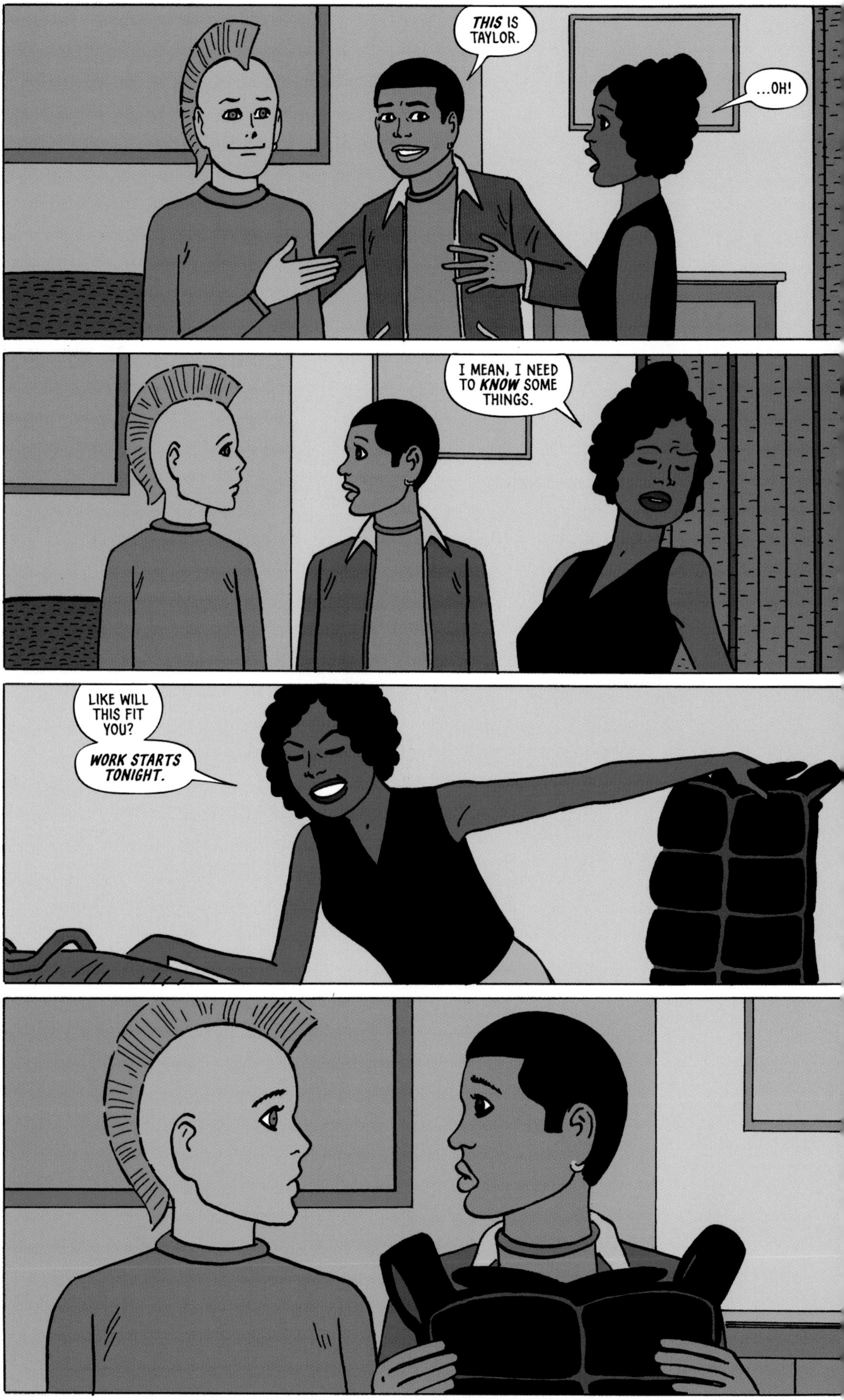
THIS IS TAYLOR.
...OH!
I MEAN, I NEED TO KNOW SOME THINGS.
LIKE WILL THIS FIT YOU?
WORK STARTS TONIGHT.

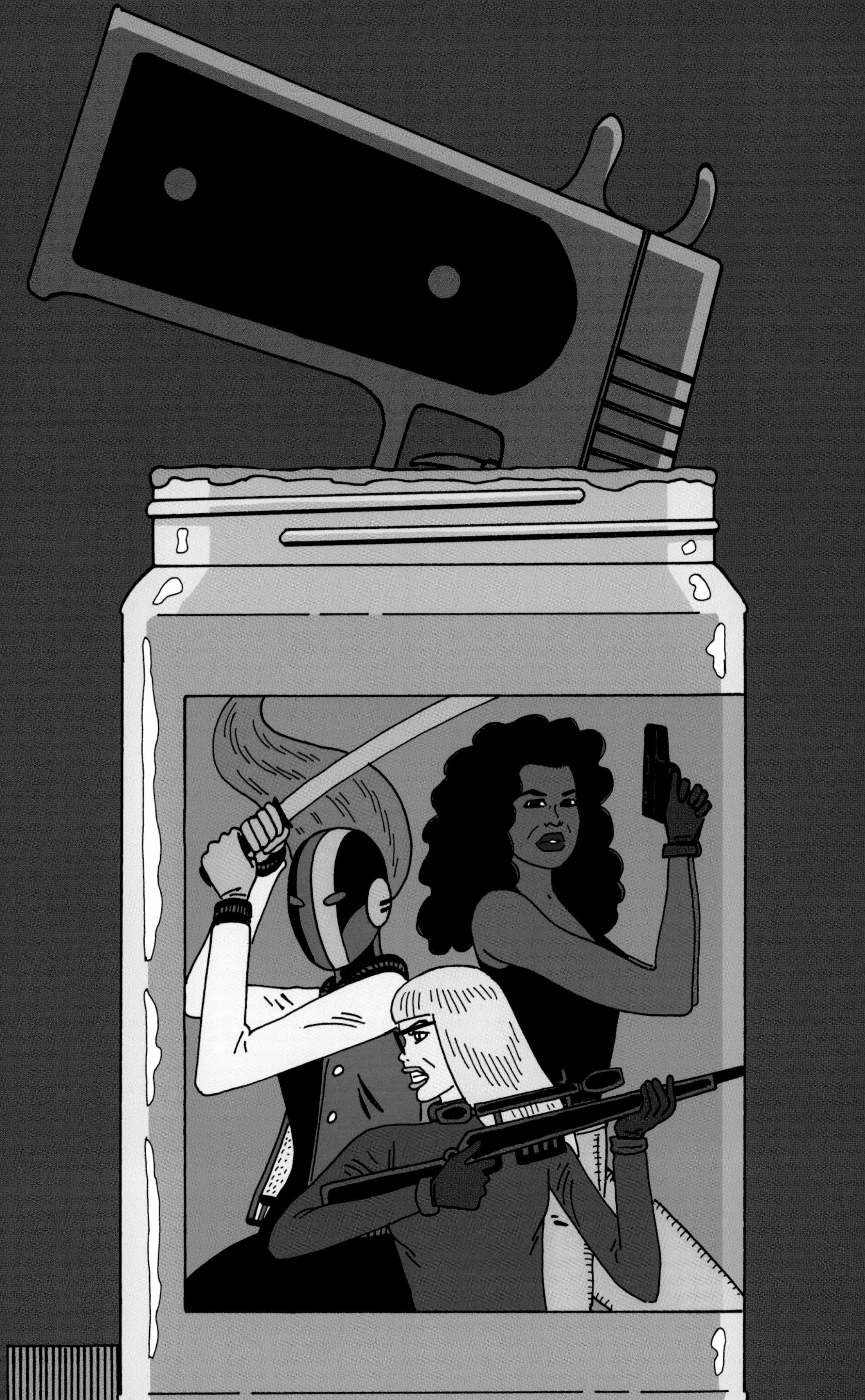
BETO-
2017

**“I don’t need interns,
I need an extraction team.”**

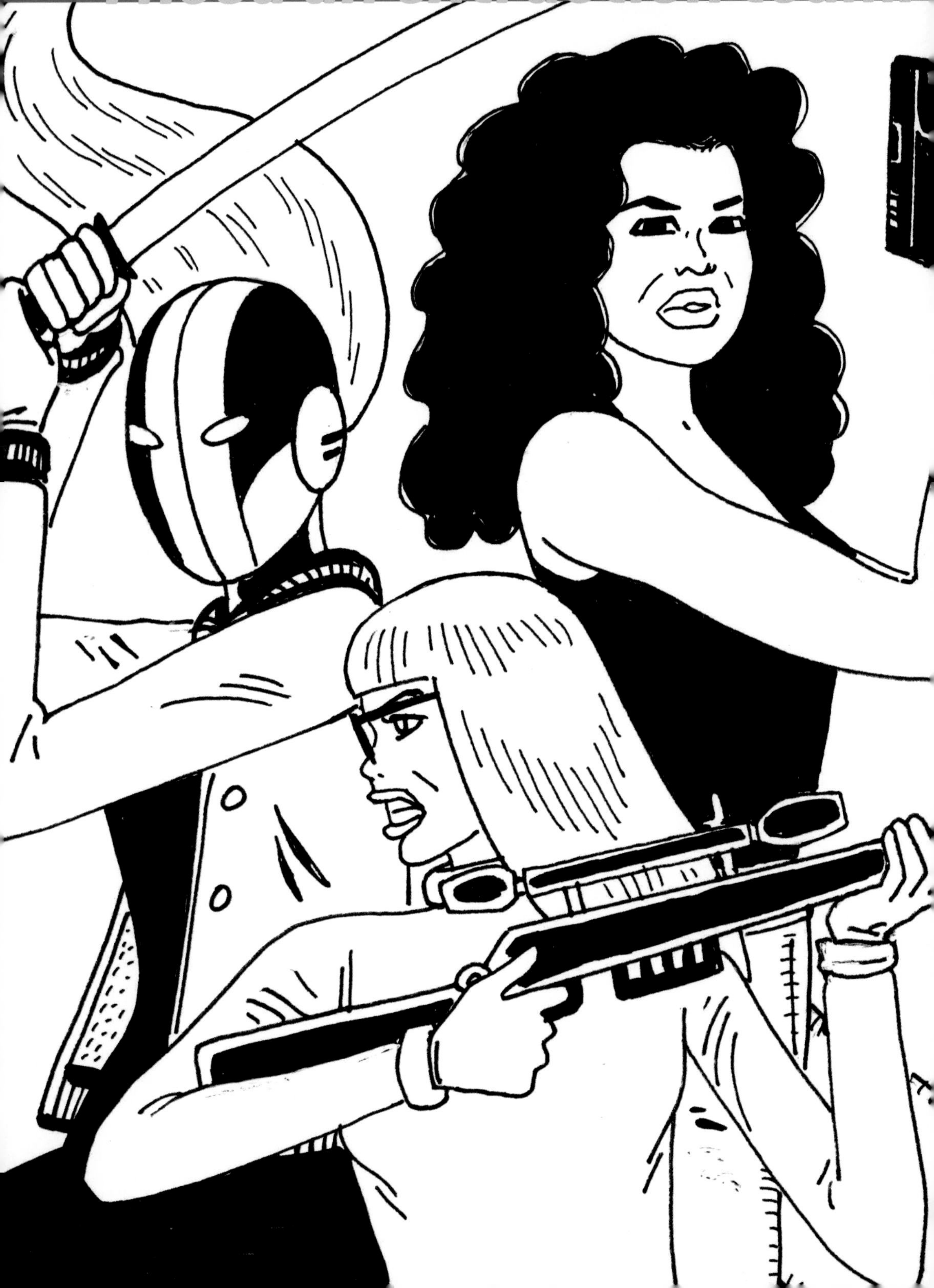

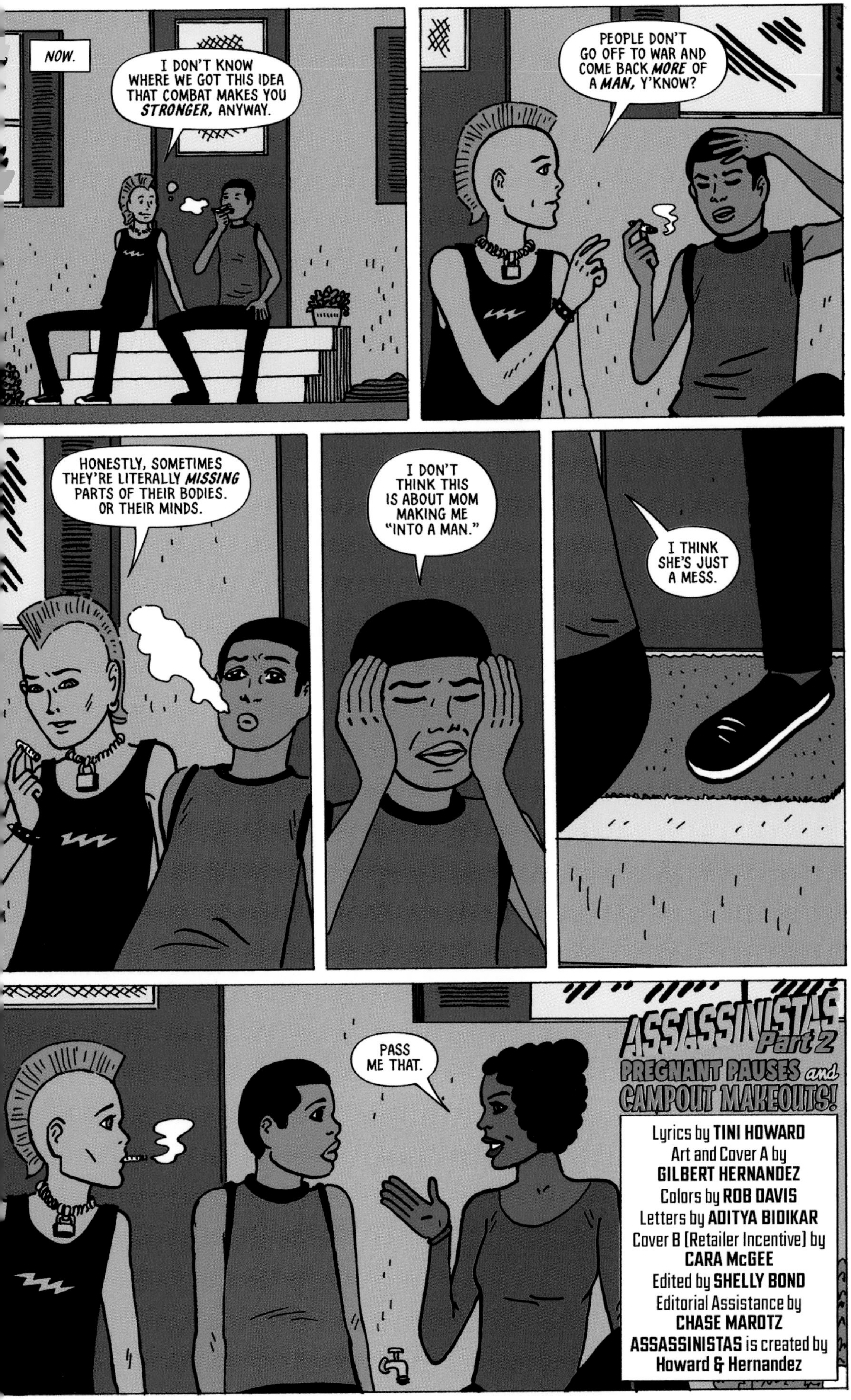
NOW.
I DON'T KNOW WHERE WE GOT THIS IDEA THAT COMBAT MAKES YOU *STRONGER,* ANYWAY.
PEOPLE DON'T GO OFF TO WAR AND COME BACK *MORE* OF A *MAN,* Y'KNOW?
HONESTLY, SOMETIMES THEY'RE LITERALLY *MISSING* PARTS OF THEIR BODIES. OR THEIR MINDS.
I DON'T THINK THIS IS ABOUT MOM MAKING ME "INTO A MAN."
I THINK SHE'S JUST A MESS.
PASS ME THAT.
ASSASSINISTAS Part 2
PREGNANT PAUSES and CAMPOUT MAKEOUTS!
Lyrics by TINI HOWARD
Art and Cover A by GILBERT HERNANDEZ
Colors by ROB DAVIS
Letters by ADITYA BIDIKAR
Cover B [Retailer Incentive] by CARA McGEE
Edited by SHELLY BOND
Editorial Assistance by CHASE MAROTZ
ASSASSINISTAS is created by Howard & Hernandez

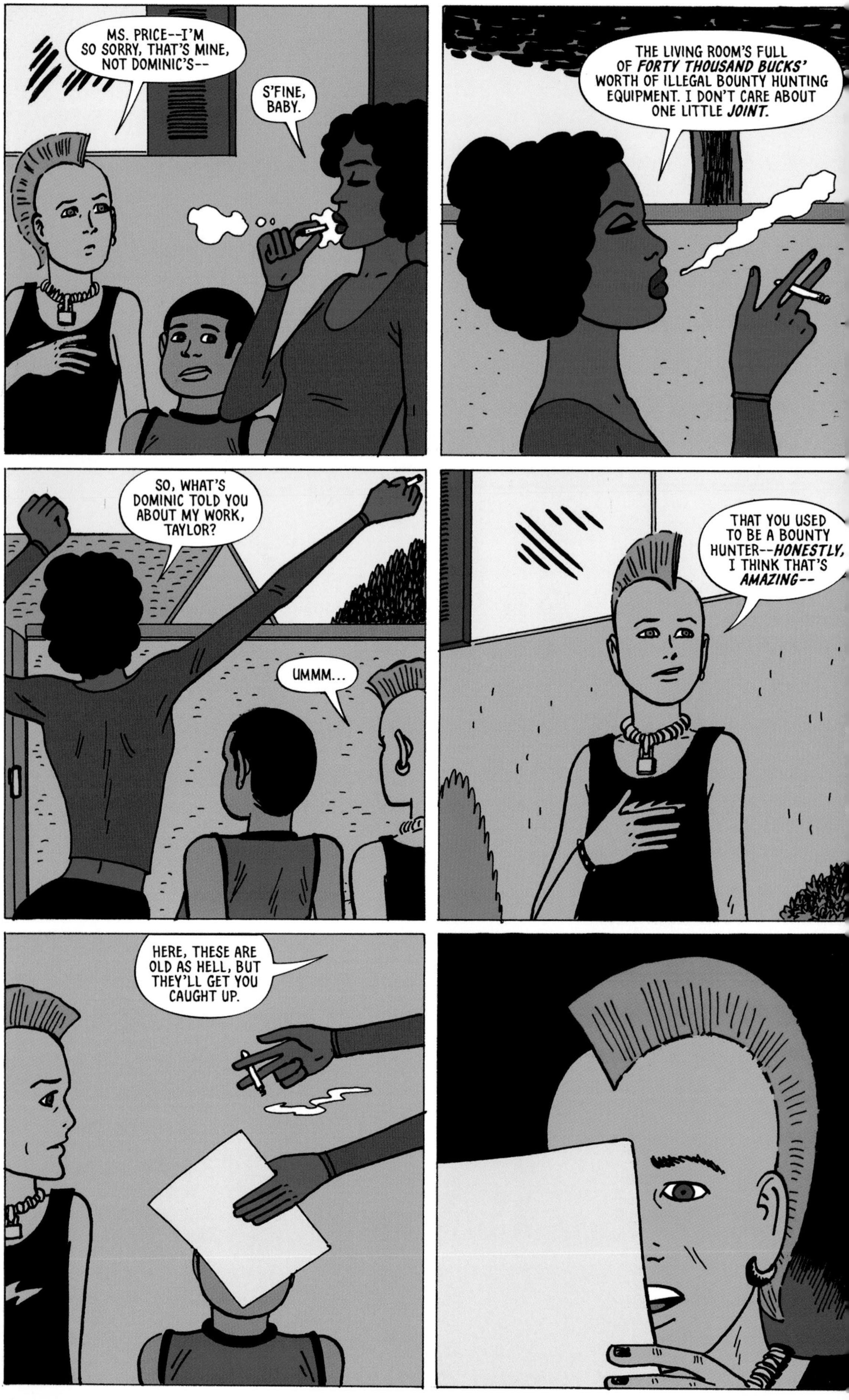
MS. PRICE--I'M SO SORRY, THAT'S MINE, NOT DOMINIC'S--
S'FINE, BABY.
THE LIVING ROOM'S FULL OF *FORTY THOUSAND BUCKS'* WORTH OF ILLEGAL BOUNTY HUNTING EQUIPMENT. I DON'T CARE ABOUT ONE LITTLE *JOINT*.
SO, WHAT'S DOMINIC TOLD YOU ABOUT MY WORK, TAYLOR?
UMMM...
THAT YOU USED TO BE A BOUNTY HUNTER--*HONESTLY,* I THINK THAT'S *AMAZING*--
HERE, THESE ARE OLD AS HELL, BUT THEY'LL GET YOU CAUGHT UP.

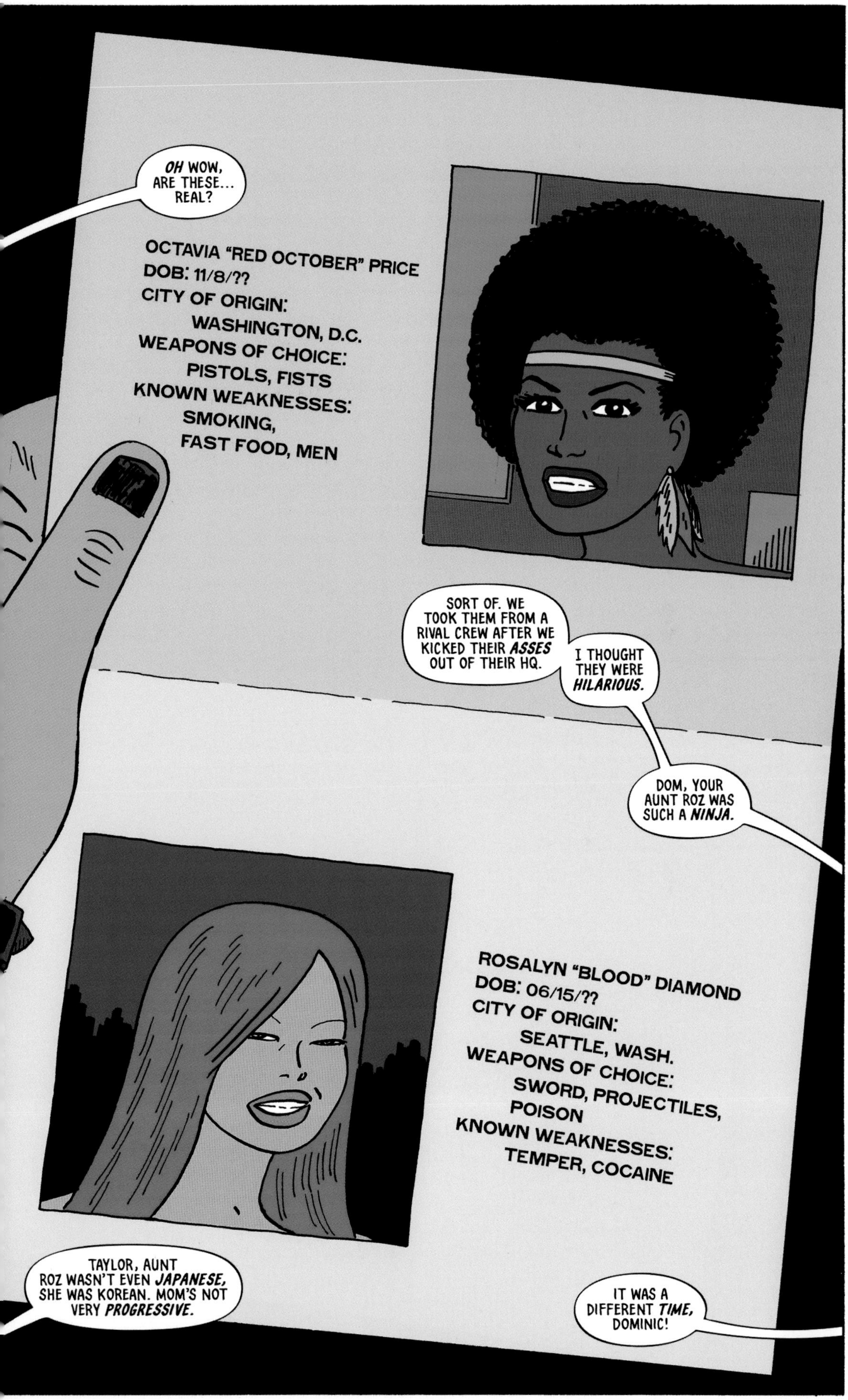

OH WOW, ARE THESE... REAL?
OCTAVIA "RED OCTOBER" PRICE
DOB: 11/8/??
CITY OF ORIGIN:
WASHINGTON, D.C.
WEAPONS OF CHOICE:
PISTOLS, FISTS
KNOWN WEAKNESSES:
SMOKING,
FAST FOOD, MEN
SORT OF. WE TOOK THEM FROM A RIVAL CREW AFTER WE KICKED THEIR ASSES OUT OF THEIR HQ.
I THOUGHT THEY WERE HILARIOUS.
DOM, YOUR AUNT ROZ WAS SUCH A NINJA.
ROSALYN "BLOOD" DIAMOND
DOB: 06/15/??
CITY OF ORIGIN:
SEATTLE, WASH.
WEAPONS OF CHOICE:
SWORD, PROJECTILES,
POISON
KNOWN WEAKNESSES:
TEMPER, COCAINE
TAYLOR, AUNT ROZ WASN'T EVEN JAPANESE, SHE WAS KOREAN. MOM'S NOT VERY PROGRESSIVE.
IT WAS A DIFFERENT TIME, DOMINIC!

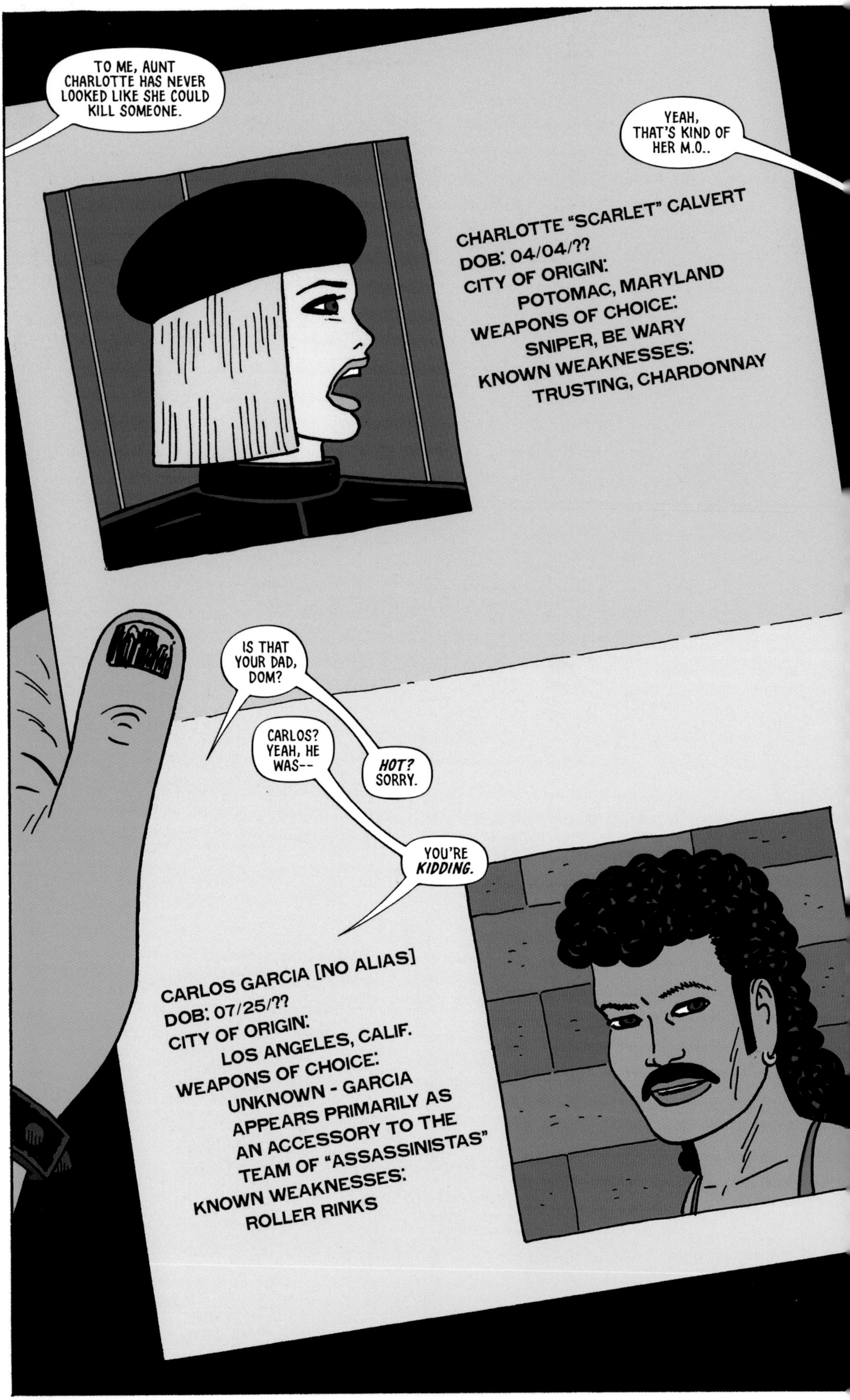
TO ME, AUNT CHARLOTTE HAS NEVER LOOKED LIKE SHE COULD KILL SOMEONE.
YEAH, THAT'S KIND OF HER M.O..
CHARLOTTE "SCARLET" CALVERT
DOB: 04/04/??
CITY OF ORIGIN:
POTOMAC, MARYLAND
WEAPONS OF CHOICE:
SNIPER, BE WARY
KNOWN WEAKNESSES:
TRUSTING, CHARDONNAY
IS THAT YOUR DAD, DOM?
CARLOS? YEAH, HE WAS--
HOT? SORRY.
YOU'RE KIDDING.
CARLOS GARCIA [NO ALIAS]
DOB: 07/25/??
CITY OF ORIGIN:
LOS ANGELES, CALIF.
WEAPONS OF CHOICE:
UNKNOWN - GARCIA APPEARS PRIMARILY AS AN ACCESSORY TO THE TEAM OF "ASSASSINISTAS"
KNOWN WEAKNESSES:
ROLLER RINKS

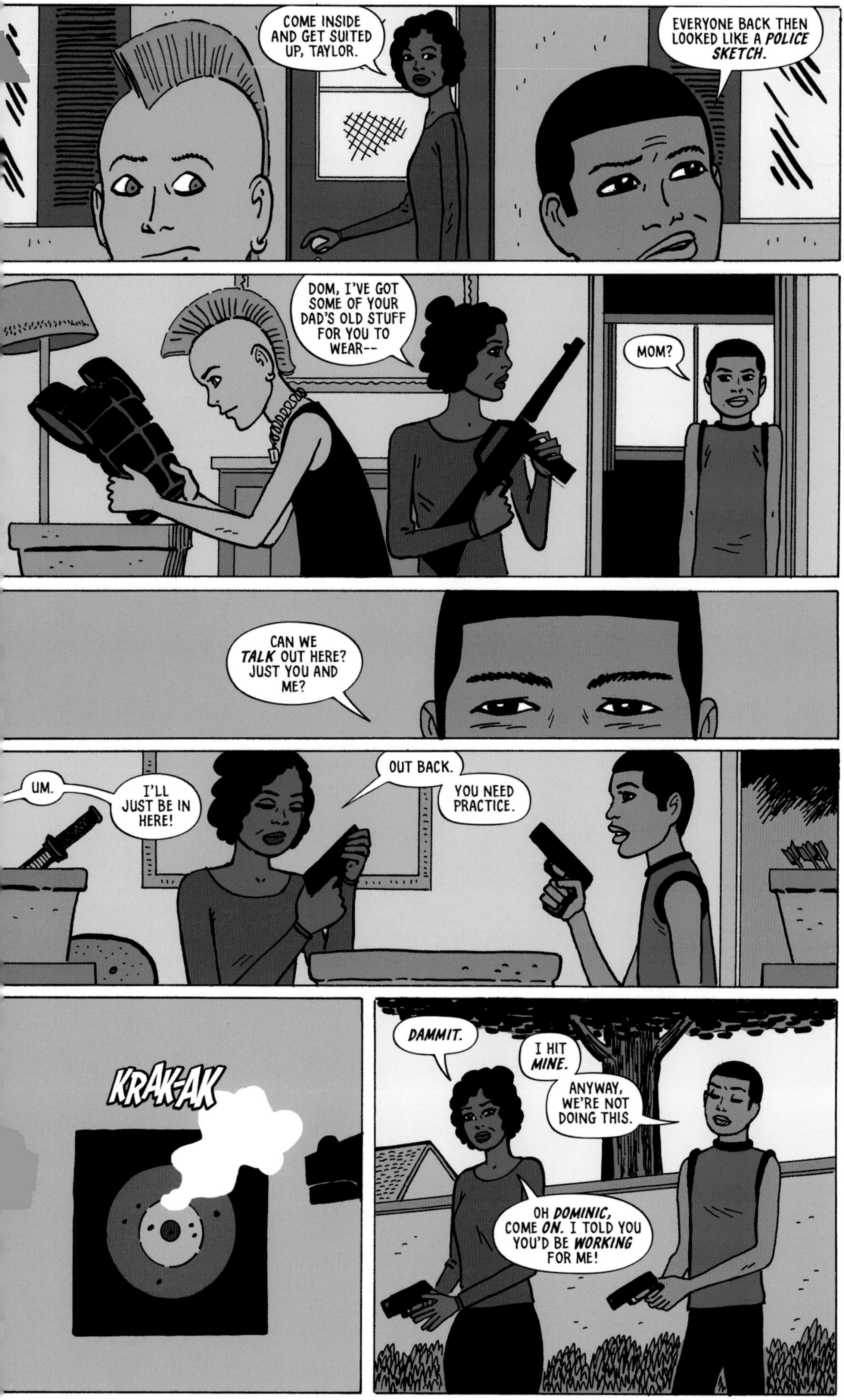
COME INSIDE AND GET SUITED UP, TAYLOR.
EVERYONE BACK THEN LOOKED LIKE A *POLICE SKETCH.*
DOM, I'VE GOT SOME OF YOUR DAD'S OLD STUFF FOR YOU TO WEAR--
MOM?
CAN WE *TALK* OUT HERE? JUST YOU AND ME?
UM.
I'LL JUST BE IN HERE!
OUT BACK.
YOU NEED PRACTICE.
KRAK-AK
DAMMIT.
I HIT *MINE.*
ANYWAY, WE'RE NOT DOING THIS.
OH *DOMINIC,* COME *ON.* I TOLD YOU YOU'D BE *WORKING* FOR ME!

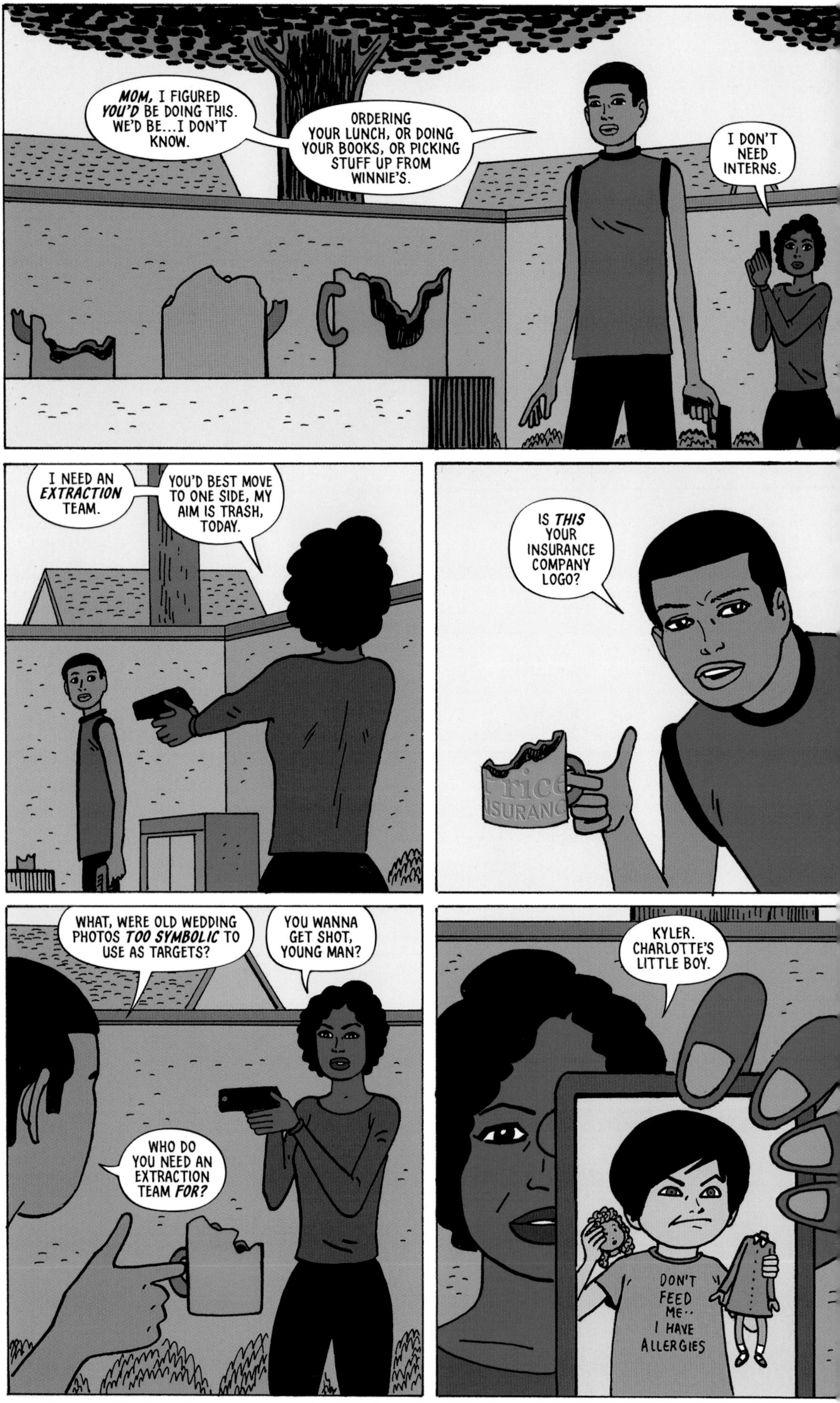
MOM, I FIGURED YOU'D BE DOING THIS. WE'D BE...I DON'T KNOW.
ORDERING YOUR LUNCH, OR DOING YOUR BOOKS, OR PICKING STUFF UP FROM WINNIE'S.
I DON'T NEED INTERNS.
I NEED AN EXTRACTION TEAM.
YOU'D BEST MOVE TO ONE SIDE, MY AIM IS TRASH, TODAY.
IS THIS YOUR INSURANCE COMPANY LOGO?
rice
SURANC
WHAT, WERE OLD WEDDING PHOTOS TOO SYMBOLIC TO USE AS TARGETS?
YOU WANNA GET SHOT, YOUNG MAN?
WHO DO YOU NEED AN EXTRACTION TEAM FOR?
KYLER. CHARLOTTE'S LITTLE BOY.
DON'T FEED ME.. I HAVE ALLERGIES

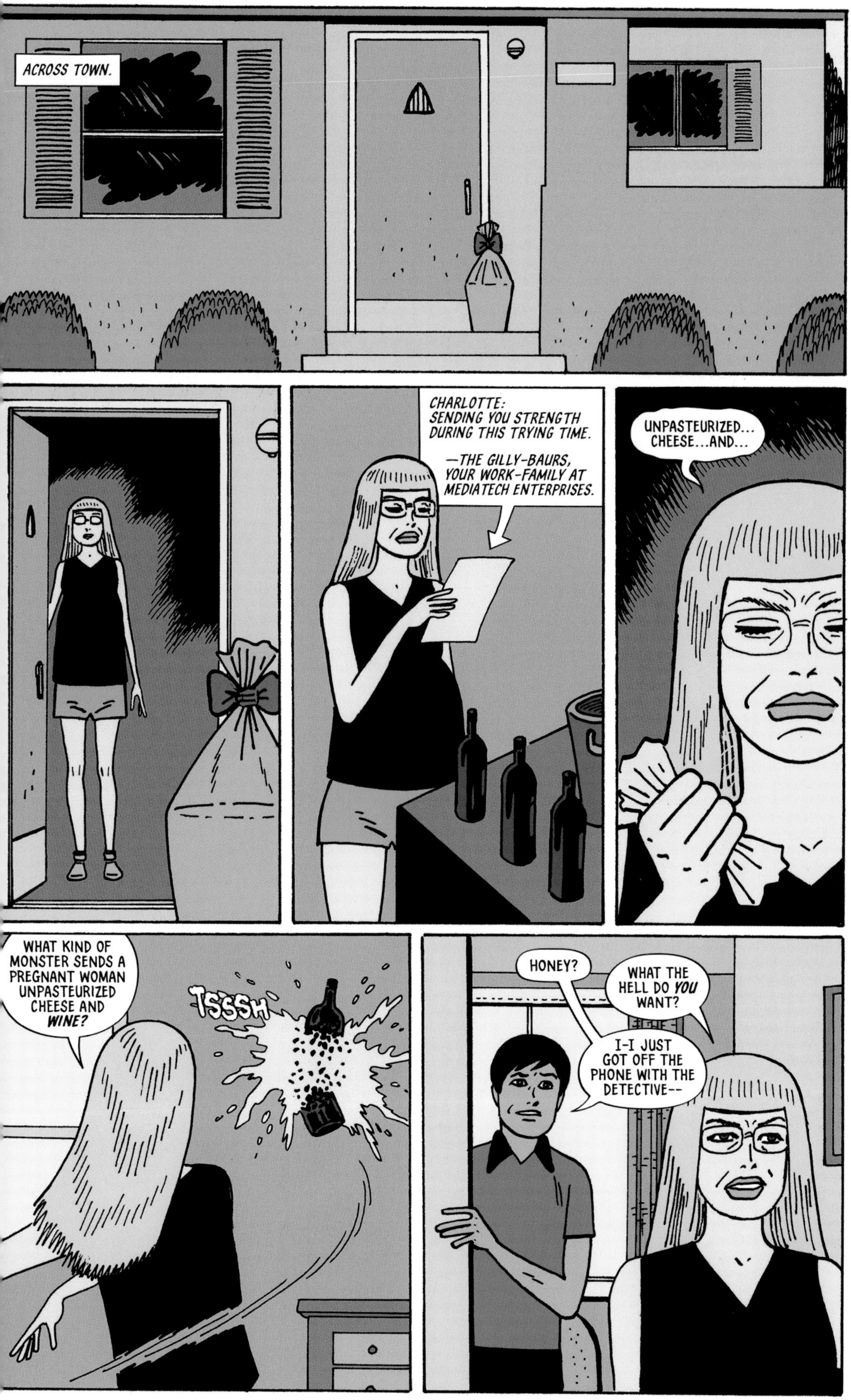
ACROSS TOWN.
CHARLOTTE: SENDING YOU STRENGTH DURING THIS TRYING TIME.
—THE GILLY-BAURS, YOUR WORK-FAMILY AT MEDIATECH ENTERPRISES.
UNPASTEURIZED... CHEESE...AND...
WHAT KIND OF MONSTER SENDS A PREGNANT WOMAN UNPASTEURIZED CHEESE AND WINE?
TSSSH
HONEY?
WHAT THE HELL DO YOU WANT?
I-I JUST GOT OFF THE PHONE WITH THE DETECTIVE--

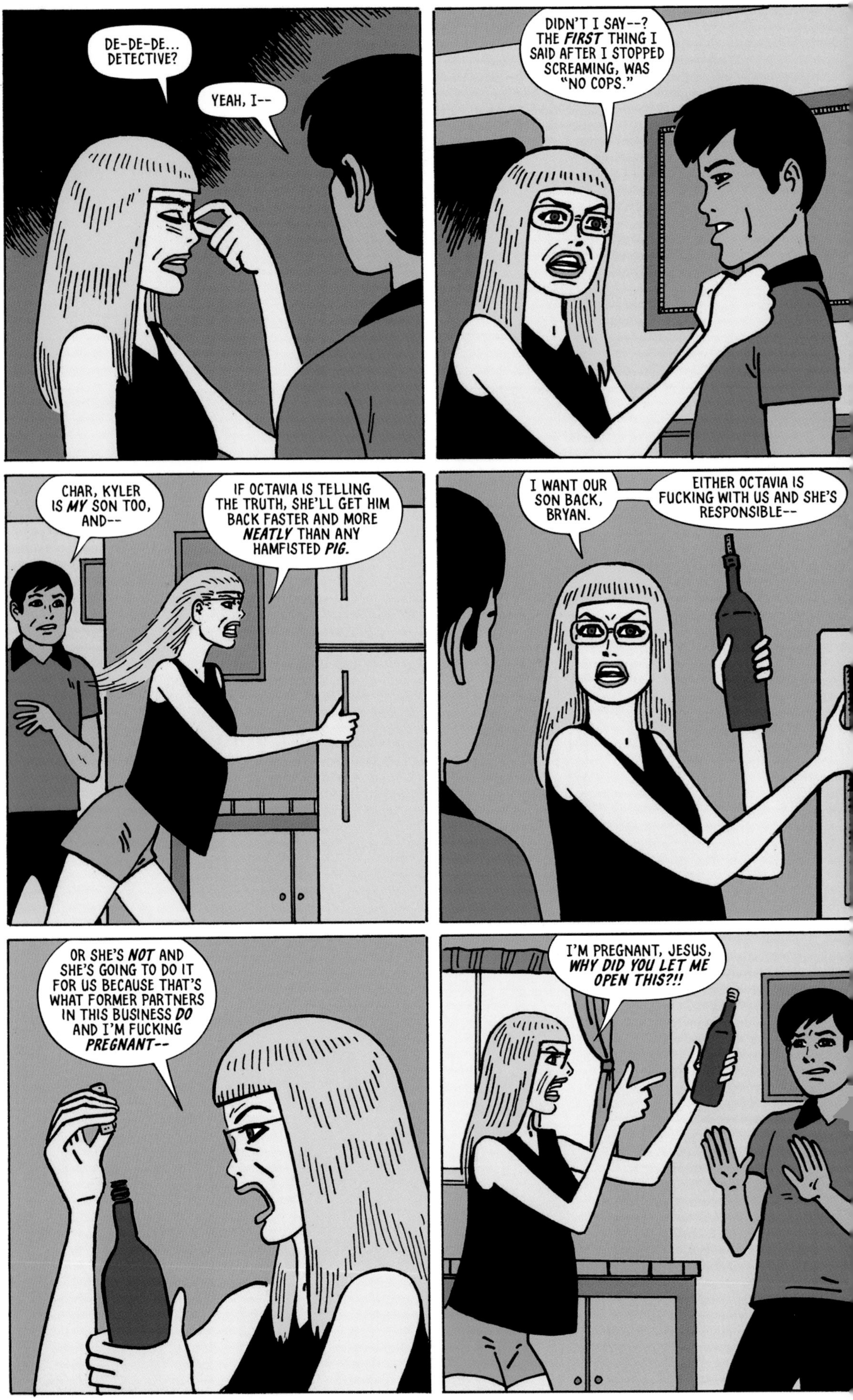
DE-DE-DE... DETECTIVE?
YEAH, I--
DIDN'T I SAY--? THE *FIRST* THING I SAID AFTER I STOPPED SCREAMING, WAS "NO COPS."
CHAR, KYLER IS *MY* SON TOO, AND--
IF OCTAVIA IS TELLING THE TRUTH, SHE'LL GET HIM BACK FASTER AND MORE *NEATLY* THAN ANY HAMFISTED *PIG.*
I WANT OUR SON BACK, BRYAN.
EITHER OCTAVIA IS FUCKING WITH US AND SHE'S RESPONSIBLE--
OR SHE'S *NOT* AND SHE'S GOING TO DO IT FOR US BECAUSE THAT'S WHAT FORMER PARTNERS IN THIS BUSINESS *DO* AND I'M FUCKING *PREGNANT*--
I'M PREGNANT, JESUS, *WHY DID YOU LET ME OPEN THIS?!!*

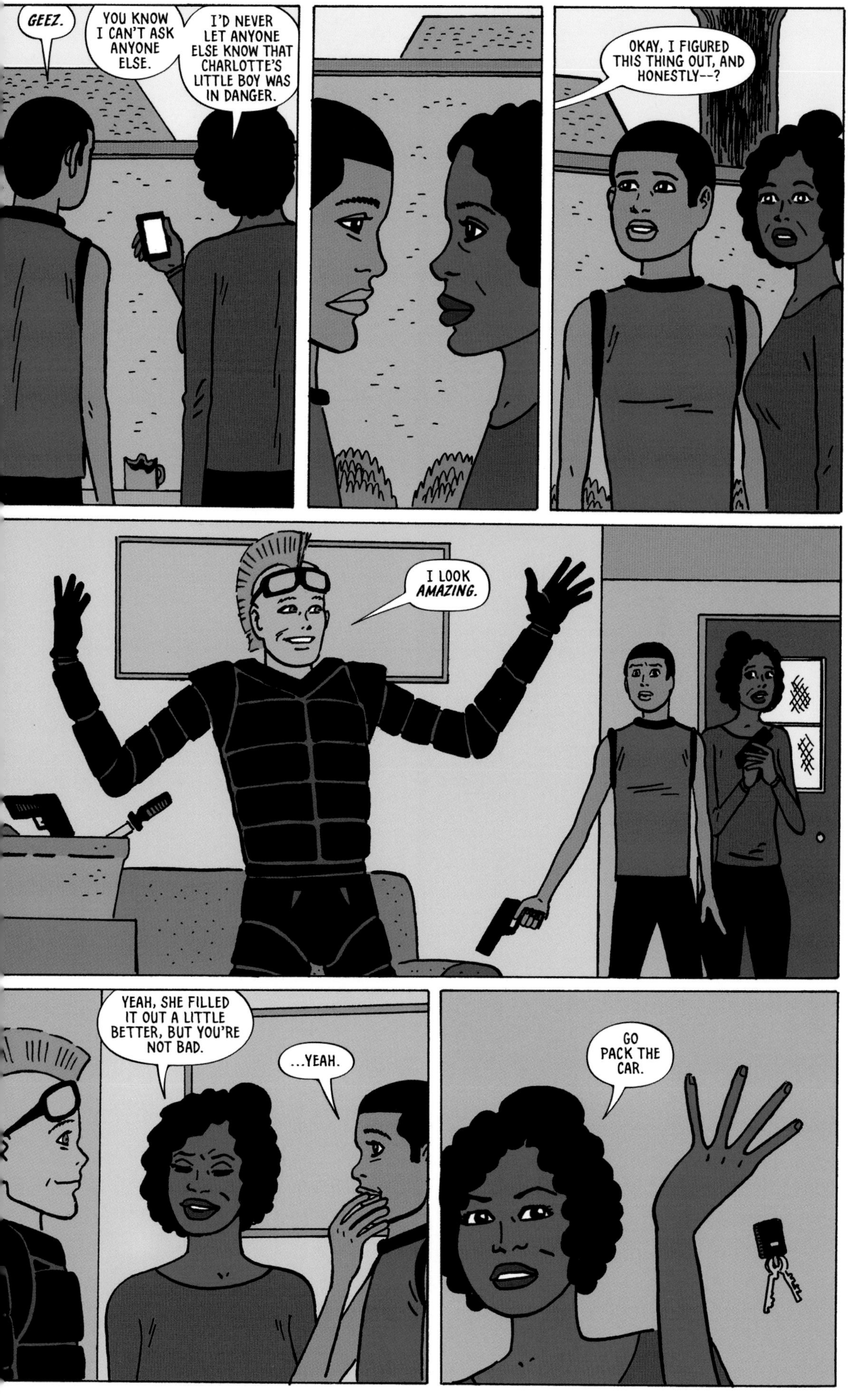
GEEZ.
YOU KNOW I CAN'T ASK ANYONE ELSE.
I'D NEVER LET ANYONE ELSE KNOW THAT CHARLOTTE'S LITTLE BOY WAS IN DANGER.
OKAY, I FIGURED THIS THING OUT, AND HONESTLY--?
I LOOK *AMAZING.*
YEAH, SHE FILLED IT OUT A LITTLE BETTER, BUT YOU'RE NOT BAD.
...YEAH.
GO PACK THE CAR.

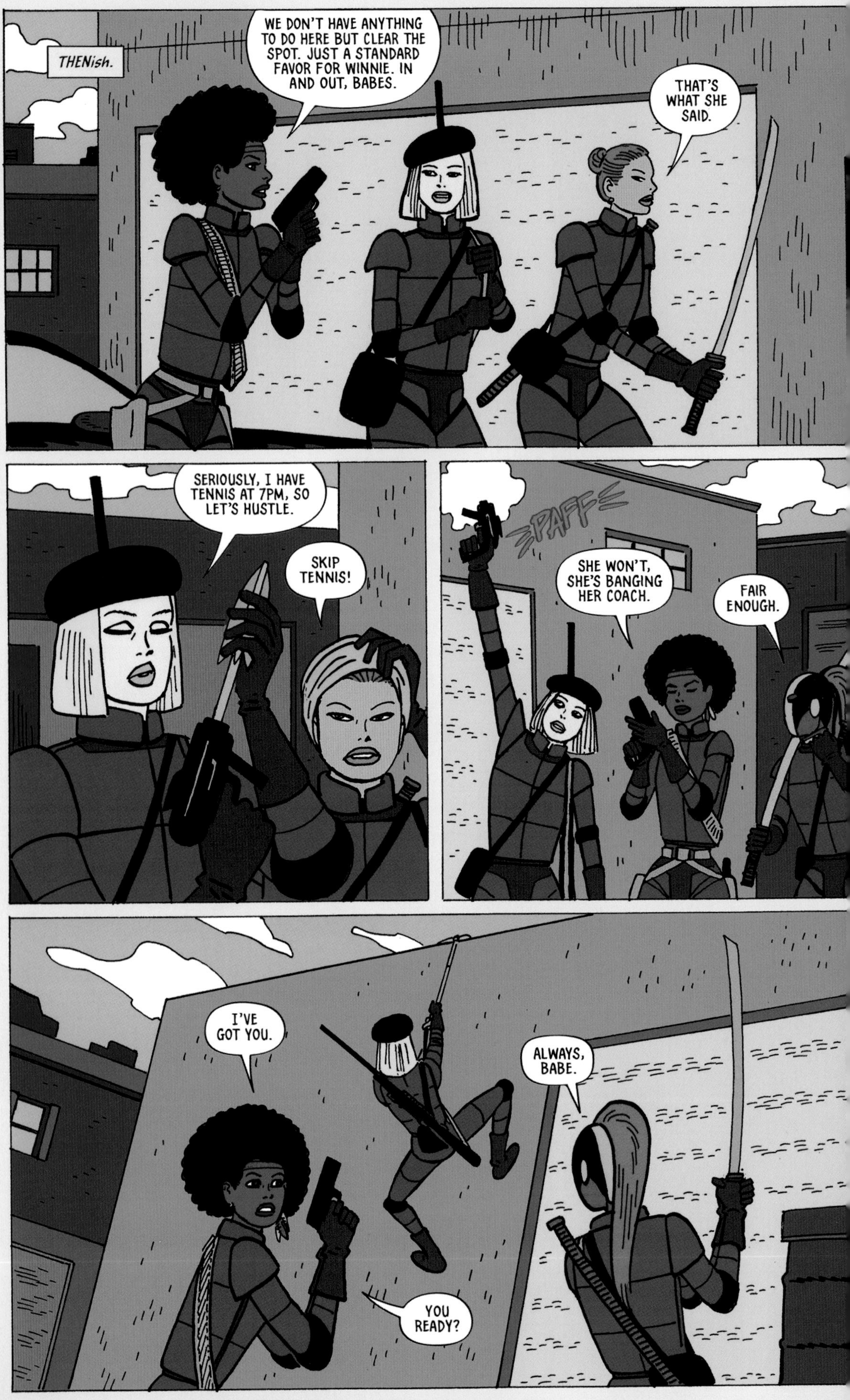
THENish.
WE DON'T HAVE ANYTHING TO DO HERE BUT CLEAR THE SPOT. JUST A STANDARD FAVOR FOR WINNIE. IN AND OUT, BABES.
THAT'S WHAT SHE SAID.
SERIOUSLY, I HAVE TENNIS AT 7PM, SO LET'S HUSTLE.
SKIP TENNIS!
PAFF
SHE WON'T, SHE'S BANGING HER COACH.
FAIR ENOUGH.
I'VE GOT YOU.
ALWAYS, BABE.
YOU READY?

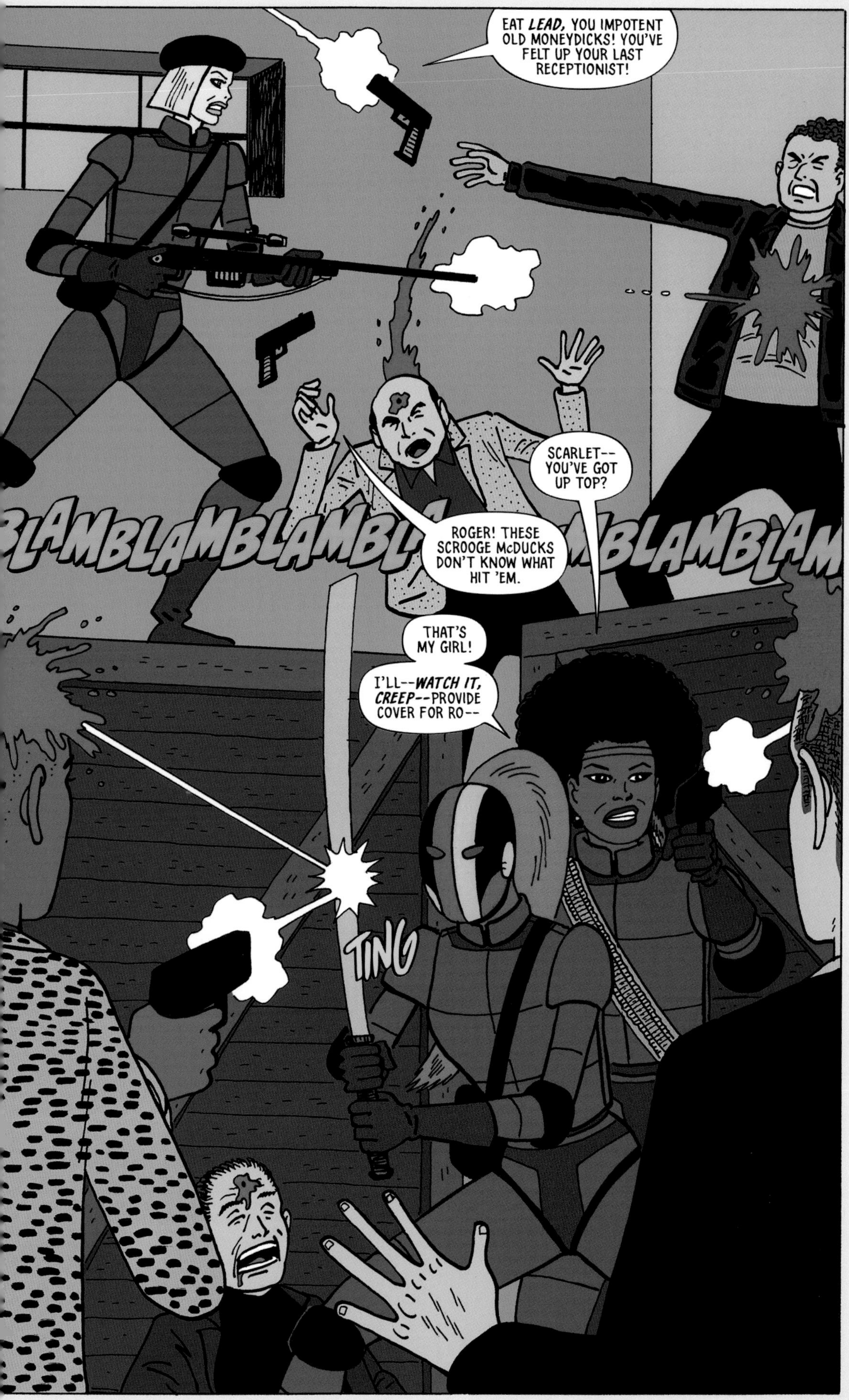

EAT *LEAD,* YOU IMPOTENT OLD MONEYDICKS! YOU'VE FELT UP YOUR LAST RECEPTIONIST!
SCARLET-- YOU'VE GOT UP TOP?
BLAMBLAMBLAMBLA MBLAMBLAM
ROGER! THESE SCROOGE McDUCKS DON'T KNOW WHAT HIT 'EM.
THAT'S MY GIRL!
I'LL--*WATCH IT, CREEP*--PROVIDE COVER FOR RO--
TING

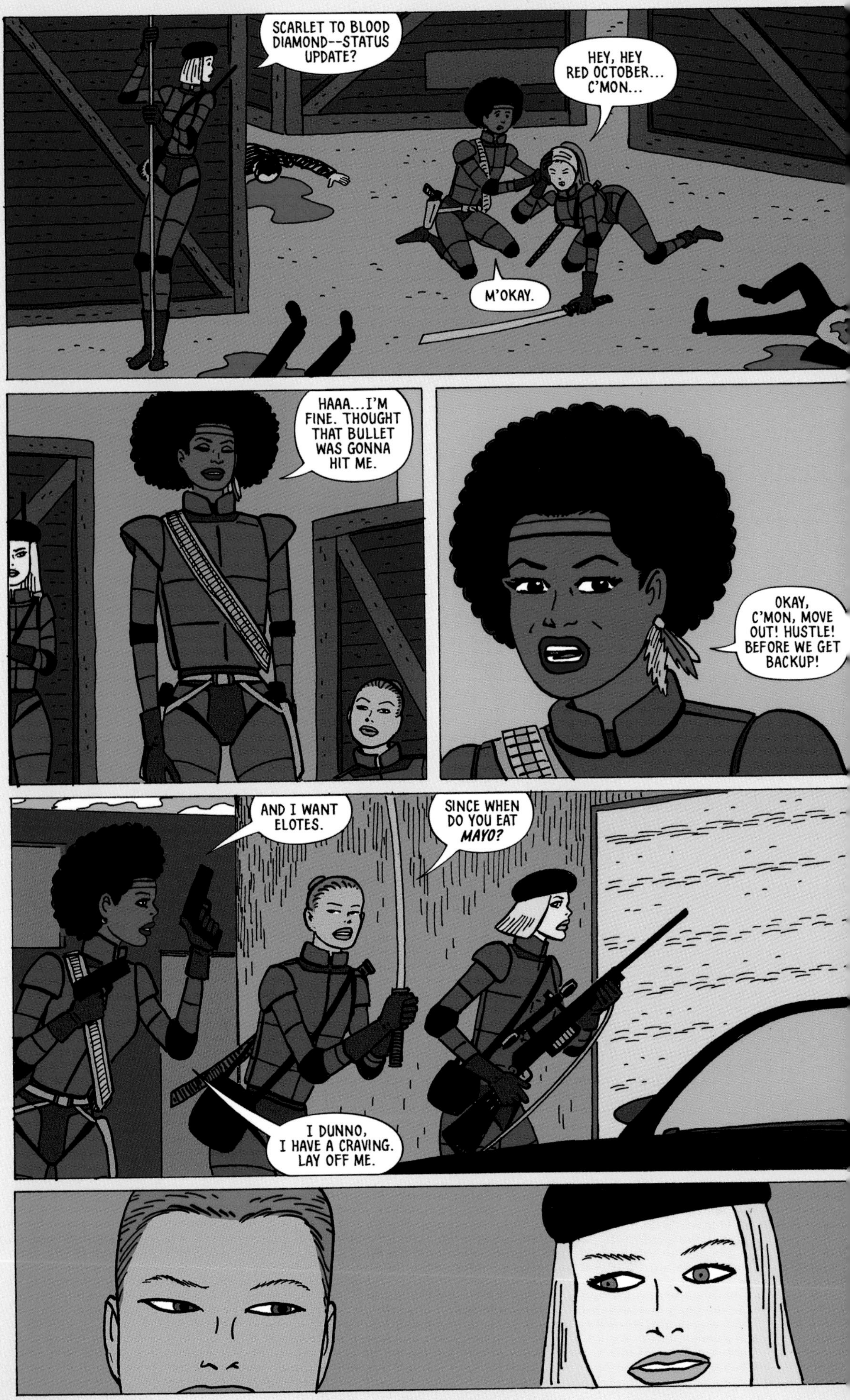
SCARLET TO BLOOD DIAMOND--STATUS UPDATE?
HEY, HEY RED OCTOBER... C'MON...
M'OKAY.
HAAA...I'M FINE. THOUGHT THAT BULLET WAS GONNA HIT ME.
OKAY, C'MON, MOVE OUT! HUSTLE! BEFORE WE GET BACKUP!
AND I WANT ELOTES.
SINCE WHEN DO YOU EAT *MAYO?*
I DUNNO, I HAVE A CRAVING. LAY OFF ME.

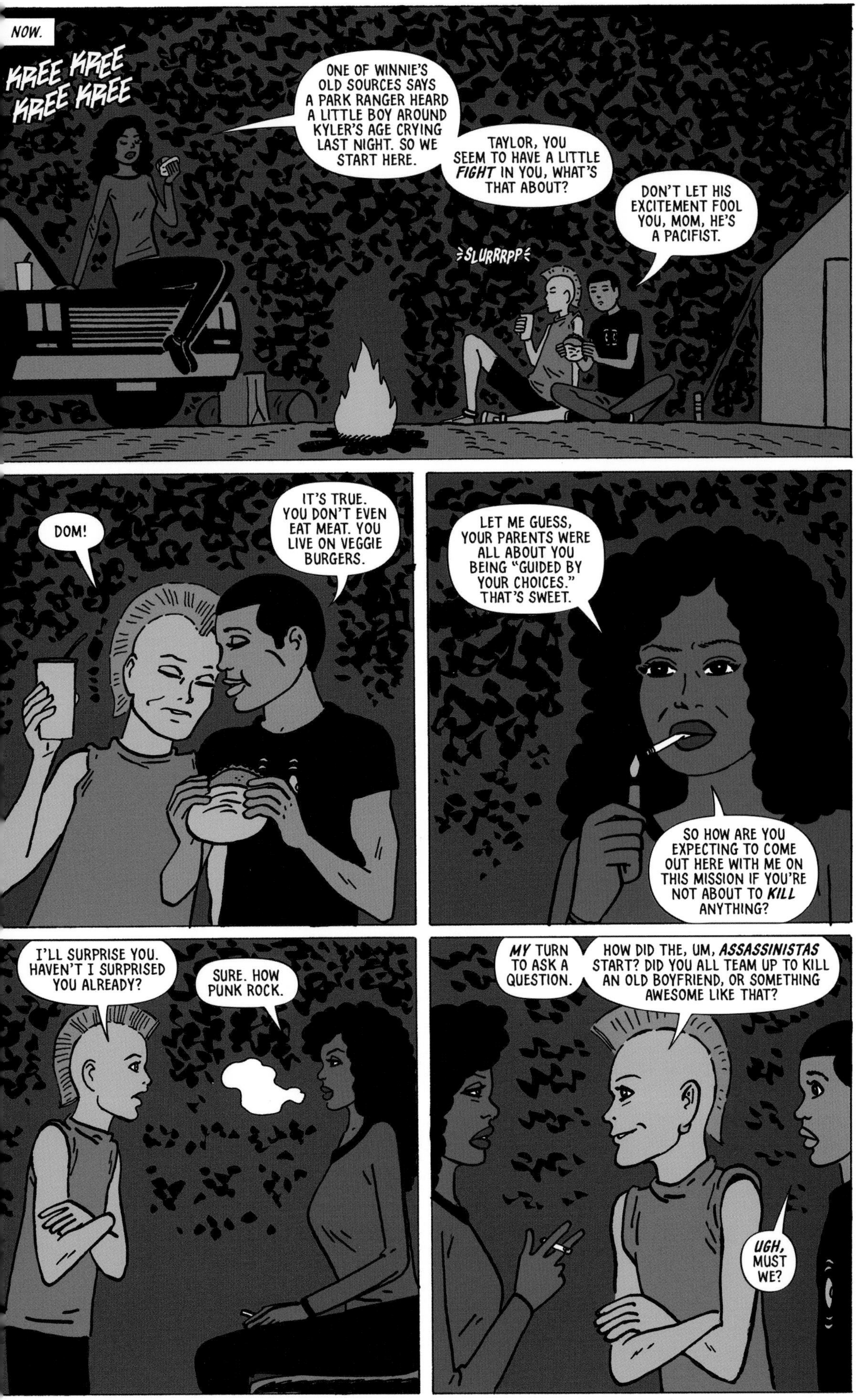
NOW.
KREE KREE KREE KREE
ONE OF WINNIE'S OLD SOURCES SAYS A PARK RANGER HEARD A LITTLE BOY AROUND KYLER'S AGE CRYING LAST NIGHT. SO WE START HERE.
TAYLOR, YOU SEEM TO HAVE A LITTLE *FIGHT* IN YOU, WHAT'S THAT ABOUT?
SLURRRPP
DON'T LET HIS EXCITEMENT FOOL YOU, MOM, HE'S A PACIFIST.
DOM!
IT'S TRUE. YOU DON'T EVEN EAT MEAT. YOU LIVE ON VEGGIE BURGERS.
LET ME GUESS, YOUR PARENTS WERE ALL ABOUT YOU BEING "GUIDED BY YOUR CHOICES." THAT'S SWEET.
SO HOW ARE YOU EXPECTING TO COME OUT HERE WITH ME ON THIS MISSION IF YOU'RE NOT ABOUT TO *KILL* ANYTHING?
I'LL SURPRISE YOU. HAVEN'T I SURPRISED YOU ALREADY?
SURE. HOW PUNK ROCK.
MY TURN TO ASK A QUESTION.
HOW DID THE, UM, *ASSASSINISTAS* START? DID YOU ALL TEAM UP TO KILL AN OLD BOYFRIEND, OR SOMETHING AWESOME LIKE THAT?
UGH, MUST WE?

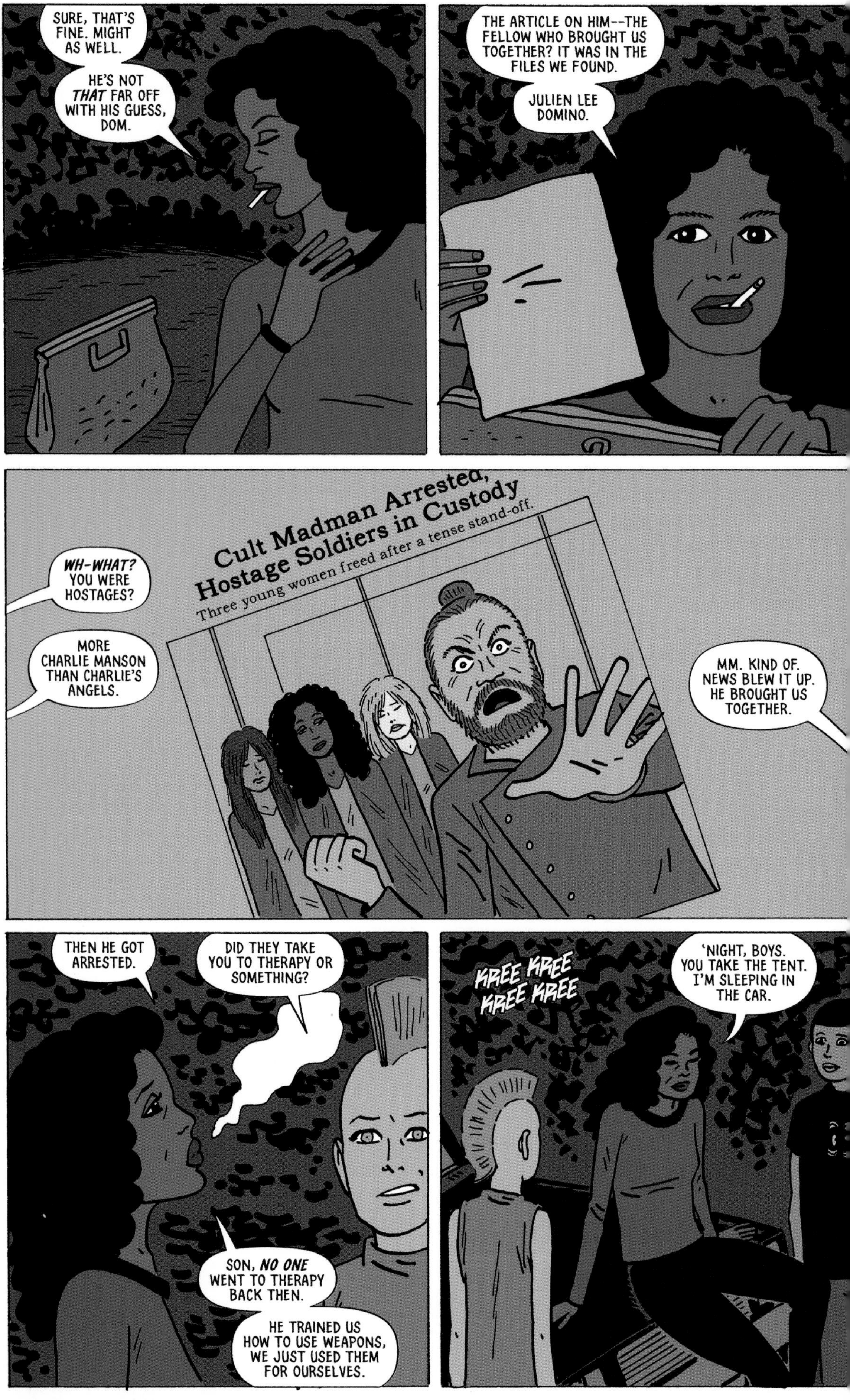
SURE, THAT'S FINE. MIGHT AS WELL.
HE'S NOT *THAT* FAR OFF WITH HIS GUESS, DOM.
THE ARTICLE ON HIM--THE FELLOW WHO BROUGHT US TOGETHER? IT WAS IN THE FILES WE FOUND.
JULIEN LEE DOMINO.
Cult Madman Arrested, Hostage Soldiers in Custody
Three young women freed after a tense stand-off.
WH-WHAT? YOU WERE HOSTAGES?
MORE CHARLIE MANSON THAN CHARLIE'S ANGELS.
MM. KIND OF. NEWS BLEW IT UP. HE BROUGHT US TOGETHER.
THEN HE GOT ARRESTED.
DID THEY TAKE YOU TO THERAPY OR SOMETHING?
SON, *NO ONE* WENT TO THERAPY BACK THEN.
HE TRAINED US HOW TO USE WEAPONS, WE JUST USED THEM FOR OURSELVES.
KREE KREE KREE KREE
'NIGHT, BOYS. YOU TAKE THE TENT. I'M SLEEPING IN THE CAR.

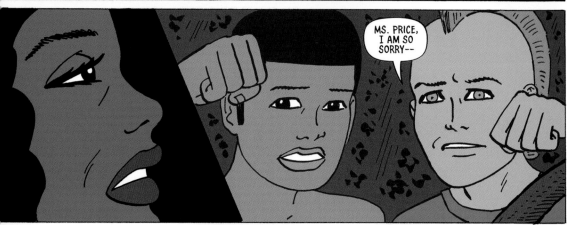

BANG BANG
BANG BANG

MOM, MOM, OPEN THE DOOR! SOMETHING GRABBED THE TENT, IT SOUNDED LIKE *METAL*, WE HEARD A *ROAR--* MOM--

MS. PRICE, I AM SO SORRY--

GET DRESSED, FOR FUCK'S SAKE!

AND CALL ME OCTAVIA, *ALSO* FOR FUCK'S SAKE!

WHAT DO WE DO?

WELL, DOMINIC, THAT DEPENDS, DID YOU FEEL LIKE *DYING* TONIGHT?

MOM!

I WAS JUST *ASKING!* WHY DO YOU HAVE TO BE SO *NASTY?*

I WAS JUST *TELLING YOU*, DOMINIC, I--

IS THERE MAYBE A *SLEEP DART* OR SOMETHING *NON-LETHAL* IN HERE?

LIKE A NET? OR TEAR GAS? THOUGH I DON'T LIKE USING TEAR GAS...

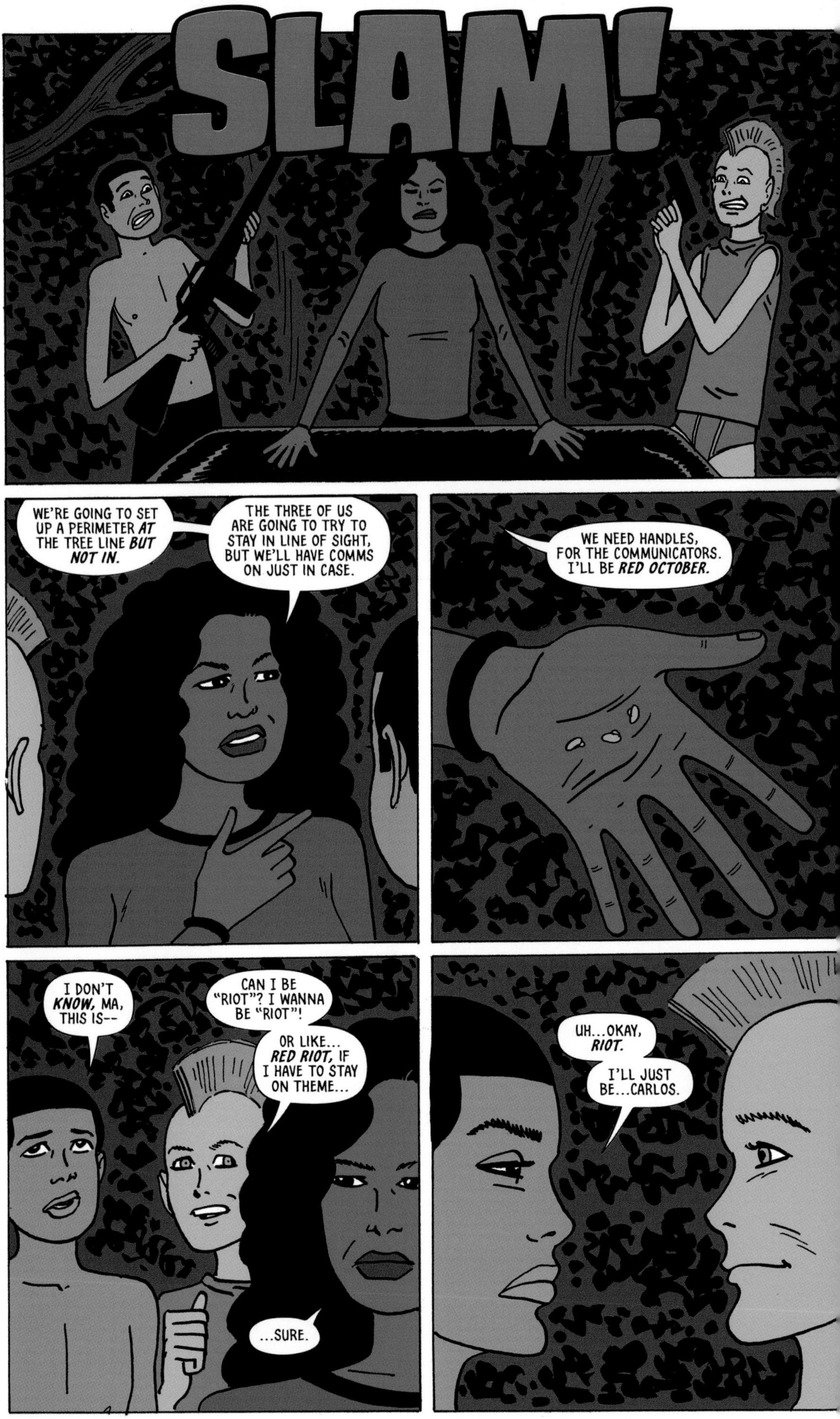
SLAM!
WE'RE GOING TO SET UP A PERIMETER *AT* THE TREE LINE *BUT NOT IN.*
THE THREE OF US ARE GOING TO TRY TO STAY IN LINE OF SIGHT, BUT WE'LL HAVE COMMS ON JUST IN CASE.
WE NEED HANDLES, FOR THE COMMUNICATORS. I'LL BE *RED OCTOBER.*
I DON'T *KNOW,* MA, THIS IS--
CAN I BE "RIOT"? I WANNA BE "RIOT"!
OR LIKE... *RED RIOT,* IF I HAVE TO STAY ON THEME...
...SURE.
UH...OKAY, *RIOT.*
I'LL JUST BE...CARLOS.

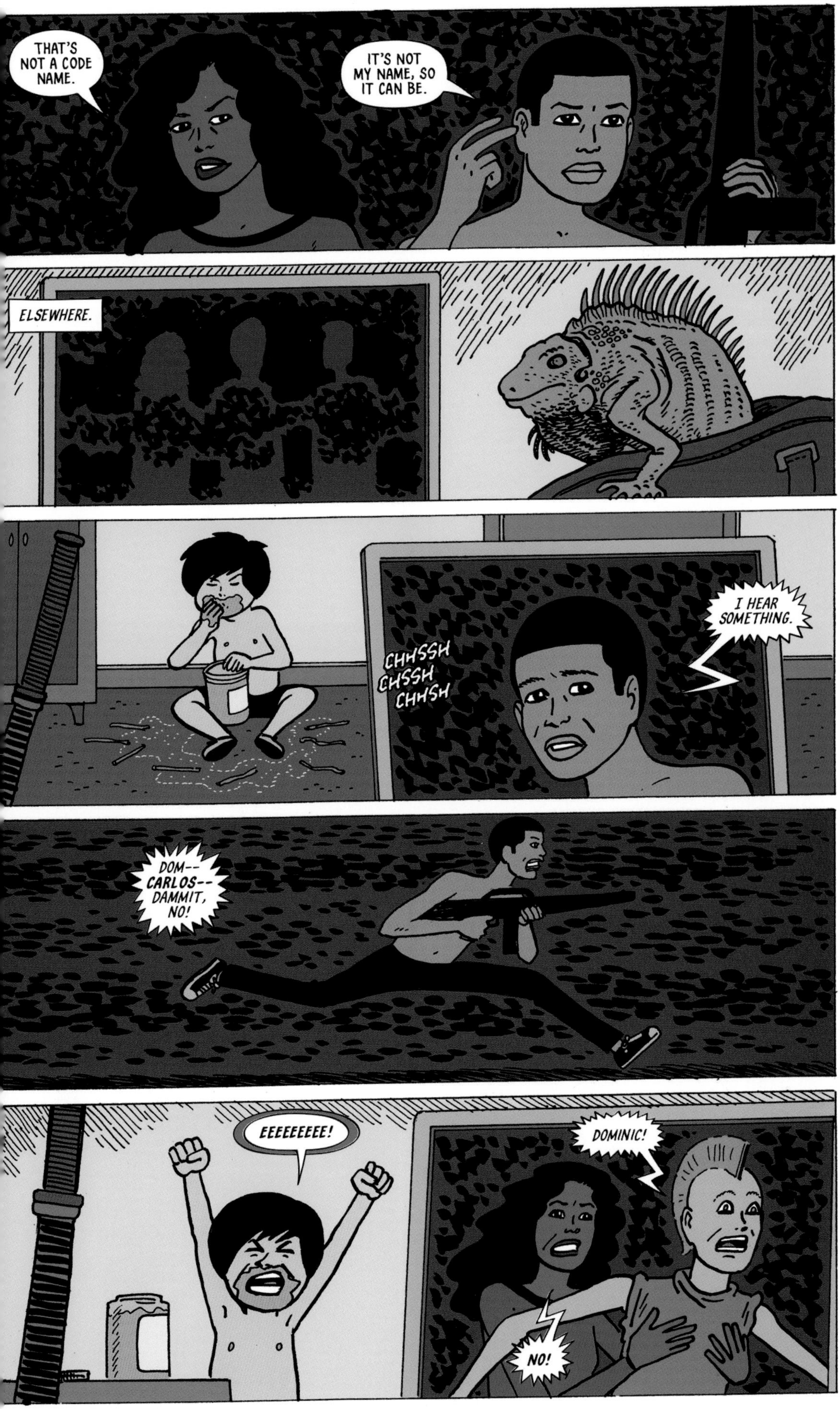
THAT'S NOT A CODE NAME.
IT'S NOT MY NAME, SO IT CAN BE.
ELSEWHERE.
CHHSSH CHSSH CHHSH
I HEAR SOMETHING.
DOM-- CARLOS-- DAMMIT, NO!
EEEEEEEEE!
DOMINIC!
NO!

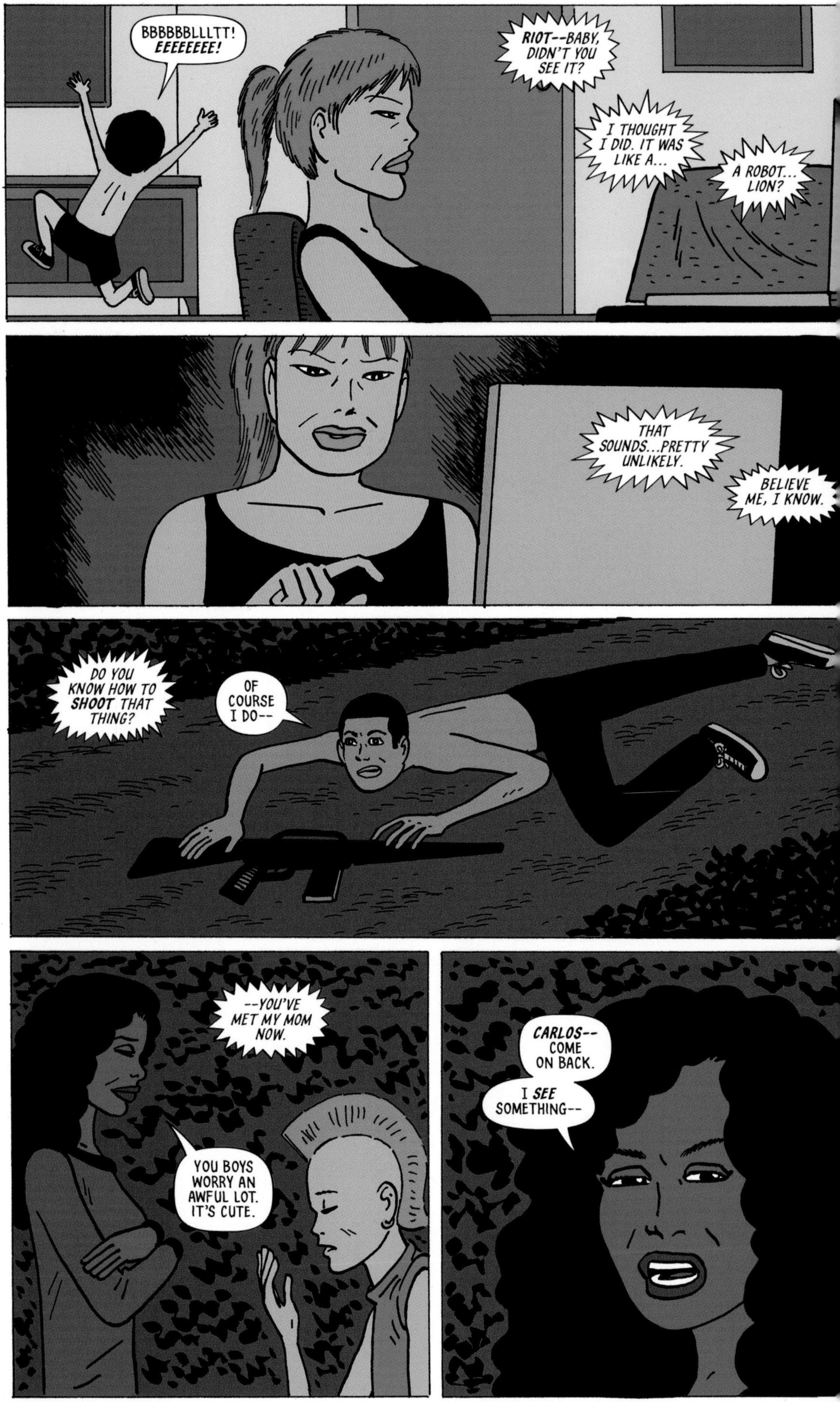
BBBBBBLLLTT! EEEEEEEE!
RIOT--BABY, DIDN'T YOU SEE IT?
I THOUGHT I DID. IT WAS LIKE A...
A ROBOT... LION?
THAT SOUNDS...PRETTY UNLIKELY.
BELIEVE ME, I KNOW.
DO YOU KNOW HOW TO SHOOT THAT THING?
OF COURSE I DO--
--YOU'VE MET MY MOM NOW.
YOU BOYS WORRY AN AWFUL LOT. IT'S CUTE.
CARLOS-- COME ON BACK.
I SEE SOMETHING--

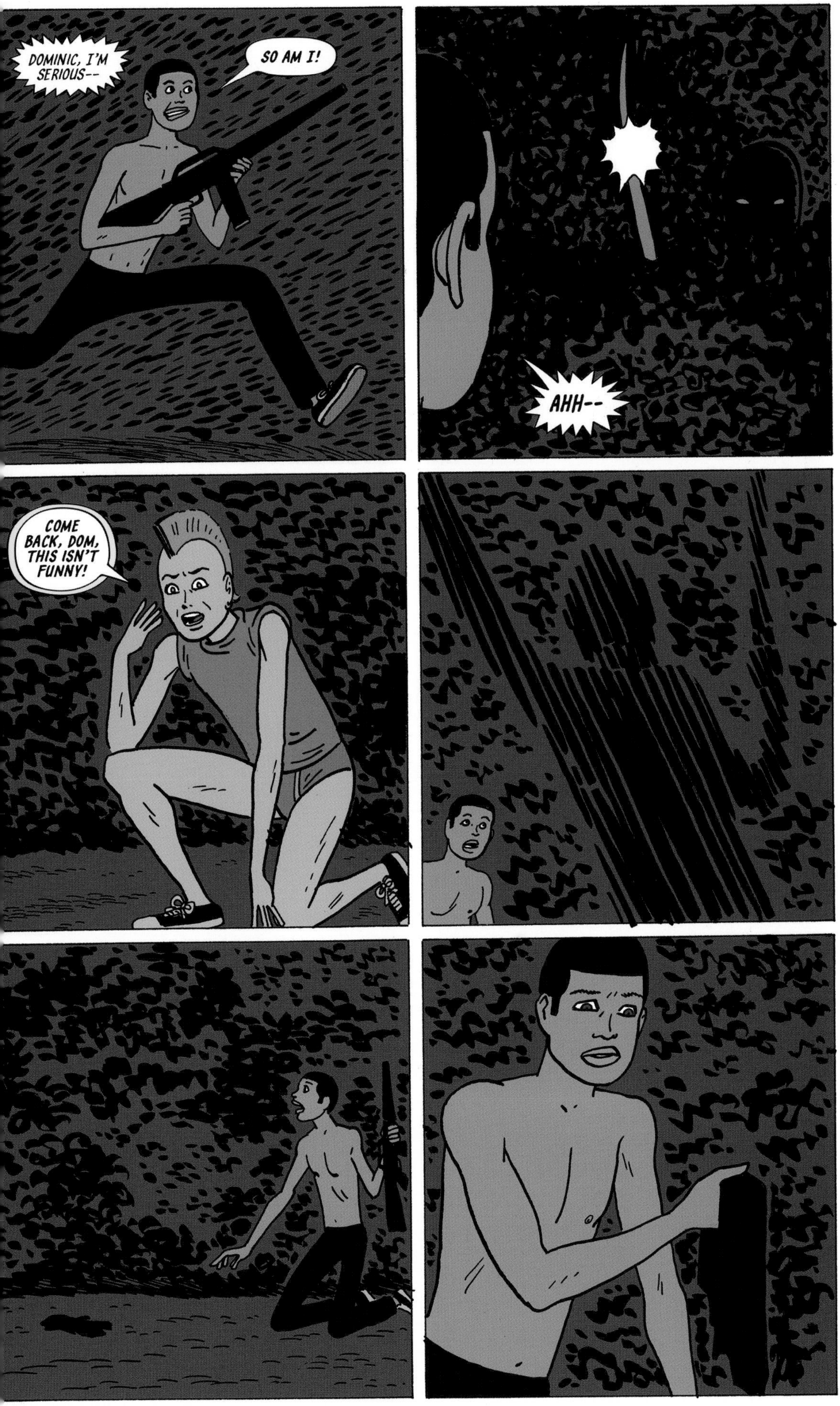
DOMINIC, I'M SERIOUS--
SO AM I!
AHH--
COME BACK, DOM, THIS ISN'T FUNNY!

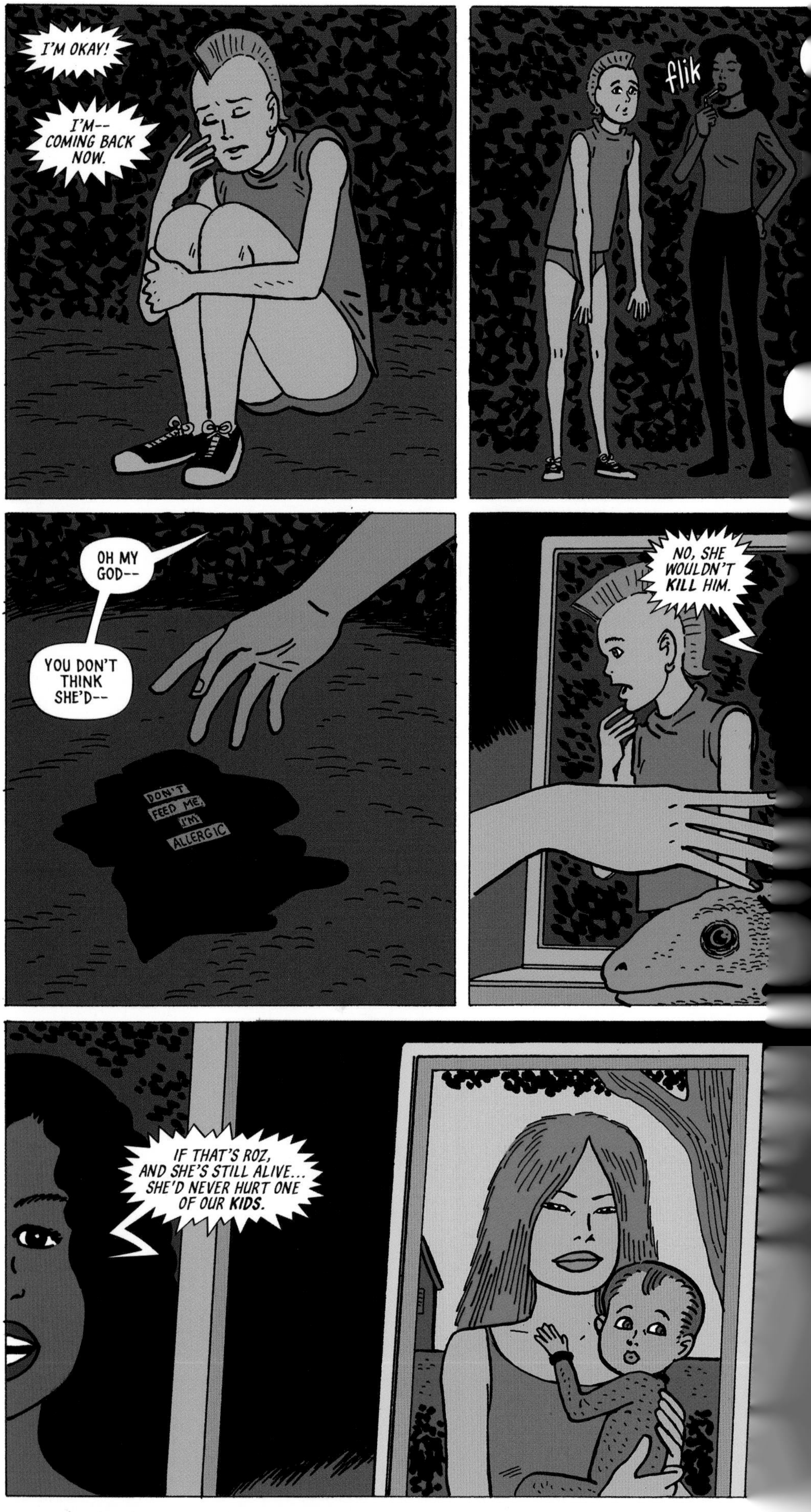

I'M OKAY!
I'M-- COMING BACK NOW.
flik
OH MY GOD--
YOU DON'T THINK SHE'D--
DON'T FEED ME, I'M ALLERGIC
NO, SHE WOULDN'T KILL HIM.
IF THAT'S ROZ, AND SHE'S STILL ALIVE... SHE'D NEVER HURT ONE OF OUR KIDS.

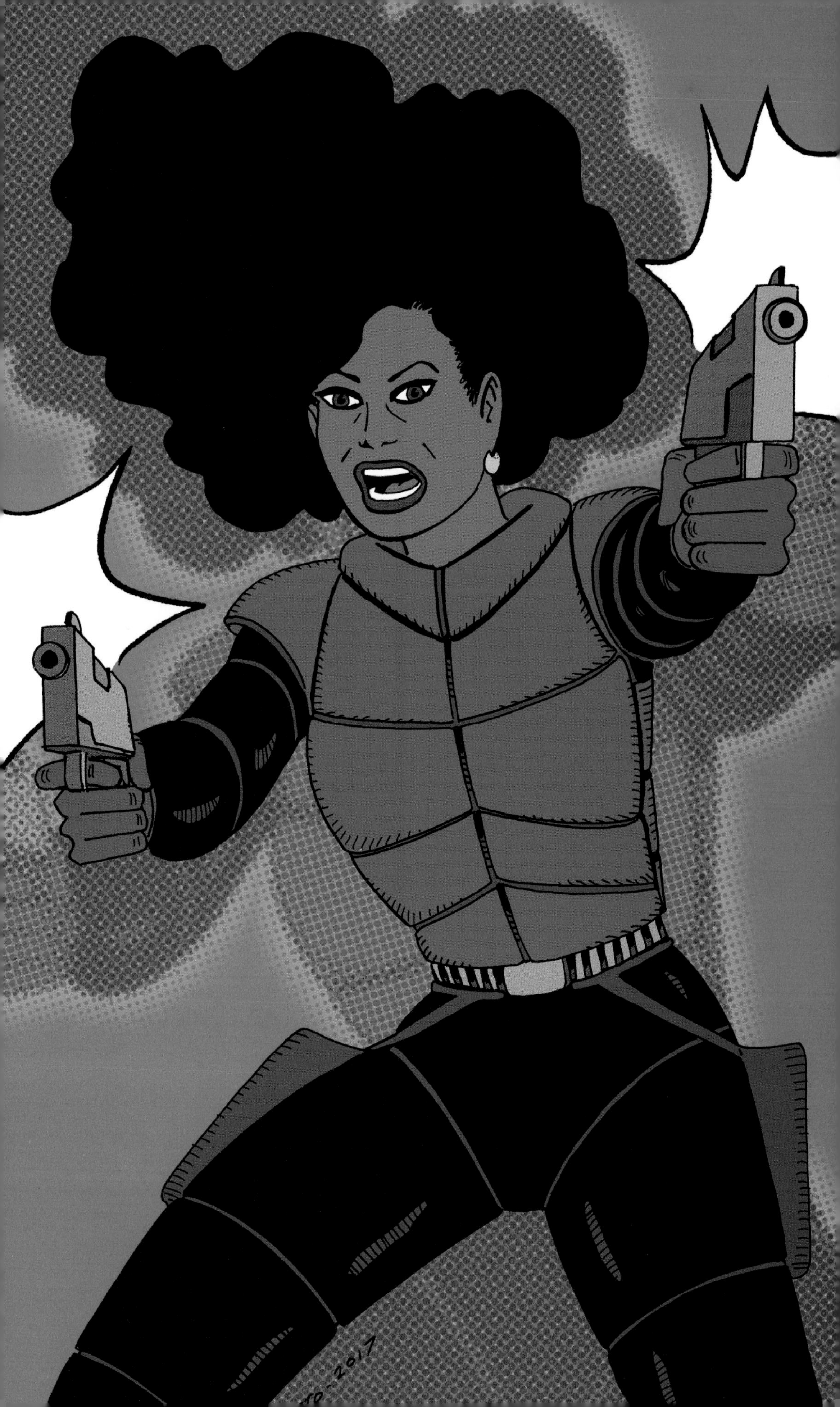

"This isn't about you getting to run wild and eat processed sugar."

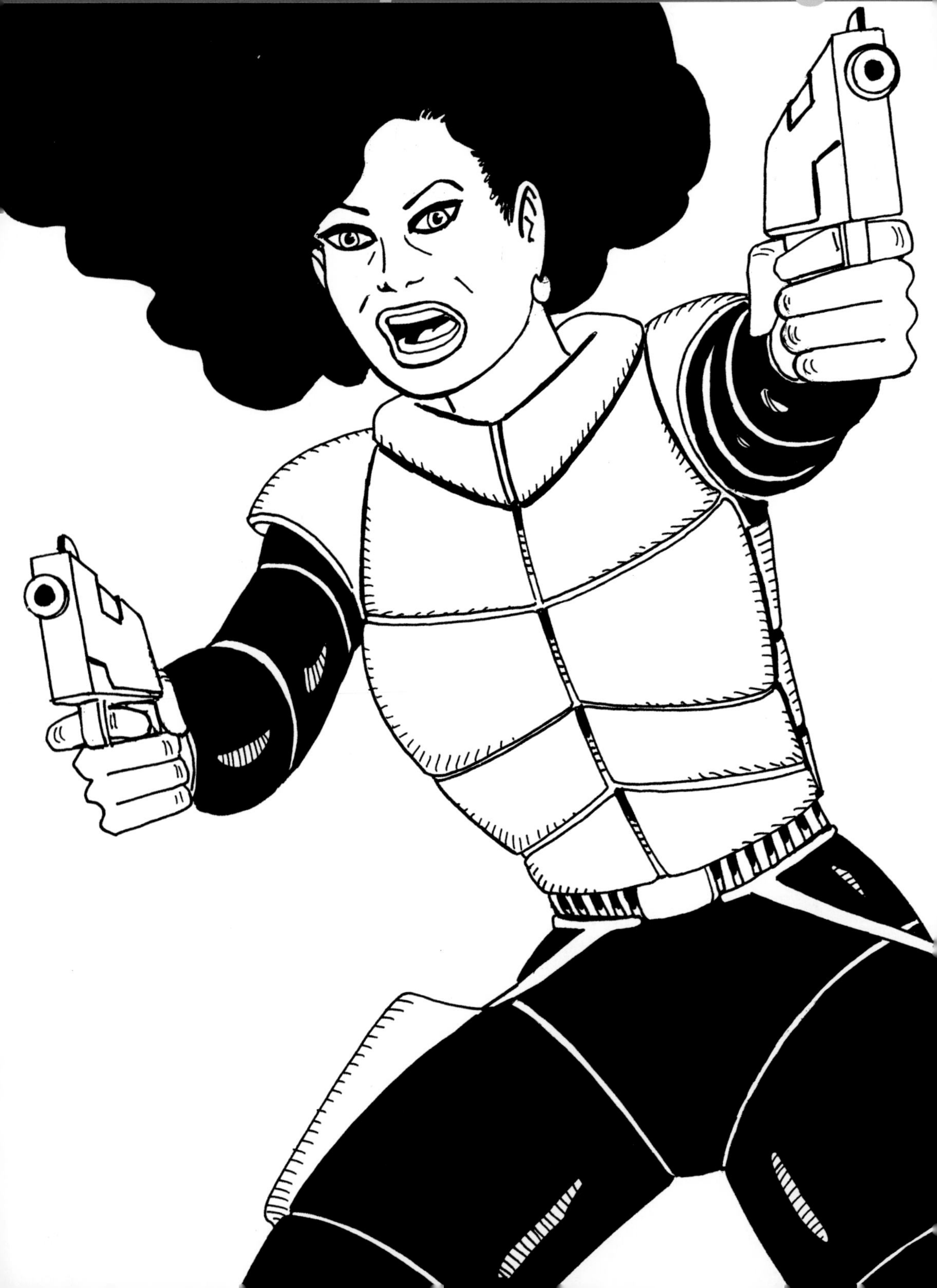

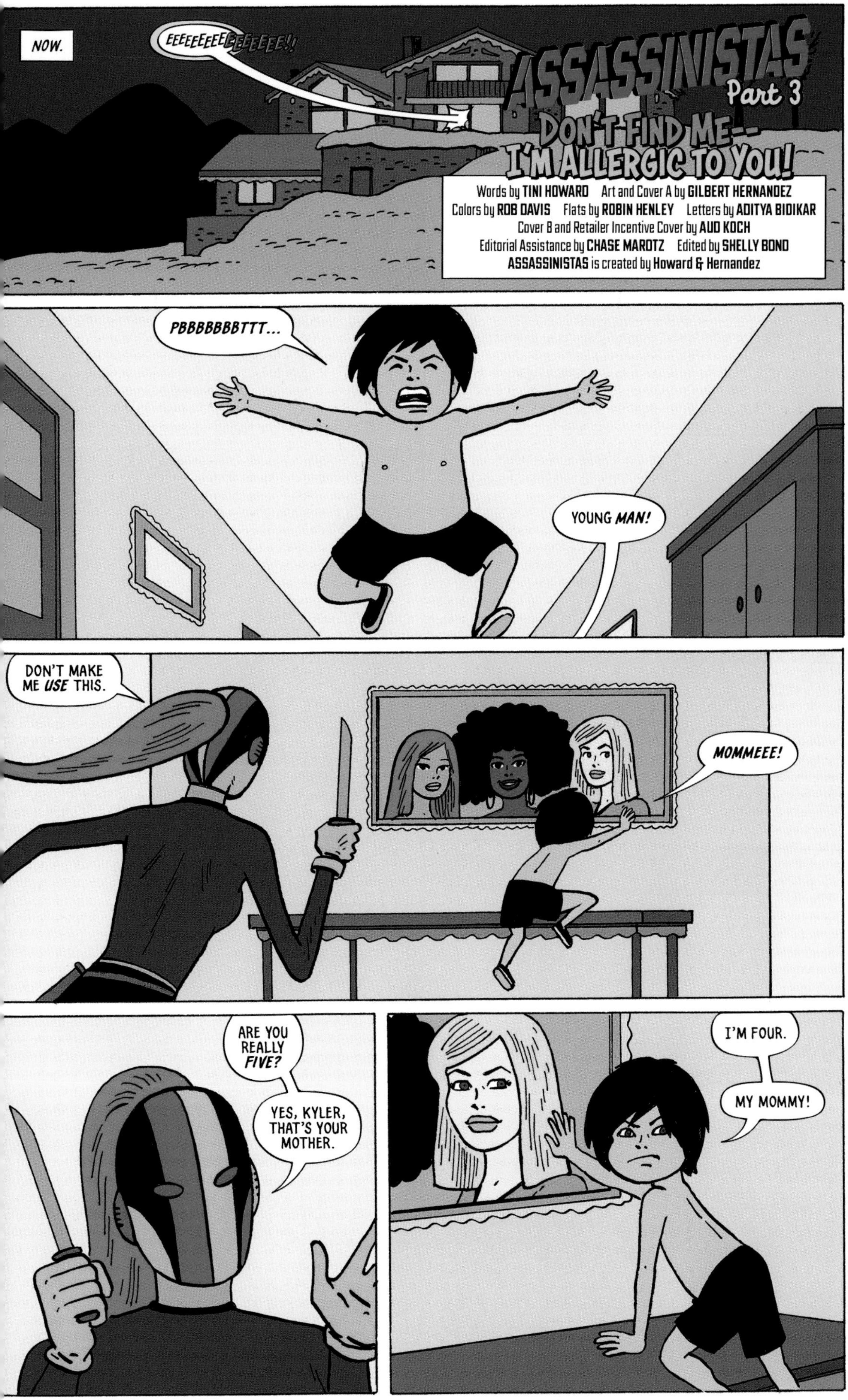
NOW.
EEEEEEEEEEEEEEEE!!
ASSASSINISTAS Part 3
DON'T FIND ME-- I'M ALLERGIC TO YOU!
Words by TINI HOWARD Art and Cover A by GILBERT HERNANDEZ
Colors by ROB DAVIS Flats by ROBIN HENLEY Letters by ADITYA BIDIKAR
Cover B and Retailer Incentive Cover by AUD KOCH
Editorial Assistance by CHASE MAROTZ Edited by SHELLY BOND
ASSASSINISTAS is created by Howard & Hernandez
PBBBBBBBTTT...
YOUNG MAN!
DON'T MAKE ME USE THIS.
MOMMEEE!
ARE YOU REALLY FIVE?
YES, KYLER, THAT'S YOUR MOTHER.
I'M FOUR.
MY MOMMY!

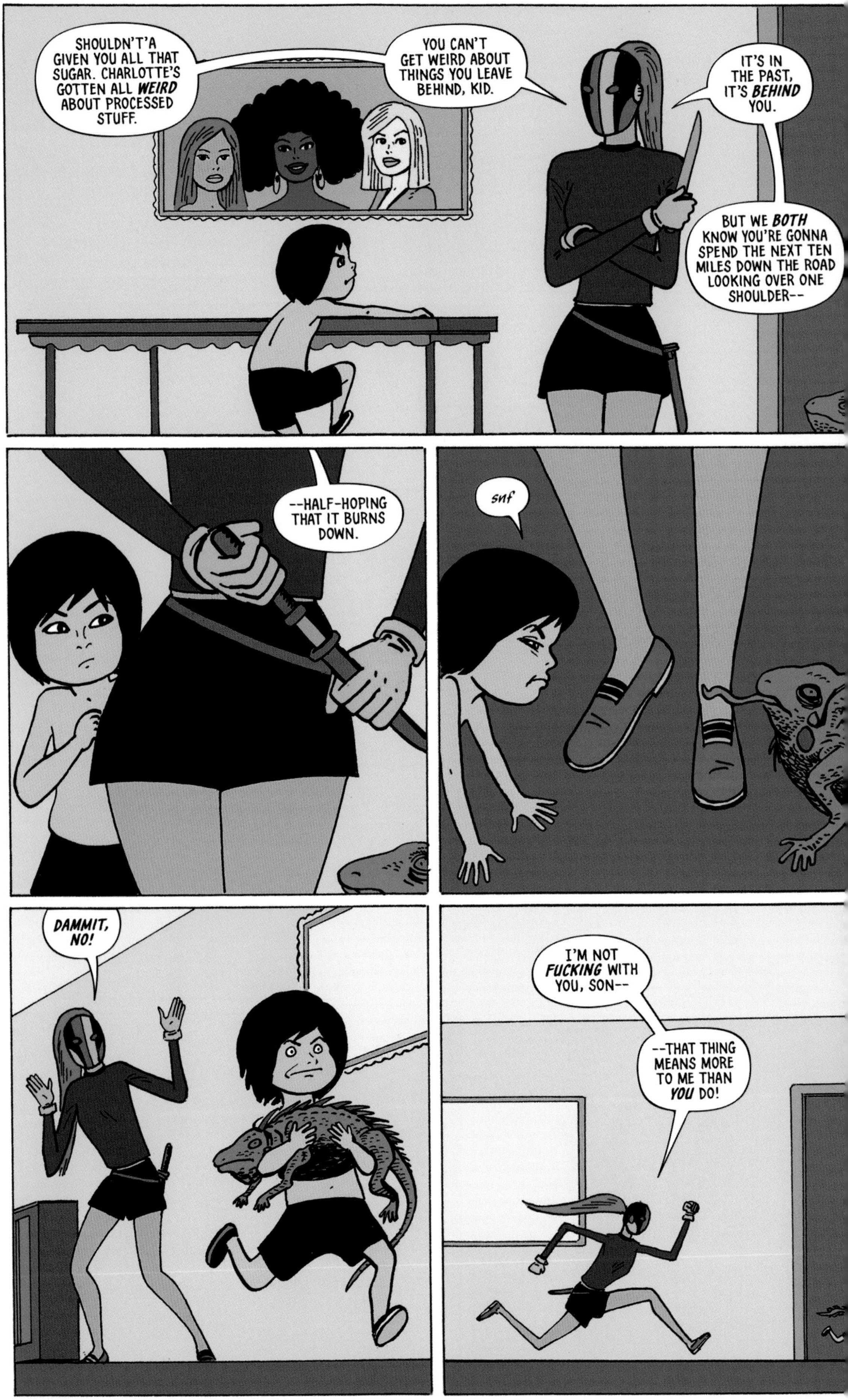
SHOULDN'T'A GIVEN YOU ALL THAT SUGAR. CHARLOTTE'S GOTTEN ALL *WEIRD* ABOUT PROCESSED STUFF.
YOU CAN'T GET WEIRD ABOUT THINGS YOU LEAVE BEHIND, KID.
IT'S IN THE PAST, IT'S *BEHIND* YOU.
BUT WE *BOTH* KNOW YOU'RE GONNA SPEND THE NEXT TEN MILES DOWN THE ROAD LOOKING OVER ONE SHOULDER--
--HALF-HOPING THAT IT BURNS DOWN.
snf
DAMMIT, NO!
I'M NOT *FUCKING* WITH YOU, SON--
--THAT THING MEANS MORE TO ME THAN *YOU* DO!

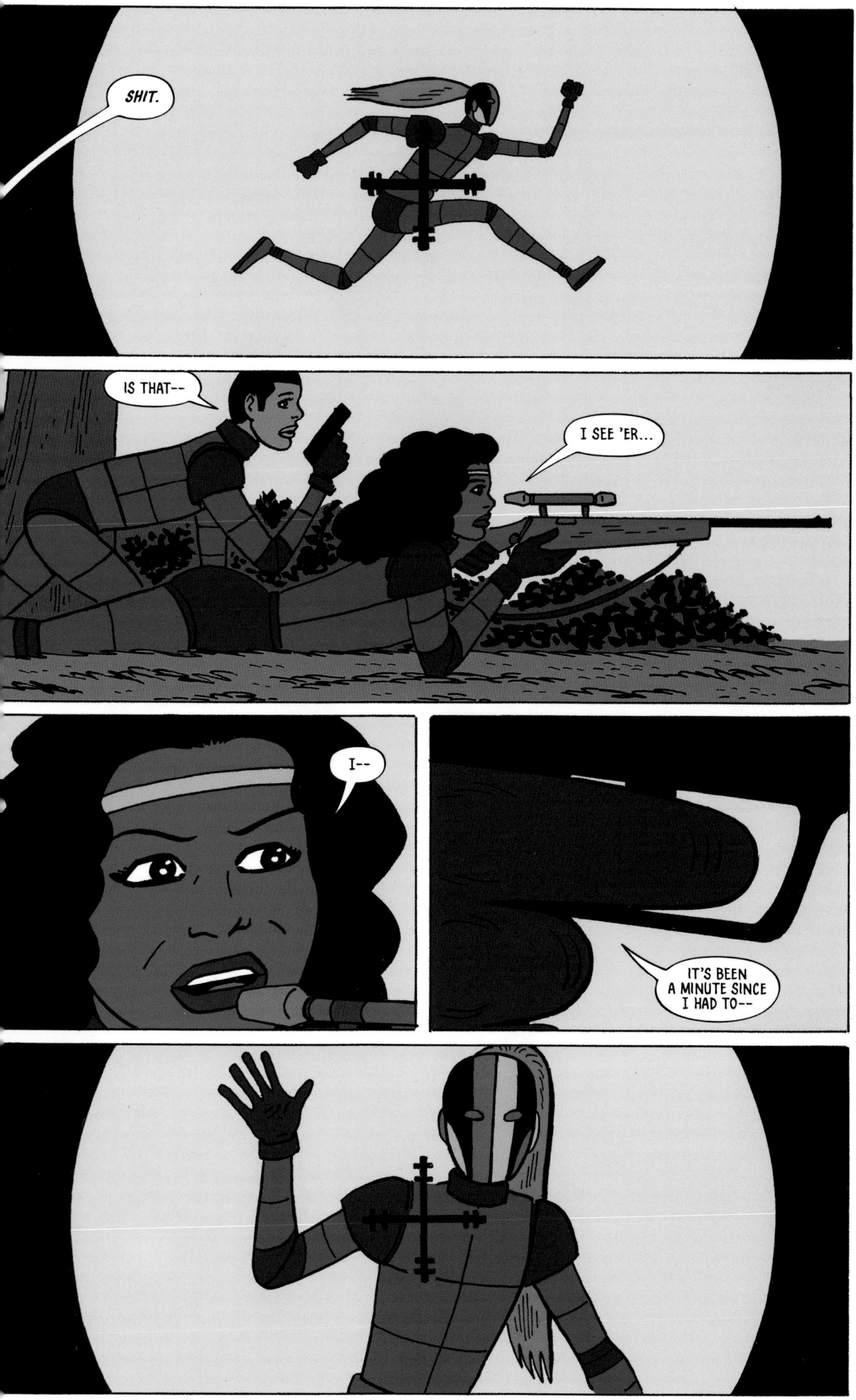
SHIT.
IS THAT--
I SEE 'ER...
I--
IT'S BEEN A MINUTE SINCE I HAD TO--

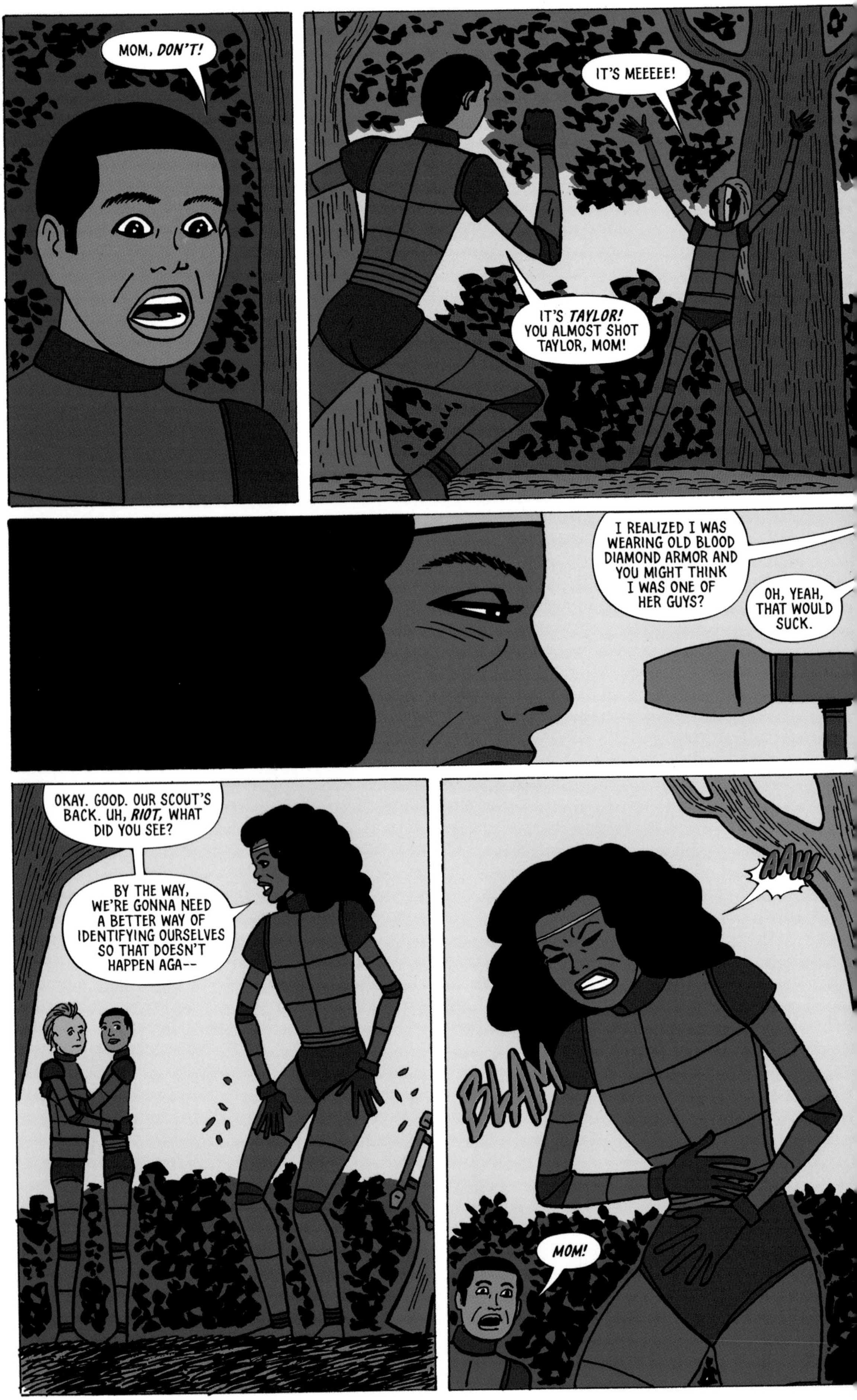
MOM, *DON'T!*
IT'S MEEEEE!
IT'S *TAYLOR!* YOU ALMOST SHOT TAYLOR, MOM!
I REALIZED I WAS WEARING OLD BLOOD DIAMOND ARMOR AND YOU MIGHT THINK I WAS ONE OF HER GUYS?
OH, YEAH, THAT WOULD SUCK.
OKAY. GOOD. OUR SCOUT'S BACK. UH, *RIOT,* WHAT DID YOU SEE?
BY THE WAY, WE'RE GONNA NEED A BETTER WAY OF IDENTIFYING OURSELVES SO THAT DOESN'T HAPPEN AGA--
AAH!
BLAM
MOM!

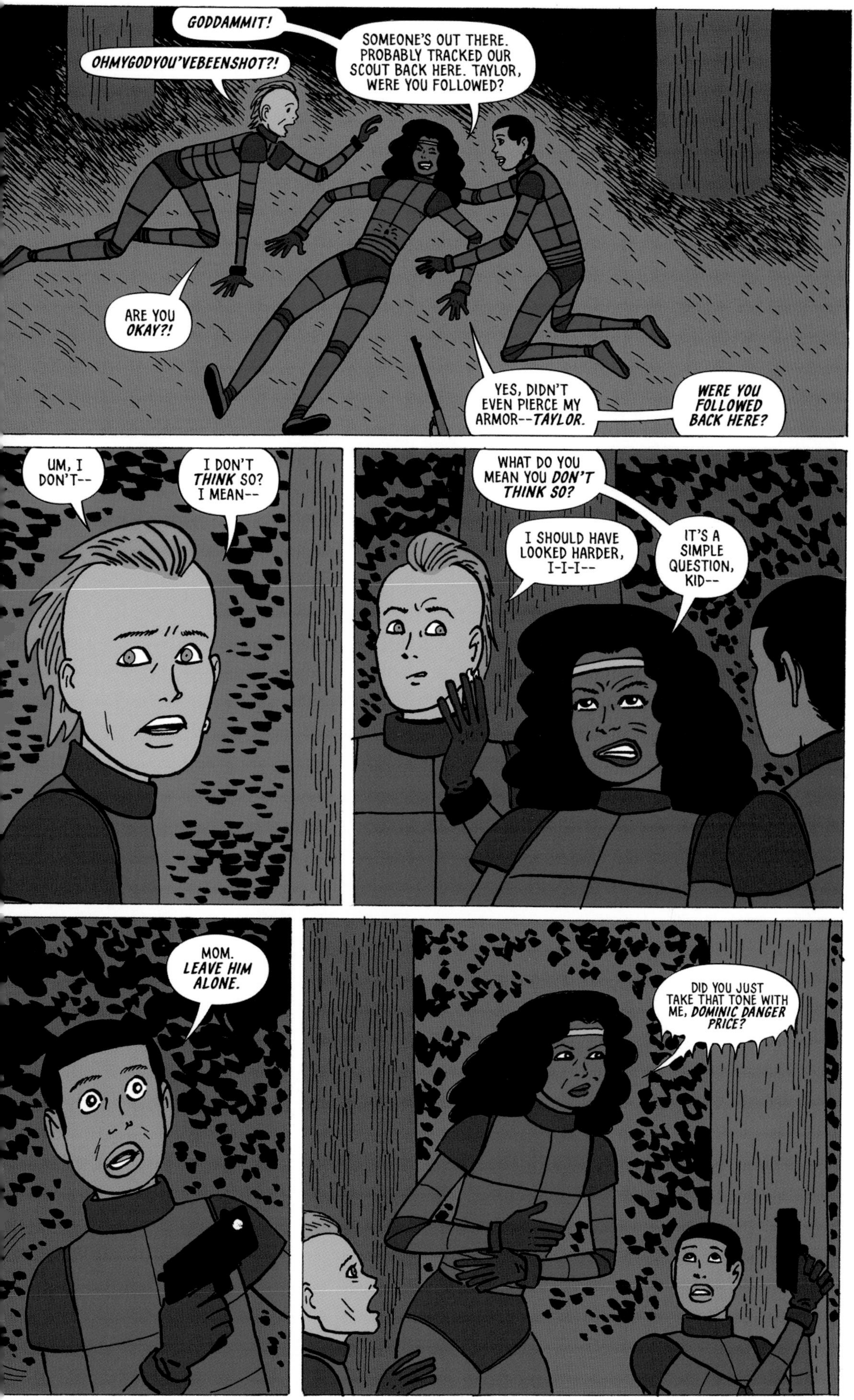
GODDAMMIT!
OHMYGODYOU'VEBEENSHOT?!
SOMEONE'S OUT THERE. PROBABLY TRACKED OUR SCOUT BACK HERE. TAYLOR, WERE YOU FOLLOWED?
ARE YOU OKAY?!
YES, DIDN'T EVEN PIERCE MY ARMOR--TAYLOR.
WERE YOU FOLLOWED BACK HERE?
UM, I DON'T--
I DON'T THINK SO? I MEAN--
WHAT DO YOU MEAN YOU DON'T THINK SO?
I SHOULD HAVE LOOKED HARDER, I-I-I--
IT'S A SIMPLE QUESTION, KID--
MOM. LEAVE HIM ALONE.
DID YOU JUST TAKE THAT TONE WITH ME, DOMINIC DANGER PRICE?

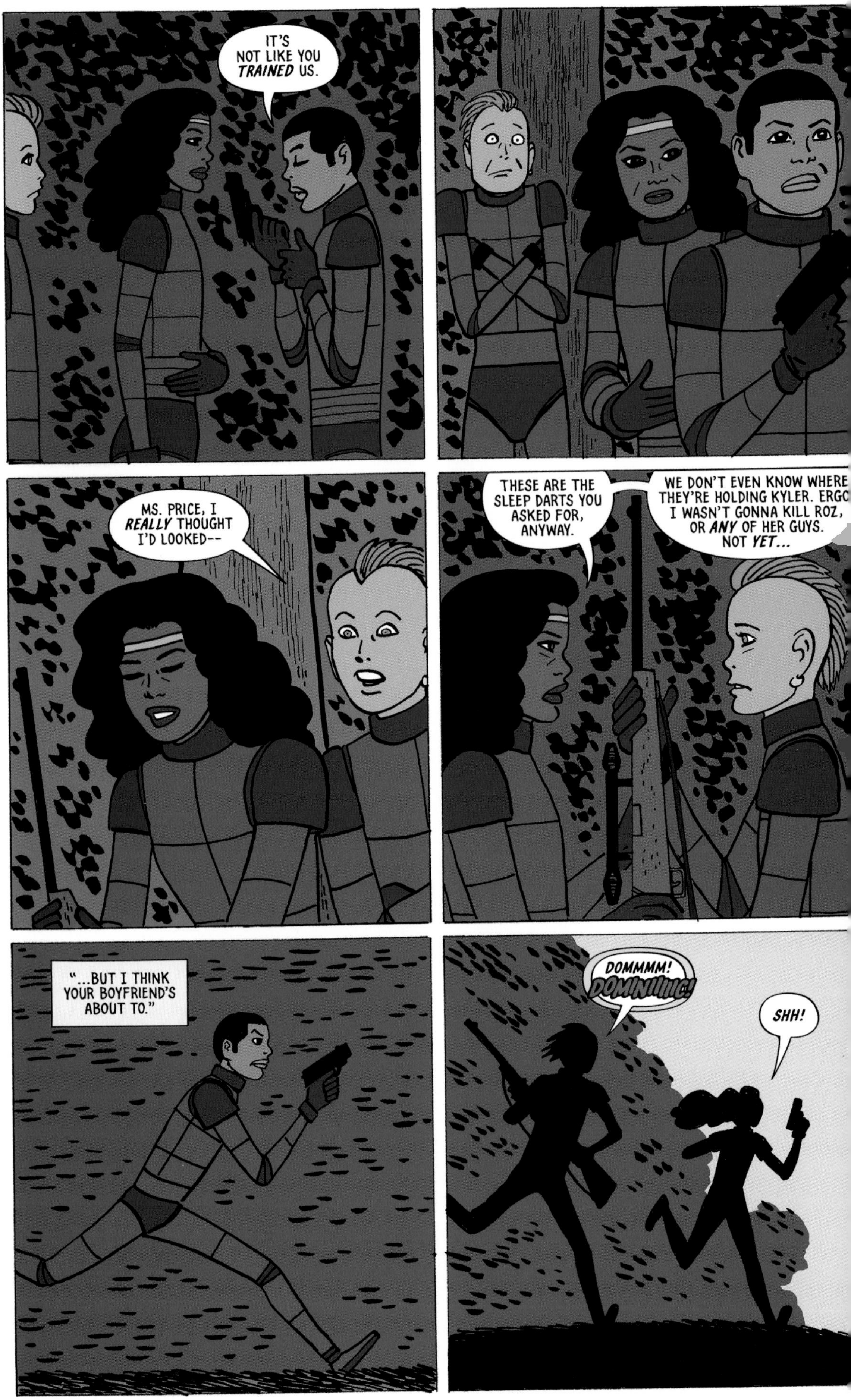
IT'S NOT LIKE YOU *TRAINED* US.
MS. PRICE, I *REALLY* THOUGHT I'D LOOKED--
THESE ARE THE SLEEP DARTS YOU ASKED FOR, ANYWAY.
WE DON'T EVEN KNOW WHERE THEY'RE HOLDING KYLER. ERGO I WASN'T GONNA KILL ROZ, OR *ANY* OF HER GUYS. NOT *YET*...
"...BUT I THINK YOUR BOYFRIEND'S ABOUT TO."
DOMMMM! DOMINIIIIIC!
SHH!

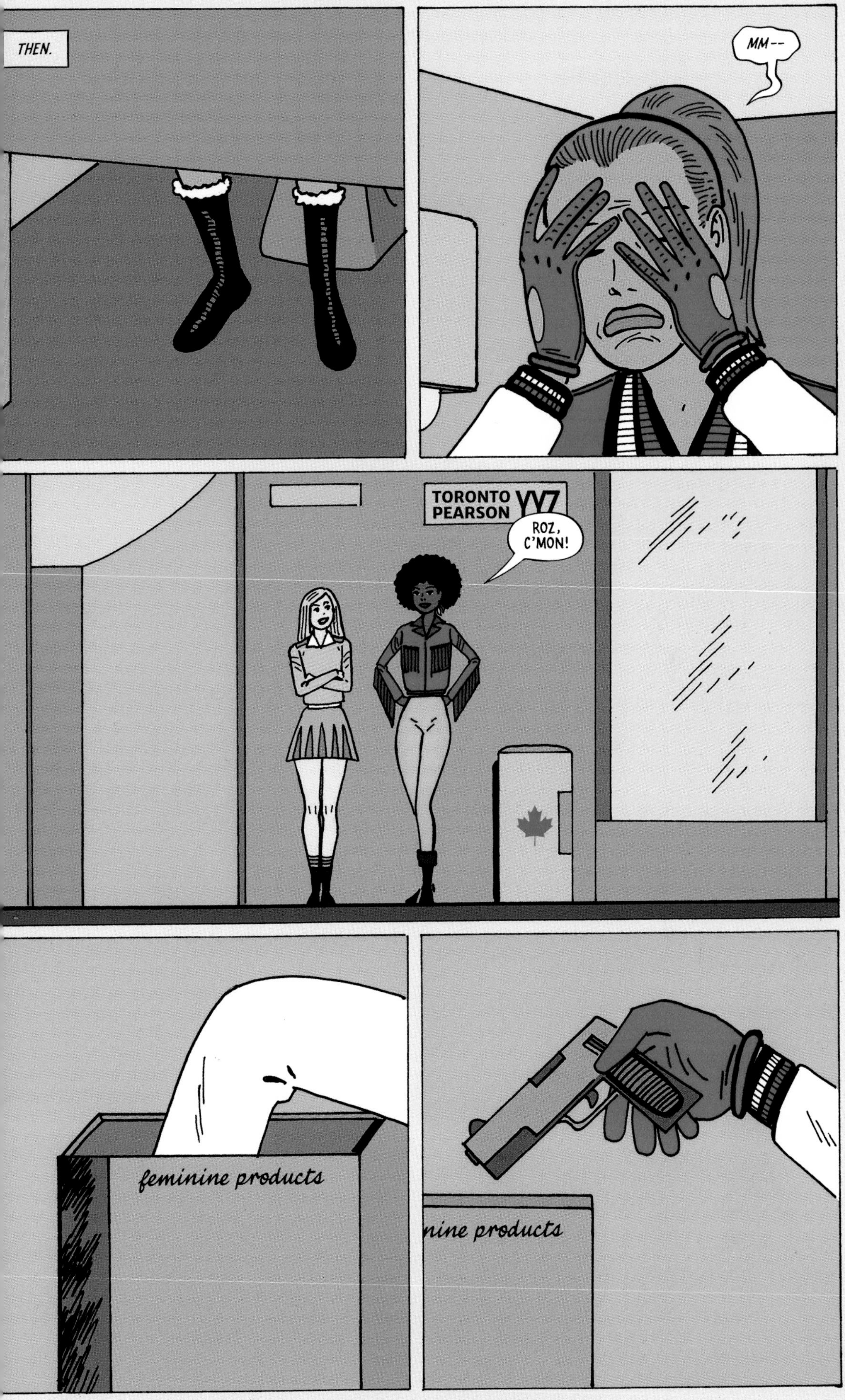
THEN.
MM--
TORONTO PEARSON YYZ
ROZ, C'MON!
feminine products
nine products

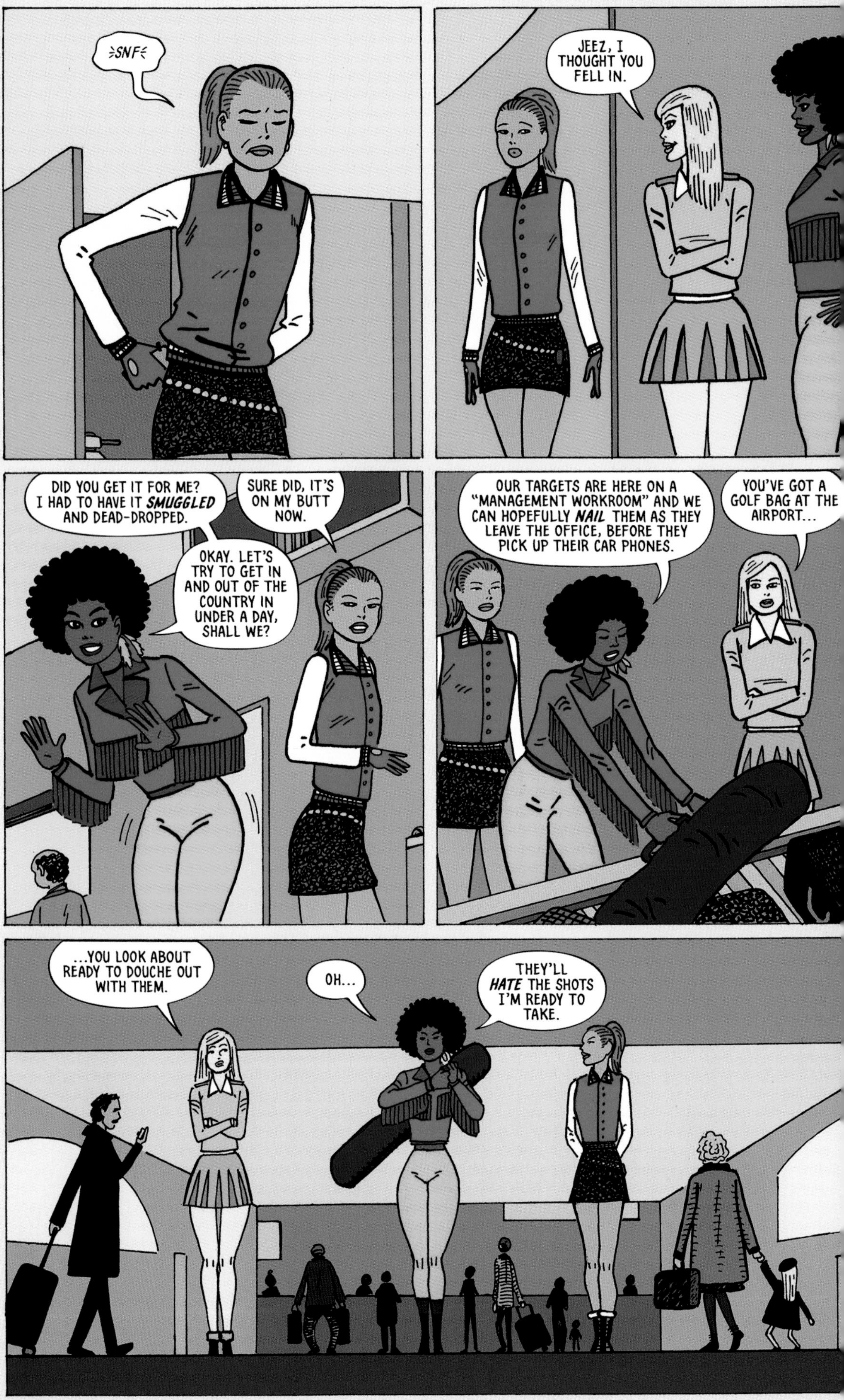
SNF
JEEZ, I THOUGHT YOU FELL IN.
DID YOU GET IT FOR ME? I HAD TO HAVE IT SMUGGLED AND DEAD-DROPPED.
SURE DID, IT'S ON MY BUTT NOW.
OKAY. LET'S TRY TO GET IN AND OUT OF THE COUNTRY IN UNDER A DAY, SHALL WE?
OUR TARGETS ARE HERE ON A "MANAGEMENT WORKROOM" AND WE CAN HOPEFULLY NAIL THEM AS THEY LEAVE THE OFFICE, BEFORE THEY PICK UP THEIR CAR PHONES.
YOU'VE GOT A GOLF BAG AT THE AIRPORT...
...YOU LOOK ABOUT READY TO DOUCHE OUT WITH THEM.
OH...
THEY'LL HATE THE SHOTS I'M READY TO TAKE.

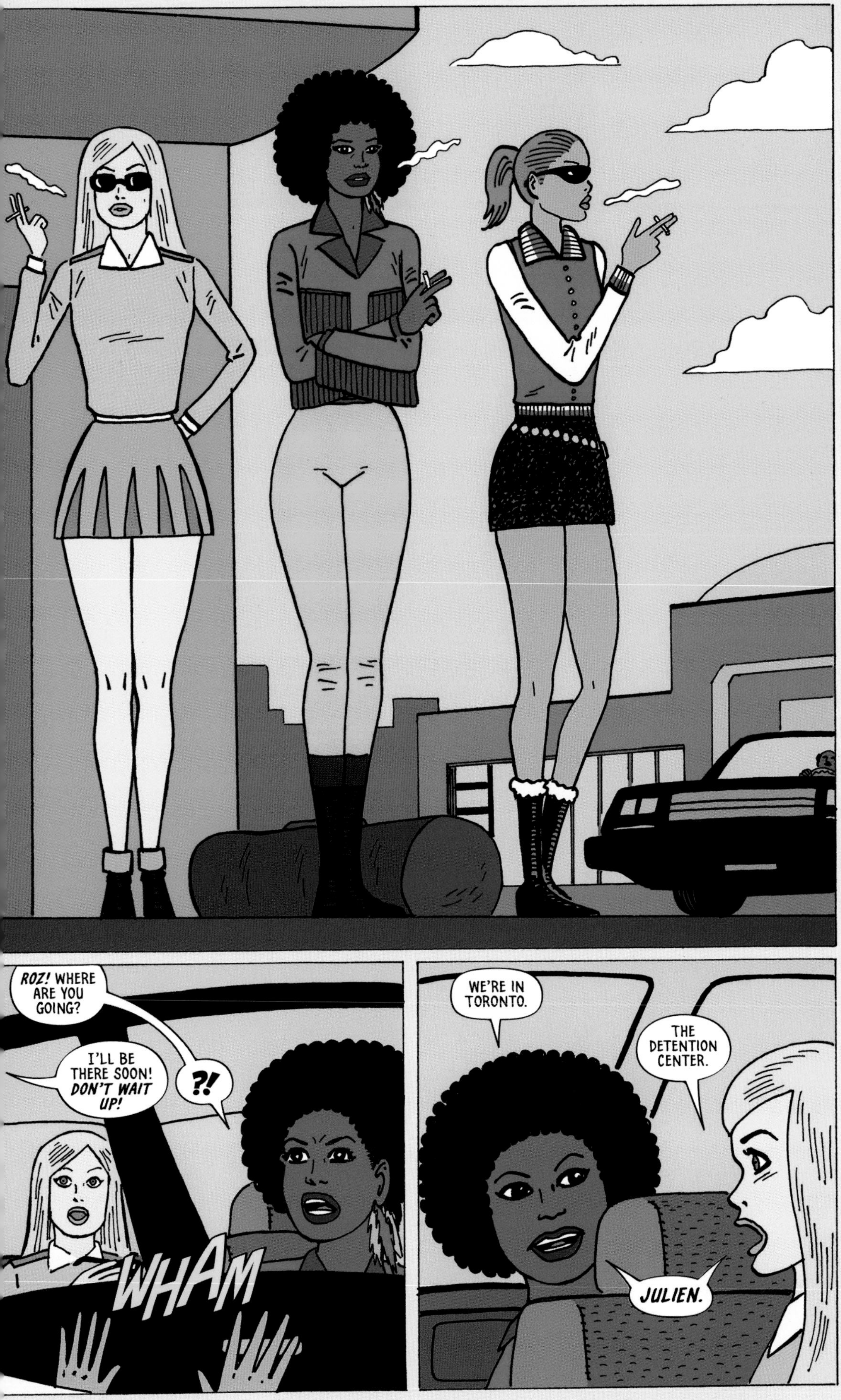
ROZ! WHERE ARE YOU GOING?
I'LL BE THERE SOON! DON'T WAIT UP!
?!
WHAM
WE'RE IN TORONTO.
THE DETENTION CENTER.
JULIEN.

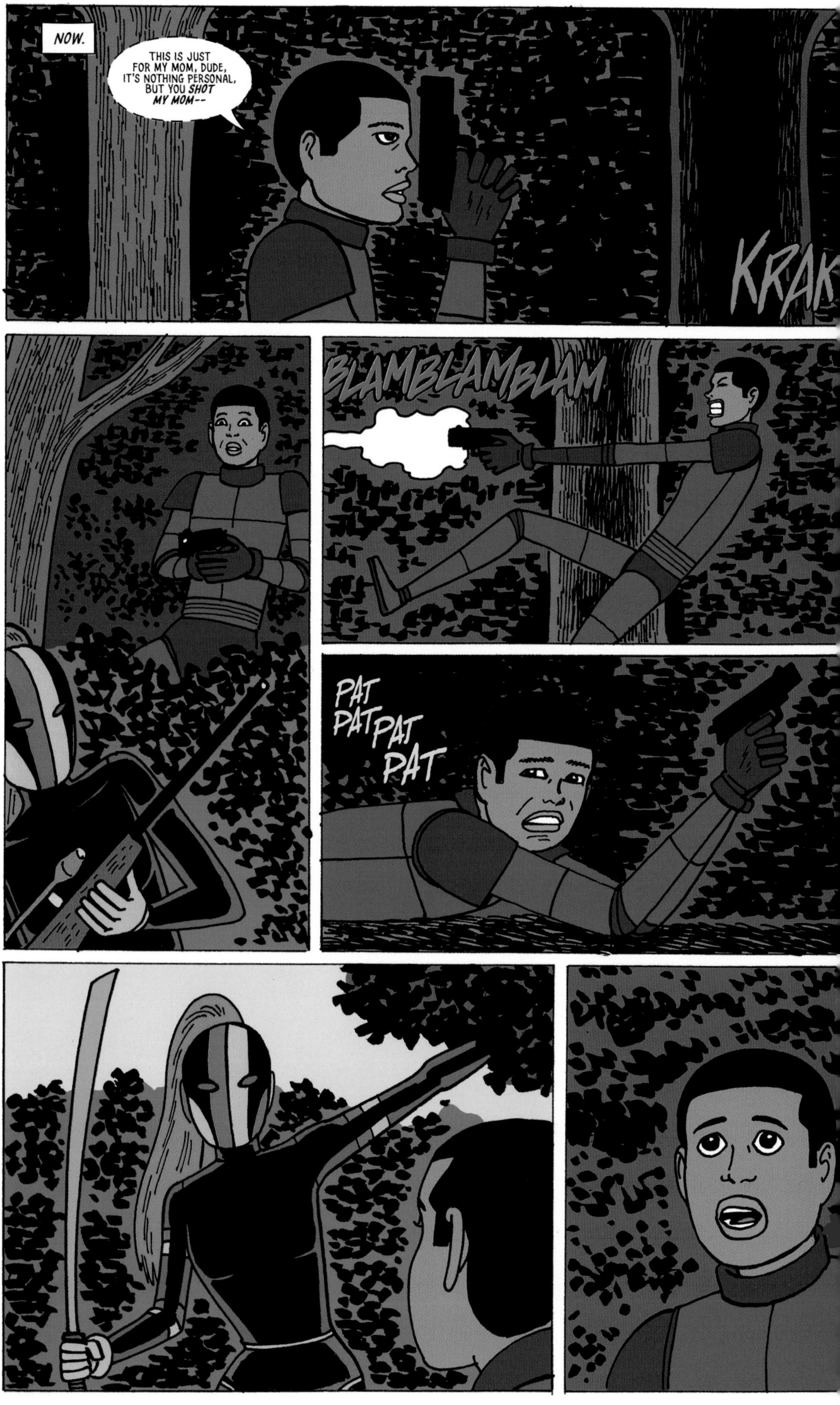

NOW.
THIS IS JUST FOR MY MOM, DUDE, IT'S NOTHING PERSONAL, BUT YOU SHOT MY MOM--
KRAK
BLAMBLAMBLAM
PAT PAT PAT PAT

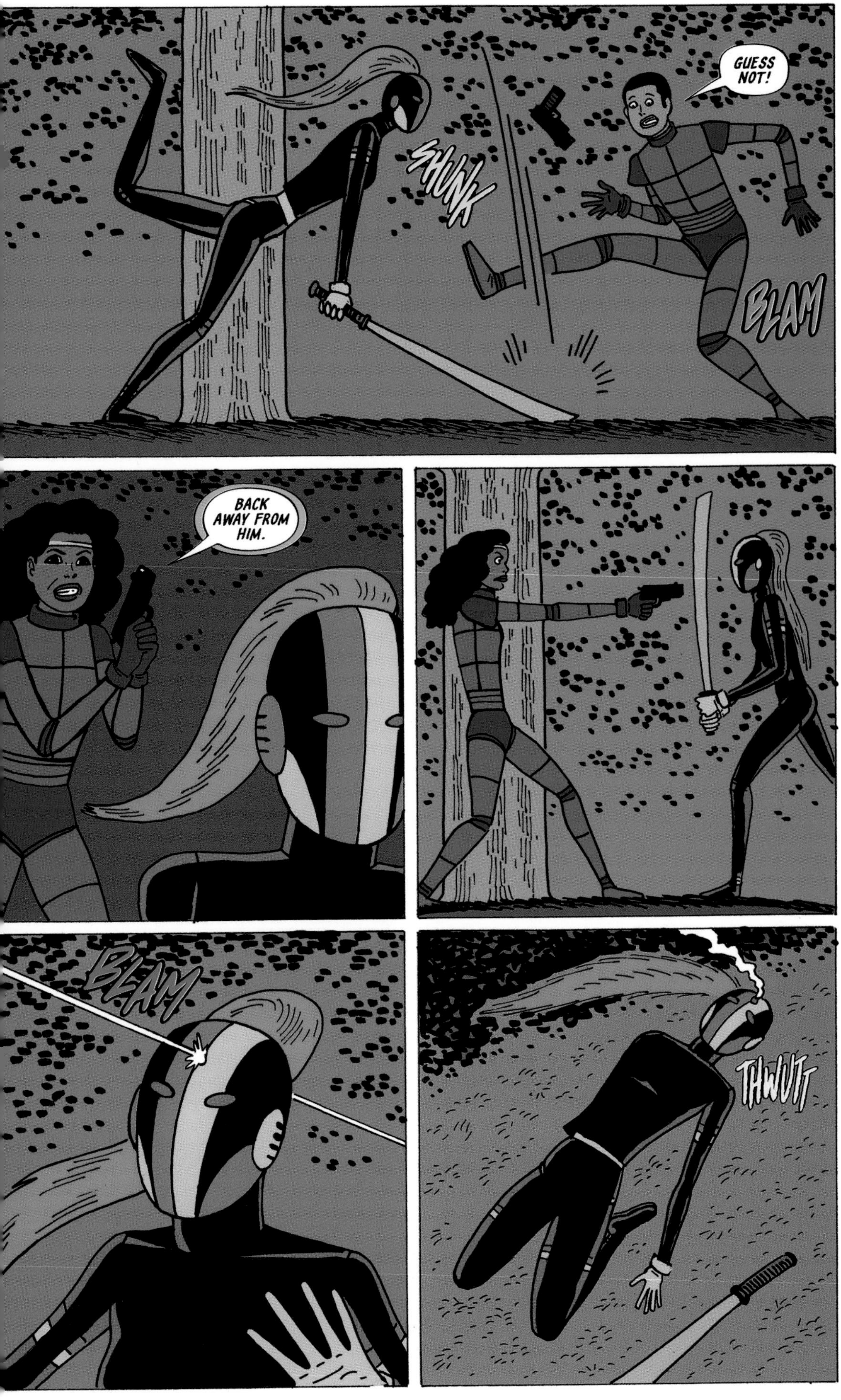
SHUNK
GUESS NOT!
BLAM
BACK AWAY FROM HIM.
BLAM
THWUTT

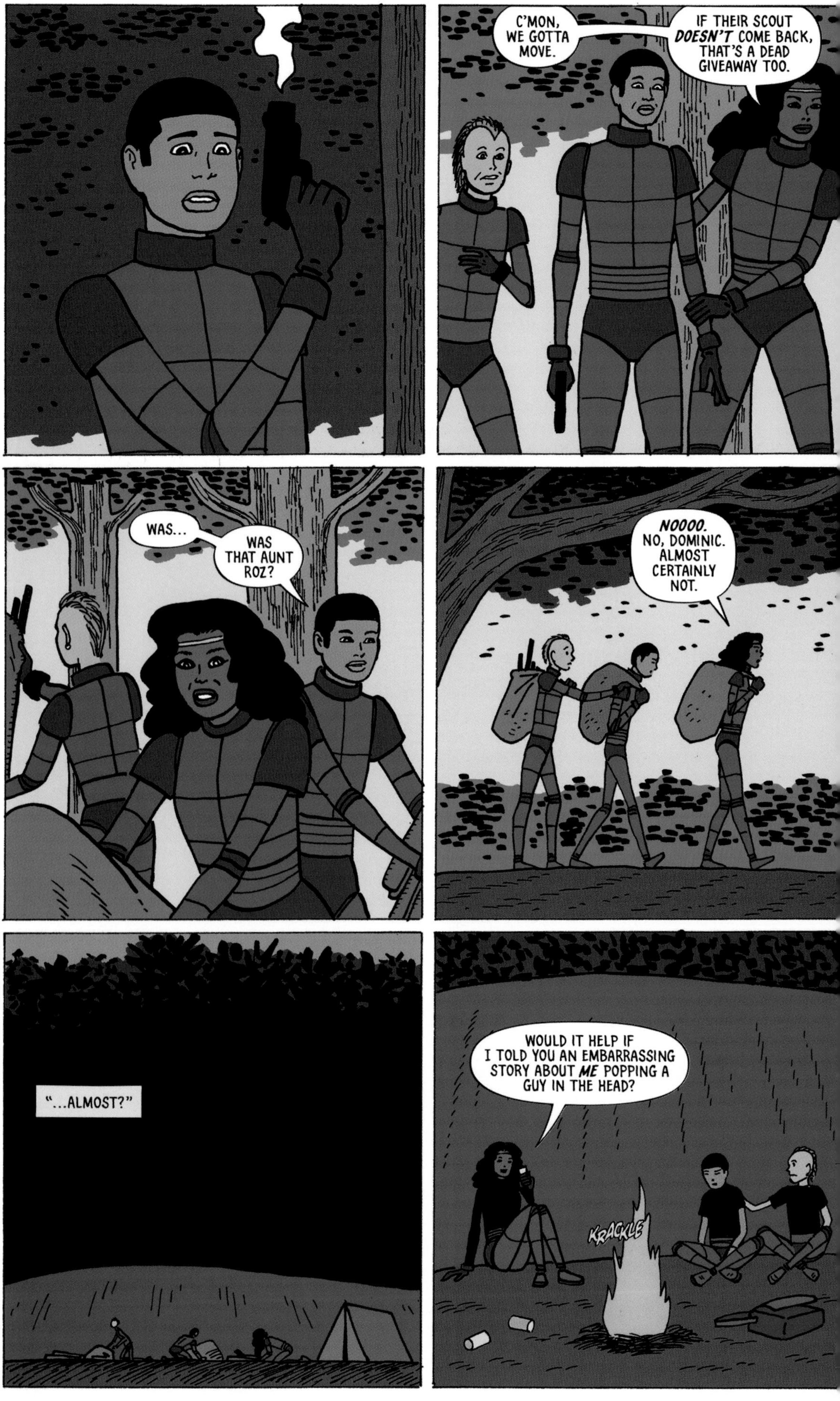

C'MON, WE GOTTA MOVE.
IF THEIR SCOUT *DOESN'T* COME BACK, THAT'S A DEAD GIVEAWAY TOO.
WAS...
WAS THAT AUNT ROZ?
NOOOO. NO, DOMINIC. ALMOST CERTAINLY NOT.
"...ALMOST?"
WOULD IT HELP IF I TOLD YOU AN EMBARRASSING STORY ABOUT *ME* POPPING A GUY IN THE HEAD?
KRACKLE

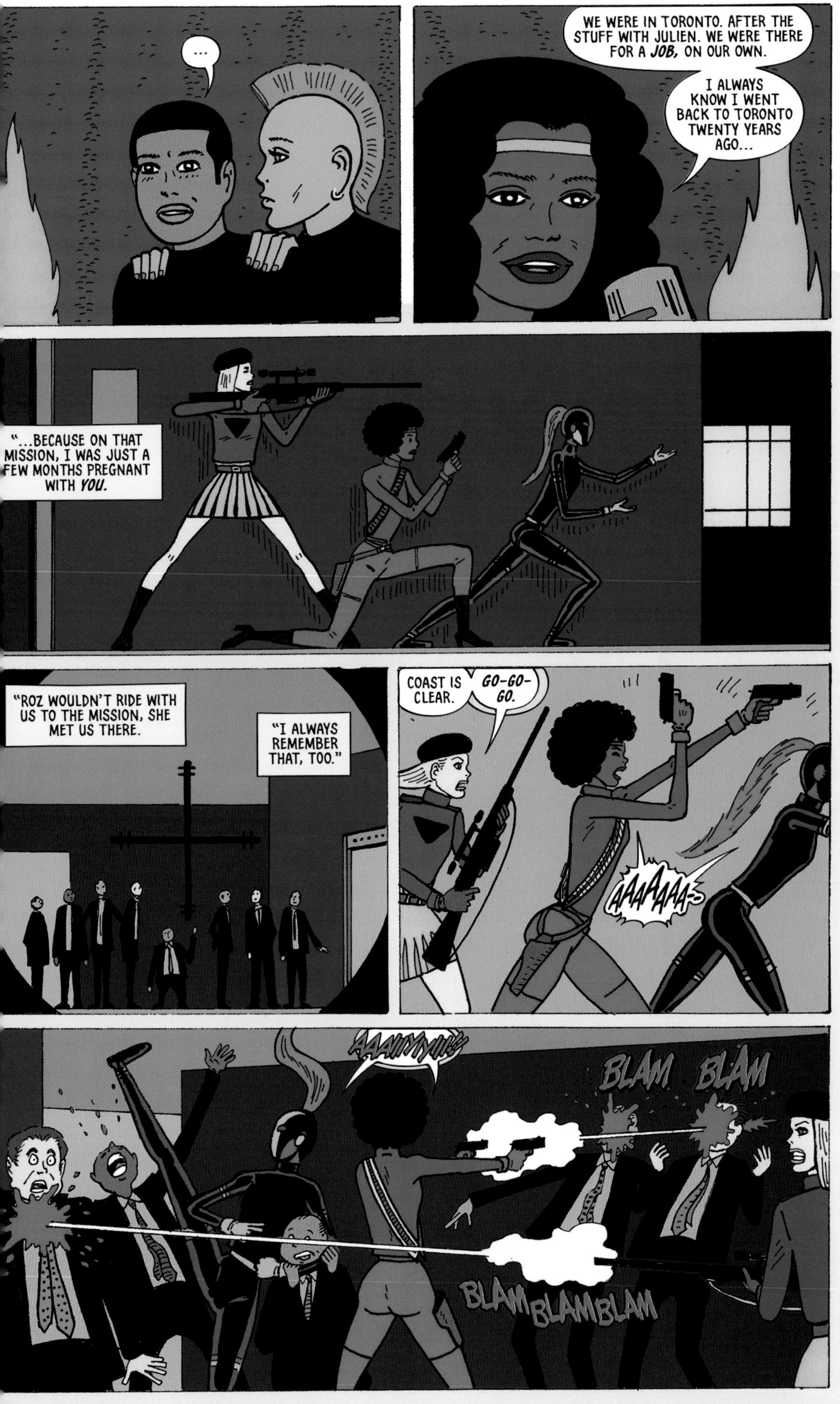
...
WE WERE IN TORONTO. AFTER THE STUFF WITH JULIEN. WE WERE THERE FOR A *JOB,* ON OUR OWN.
I ALWAYS KNOW I WENT BACK TO TORONTO TWENTY YEARS AGO...
"...BECAUSE ON THAT MISSION, I WAS JUST A FEW MONTHS PREGNANT WITH *YOU.*
"ROZ WOULDN'T RIDE WITH US TO THE MISSION, SHE MET US THERE.
"I ALWAYS REMEMBER THAT, TOO."
COAST IS CLEAR.
GO-GO-GO.
AAAAAAA-
AAAIIYYIII!
BLAM BLAM
BLAM BLAM BLAM

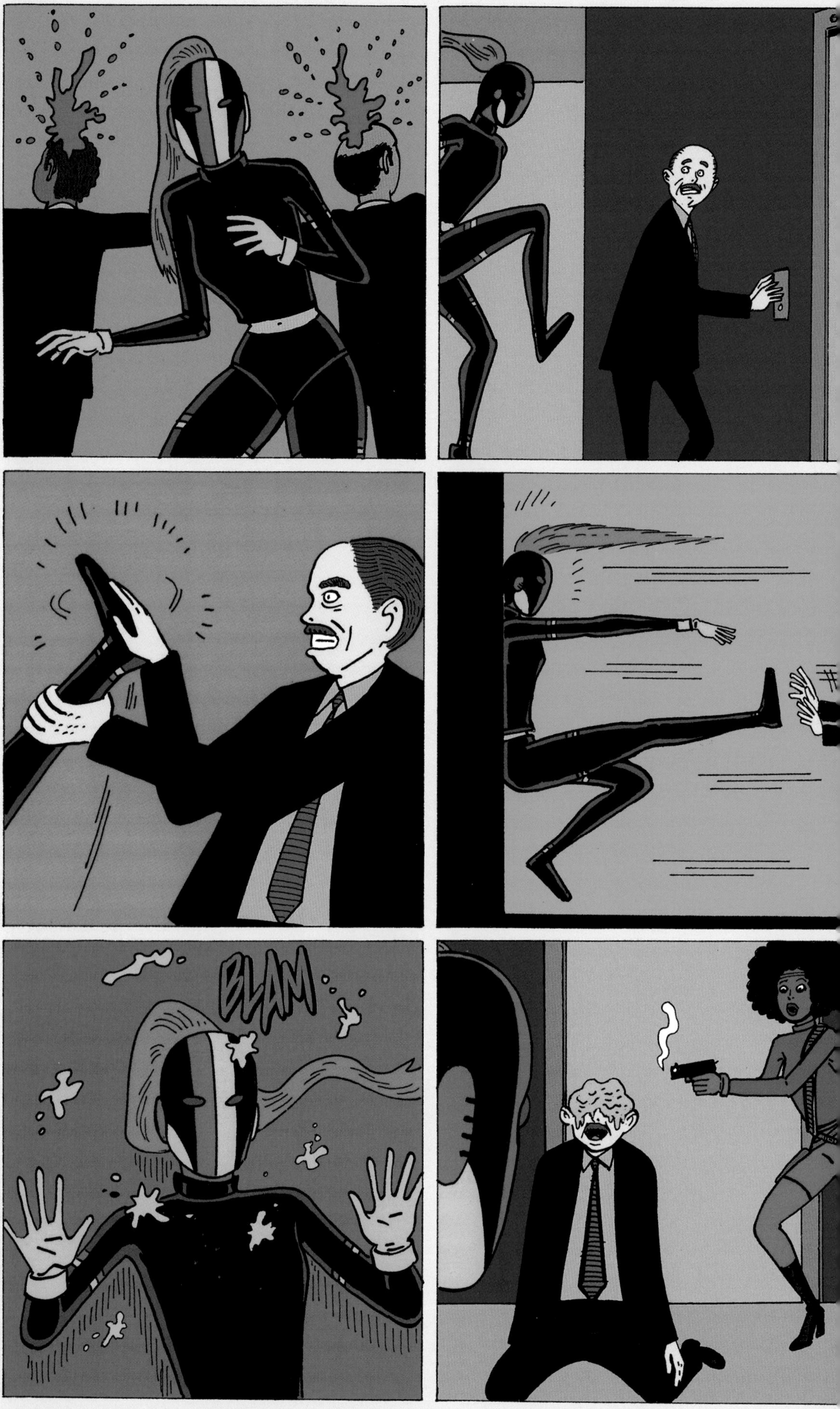
BLAM

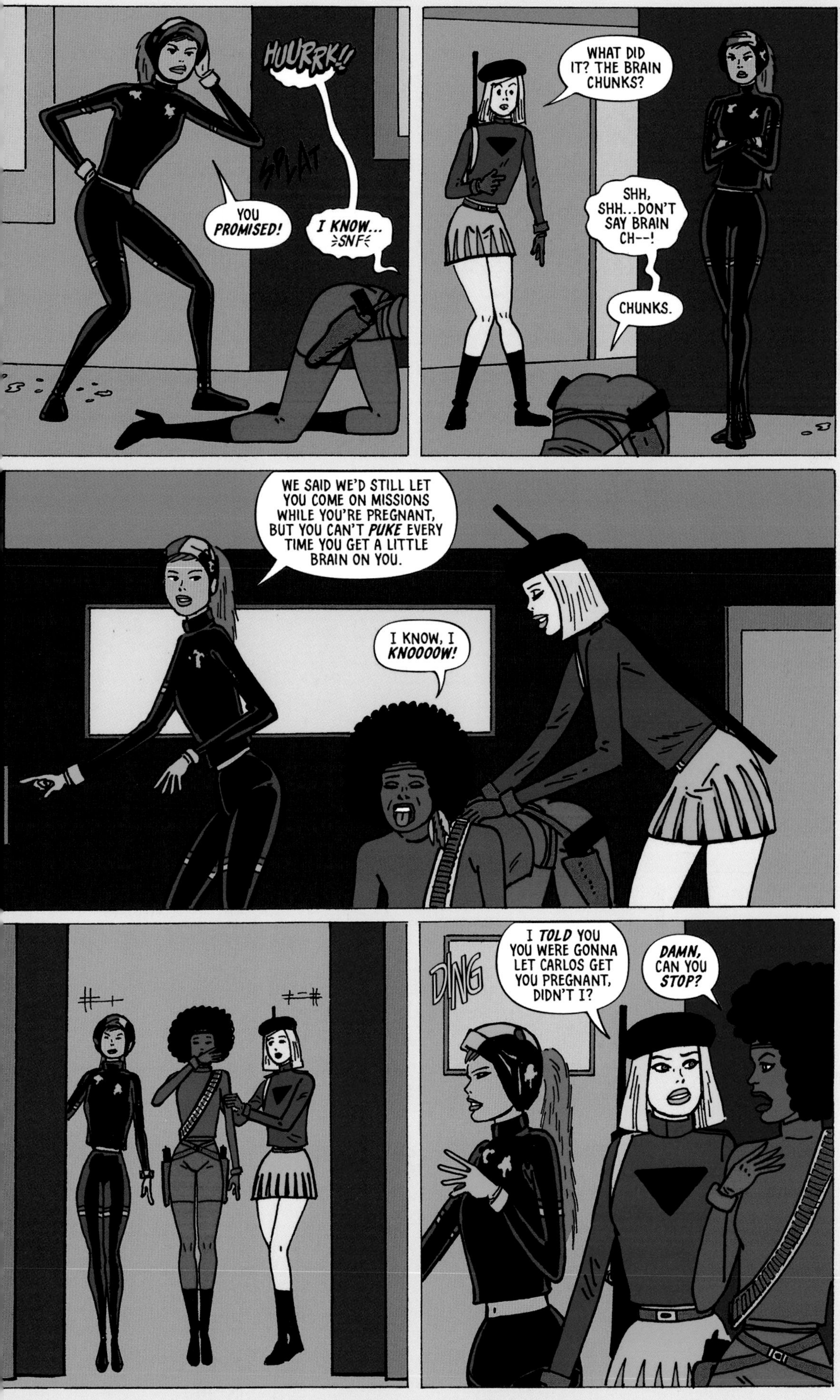
HUURRK!!
SPLAT
YOU *PROMISED!*
I KNOW... SNF
WHAT DID IT? THE BRAIN CHUNKS?
SHH, SHH...DON'T SAY BRAIN CH--!
CHUNKS.
WE SAID WE'D STILL LET YOU COME ON MISSIONS WHILE YOU'RE PREGNANT, BUT YOU CAN'T *PUKE* EVERY TIME YOU GET A LITTLE BRAIN ON YOU.
I KNOW, I *KNOOOOW!*
DING
I *TOLD* YOU YOU WERE GONNA LET CARLOS GET YOU PREGNANT, DIDN'T I?
DAMN, CAN YOU *STOP?*

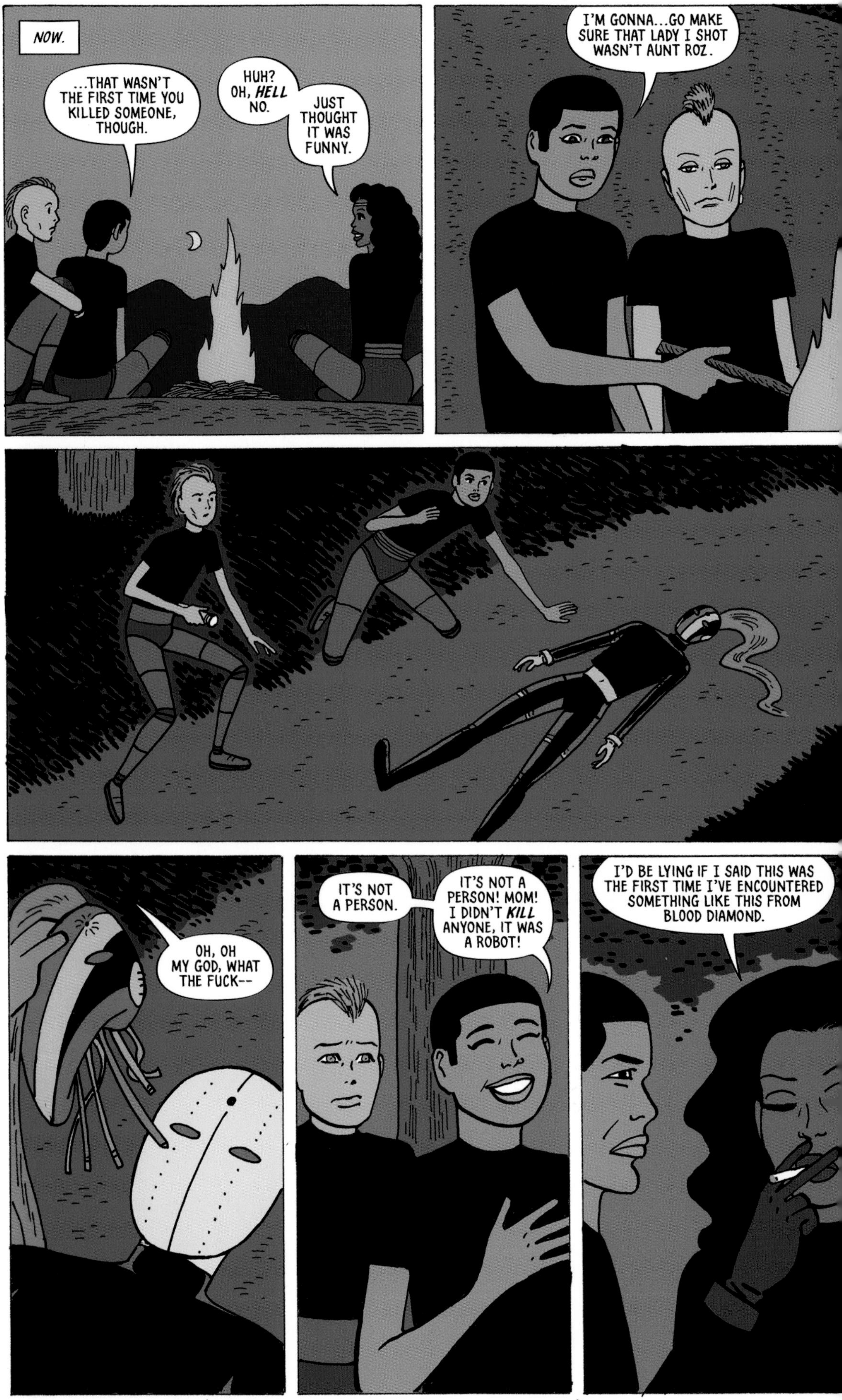
NOW.
...THAT WASN'T THE FIRST TIME YOU KILLED SOMEONE, THOUGH.
HUH? OH, HELL NO.
JUST THOUGHT IT WAS FUNNY.
I'M GONNA...GO MAKE SURE THAT LADY I SHOT WASN'T AUNT ROZ.
OH, OH MY GOD, WHAT THE FUCK--
IT'S NOT A PERSON.
IT'S NOT A PERSON! MOM! I DIDN'T KILL ANYONE, IT WAS A ROBOT!
I'D BE LYING IF I SAID THIS WAS THE FIRST TIME I'VE ENCOUNTERED SOMETHING LIKE THIS FROM BLOOD DIAMOND.

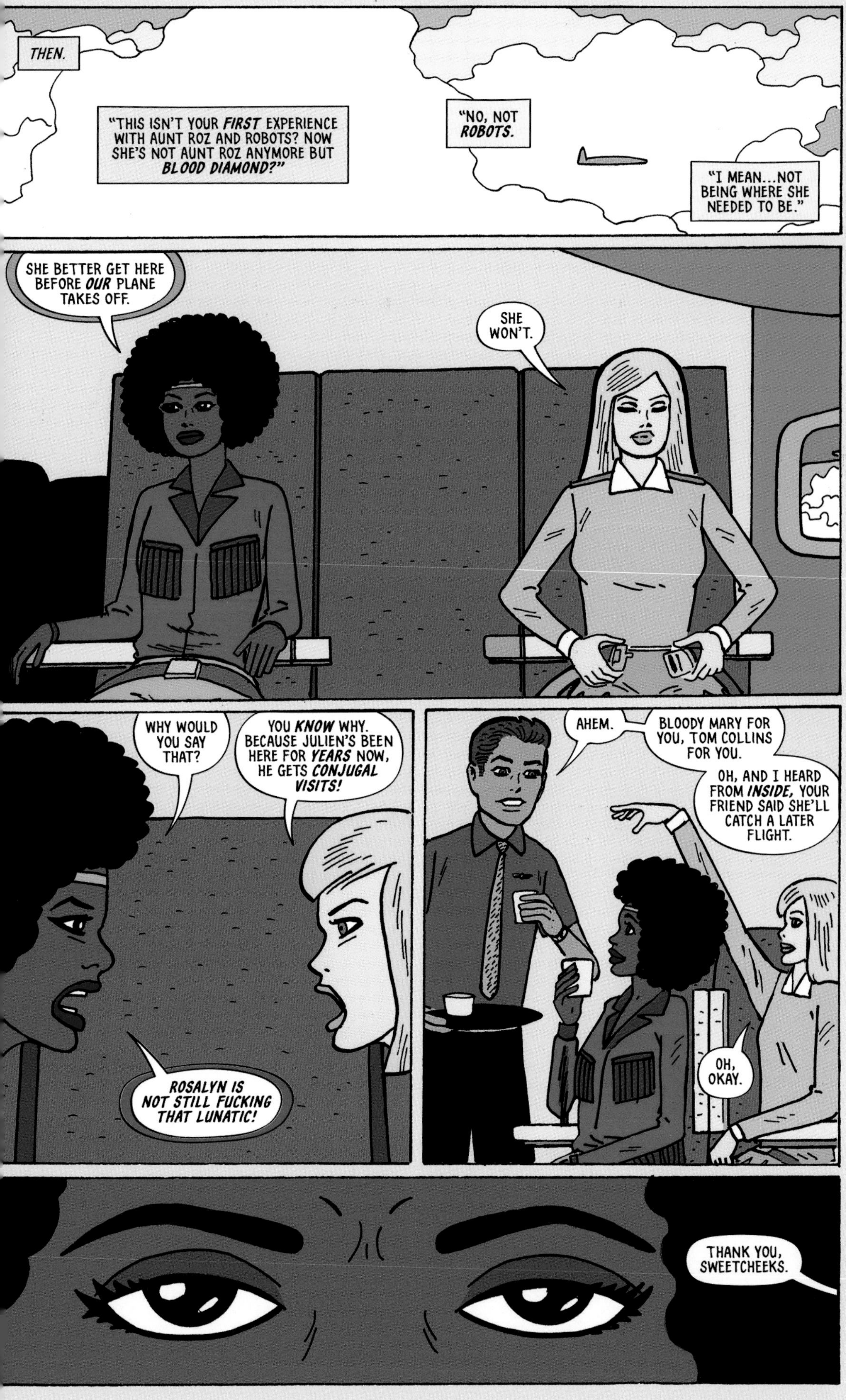
THEN.
"THIS ISN'T YOUR FIRST EXPERIENCE WITH AUNT ROZ AND ROBOTS? NOW SHE'S NOT AUNT ROZ ANYMORE BUT BLOOD DIAMOND?"
"NO, NOT ROBOTS.
"I MEAN...NOT BEING WHERE SHE NEEDED TO BE."
SHE BETTER GET HERE BEFORE OUR PLANE TAKES OFF.
SHE WON'T.
WHY WOULD YOU SAY THAT?
YOU KNOW WHY. BECAUSE JULIEN'S BEEN HERE FOR YEARS NOW, HE GETS CONJUGAL VISITS!
ROSALYN IS NOT STILL FUCKING THAT LUNATIC!
AHEM.
BLOODY MARY FOR YOU, TOM COLLINS FOR YOU.
OH, AND I HEARD FROM INSIDE, YOUR FRIEND SAID SHE'LL CATCH A LATER FLIGHT.
OH, OKAY.
THANK YOU, SWEETCHEEKS.

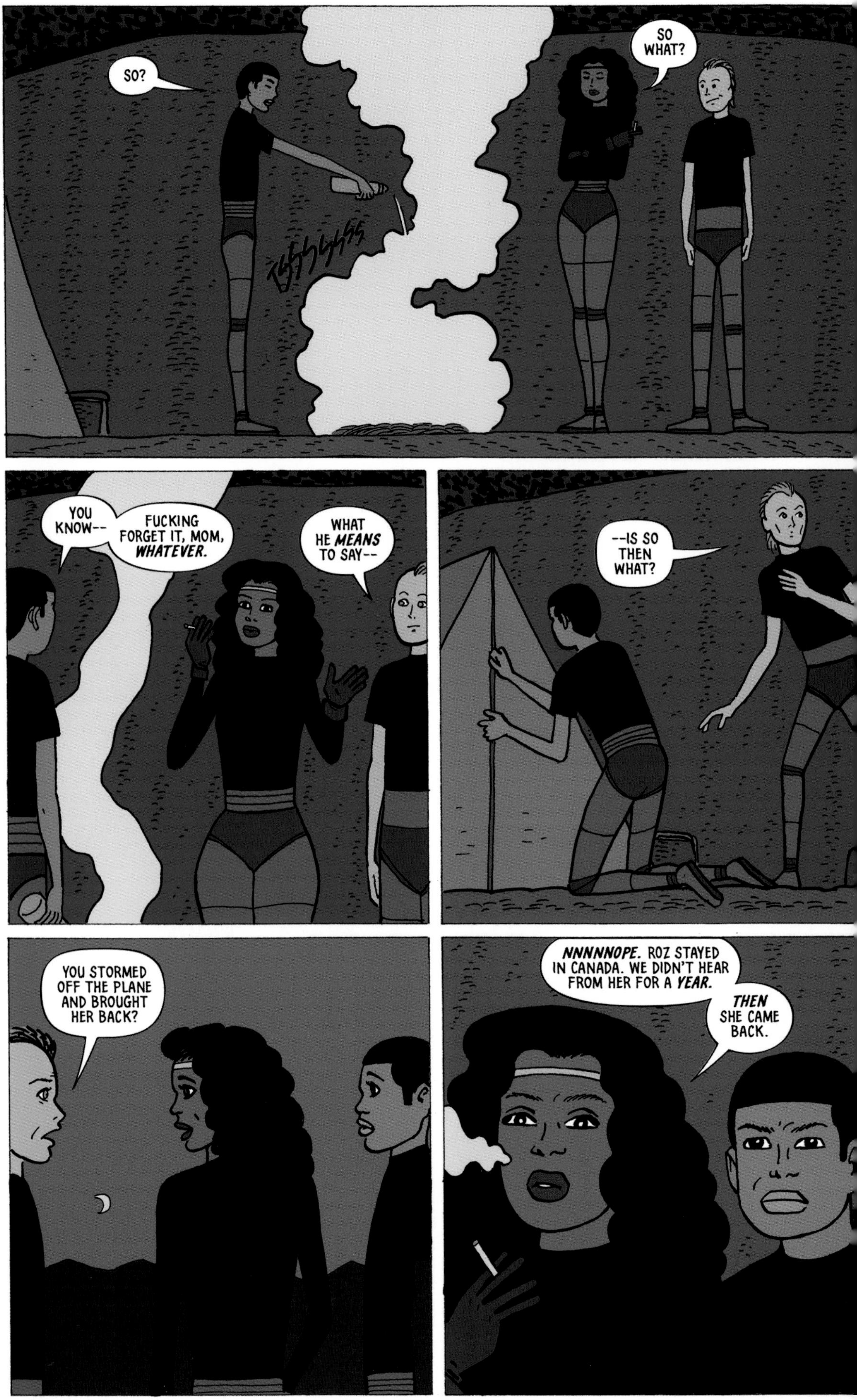
SO?
SO WHAT?
TSSSSSSSS
YOU KNOW--
FUCKING FORGET IT, MOM, *WHATEVER.*
WHAT HE *MEANS* TO SAY--
--IS SO THEN WHAT?
YOU STORMED OFF THE PLANE AND BROUGHT HER BACK?
NNNNNOPE. ROZ STAYED IN CANADA. WE DIDN'T HEAR FROM HER FOR A *YEAR.*
THEN SHE CAME BACK.

THEN, AGAIN.

PARDON!

KA-KLINK

GODDAMMIT, ROSALYN!

"SHE WAS GONE THE WHOLE TIME I WAS PREGNANT WITH YOU, DOMINIC.

"DIDN'T HEAR FROM HER 'TIL AFTER YOU WERE BORN.

WHAM

"WHEN I DISCOVERED YOU HAVE A COUSIN, AFTER A FASHION.

feminine products

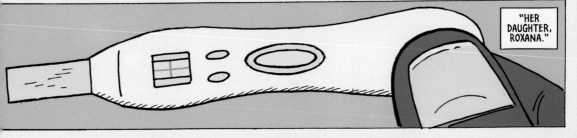

"HER DAUGHTER, ROXANA."

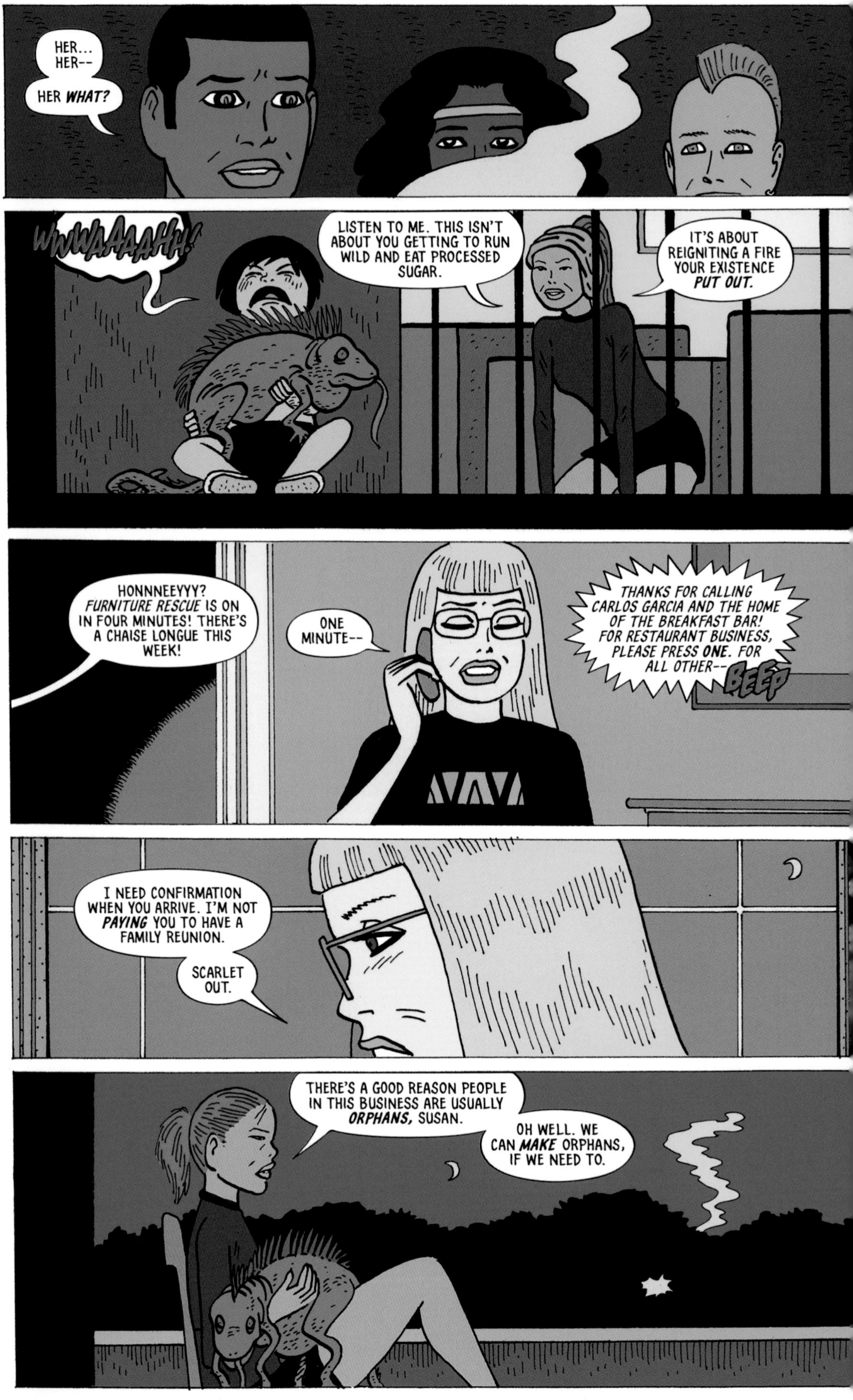
HER... HER--
HER WHAT?
WWWAAAAHH!
LISTEN TO ME. THIS ISN'T ABOUT YOU GETTING TO RUN WILD AND EAT PROCESSED SUGAR.
IT'S ABOUT REIGNITING A FIRE YOUR EXISTENCE PUT OUT.
HONNNEEYYY? FURNITURE RESCUE IS ON IN FOUR MINUTES! THERE'S A CHAISE LONGUE THIS WEEK!
ONE MINUTE--
THANKS FOR CALLING CARLOS GARCIA AND THE HOME OF THE BREAKFAST BAR! FOR RESTAURANT BUSINESS, PLEASE PRESS ONE. FOR ALL OTHER--
BEEP
I NEED CONFIRMATION WHEN YOU ARRIVE. I'M NOT PAYING YOU TO HAVE A FAMILY REUNION.
SCARLET OUT.
THERE'S A GOOD REASON PEOPLE IN THIS BUSINESS ARE USUALLY ORPHANS, SUSAN.
OH WELL. WE CAN MAKE ORPHANS, IF WE NEED TO.

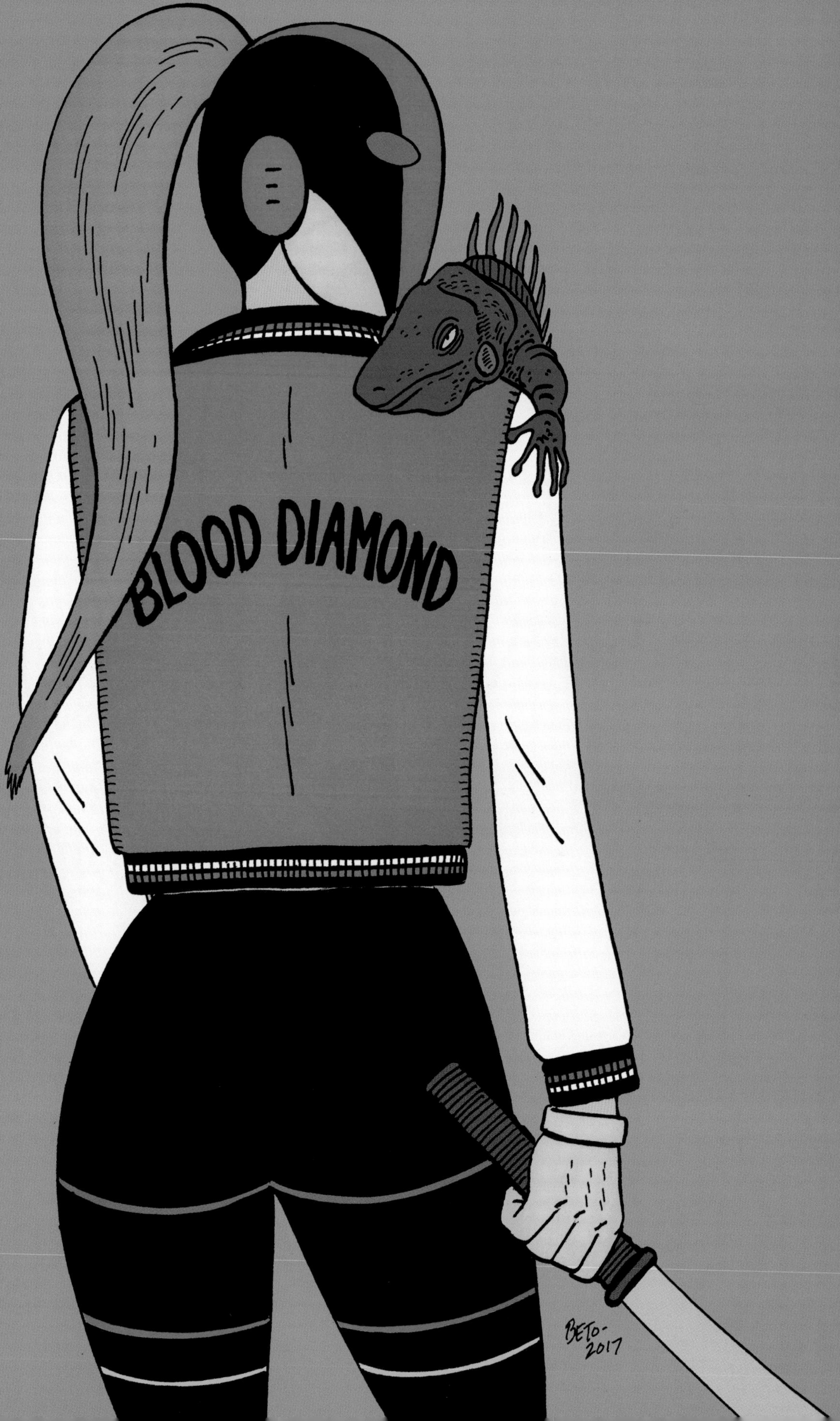
BLOOD DIAMOND
BETO-
2017

“Once you’re photographed for the papers in a place, you should stop committing felonies there.”

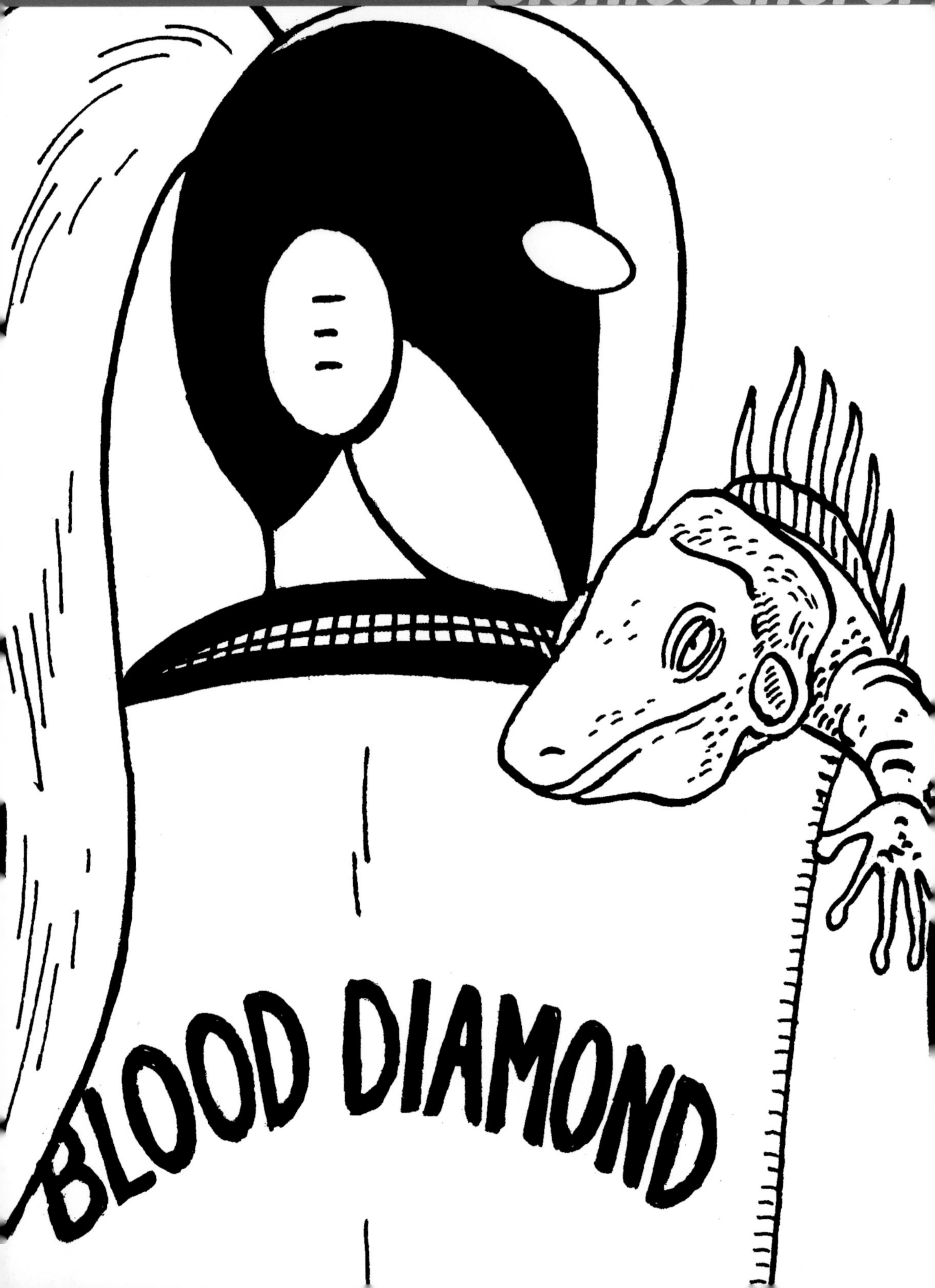

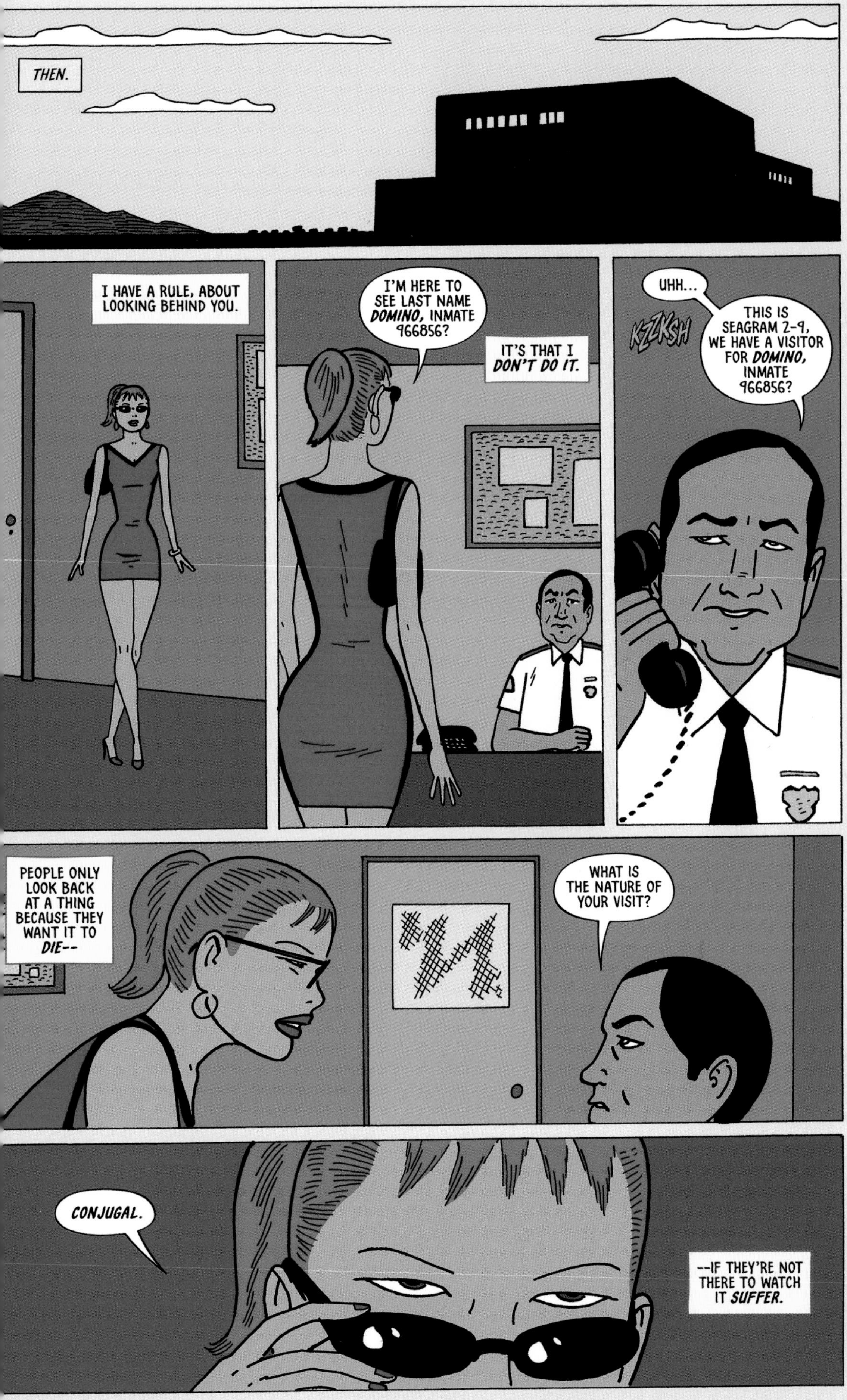

THEN.
I HAVE A RULE, ABOUT LOOKING BEHIND YOU.
I'M HERE TO SEE LAST NAME *DOMINO,* INMATE 966856?
IT'S THAT I *DON'T DO IT.*
UHH...
KZZKSH
THIS IS SEAGRAM 2-9, WE HAVE A VISITOR FOR *DOMINO,* INMATE 966856?
PEOPLE ONLY LOOK BACK AT A THING BECAUSE THEY WANT IT TO *DIE--*
WHAT IS THE NATURE OF YOUR VISIT?
CONJUGAL.
--IF THEY'RE NOT THERE TO WATCH IT *SUFFER.*

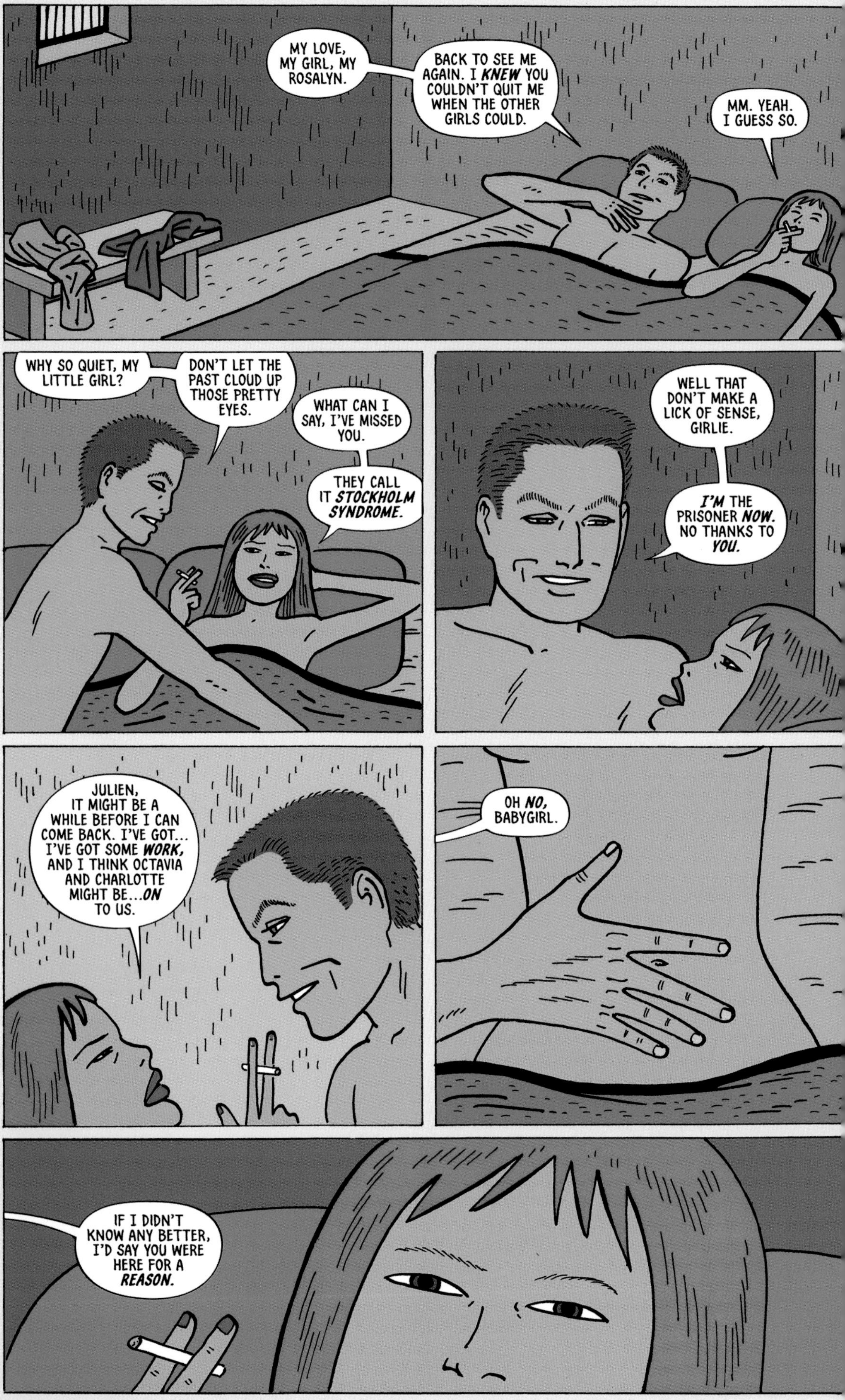
MY LOVE, MY GIRL, MY ROSALYN.
BACK TO SEE ME AGAIN. I *KNEW* YOU COULDN'T QUIT ME WHEN THE OTHER GIRLS COULD.
MM. YEAH. I GUESS SO.
WHY SO QUIET, MY LITTLE GIRL?
DON'T LET THE PAST CLOUD UP THOSE PRETTY EYES.
WHAT CAN I SAY, I'VE MISSED YOU.
THEY CALL IT *STOCKHOLM SYNDROME.*
WELL THAT DON'T MAKE A LICK OF SENSE, GIRLIE.
I'M THE PRISONER *NOW.* NO THANKS TO *YOU.*
JULIEN, IT MIGHT BE A WHILE BEFORE I CAN COME BACK. I'VE GOT... I'VE GOT SOME *WORK,* AND I THINK OCTAVIA AND CHARLOTTE MIGHT BE...*ON* TO US.
OH *NO,* BABYGIRL.
IF I DIDN'T KNOW ANY BETTER, I'D SAY YOU WERE HERE FOR A *REASON.*

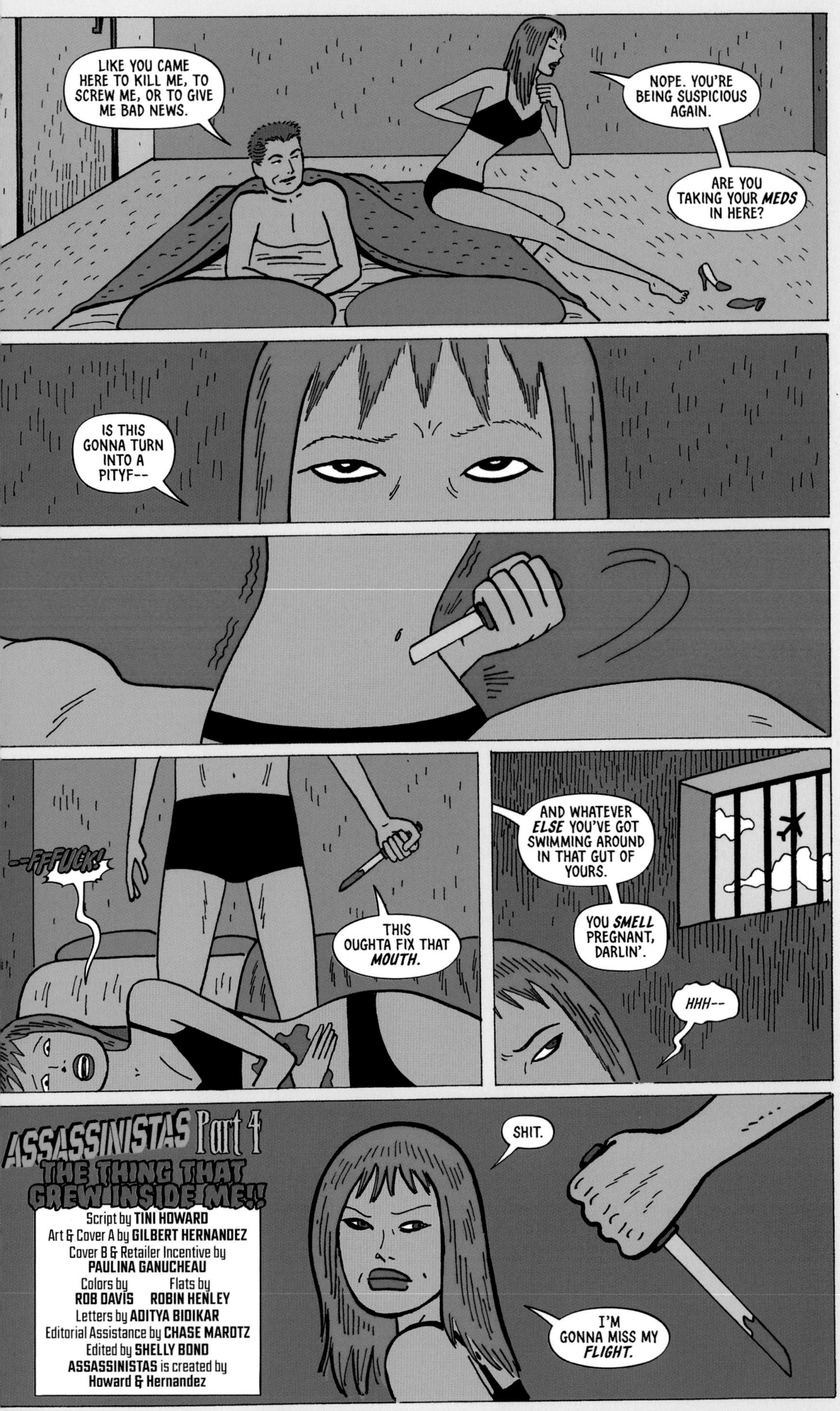

LIKE YOU CAME HERE TO KILL ME, TO SCREW ME, OR TO GIVE ME BAD NEWS.
NOPE. YOU'RE BEING SUSPICIOUS AGAIN.
ARE YOU TAKING YOUR MEDS IN HERE?
IS THIS GONNA TURN INTO A PITYF--
--FFFUCK!
THIS OUGHTA FIX THAT MOUTH.
AND WHATEVER ELSE YOU'VE GOT SWIMMING AROUND IN THAT GUT OF YOURS.
YOU SMELL PREGNANT, DARLIN'.
HHH--
ASSASSINISTAS Part 4
THE THING THAT GREW INSIDE ME!!
Script by TINI HOWARD
Art & Cover A by GILBERT HERNANDEZ
Cover B & Retailer Incentive by PAULINA GANUCHEAU
Colors by ROB DAVIS
Flats by ROBIN HENLEY
Letters by ADITYA BIDIKAR
Editorial Assistance by CHASE MAROTZ
Edited by SHELLY BOND
ASSASSINISTAS is created by Howard & Hernandez
SHIT.
I'M GONNA MISS MY FLIGHT.

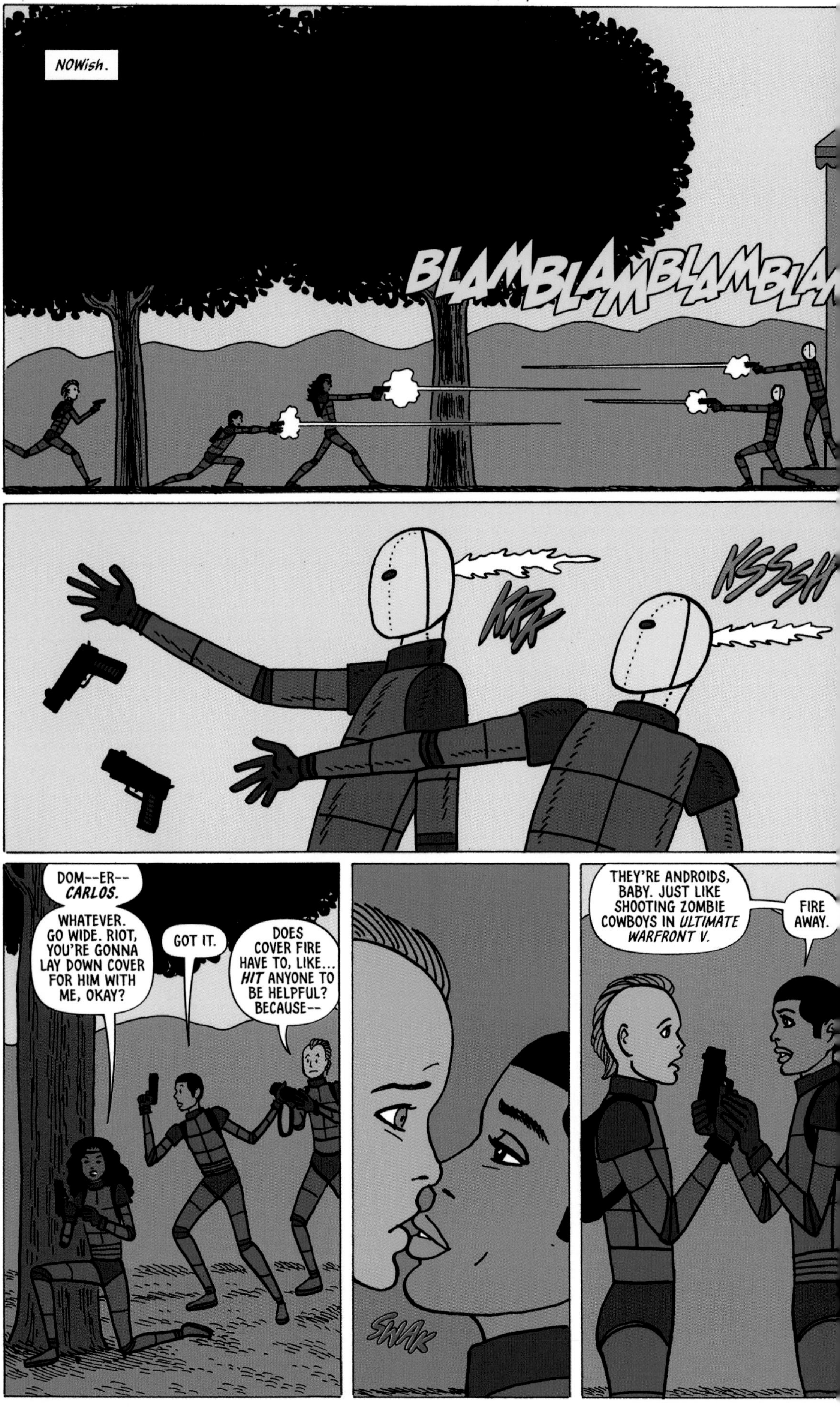
NOWish.
BLAMBLAMBLAMBLAM
KRK
KSSSH
DOM--ER--CARLOS.
WHATEVER. GO WIDE. RIOT, YOU'RE GONNA LAY DOWN COVER FOR HIM WITH ME, OKAY?
GOT IT.
DOES COVER FIRE HAVE TO, LIKE... HIT ANYONE TO BE HELPFUL? BECAUSE--
SMAK
THEY'RE ANDROIDS, BABY. JUST LIKE SHOOTING ZOMBIE COWBOYS IN ULTIMATE WARFRONT V.
FIRE AWAY.

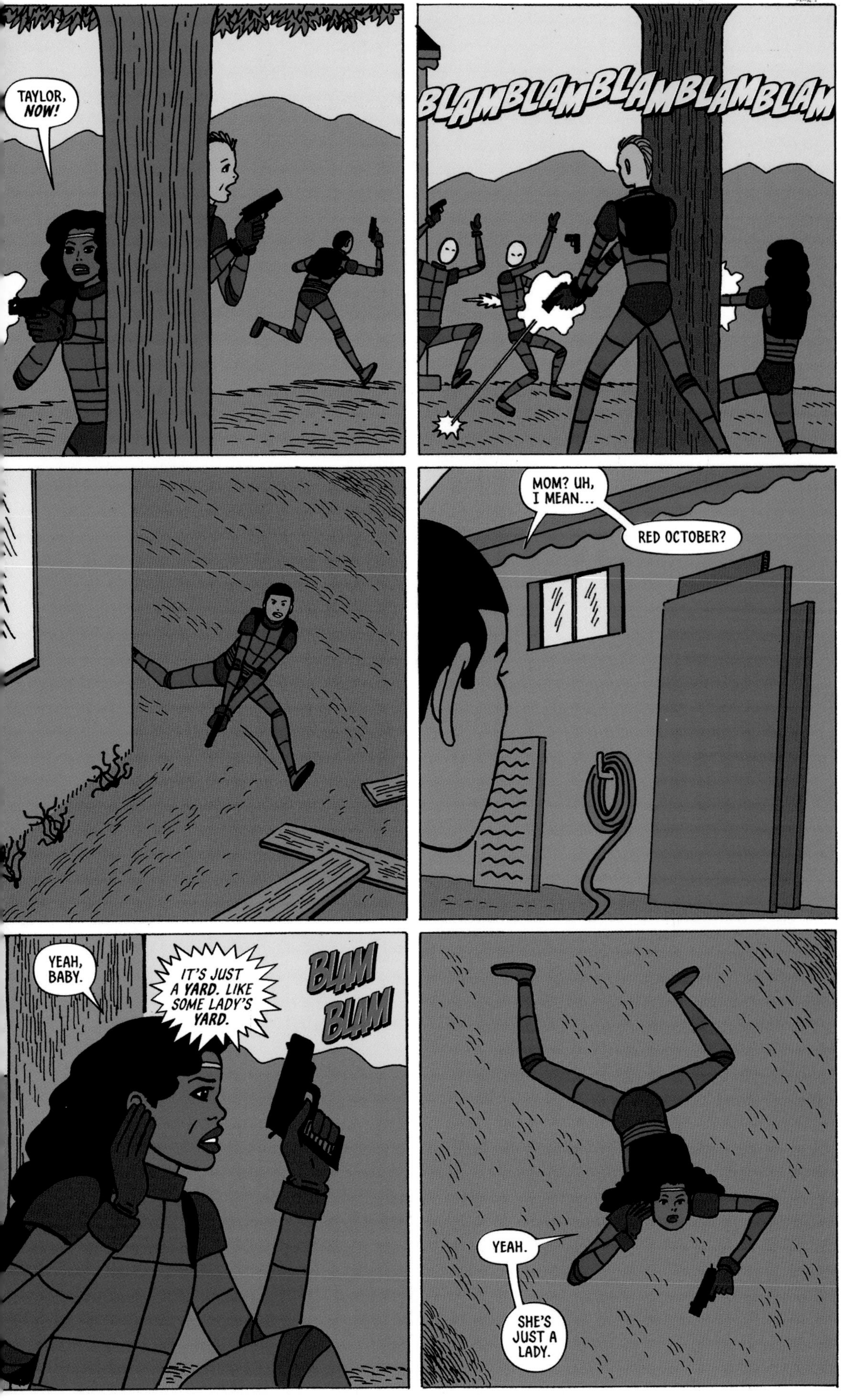
TAYLOR, NOW!
BLAMBLAMBLAMBLAMBLAM
MOM? UH, I MEAN...
RED OCTOBER?
YEAH, BABY.
IT'S JUST A YARD. LIKE SOME LADY'S YARD.
BLAM BLAM
YEAH.
SHE'S JUST A LADY.

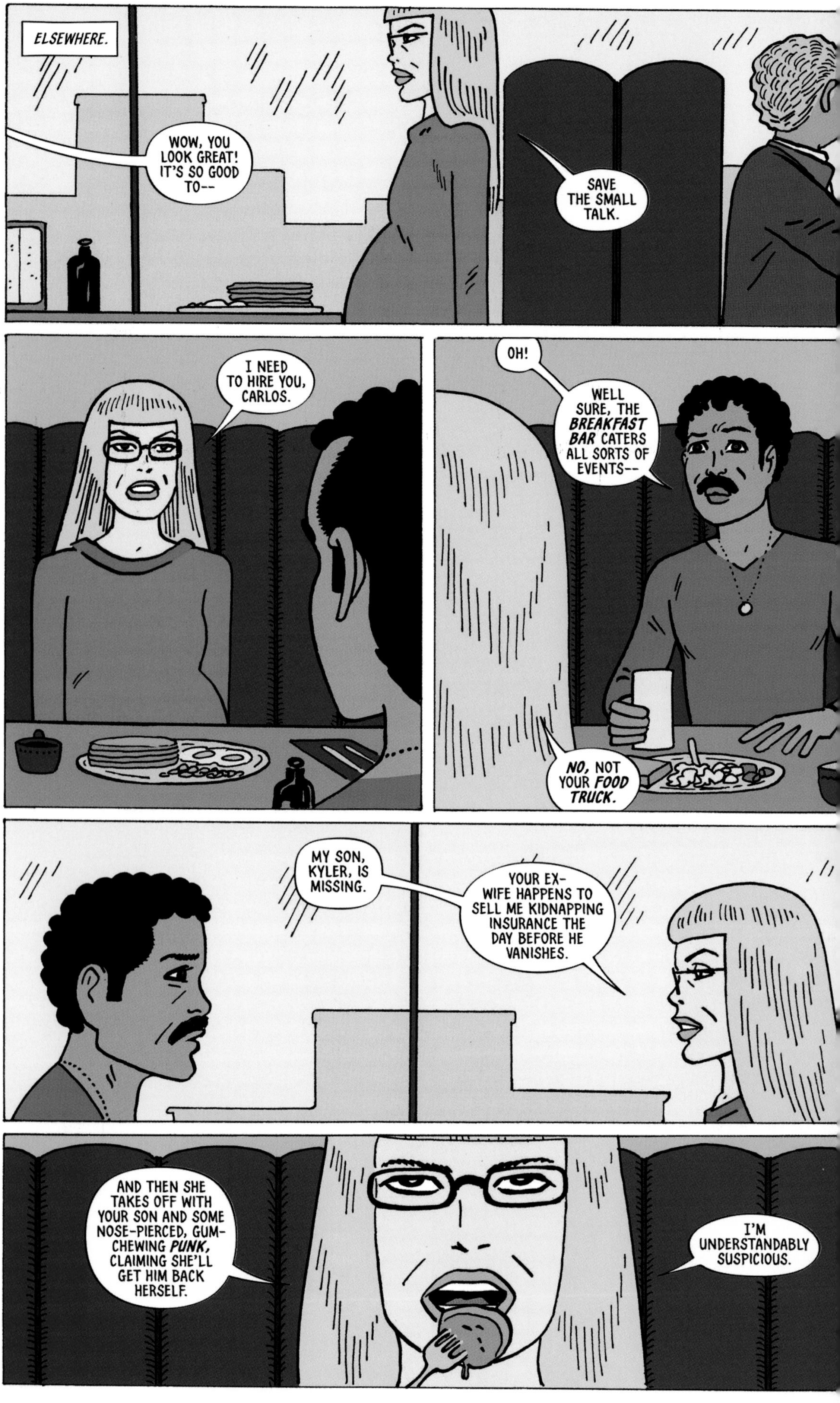
ELSEWHERE.
WOW, YOU LOOK GREAT! IT'S SO GOOD TO--
SAVE THE SMALL TALK.
I NEED TO HIRE YOU, CARLOS.
OH!
WELL SURE, THE *BREAKFAST BAR* CATERS ALL SORTS OF EVENTS--
NO, NOT YOUR *FOOD TRUCK.*
MY SON, KYLER, IS MISSING.
YOUR EX-WIFE HAPPENS TO SELL ME KIDNAPPING INSURANCE THE DAY BEFORE HE VANISHES.
AND THEN SHE TAKES OFF WITH YOUR SON AND SOME NOSE-PIERCED, GUM-CHEWING *PUNK,* CLAIMING SHE'LL GET HIM BACK HERSELF.
I'M UNDERSTANDABLY SUSPICIOUS.

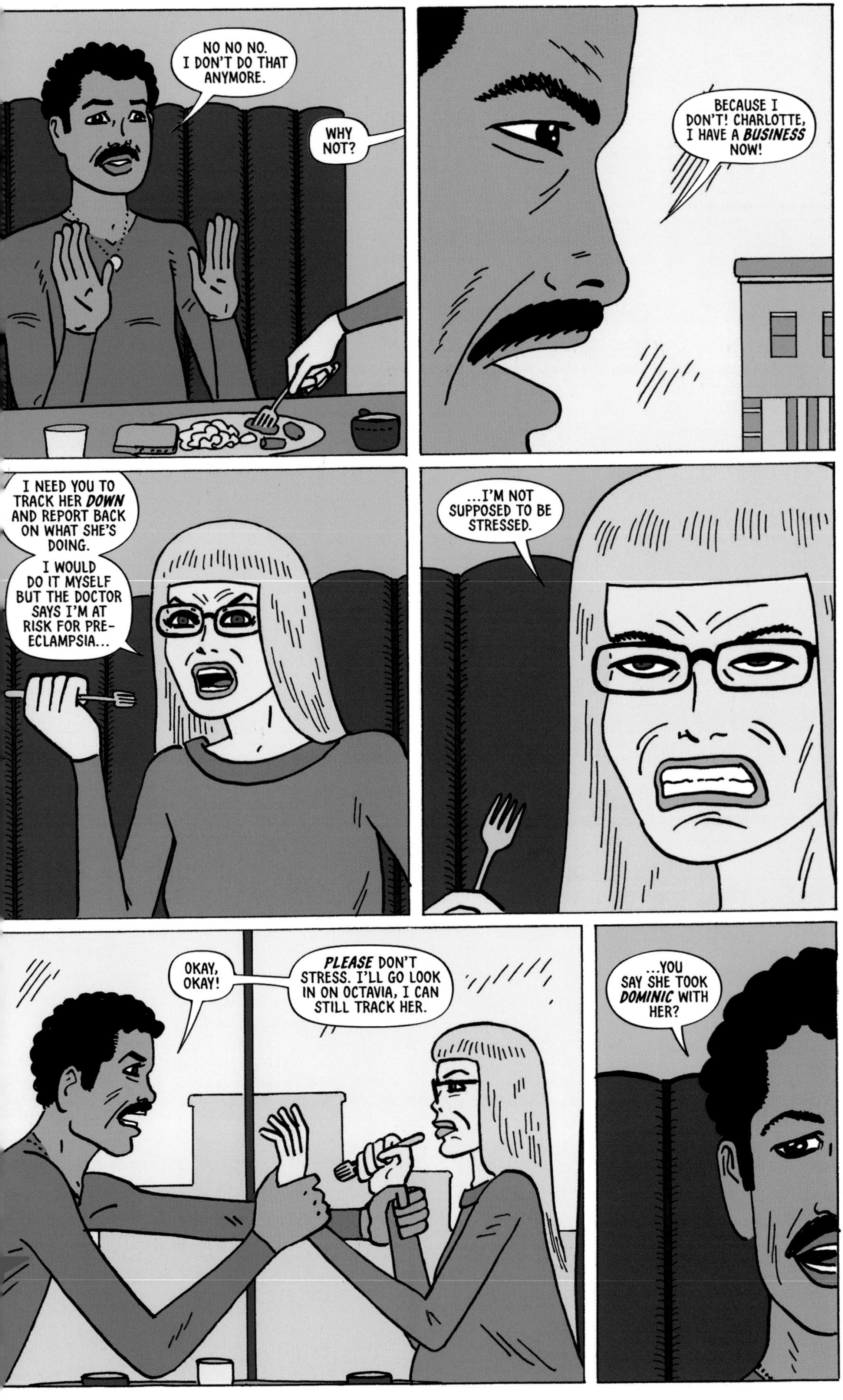
NO NO NO. I DON'T DO THAT ANYMORE.
WHY NOT?
BECAUSE I DON'T! CHARLOTTE, I HAVE A *BUSINESS* NOW!
I NEED YOU TO TRACK HER *DOWN* AND REPORT BACK ON WHAT SHE'S DOING.
I WOULD DO IT MYSELF BUT THE DOCTOR SAYS I'M AT RISK FOR PRE-ECLAMPSIA...
...I'M NOT SUPPOSED TO BE STRESSED.
OKAY, OKAY!
PLEASE DON'T STRESS. I'LL GO LOOK IN ON OCTAVIA, I CAN STILL TRACK HER.
...YOU SAY SHE TOOK *DOMINIC* WITH HER?

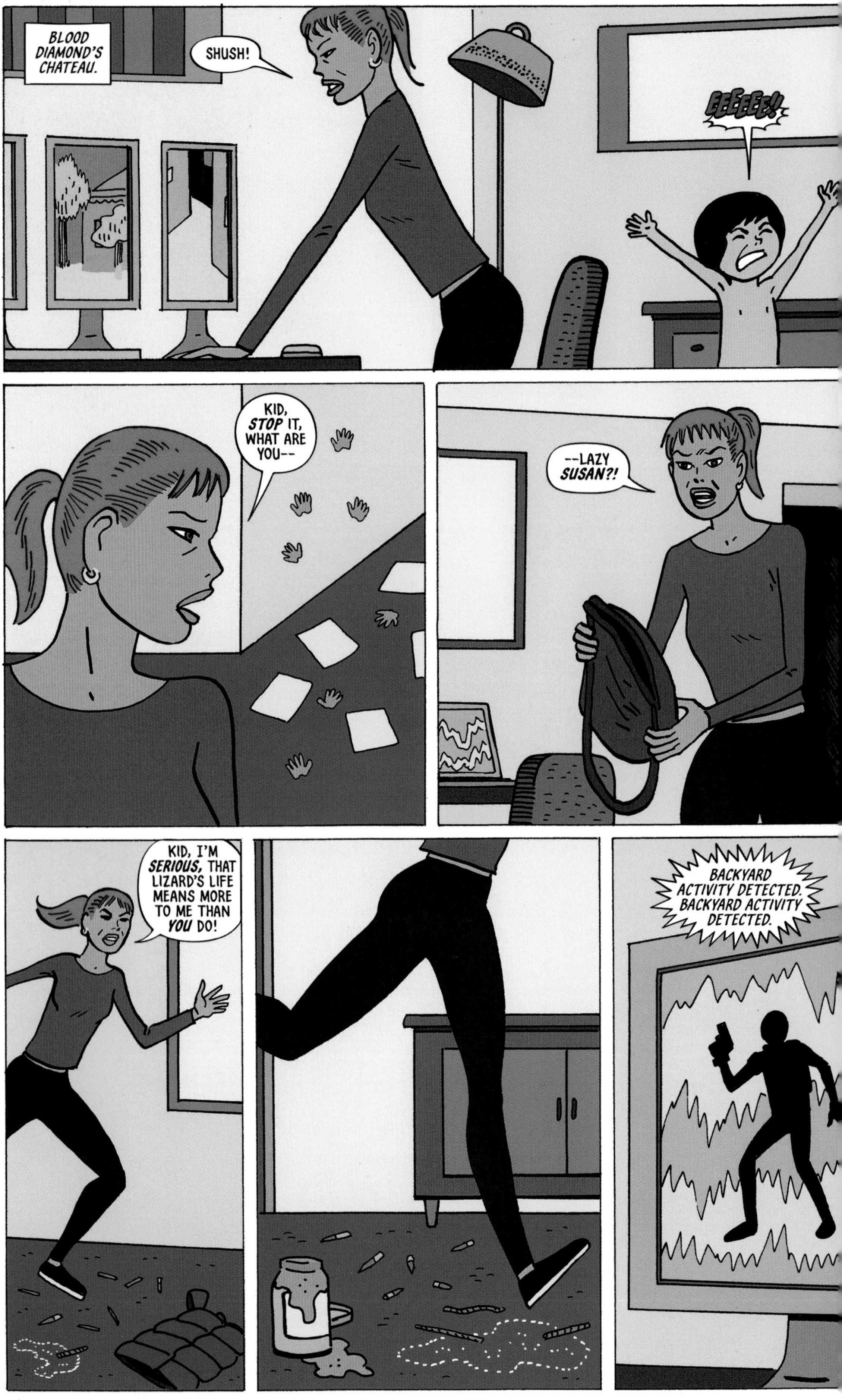
BLOOD DIAMOND'S CHATEAU.
SHUSH!
EEEEEE!!
KID, STOP IT, WHAT ARE YOU--
--LAZY SUSAN?!
KID, I'M SERIOUS, THAT LIZARD'S LIFE MEANS MORE TO ME THAN YOU DO!
BACKYARD ACTIVITY DETECTED. BACKYARD ACTIVITY DETECTED.

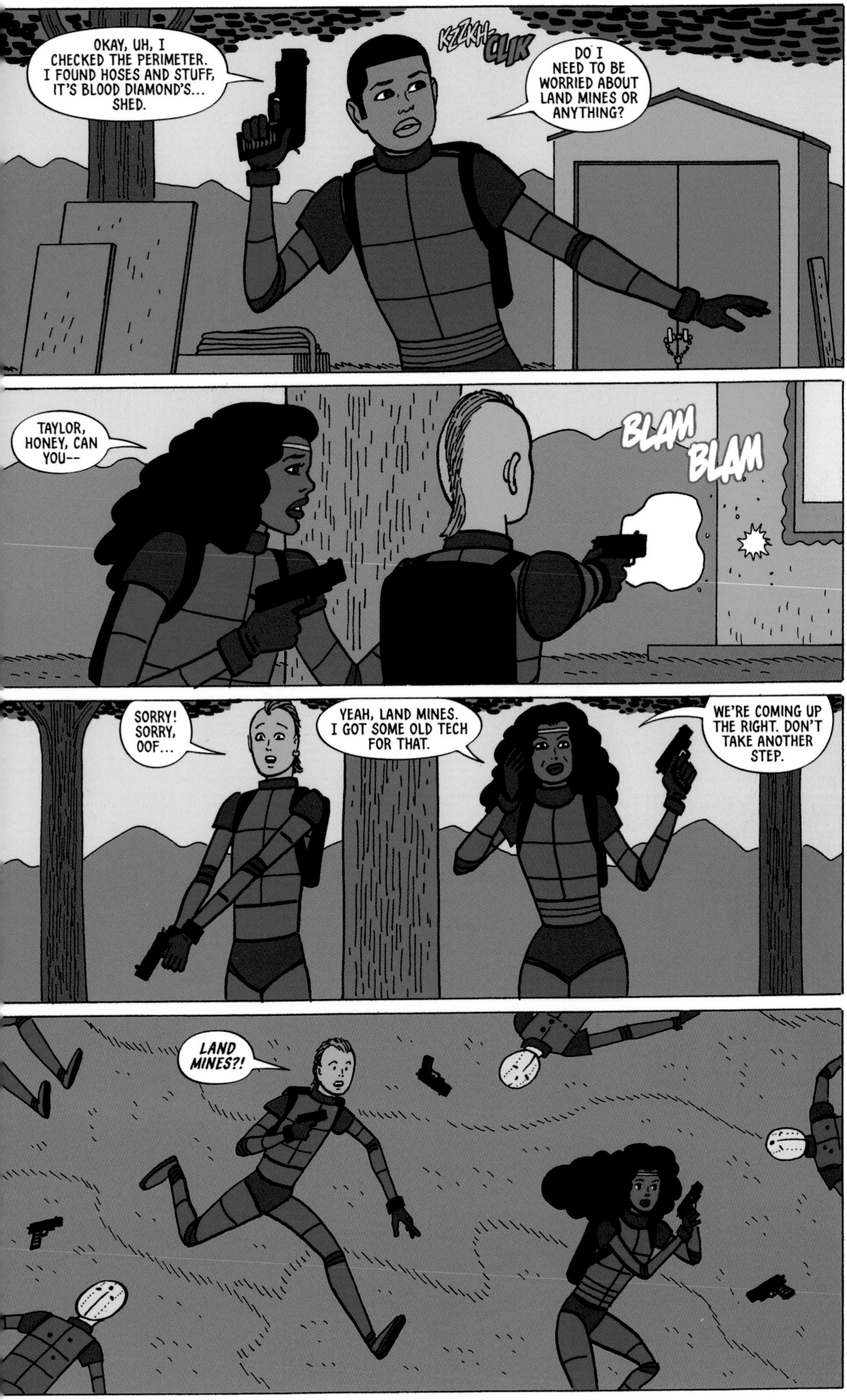
OKAY, UH, I CHECKED THE PERIMETER. I FOUND HOSES AND STUFF, IT'S BLOOD DIAMOND'S... SHED.
KZZKH-CLIK
DO I NEED TO BE WORRIED ABOUT LAND MINES OR ANYTHING?
TAYLOR, HONEY, CAN YOU--
BLAM
BLAM
SORRY! SORRY, OOF...
YEAH, LAND MINES. I GOT SOME OLD TECH FOR THAT.
WE'RE COMING UP THE RIGHT. DON'T TAKE ANOTHER STEP.
LAND MINES?!

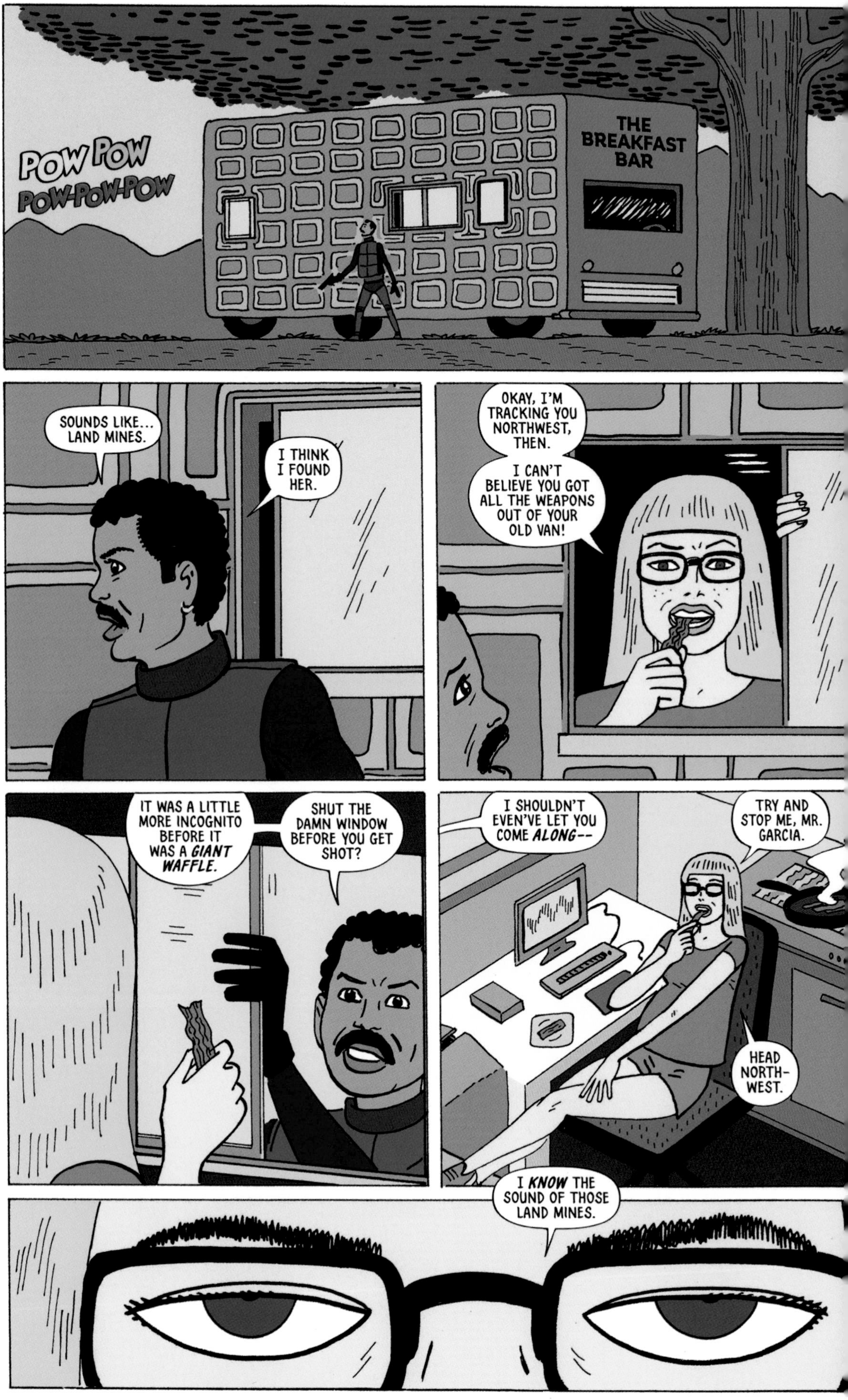
POW POW
POW-POW-POW
THE BREAKFAST BAR
SOUNDS LIKE... LAND MINES.
I THINK I FOUND HER.
OKAY, I'M TRACKING YOU NORTHWEST, THEN.
I CAN'T BELIEVE YOU GOT ALL THE WEAPONS OUT OF YOUR OLD VAN!
IT WAS A LITTLE MORE INCOGNITO BEFORE IT WAS A *GIANT WAFFLE.*
SHUT THE DAMN WINDOW BEFORE YOU GET SHOT?
I SHOULDN'T EVEN'VE LET YOU COME *ALONG*--
TRY AND STOP ME, MR. GARCIA.
HEAD NORTH-WEST.
I *KNOW* THE SOUND OF THOSE LAND MINES.

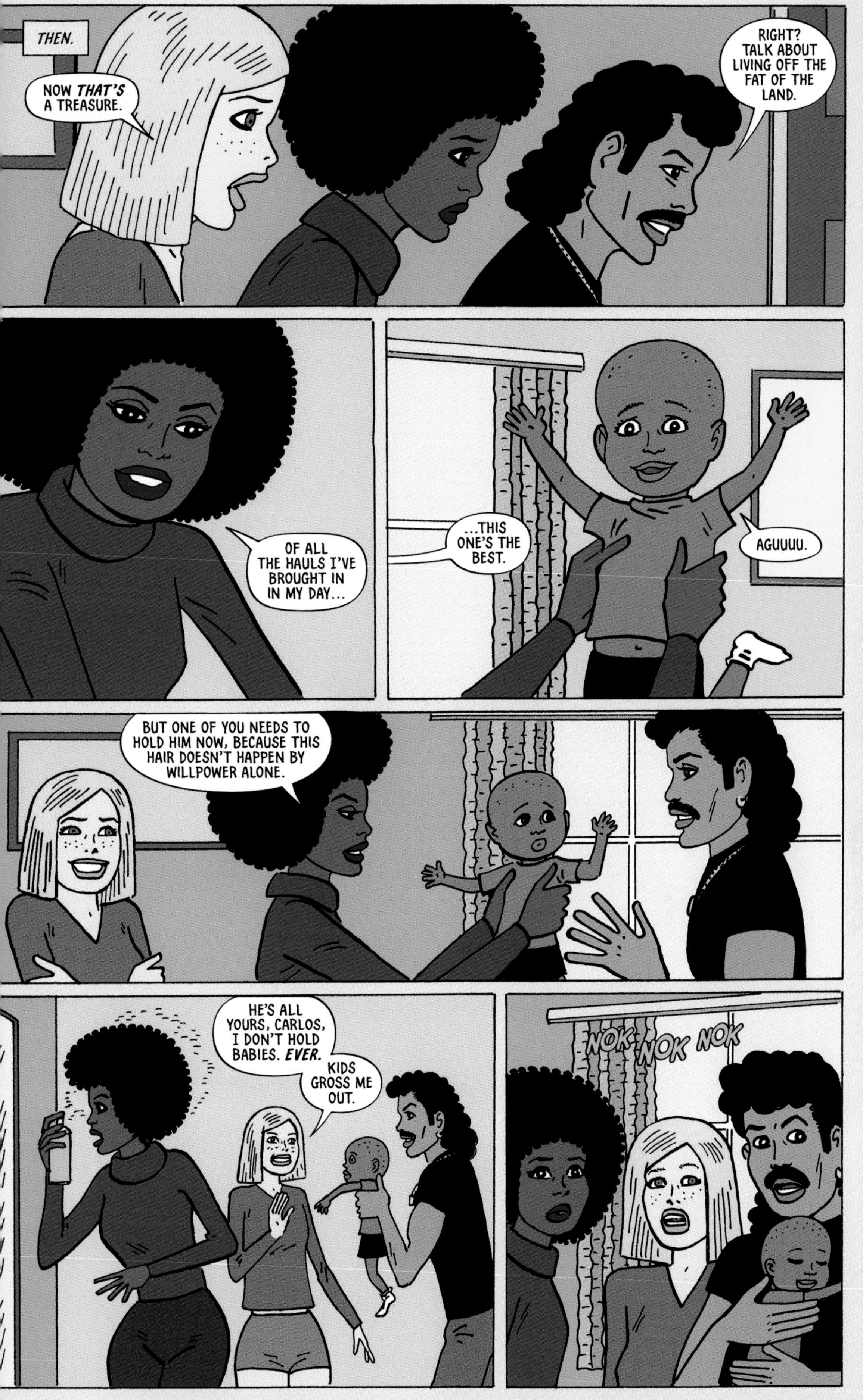
THEN.
NOW THAT'S A TREASURE.
RIGHT? TALK ABOUT LIVING OFF THE FAT OF THE LAND.
OF ALL THE HAULS I'VE BROUGHT IN IN MY DAY...
...THIS ONE'S THE BEST.
AGUUUU.
BUT ONE OF YOU NEEDS TO HOLD HIM NOW, BECAUSE THIS HAIR DOESN'T HAPPEN BY WILLPOWER ALONE.
HE'S ALL YOURS, CARLOS, I DON'T HOLD BABIES. EVER.
KIDS GROSS ME OUT.
NOK NOK NOK

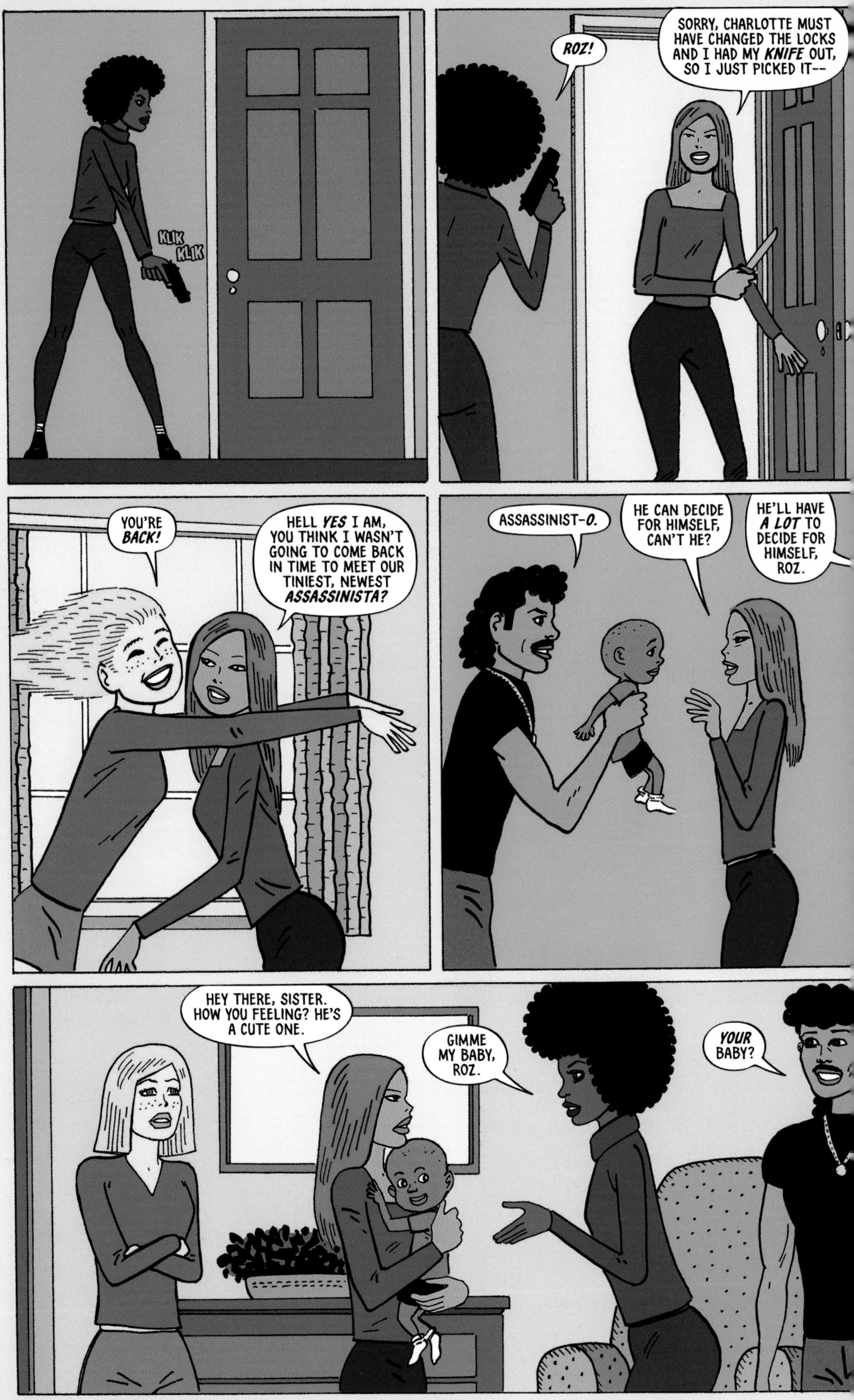
KLIK
KLIK
ROZ!
SORRY, CHARLOTTE MUST HAVE CHANGED THE LOCKS AND I HAD MY *KNIFE* OUT, SO I JUST PICKED IT--
YOU'RE *BACK!*
HELL *YES* I AM, YOU THINK I WASN'T GOING TO COME BACK IN TIME TO MEET OUR TINIEST, NEWEST *ASSASSINISTA?*
ASSASSINIST-*O*.
HE CAN DECIDE FOR HIMSELF, CAN'T HE?
HE'LL HAVE *A LOT* TO DECIDE FOR HIMSELF, ROZ.
HEY THERE, SISTER. HOW YOU FEELING? HE'S A CUTE ONE.
GIMME MY BABY, ROZ.
YOUR BABY?

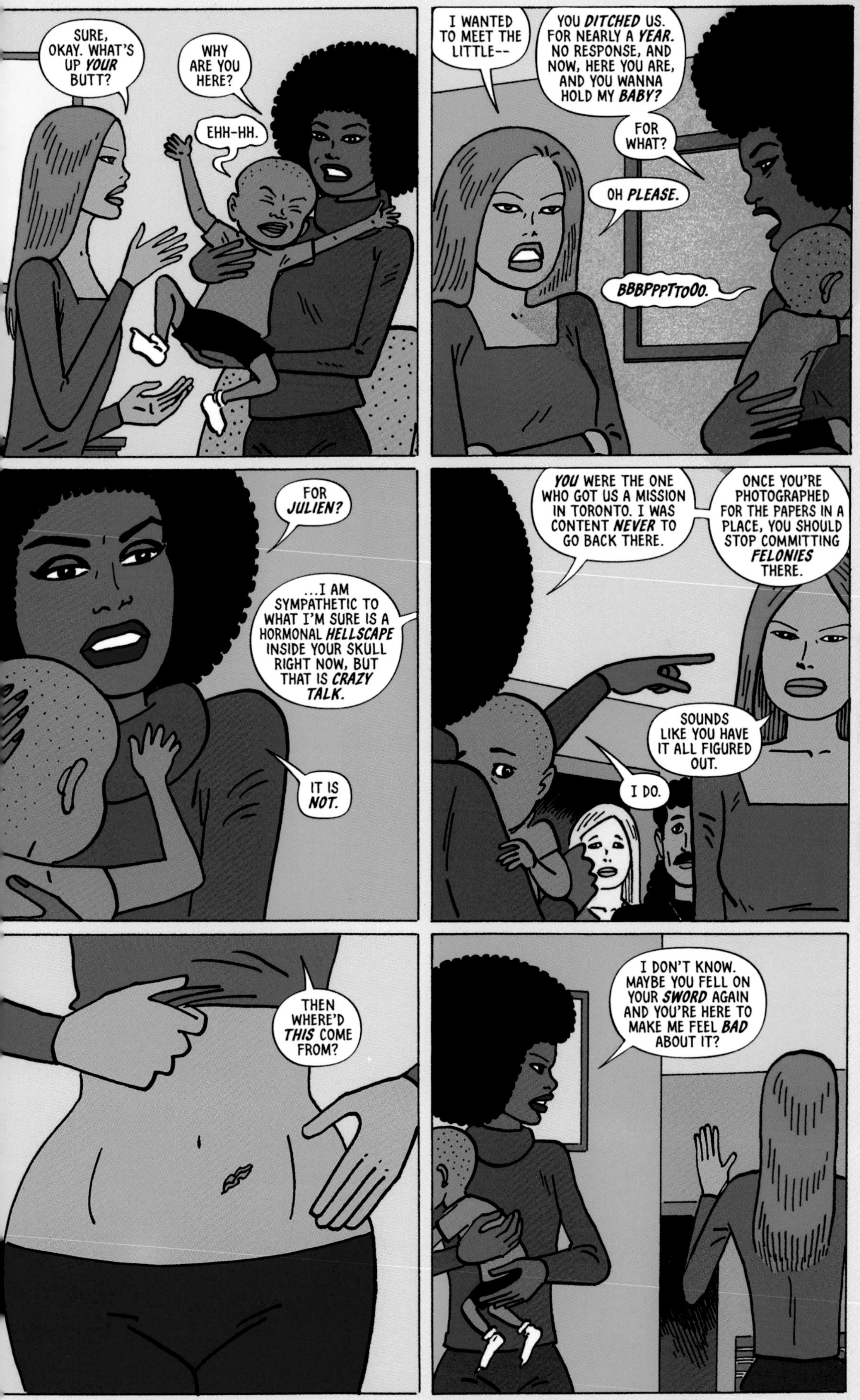

SURE, OKAY. WHAT'S UP *YOUR* BUTT?
WHY ARE YOU HERE?
EHH-HH.
I WANTED TO MEET THE LITTLE--
YOU *DITCHED* US. FOR NEARLY A *YEAR.* NO RESPONSE, AND NOW, HERE YOU ARE, AND YOU WANNA HOLD MY *BABY?*
FOR WHAT?
OH *PLEASE.*
BBBPPPTTOOO.
FOR *JULIEN?*
...I AM SYMPATHETIC TO WHAT I'M SURE IS A HORMONAL *HELLSCAPE* INSIDE YOUR SKULL RIGHT NOW, BUT THAT IS *CRAZY TALK.*
IT IS *NOT.*
YOU WERE THE ONE WHO GOT US A MISSION IN TORONTO. I WAS CONTENT *NEVER* TO GO BACK THERE.
ONCE YOU'RE PHOTOGRAPHED FOR THE PAPERS IN A PLACE, YOU SHOULD STOP COMMITTING *FELONIES* THERE.
SOUNDS LIKE YOU HAVE IT ALL FIGURED OUT.
I DO.
THEN WHERE'D *THIS* COME FROM?
I DON'T KNOW. MAYBE YOU FELL ON YOUR *SWORD* AGAIN AND YOU'RE HERE TO MAKE ME FEEL *BAD* ABOUT IT?

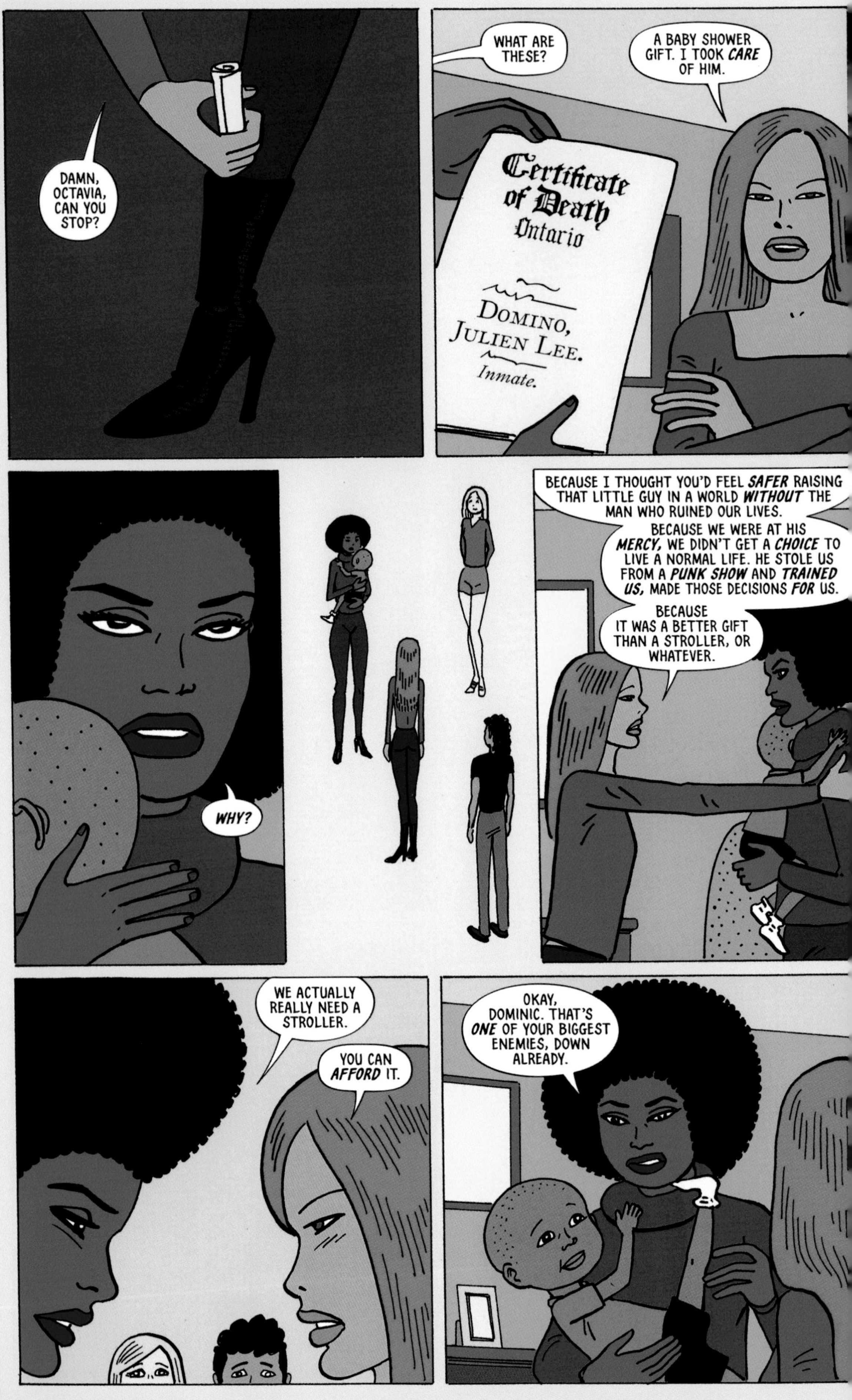
DAMN, OCTAVIA, CAN YOU STOP?
WHAT ARE THESE?
A BABY SHOWER GIFT. I TOOK *CARE* OF HIM.
Certificate of Death
Ontario
DOMINO, JULIEN LEE.
Inmate.
WHY?
BECAUSE I THOUGHT YOU'D FEEL *SAFER* RAISING THAT LITTLE GUY IN A WORLD *WITHOUT* THE MAN WHO RUINED OUR LIVES.
BECAUSE WE WERE AT HIS *MERCY,* WE DIDN'T GET A *CHOICE* TO LIVE A NORMAL LIFE. HE STOLE US FROM A *PUNK SHOW* AND *TRAINED US,* MADE THOSE DECISIONS *FOR* US.
BECAUSE IT WAS A BETTER GIFT THAN A STROLLER, OR WHATEVER.
WE ACTUALLY REALLY NEED A STROLLER.
YOU CAN *AFFORD* IT.
OKAY, DOMINIC. THAT'S *ONE* OF YOUR BIGGEST ENEMIES, DOWN ALREADY.

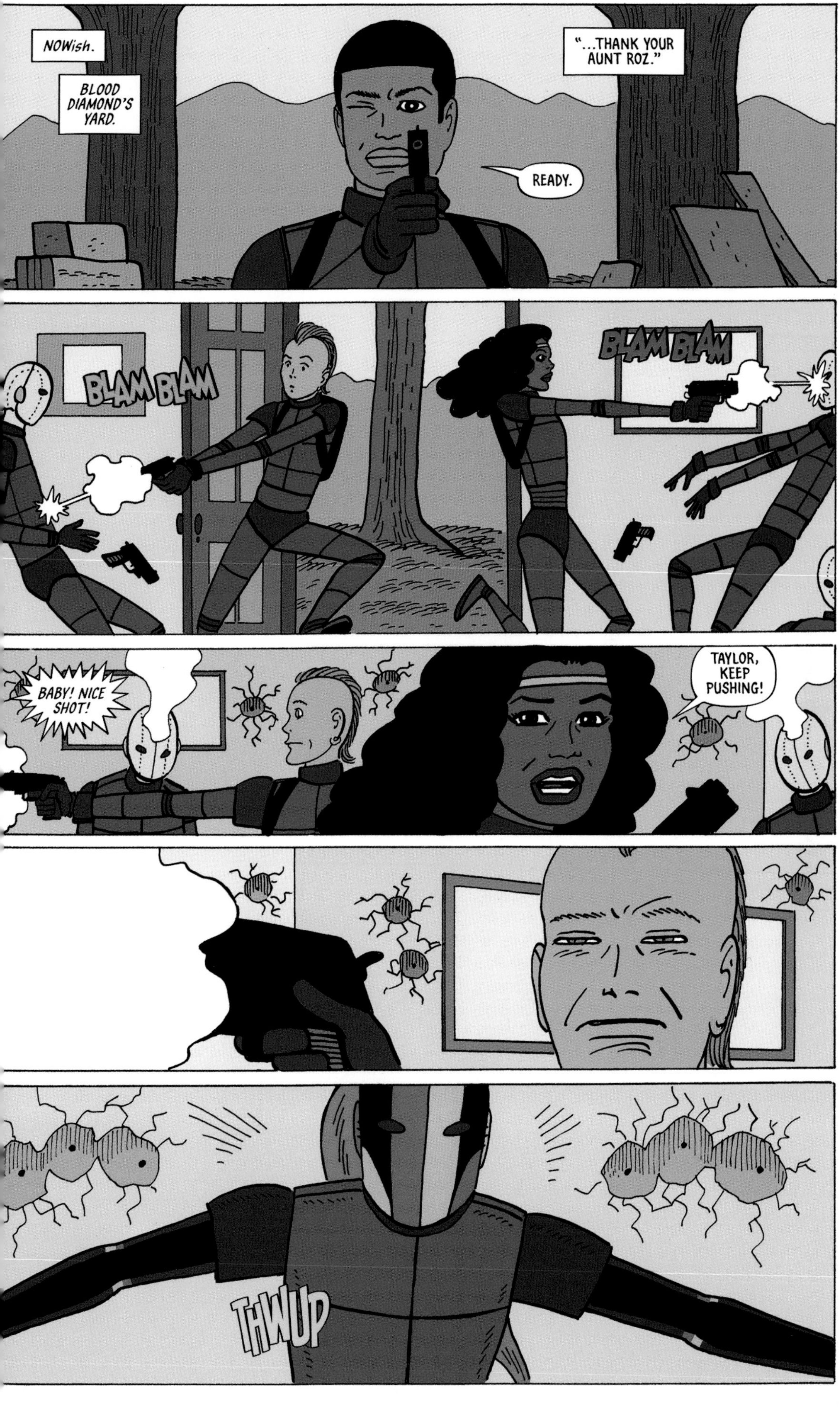
NOWish.
BLOOD DIAMOND'S YARD.
"...THANK YOUR AUNT ROZ."
READY.
BLAM BLAM
BLAM BLAM
BABY! NICE SHOT!
TAYLOR, KEEP PUSHING!
THWUP

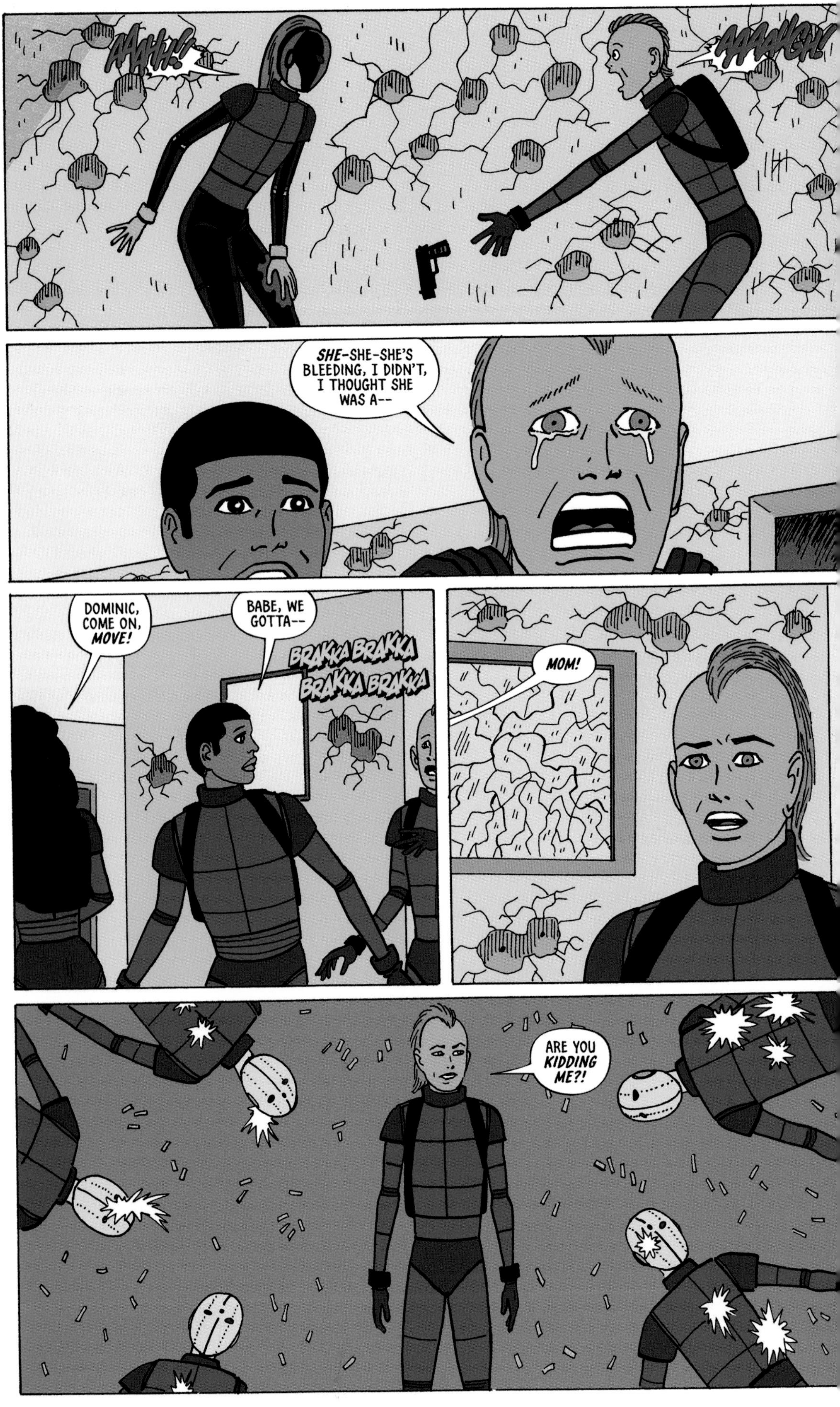
AAHH!
AAAAHGH!
SHE-SHE-SHE'S BLEEDING, I DIDN'T, I THOUGHT SHE WAS A--
DOMINIC, COME ON, MOVE!
BABE, WE GOTTA--
BRAKKA BRAKKA BRAKKA BRAKKA
MOM!
ARE YOU KIDDING ME?!

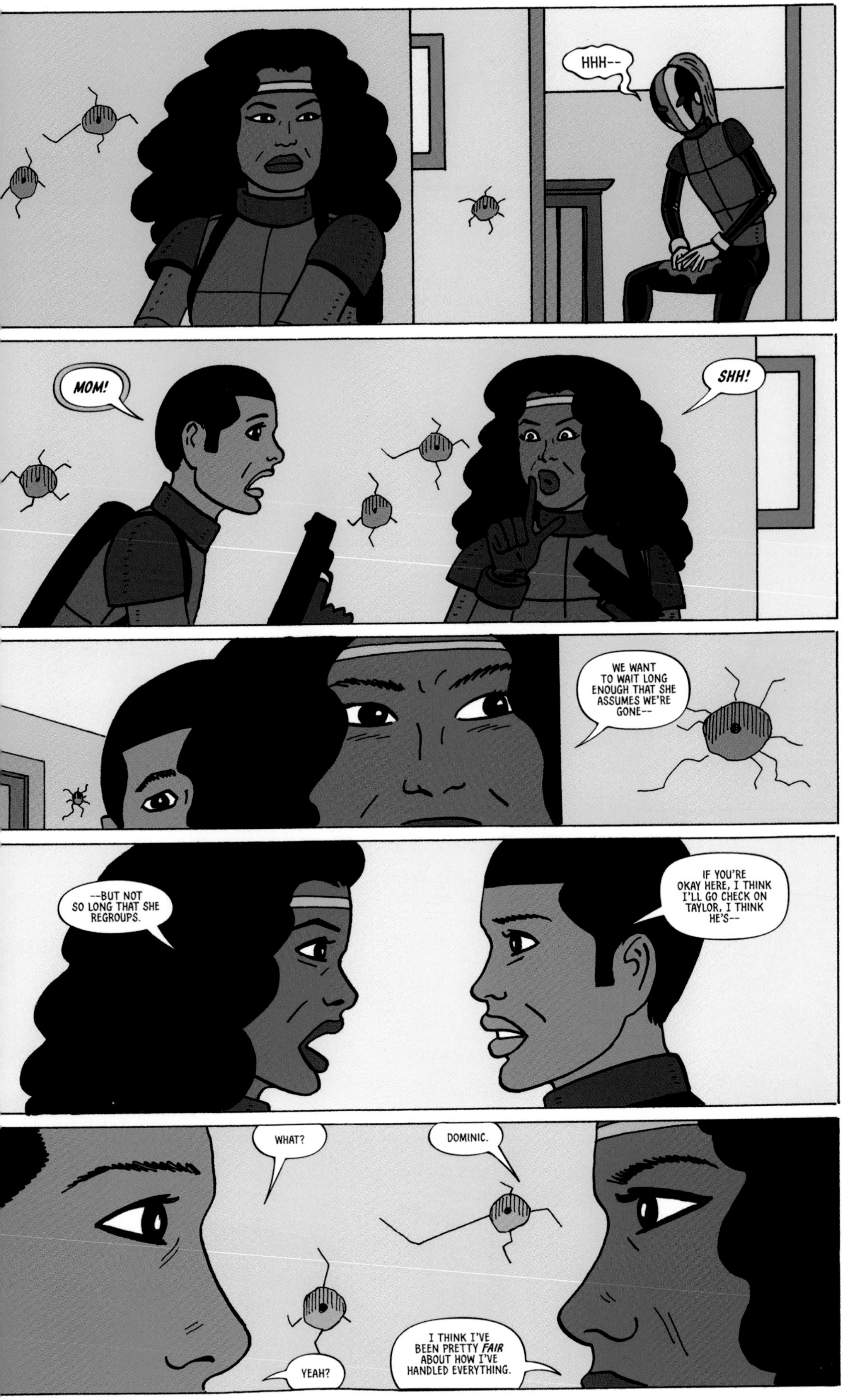
HHH--
MOM!
SHH!
WE WANT TO WAIT LONG ENOUGH THAT SHE ASSUMES WE'RE GONE--
--BUT NOT SO LONG THAT SHE REGROUPS.
IF YOU'RE OKAY HERE, I THINK I'LL GO CHECK ON TAYLOR, I THINK HE'S--
DOMINIC.
WHAT?
I THINK I'VE BEEN PRETTY FAIR ABOUT HOW I'VE HANDLED EVERYTHING.
YEAH?

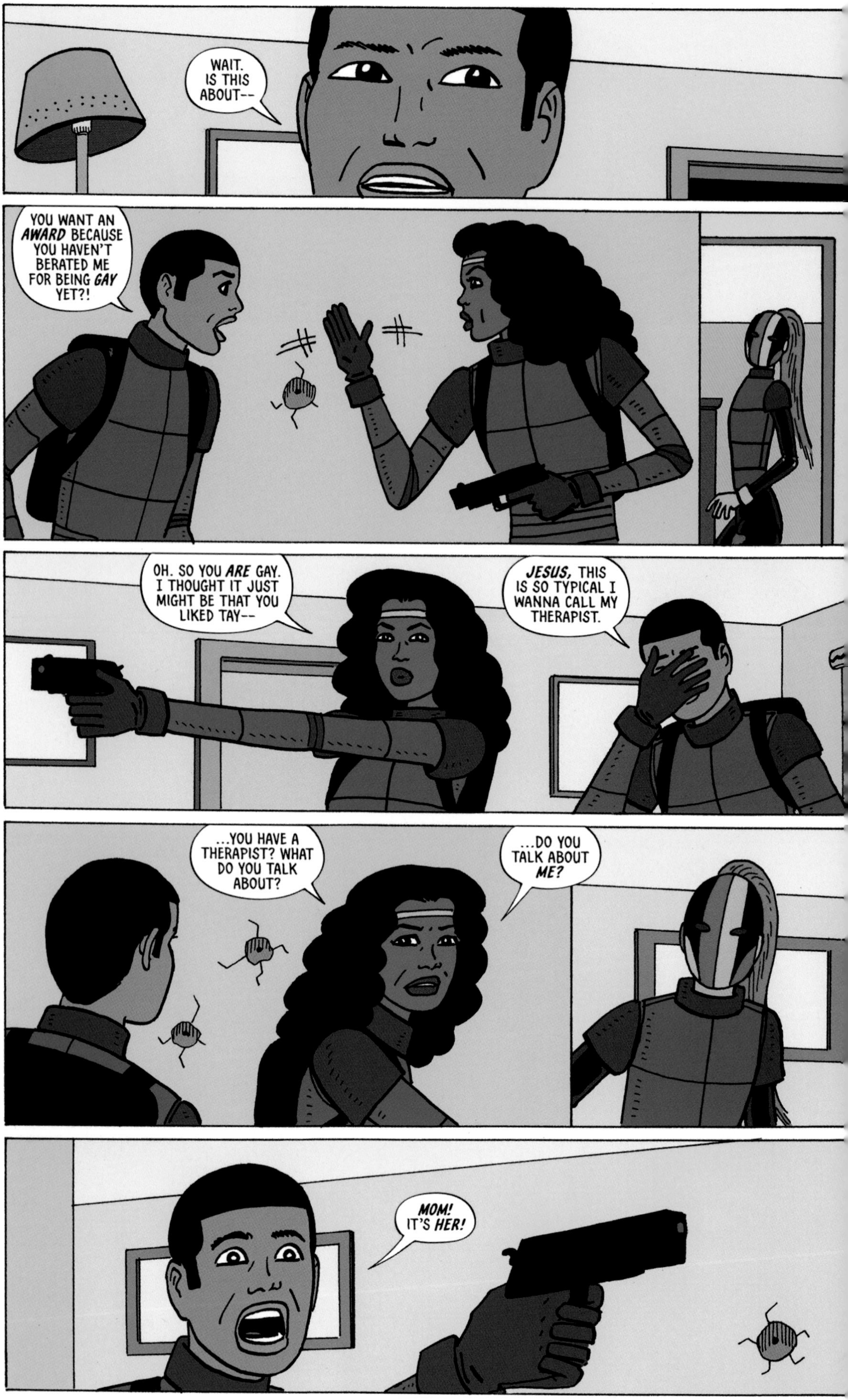

WAIT. IS THIS ABOUT--
YOU WANT AN *AWARD* BECAUSE YOU HAVEN'T BERATED ME FOR BEING *GAY* YET?!
OH. SO YOU *ARE* GAY. I THOUGHT IT JUST MIGHT BE THAT YOU LIKED TAY--
JESUS, THIS IS SO TYPICAL I WANNA CALL MY THERAPIST.
...YOU HAVE A THERAPIST? WHAT DO YOU TALK ABOUT?
...DO YOU TALK ABOUT *ME?*
MOM! IT'S *HER!*

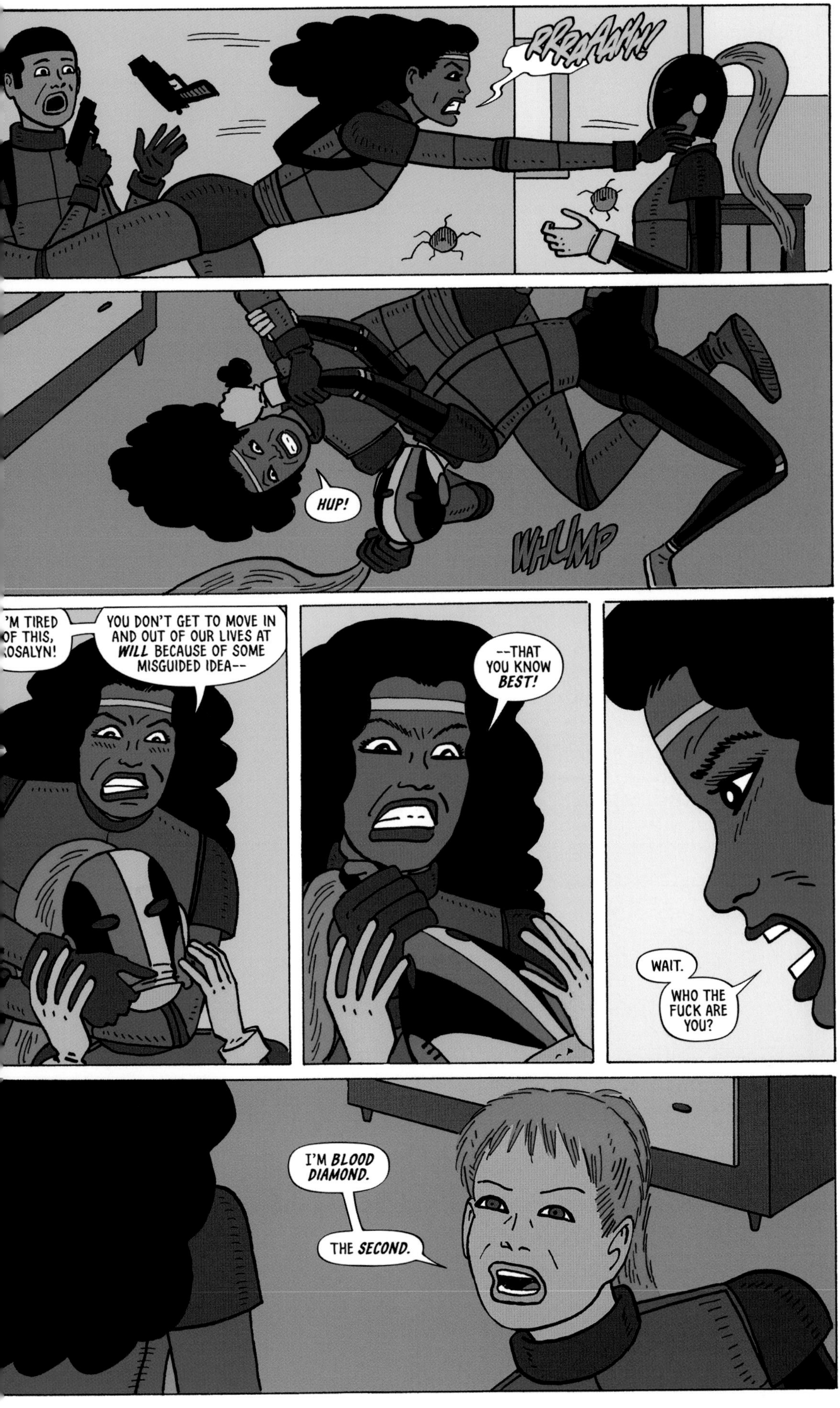

RRRAAHH!
HUP!
WHUMP
'M TIRED OF THIS, OSALYN!
YOU DON'T GET TO MOVE IN AND OUT OF OUR LIVES AT *WILL* BECAUSE OF SOME MISGUIDED IDEA--
--THAT YOU KNOW *BEST!*
WAIT.
WHO THE FUCK ARE YOU?
I'M *BLOOD DIAMOND.*
THE *SECOND.*

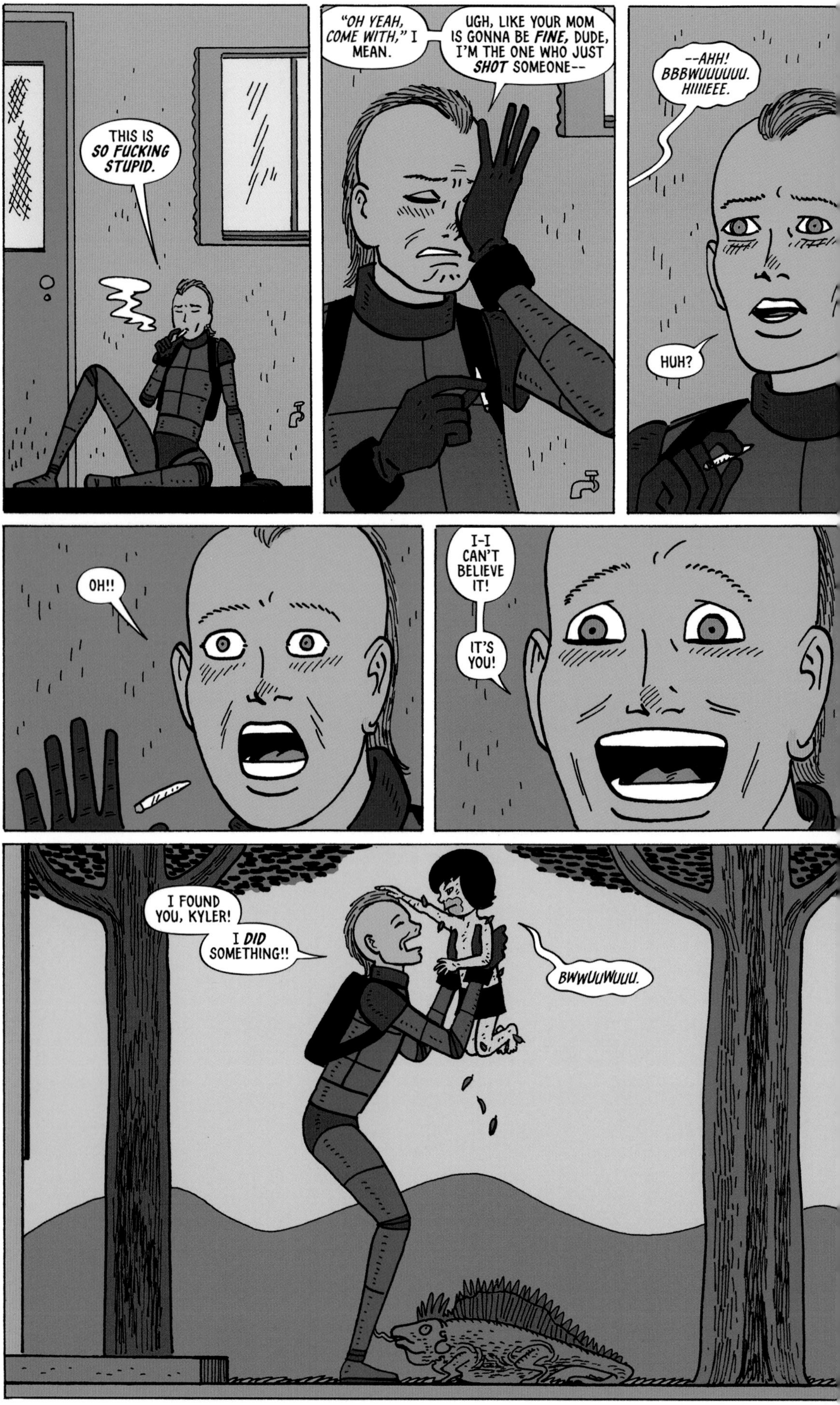

THIS IS SO FUCKING STUPID.
"OH YEAH, COME WITH," I MEAN.
UGH, LIKE YOUR MOM IS GONNA BE FINE, DUDE, I'M THE ONE WHO JUST SHOT SOMEONE--
--AHH! BBBWUUUUUU. HIIIIEEE.
HUH?
OH!!
I-I CAN'T BELIEVE IT!
IT'S YOU!
I FOUND YOU, KYLER!
I DID SOMETHING!!
BWWUUWUUU.

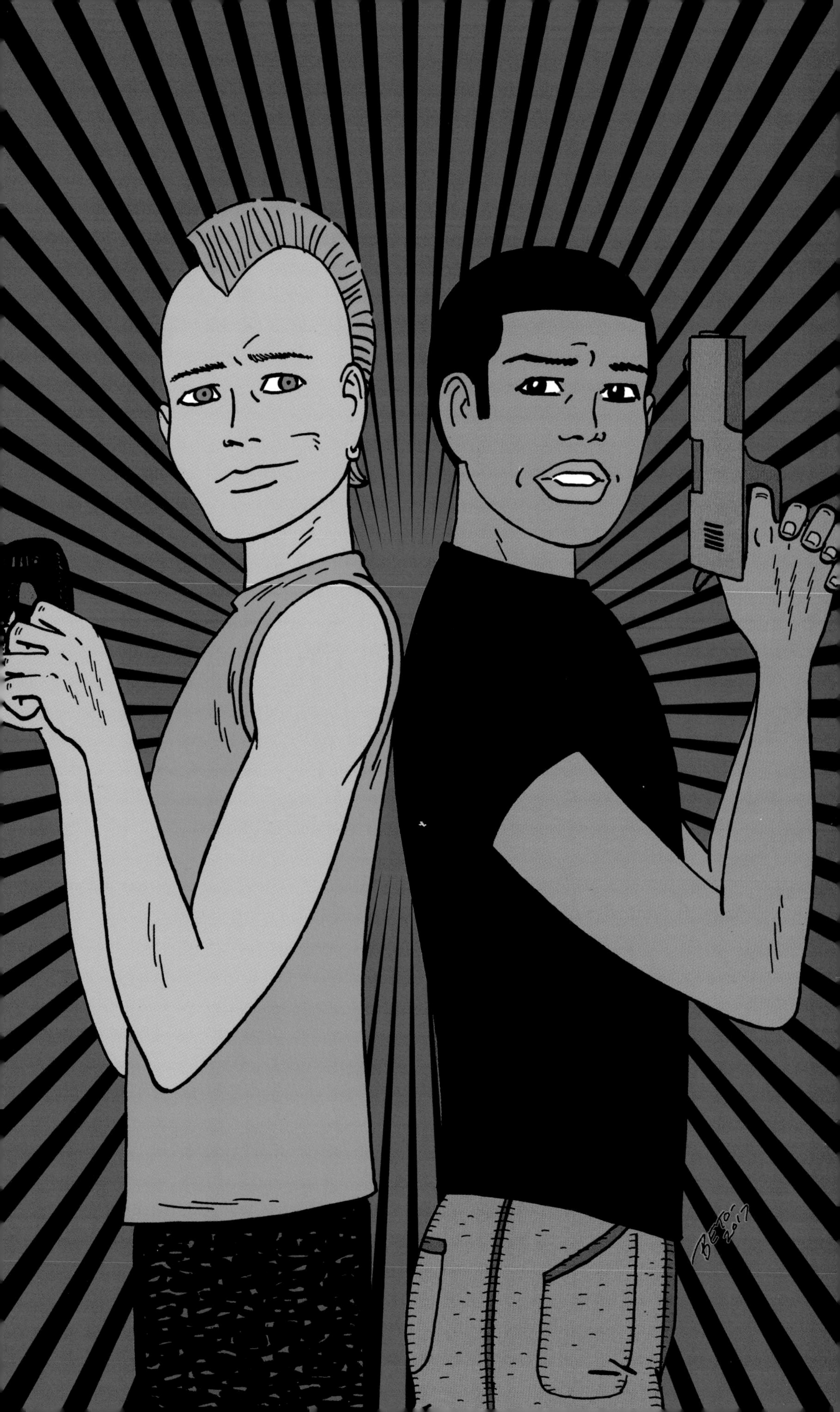
BETO 2017

“Nothing in the real world is half as lucrative as the assassination game.”

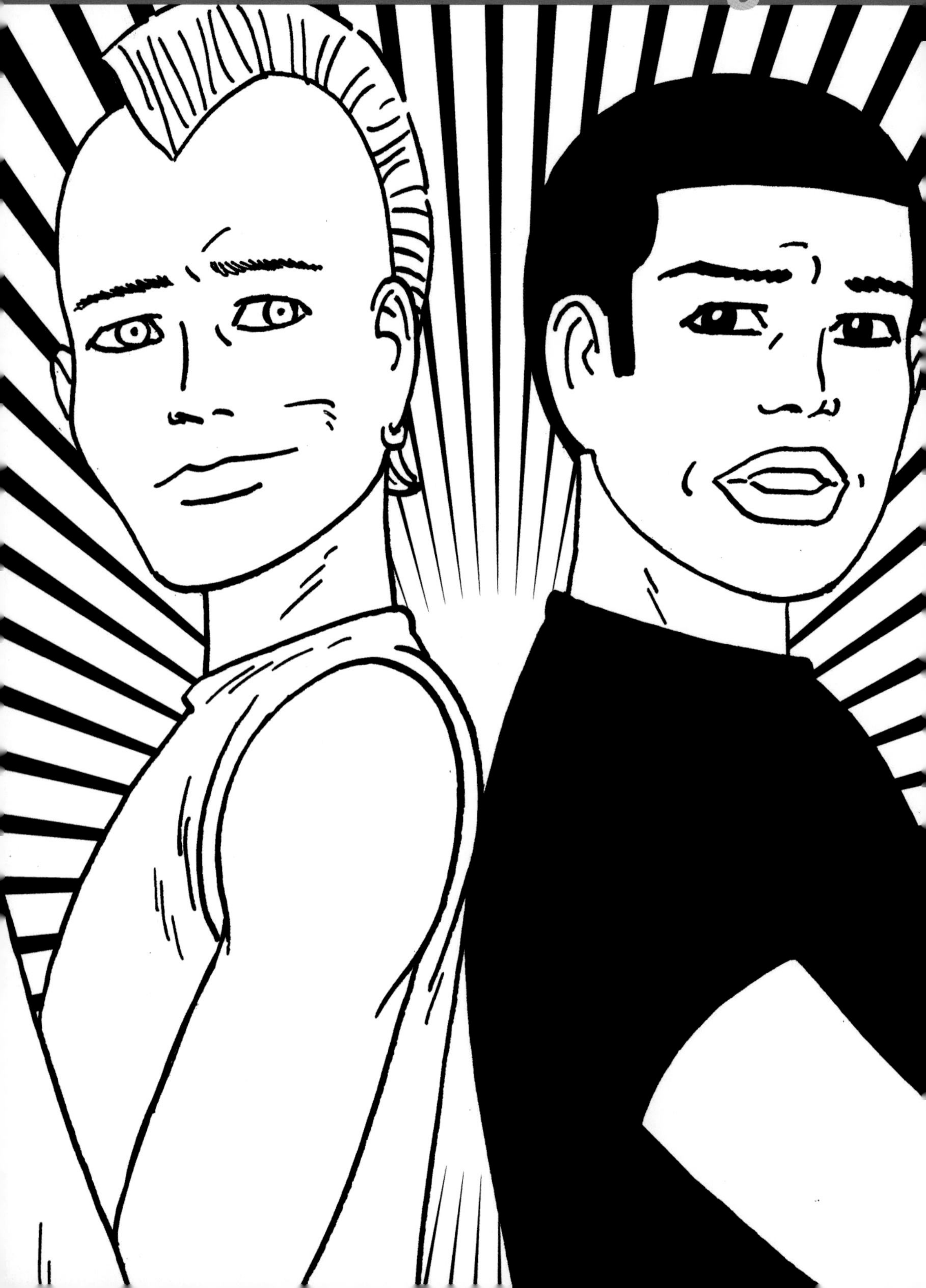

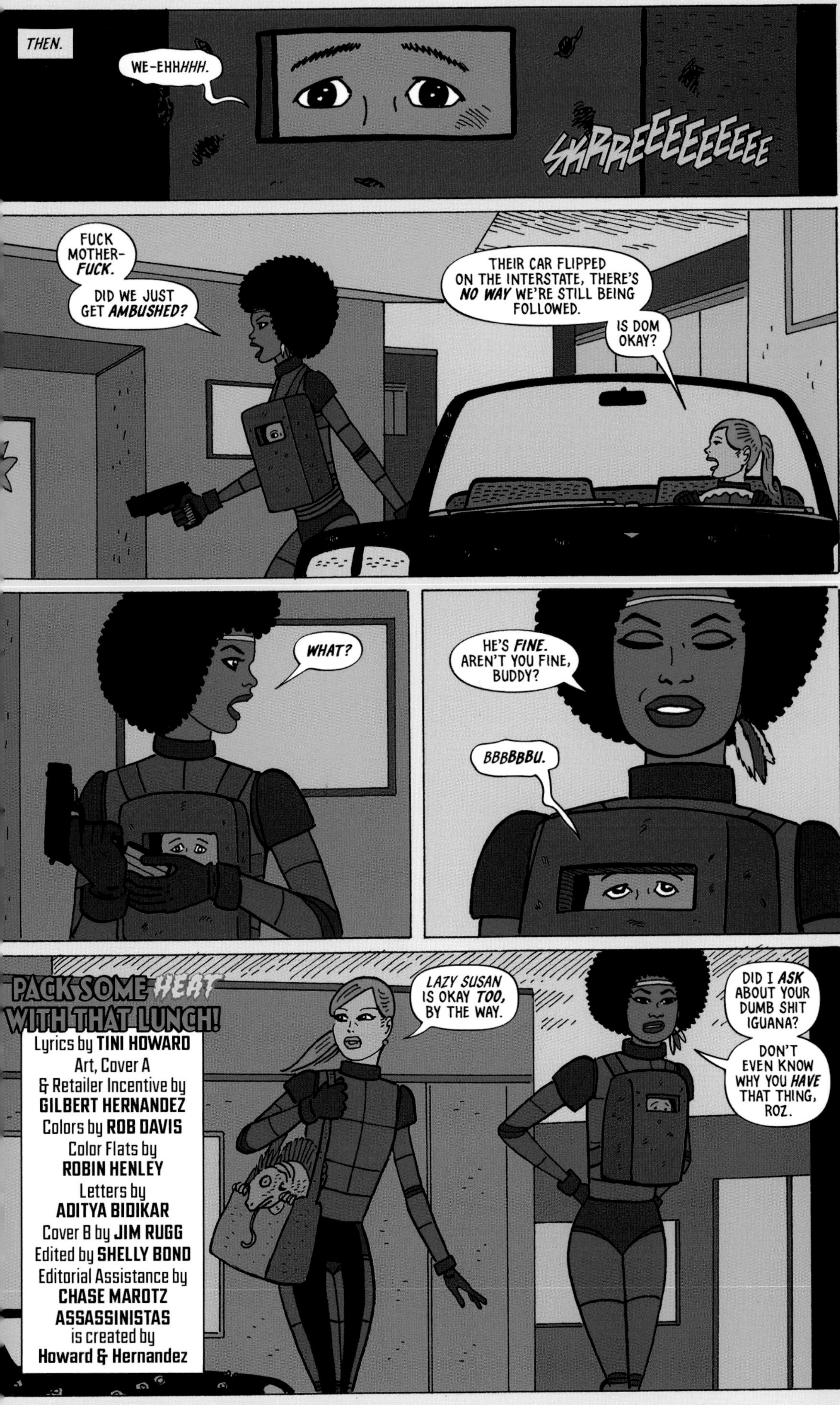
THEN.
WE-EHHHHH.
SKRREEEEEEEEE
FUCK MOTHER-FUCK.
DID WE JUST GET AMBUSHED?
THEIR CAR FLIPPED ON THE INTERSTATE, THERE'S NO WAY WE'RE STILL BEING FOLLOWED.
IS DOM OKAY?
WHAT?
HE'S FINE. AREN'T YOU FINE, BUDDY?
BBBBBBU.
PACK SOME HEAT WITH THAT LUNCH!
Lyrics by TINI HOWARD
Art, Cover A & Retailer Incentive by GILBERT HERNANDEZ
Colors by ROB DAVIS
Color Flats by ROBIN HENLEY
Letters by ADITYA BIDIKAR
Cover B by JIM RUGG
Edited by SHELLY BOND
Editorial Assistance by CHASE MAROTZ
ASSASSINISTAS is created by Howard & Hernandez
LAZY SUSAN IS OKAY TOO, BY THE WAY.
DID I ASK ABOUT YOUR DUMB SHIT IGUANA?
DON'T EVEN KNOW WHY YOU HAVE THAT THING, ROZ.

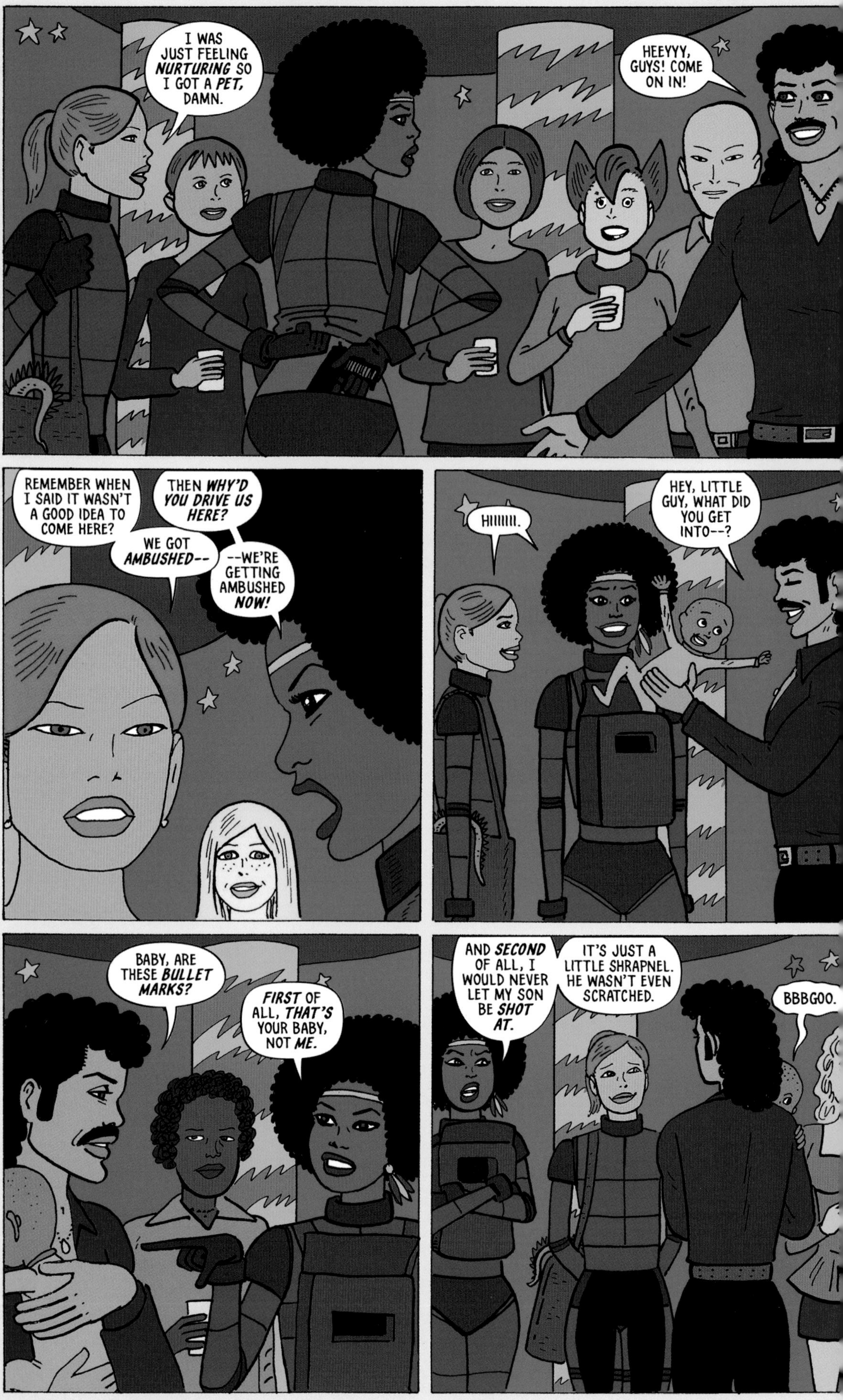
I WAS JUST FEELING NURTURING SO I GOT A PET, DAMN.
HEEYYY, GUYS! COME ON IN!
REMEMBER WHEN I SAID IT WASN'T A GOOD IDEA TO COME HERE?
THEN WHY'D YOU DRIVE US HERE?
WE GOT AMBUSHED--
--WE'RE GETTING AMBUSHED NOW!
HIIIIII.
HEY, LITTLE GUY, WHAT DID YOU GET INTO--?
BABY, ARE THESE BULLET MARKS?
FIRST OF ALL, THAT'S YOUR BABY, NOT ME.
AND SECOND OF ALL, I WOULD NEVER LET MY SON BE SHOT AT.
IT'S JUST A LITTLE SHRAPNEL. HE WASN'T EVEN SCRATCHED.
BBBGOO.

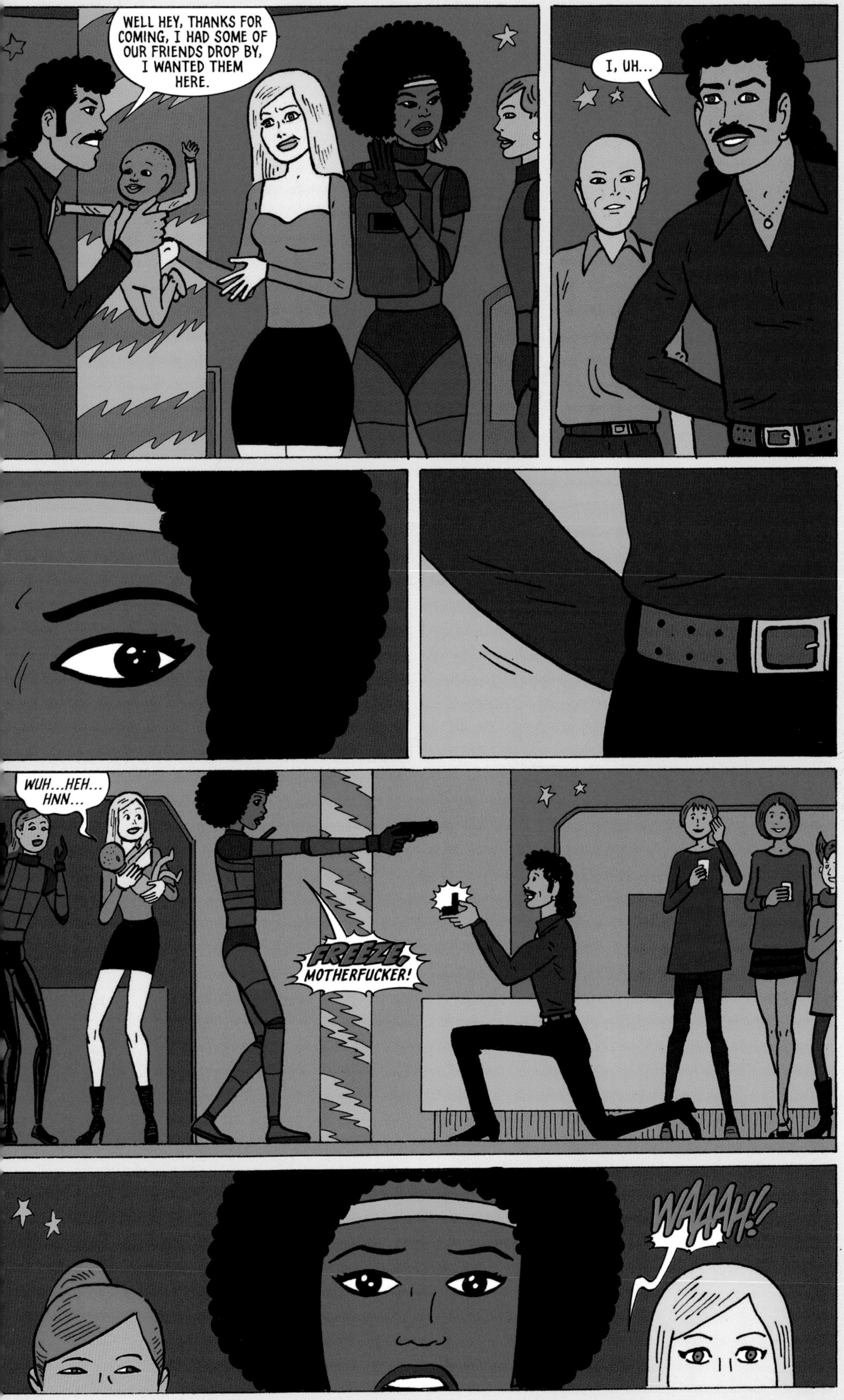
WELL HEY, THANKS FOR COMING, I HAD SOME OF OUR FRIENDS DROP BY, I WANTED THEM HERE.
I, UH...
WUH...HEH... HNN...
FREEZE, MOTHERFUCKER!
WAAAH!!

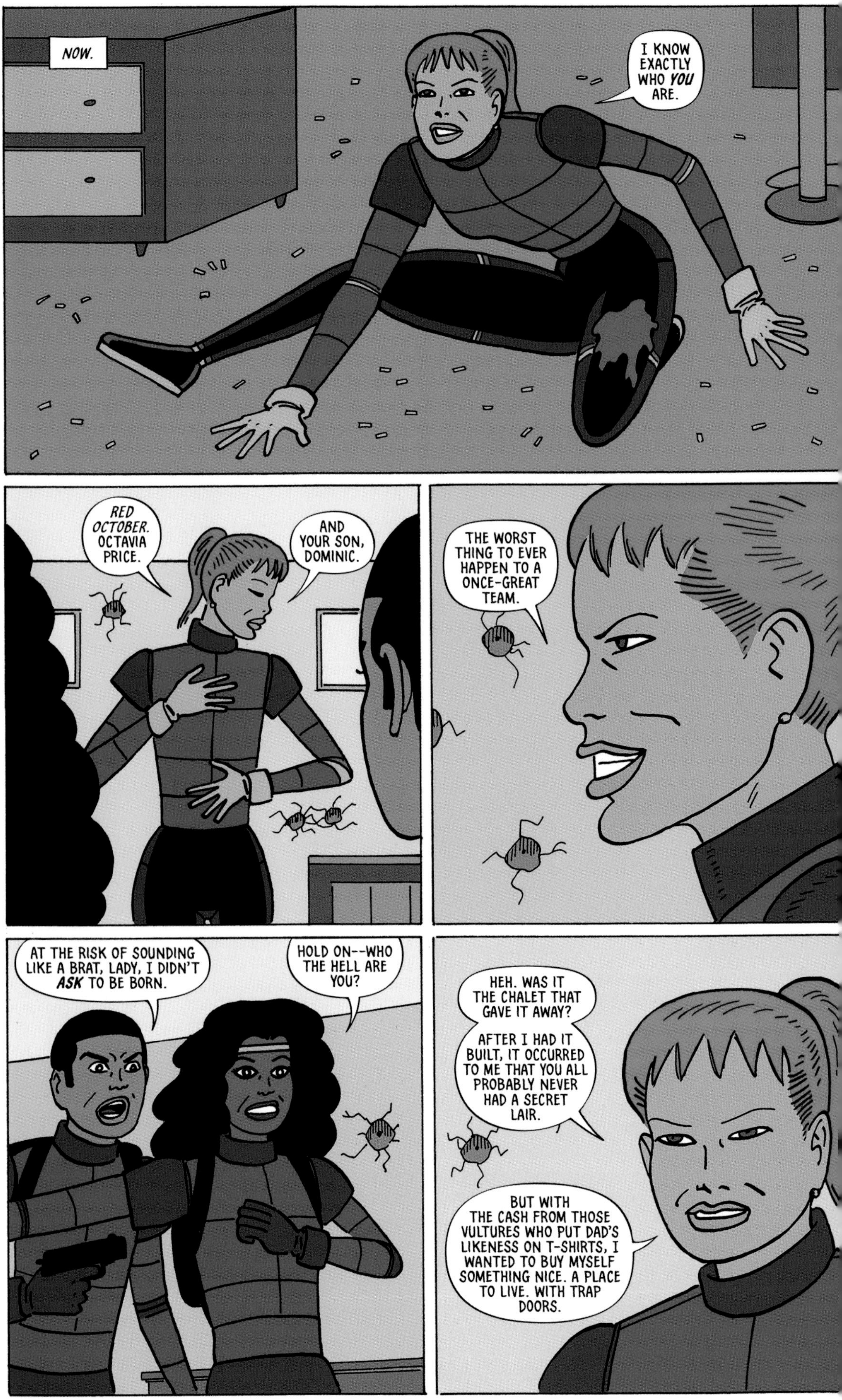
NOW.
I KNOW EXACTLY WHO *YOU* ARE.
RED OCTOBER. OCTAVIA PRICE.
AND YOUR SON, DOMINIC.
THE WORST THING TO EVER HAPPEN TO A ONCE-GREAT TEAM.
AT THE RISK OF SOUNDING LIKE A BRAT, LADY, I DIDN'T ***ASK*** TO BE BORN.
HOLD ON--WHO THE HELL ARE YOU?
HEH. WAS IT THE CHALET THAT GAVE IT AWAY?
AFTER I HAD IT BUILT, IT OCCURRED TO ME THAT YOU ALL PROBABLY NEVER HAD A SECRET LAIR.
BUT WITH THE CASH FROM THOSE VULTURES WHO PUT DAD'S LIKENESS ON T-SHIRTS, I WANTED TO BUY MYSELF SOMETHING NICE. A PLACE TO LIVE. WITH TRAP DOORS.

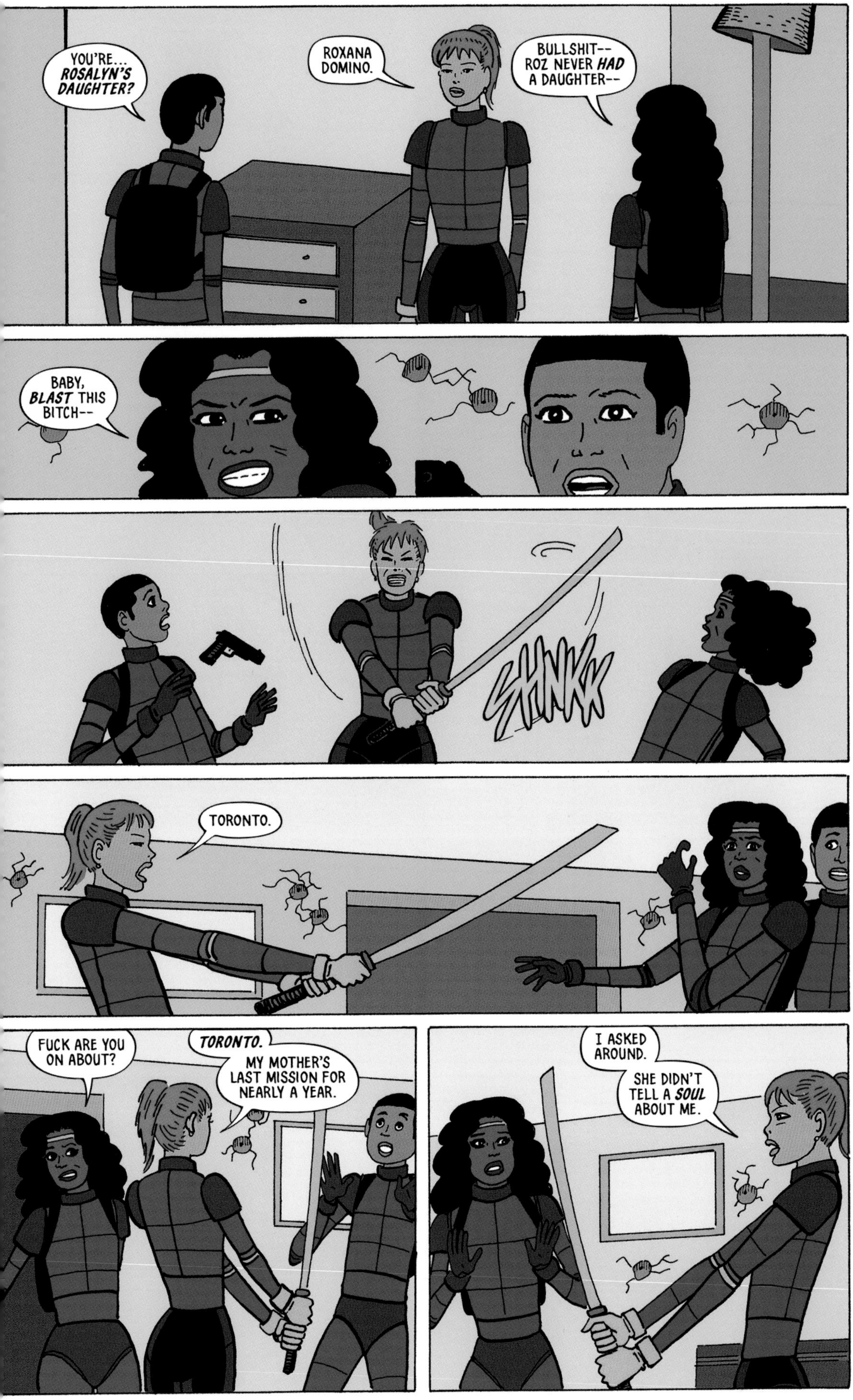

YOU'RE... ROSALYN'S DAUGHTER?
ROXANA DOMINO.
BULLSHIT-- ROZ NEVER HAD A DAUGHTER--
BABY, BLAST THIS BITCH--
SHNKK
TORONTO.
FUCK ARE YOU ON ABOUT?
TORONTO.
MY MOTHER'S LAST MISSION FOR NEARLY A YEAR.
I ASKED AROUND.
SHE DIDN'T TELL A SOUL ABOUT ME.

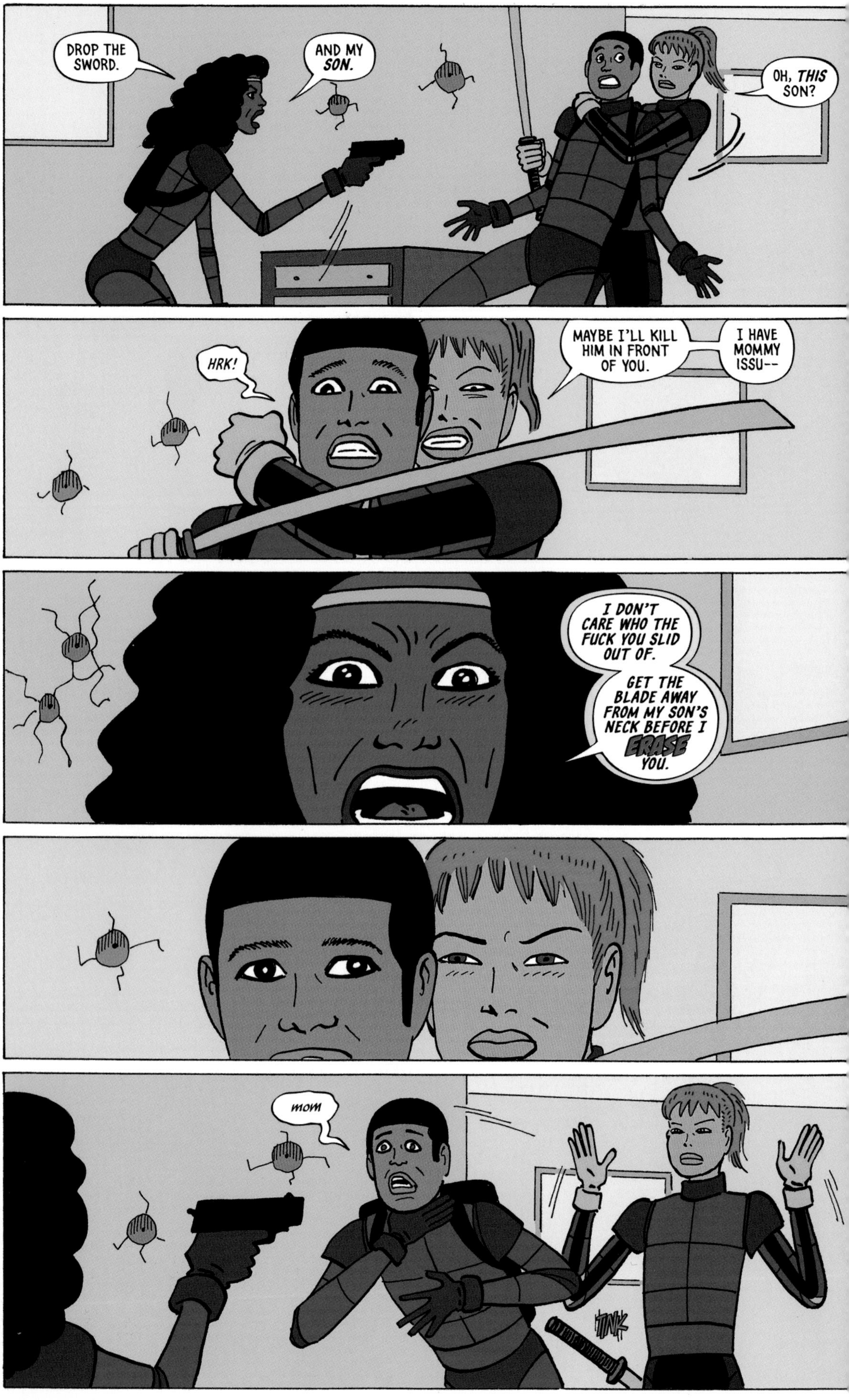
DROP THE SWORD.
AND MY SON.
OH, THIS SON?
HRK!
MAYBE I'LL KILL HIM IN FRONT OF YOU.
I HAVE MOMMY ISSU--
I DON'T CARE WHO THE FUCK YOU SLID OUT OF.
GET THE BLADE AWAY FROM MY SON'S NECK BEFORE I ERASE YOU.
mom
TINK

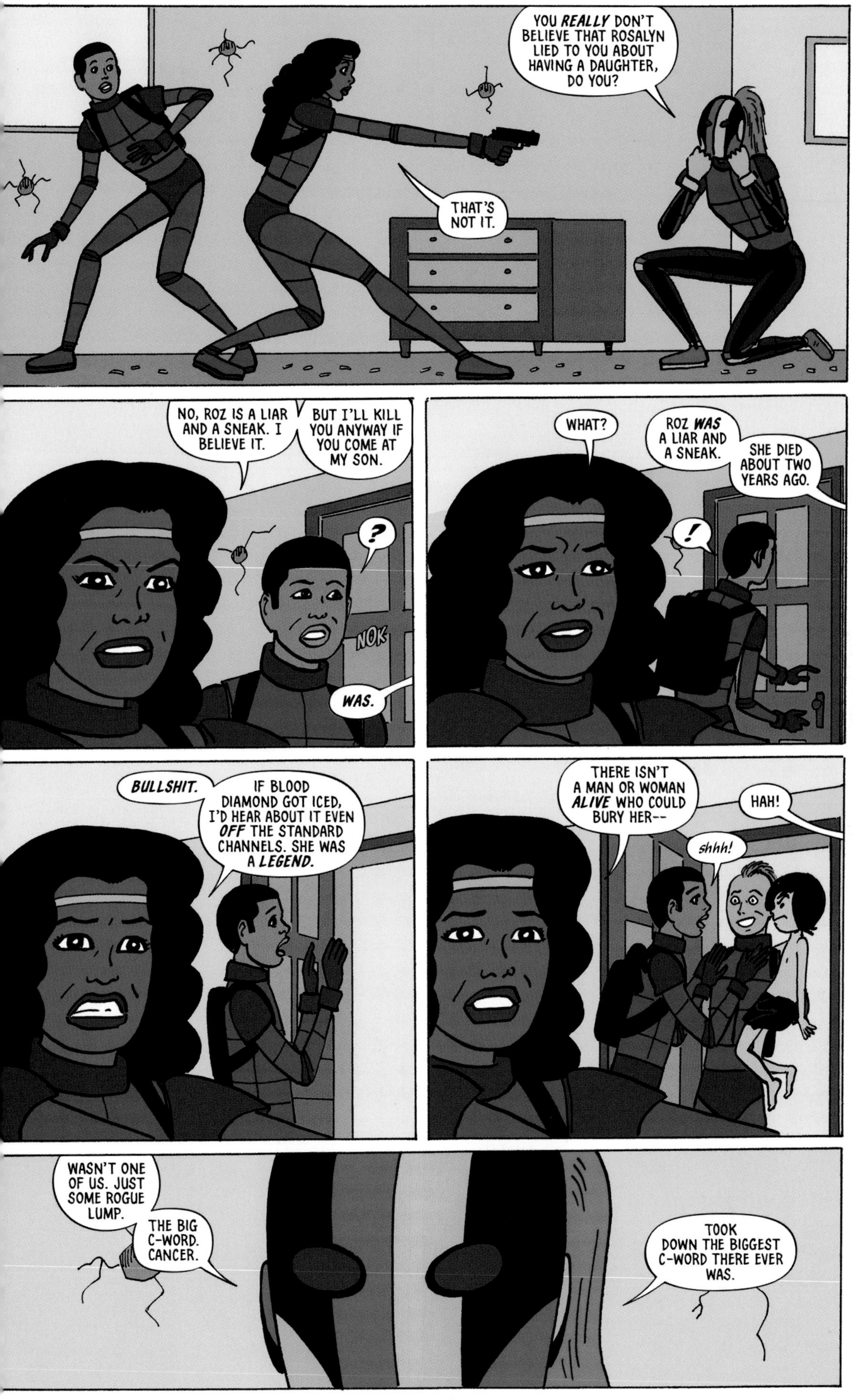
YOU *REALLY* DON'T BELIEVE THAT ROSALYN LIED TO YOU ABOUT HAVING A DAUGHTER, DO YOU?
THAT'S NOT IT.
NO, ROZ IS A LIAR AND A SNEAK. I BELIEVE IT.
BUT I'LL KILL YOU ANYWAY IF YOU COME AT MY SON.
?
NOK
WAS.
WHAT?
ROZ *WAS* A LIAR AND A SNEAK.
SHE DIED ABOUT TWO YEARS AGO.
!
BULLSHIT.
IF BLOOD DIAMOND GOT ICED, I'D HEAR ABOUT IT EVEN *OFF* THE STANDARD CHANNELS. SHE WAS A *LEGEND.*
THERE ISN'T A MAN OR WOMAN *ALIVE* WHO COULD BURY HER--
HAH!
shhh!
WASN'T ONE OF US. JUST SOME ROGUE LUMP.
THE BIG C-WORD. CANCER.
TOOK DOWN THE BIGGEST C-WORD THERE EVER WAS.

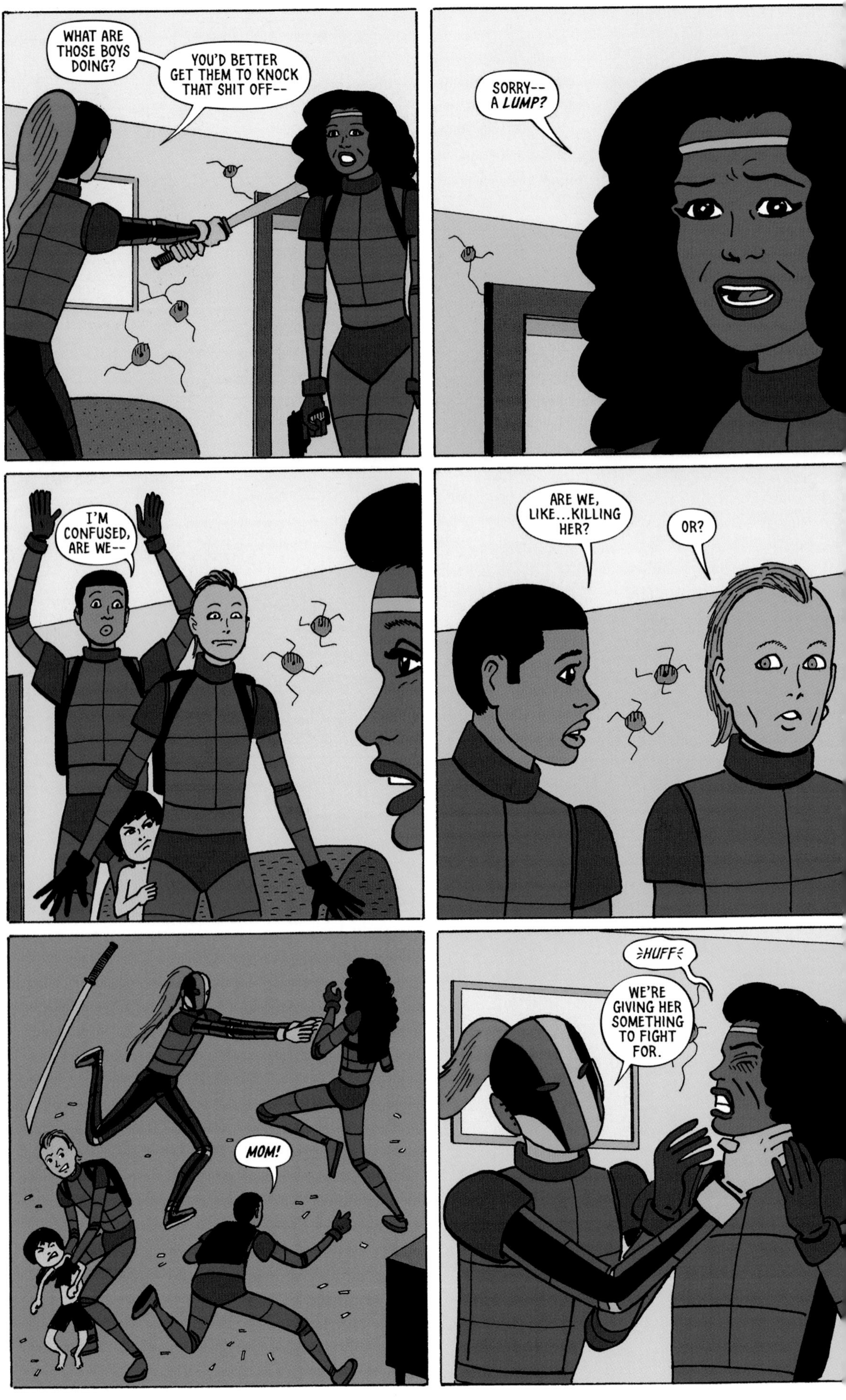

WHAT ARE THOSE BOYS DOING?
YOU'D BETTER GET THEM TO KNOCK THAT SHIT OFF--
SORRY-- A *LUMP?*
I'M CONFUSED, ARE WE--
ARE WE, LIKE...KILLING HER?
OR?
MOM!
HUFF
WE'RE GIVING HER SOMETHING TO FIGHT FOR.

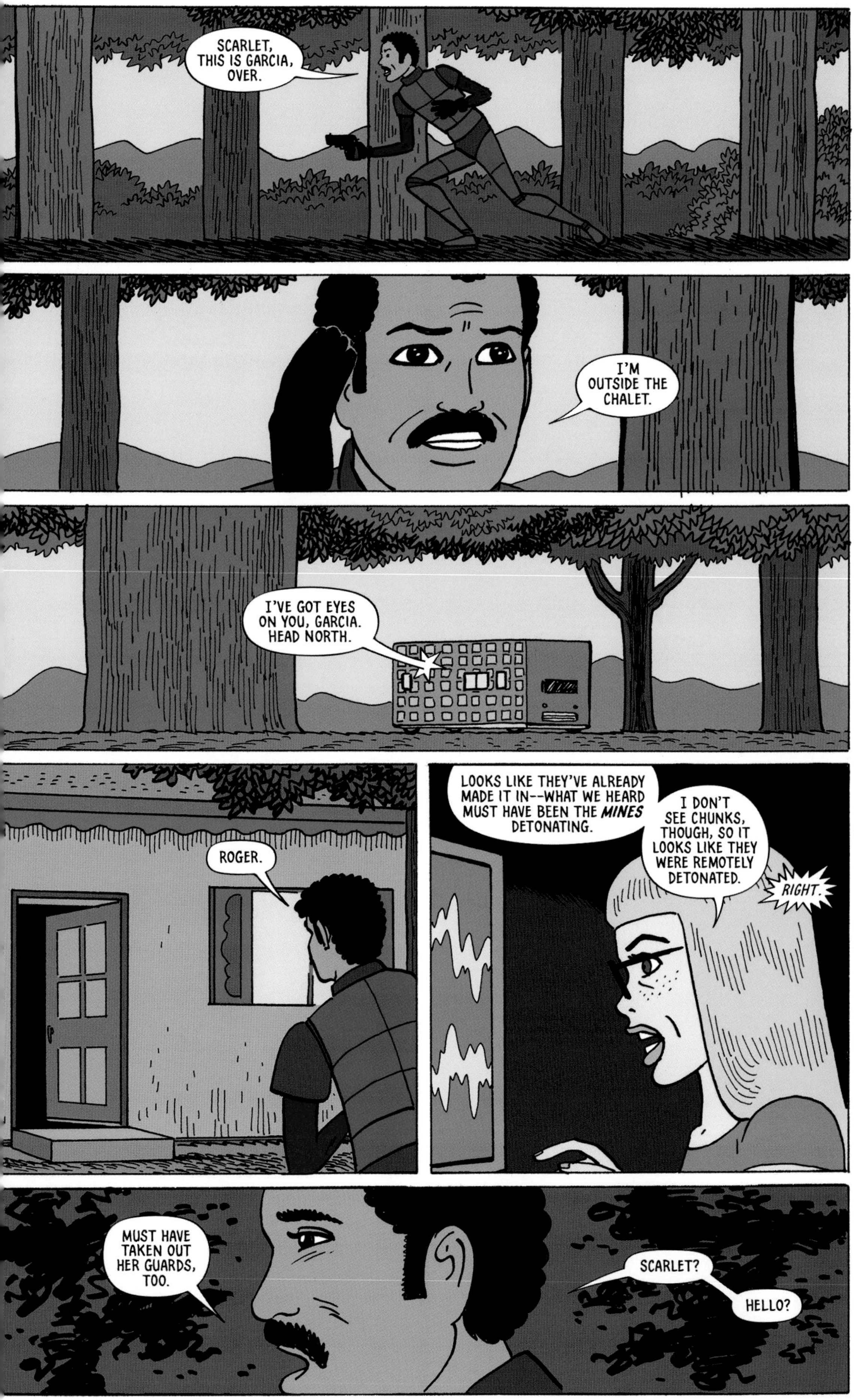
SCARLET, THIS IS GARCIA, OVER.
I'M OUTSIDE THE CHALET.
I'VE GOT EYES ON YOU, GARCIA. HEAD NORTH.
ROGER.
LOOKS LIKE THEY'VE ALREADY MADE IT IN--WHAT WE HEARD MUST HAVE BEEN THE *MINES* DETONATING.
I DON'T SEE CHUNKS, THOUGH, SO IT LOOKS LIKE THEY WERE REMOTELY DETONATED.
RIGHT.
MUST HAVE TAKEN OUT HER GUARDS, TOO.
SCARLET?
HELLO?

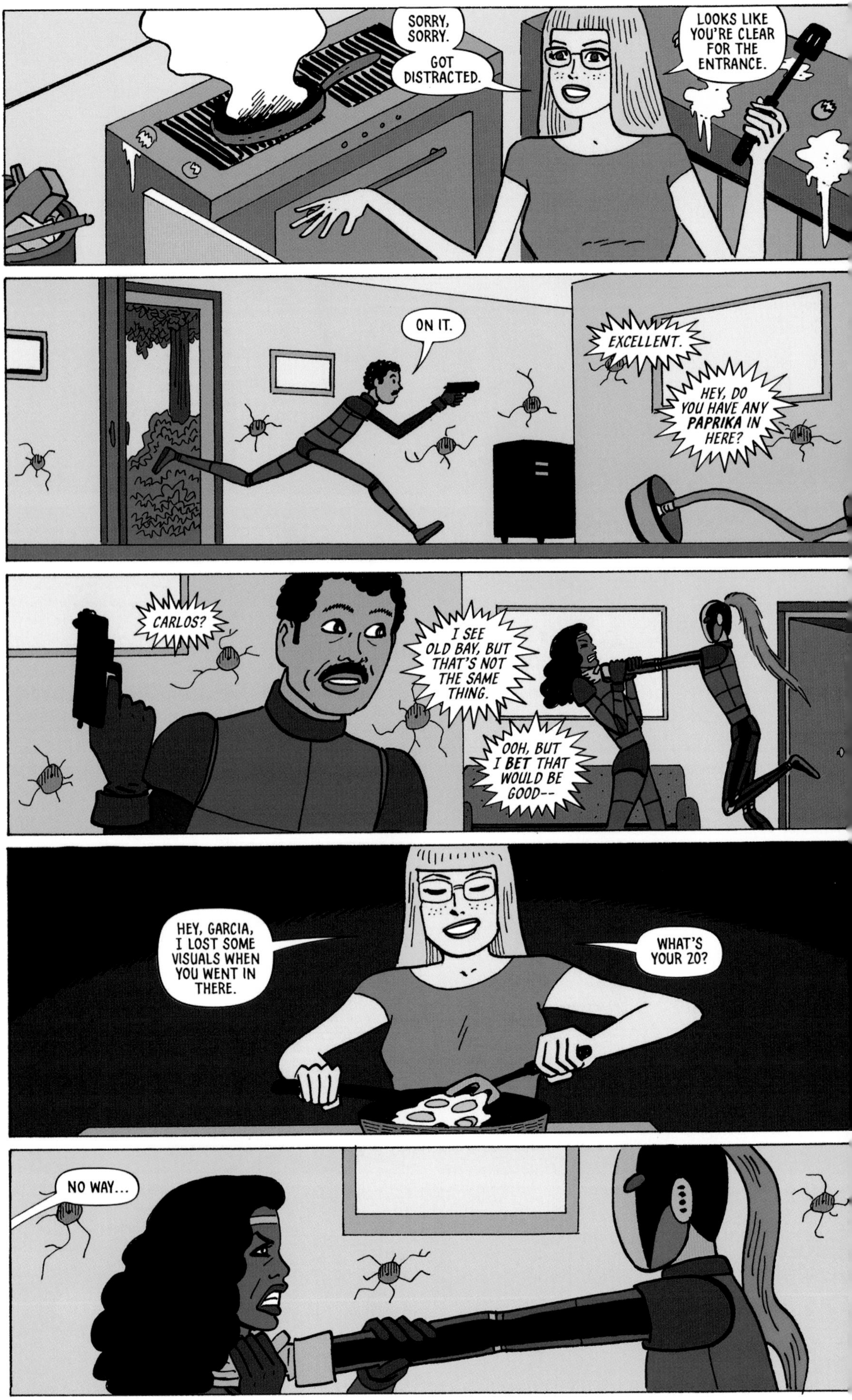

SORRY, SORRY.
GOT DISTRACTED.
LOOKS LIKE YOU'RE CLEAR FOR THE ENTRANCE.
ON IT.
EXCELLENT.
HEY, DO YOU HAVE ANY PAPRIKA IN HERE?
CARLOS?
I SEE OLD BAY, BUT THAT'S NOT THE SAME THING.
OOH, BUT I BET THAT WOULD BE GOOD--
HEY, GARCIA, I LOST SOME VISUALS WHEN YOU WENT IN THERE.
WHAT'S YOUR 20?
NO WAY...

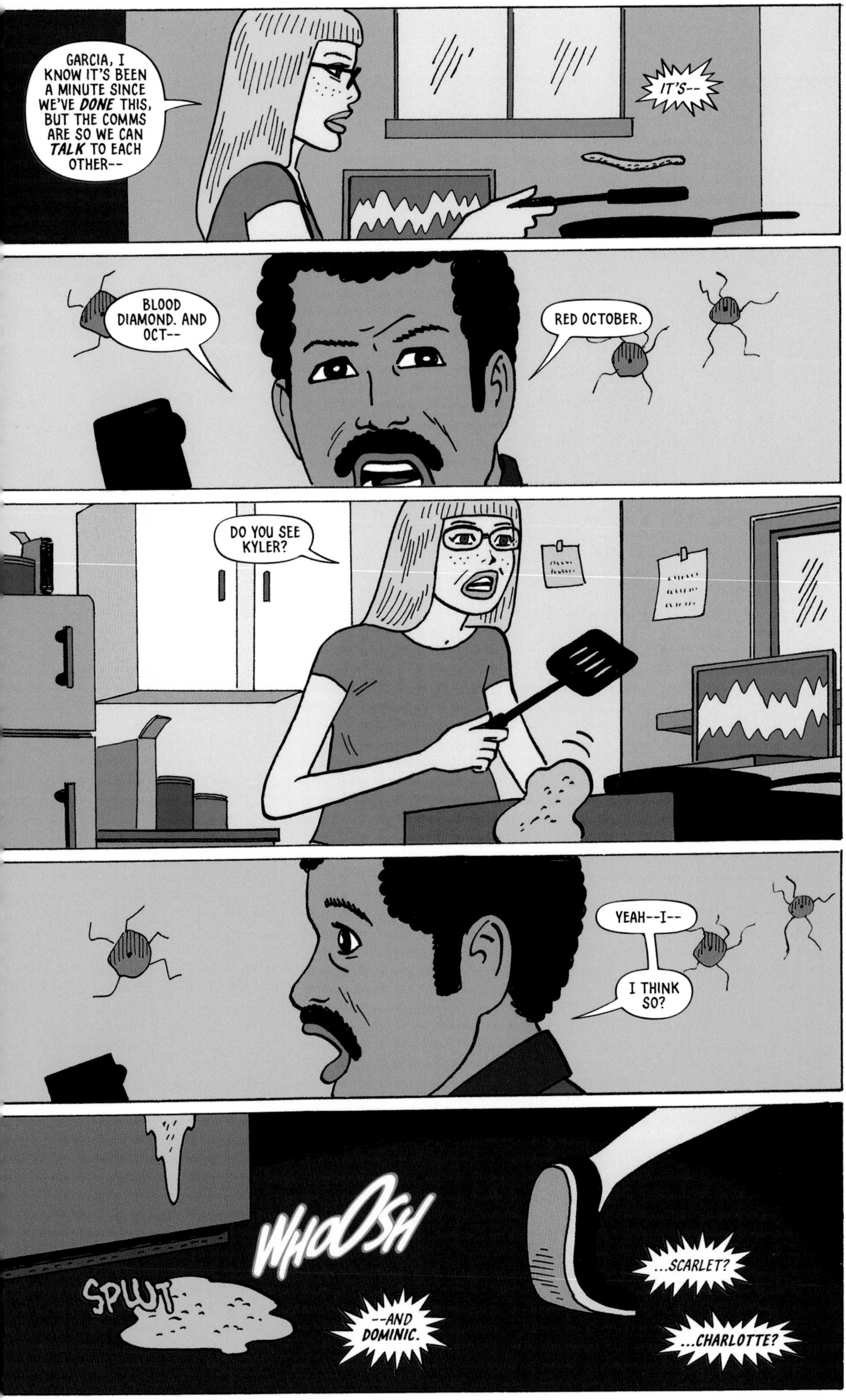
GARCIA, I KNOW IT'S BEEN A MINUTE SINCE WE'VE *DONE* THIS, BUT THE COMMS ARE SO WE CAN *TALK* TO EACH OTHER--
IT'S--
BLOOD DIAMOND. AND OCT--
RED OCTOBER.
DO YOU SEE KYLER?
YEAH--I--
I THINK SO?
WHOOSH
SPLUT
--AND DOMINIC.
...SCARLET?
...CHARLOTTE?

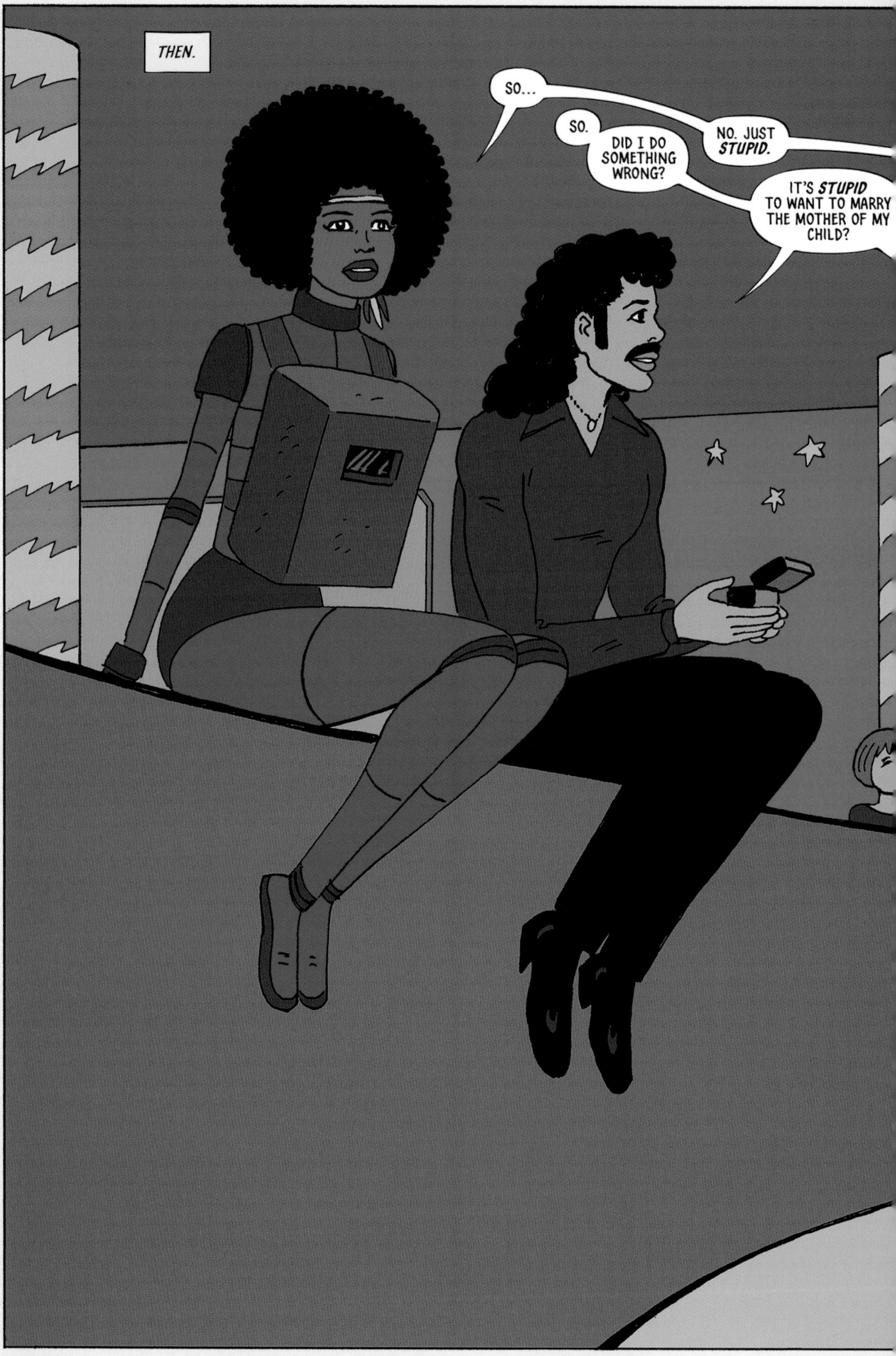
THEN.
SO...
SO.
DID I DO SOMETHING WRONG?
NO. JUST *STUPID.*
IT'S *STUPID* TO WANT TO MARRY THE MOTHER OF MY CHILD?

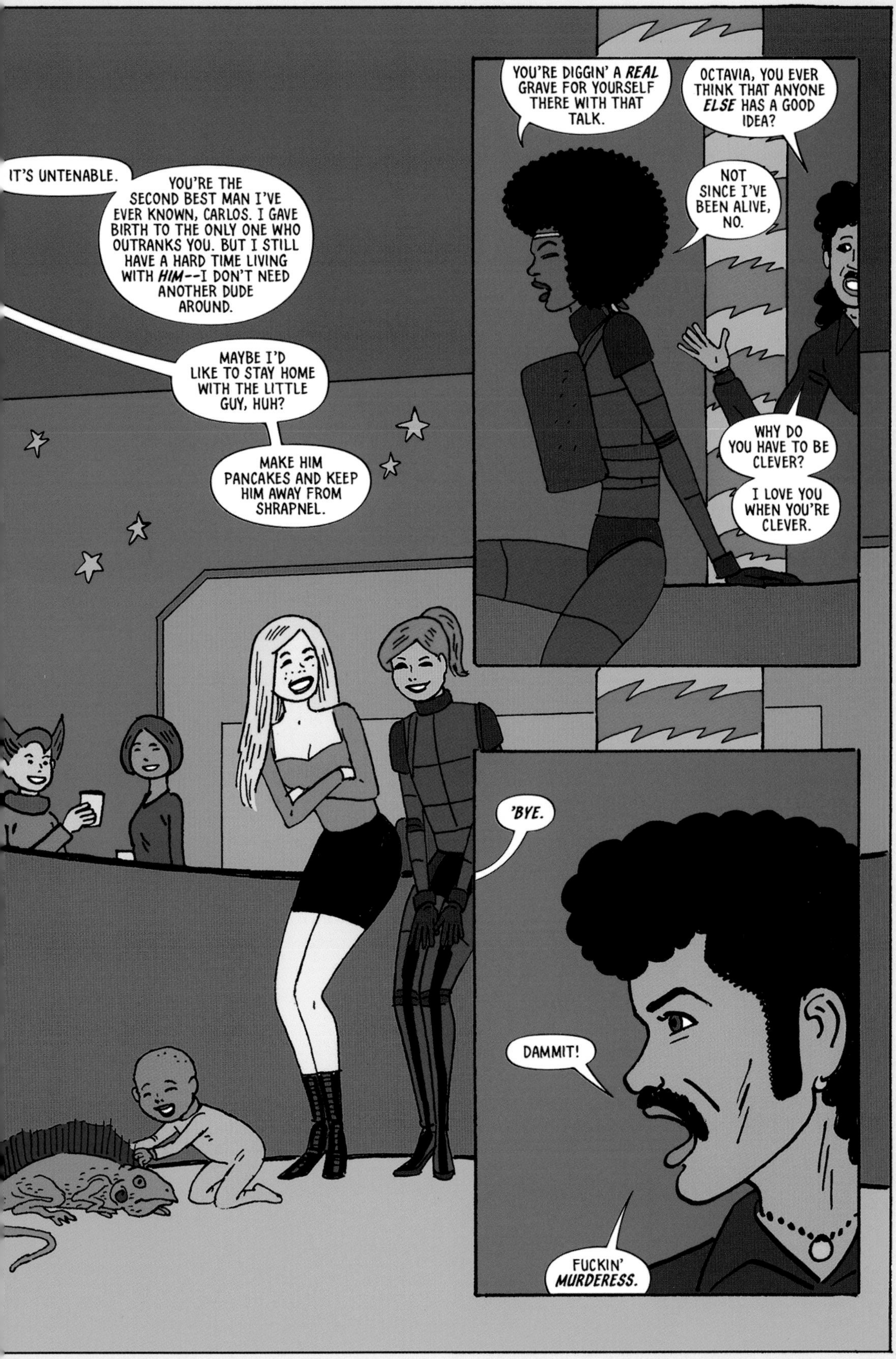
IT'S UNTENABLE.
YOU'RE THE SECOND BEST MAN I'VE EVER KNOWN, CARLOS. I GAVE BIRTH TO THE ONLY ONE WHO OUTRANKS YOU. BUT I STILL HAVE A HARD TIME LIVING WITH *HIM*--I DON'T NEED ANOTHER DUDE AROUND.
MAYBE I'D LIKE TO STAY HOME WITH THE LITTLE GUY, HUH?
MAKE HIM PANCAKES AND KEEP HIM AWAY FROM SHRAPNEL.
YOU'RE DIGGIN' A *REAL* GRAVE FOR YOURSELF THERE WITH THAT TALK.
OCTAVIA, YOU EVER THINK THAT ANYONE *ELSE* HAS A GOOD IDEA?
NOT SINCE I'VE BEEN ALIVE, NO.
WHY DO YOU HAVE TO BE CLEVER?
I LOVE YOU WHEN YOU'RE CLEVER.
'BYE.
DAMMIT!
FUCKIN' *MURDERESS.*

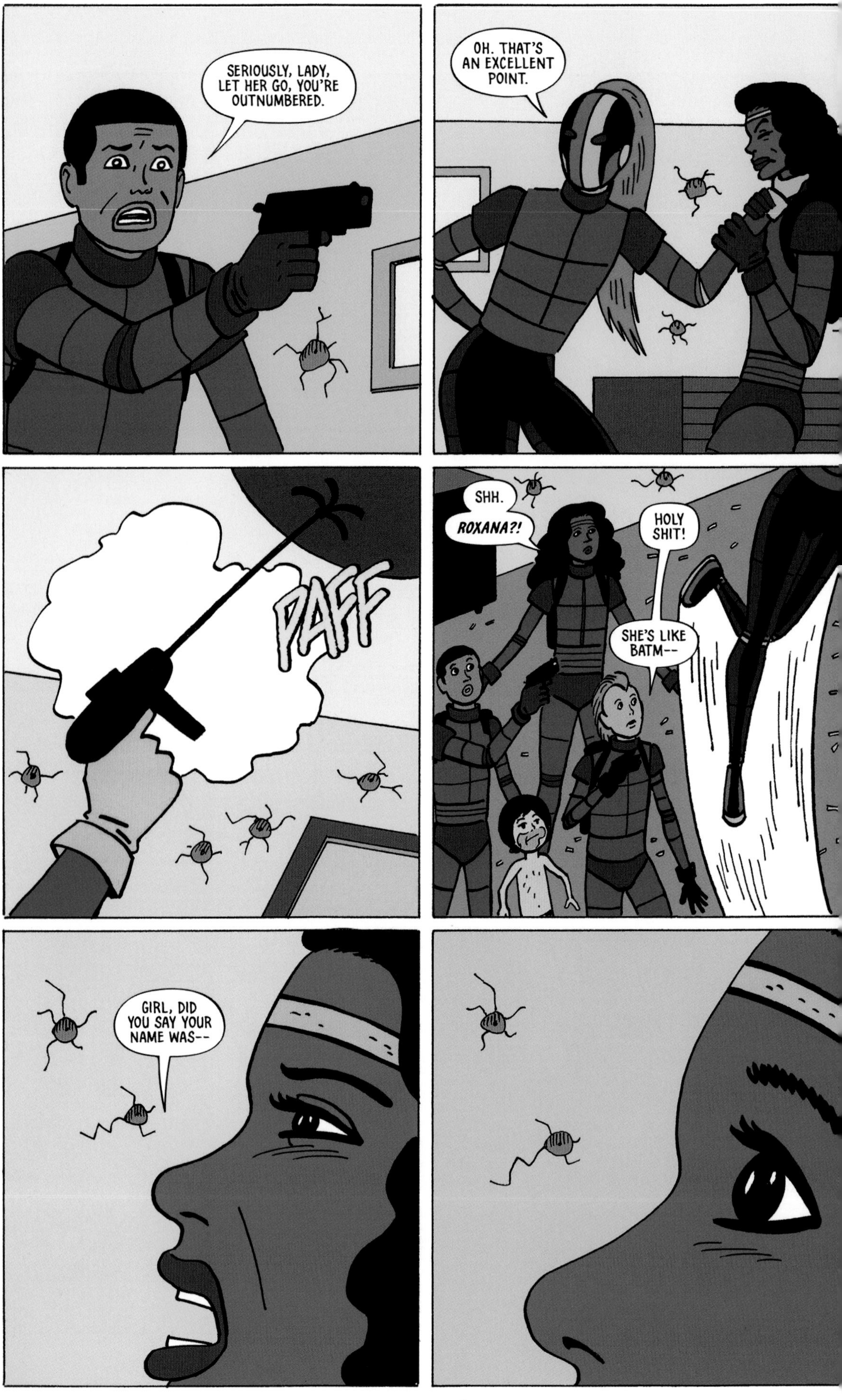

SERIOUSLY, LADY, LET HER GO, YOU'RE OUTNUMBERED.
OH. THAT'S AN EXCELLENT POINT.
PAFF
SHH.
ROXANA?!
HOLY SHIT!
SHE'S LIKE BATM--
GIRL, DID YOU SAY YOUR NAME WAS--

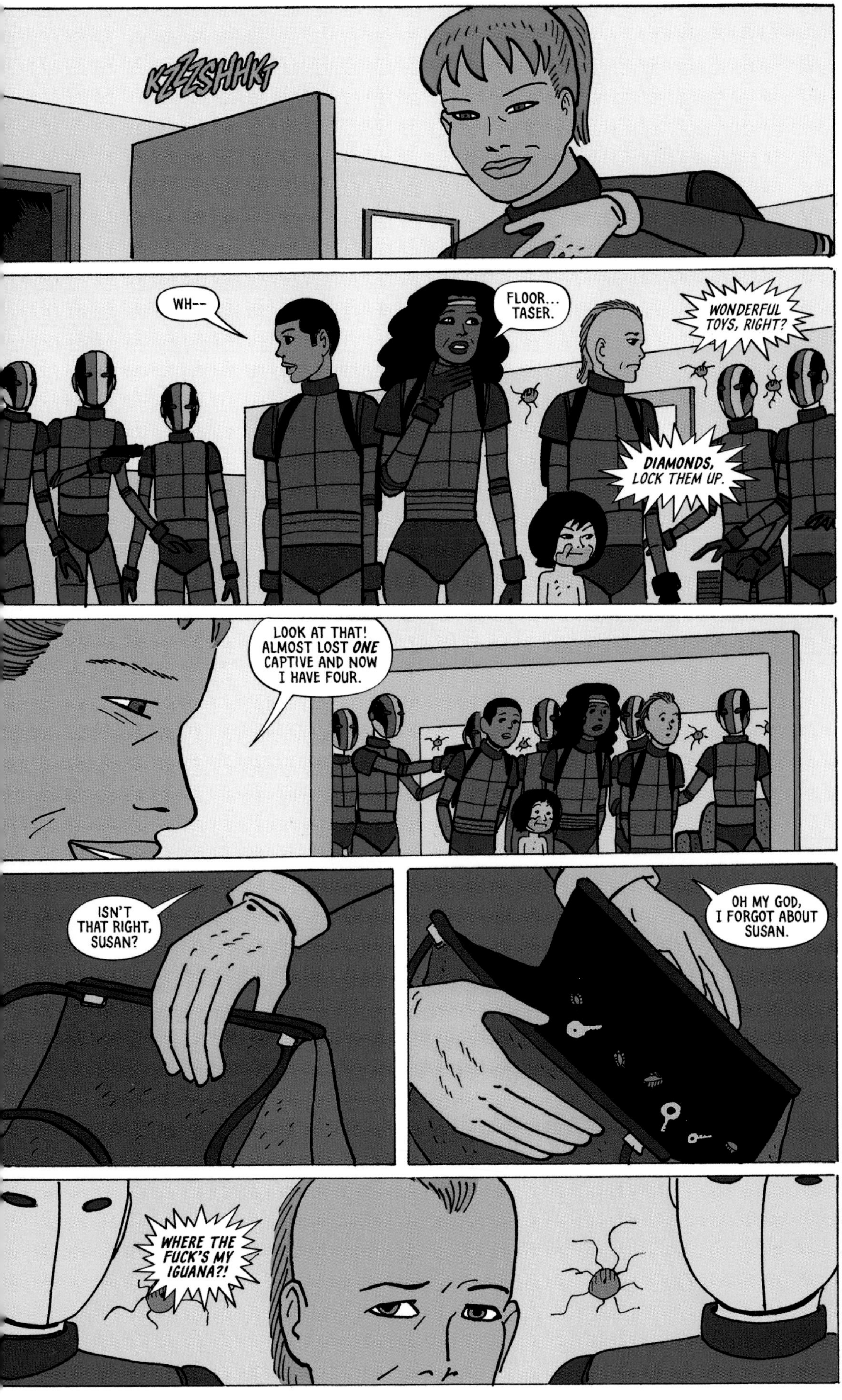
KZZZSHHKT
WH--
FLOOR... TASER.
WONDERFUL TOYS, RIGHT?
DIAMONDS, LOCK THEM UP.
LOOK AT THAT! ALMOST LOST ONE CAPTIVE AND NOW I HAVE FOUR.
ISN'T THAT RIGHT, SUSAN?
OH MY GOD, I FORGOT ABOUT SUSAN.
WHERE THE FUCK'S MY IGUANA?!

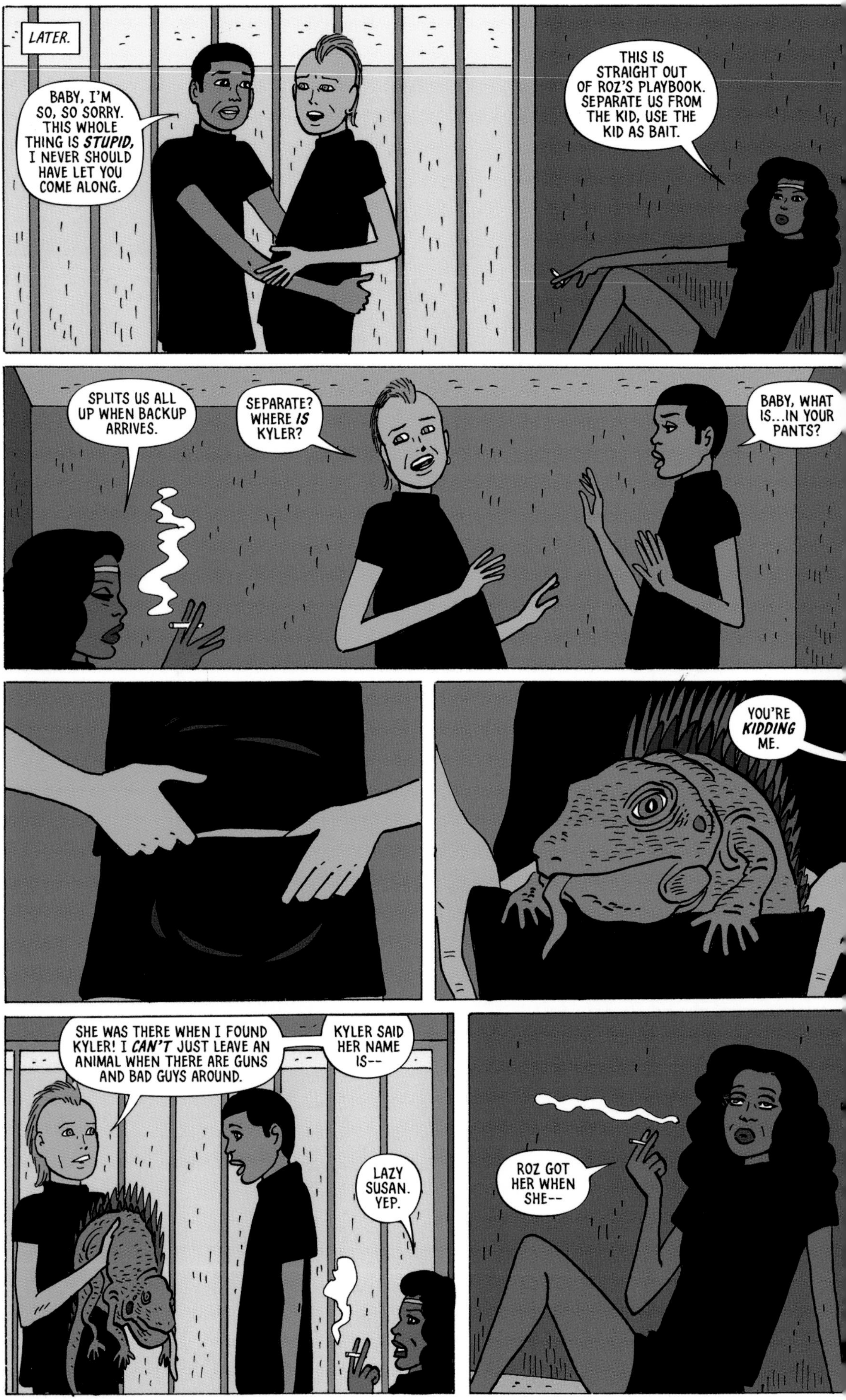
LATER.
BABY, I'M SO, SO SORRY. THIS WHOLE THING IS *STUPID,* I NEVER SHOULD HAVE LET YOU COME ALONG.
THIS IS STRAIGHT OUT OF ROZ'S PLAYBOOK. SEPARATE US FROM THE KID, USE THE KID AS BAIT.
SPLITS US ALL UP WHEN BACKUP ARRIVES.
SEPARATE? WHERE *IS* KYLER?
BABY, WHAT IS...IN YOUR PANTS?
YOU'RE *KIDDING* ME.
SHE WAS THERE WHEN I FOUND KYLER! I *CAN'T* JUST LEAVE AN ANIMAL WHEN THERE ARE GUNS AND BAD GUYS AROUND.
KYLER SAID HER NAME IS--
LAZY SUSAN. YEP.
ROZ GOT HER WHEN SHE--

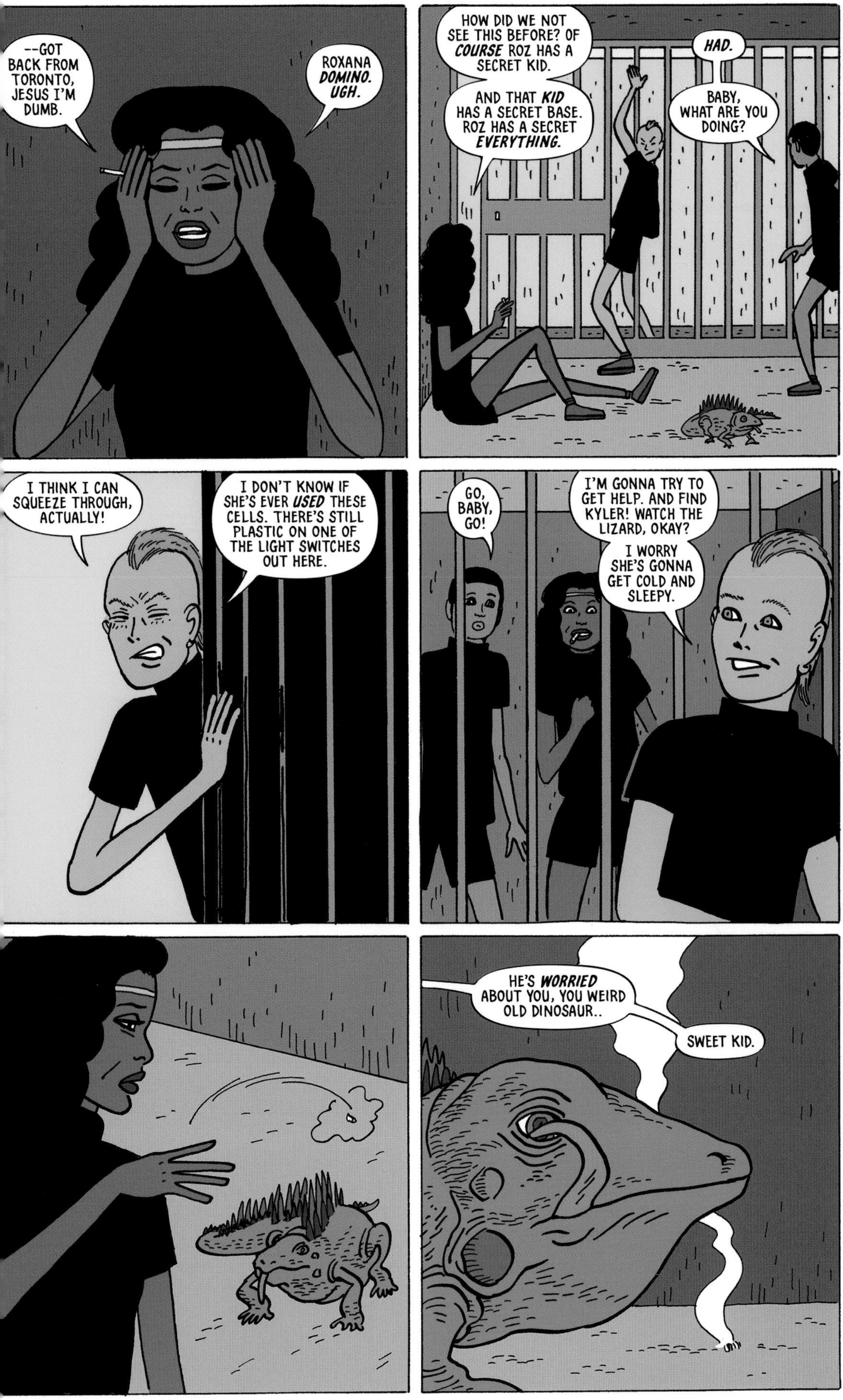
--GOT BACK FROM TORONTO, JESUS I'M DUMB.
ROXANA *DOMINO. UGH.*
HOW DID WE NOT SEE THIS BEFORE? OF *COURSE* ROZ HAS A SECRET KID.
AND THAT *KID* HAS A SECRET BASE. ROZ HAS A SECRET *EVERYTHING.*
HAD.
BABY, WHAT ARE YOU DOING?
I THINK I CAN SQUEEZE THROUGH, ACTUALLY!
I DON'T KNOW IF SHE'S EVER *USED* THESE CELLS. THERE'S STILL PLASTIC ON ONE OF THE LIGHT SWITCHES OUT HERE.
GO, BABY, GO!
I'M GONNA TRY TO GET HELP. AND FIND KYLER! WATCH THE LIZARD, OKAY?
I WORRY SHE'S GONNA GET COLD AND SLEEPY.
HE'S *WORRIED* ABOUT YOU, YOU WEIRD OLD DINOSAUR..
SWEET KID.

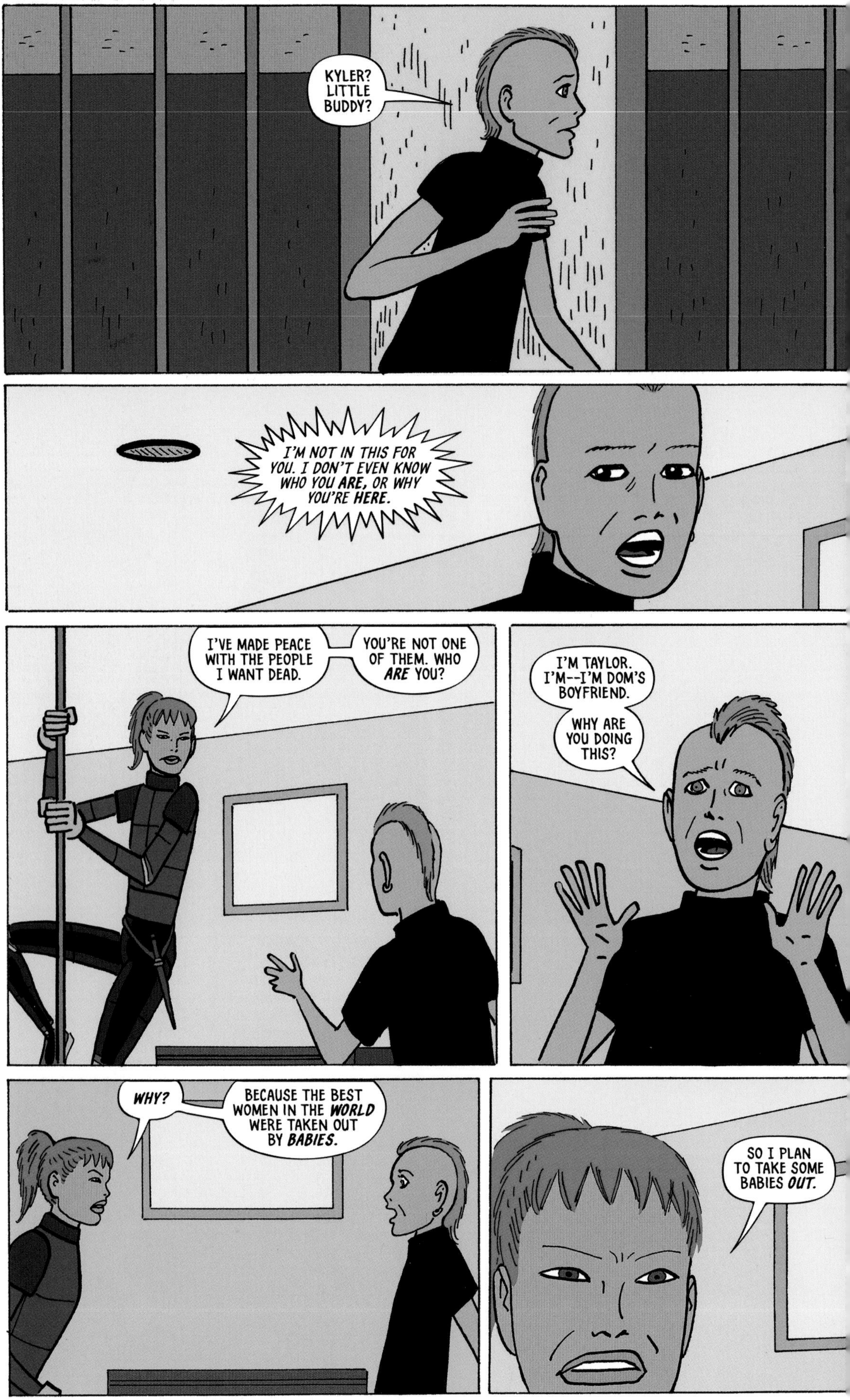
KYLER? LITTLE BUDDY?
I'M NOT IN THIS FOR YOU. I DON'T EVEN KNOW WHO YOU ARE, OR WHY YOU'RE HERE.
I'VE MADE PEACE WITH THE PEOPLE I WANT DEAD.
YOU'RE NOT ONE OF THEM. WHO ARE YOU?
I'M TAYLOR. I'M--I'M DOM'S BOYFRIEND.
WHY ARE YOU DOING THIS?
WHY?
BECAUSE THE BEST WOMEN IN THE WORLD WERE TAKEN OUT BY BABIES.
SO I PLAN TO TAKE SOME BABIES OUT.

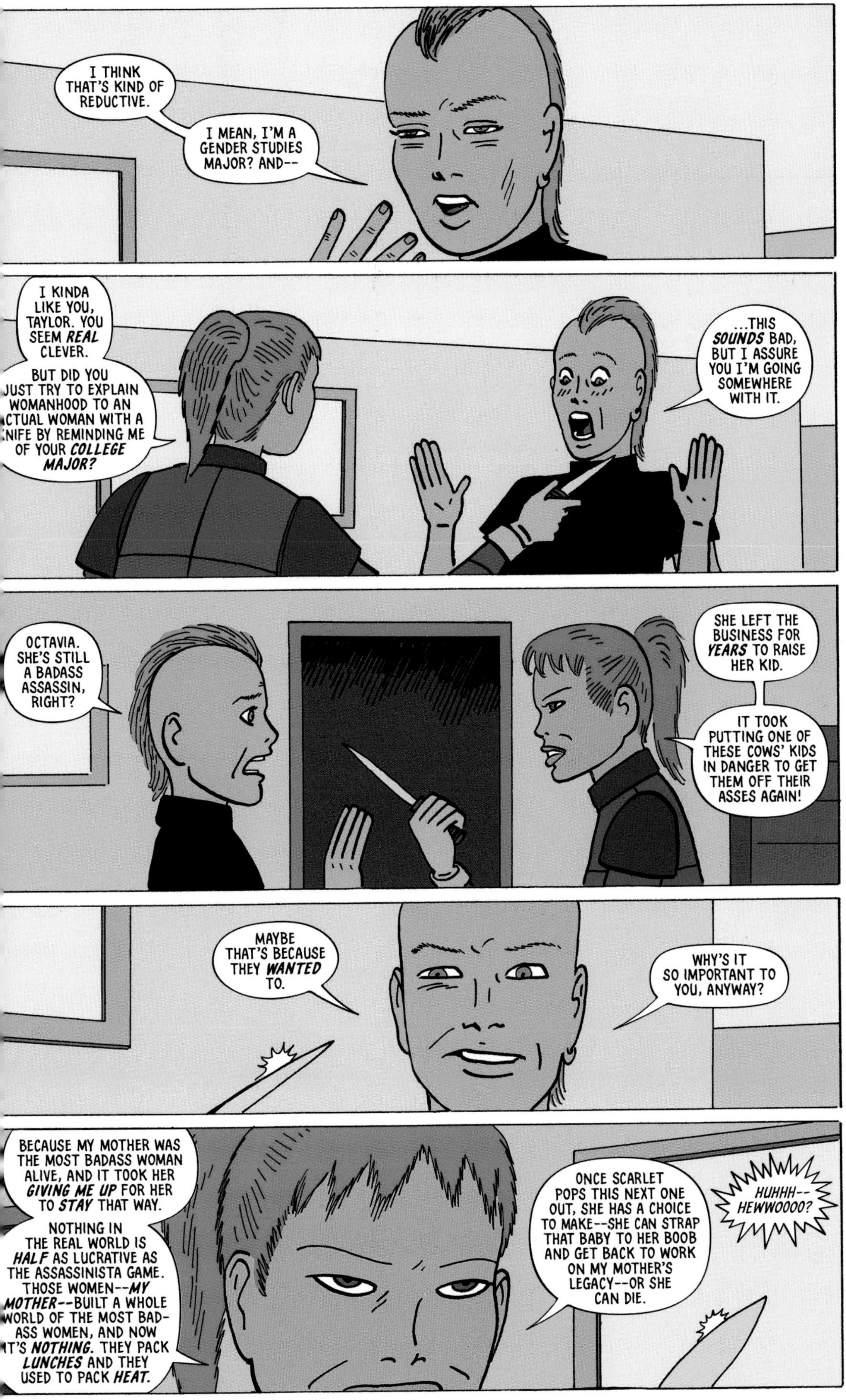
I THINK THAT'S KIND OF REDUCTIVE.
I MEAN, I'M A GENDER STUDIES MAJOR? AND--
I KINDA LIKE YOU, TAYLOR. YOU SEEM *REAL* CLEVER.
BUT DID YOU JUST TRY TO EXPLAIN WOMANHOOD TO AN ACTUAL WOMAN WITH A KNIFE BY REMINDING ME OF YOUR *COLLEGE MAJOR?*
...THIS *SOUNDS* BAD, BUT I ASSURE YOU I'M GOING SOMEWHERE WITH IT.
OCTAVIA. SHE'S STILL A BADASS ASSASSIN, RIGHT?
SHE LEFT THE BUSINESS FOR *YEARS* TO RAISE HER KID.
IT TOOK PUTTING ONE OF THESE COWS' KIDS IN DANGER TO GET THEM OFF THEIR ASSES AGAIN!
MAYBE THAT'S BECAUSE THEY *WANTED* TO.
WHY'S IT SO IMPORTANT TO YOU, ANYWAY?
BECAUSE MY MOTHER WAS THE MOST BADASS WOMAN ALIVE, AND IT TOOK HER *GIVING ME UP* FOR HER TO *STAY* THAT WAY.
NOTHING IN THE REAL WORLD IS *HALF* AS LUCRATIVE AS THE ASSASSINISTA GAME. THOSE WOMEN--*MY MOTHER*--BUILT A WHOLE WORLD OF THE MOST BAD-ASS WOMEN, AND NOW IT'S *NOTHING.* THEY PACK *LUNCHES* AND THEY USED TO PACK *HEAT.*
ONCE SCARLET POPS THIS NEXT ONE OUT, SHE HAS A CHOICE TO MAKE--SHE CAN STRAP THAT BABY TO HER BOOB AND GET BACK TO WORK ON MY MOTHER'S LEGACY--OR SHE CAN DIE.
HUHHH-- HEWWOOOO?

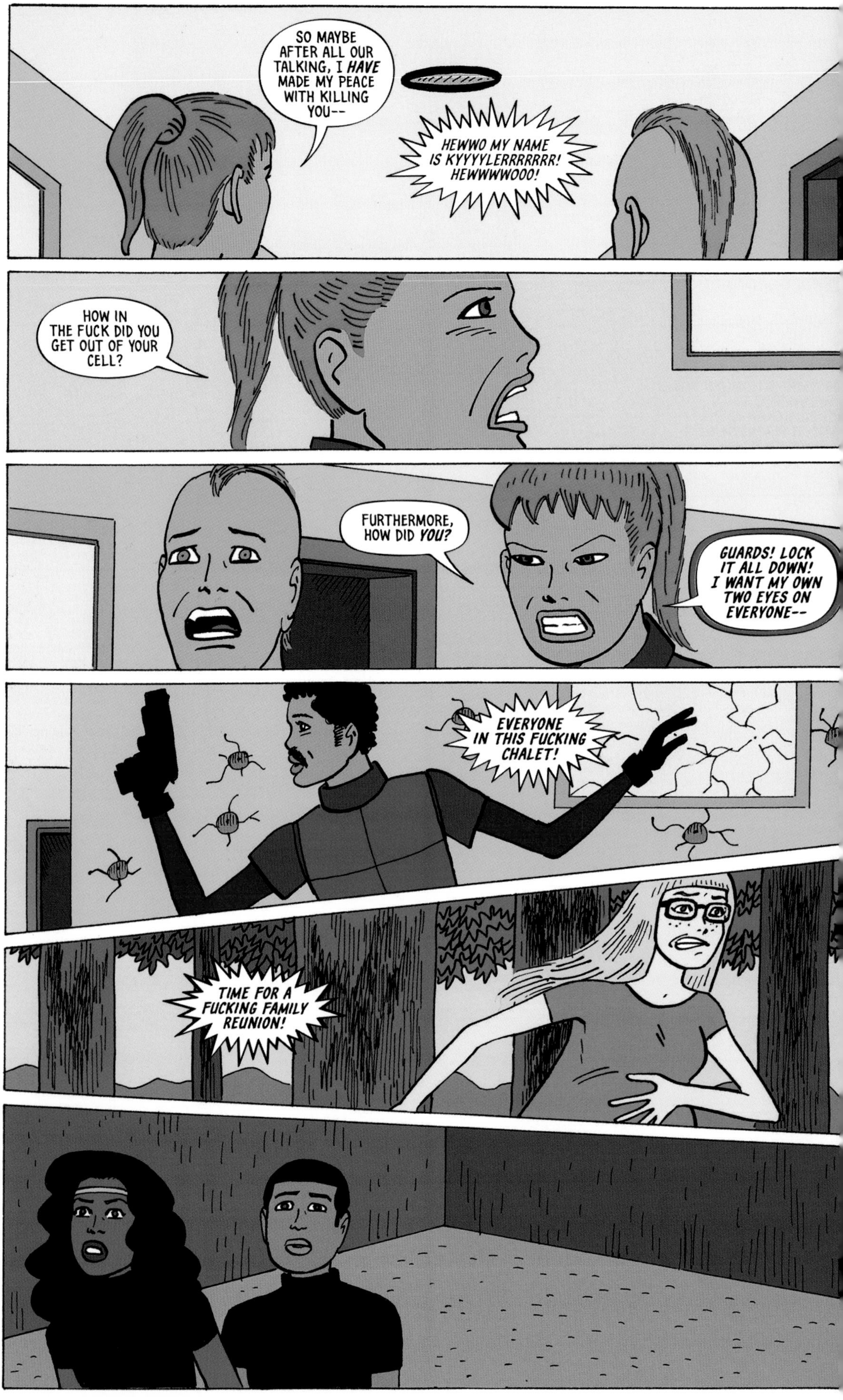
SO MAYBE AFTER ALL OUR TALKING, I *HAVE* MADE MY PEACE WITH KILLING YOU--
HEWWO MY NAME IS KYYYYLERRRRRRR! HEWWWWOOO!
HOW IN THE FUCK DID YOU GET OUT OF YOUR CELL?
FURTHERMORE, HOW DID *YOU*?
GUARDS! LOCK IT ALL DOWN! I WANT MY OWN TWO EYES ON EVERYONE--
EVERYONE IN THIS FUCKING CHALET!
TIME FOR A FUCKING FAMILY REUNION!

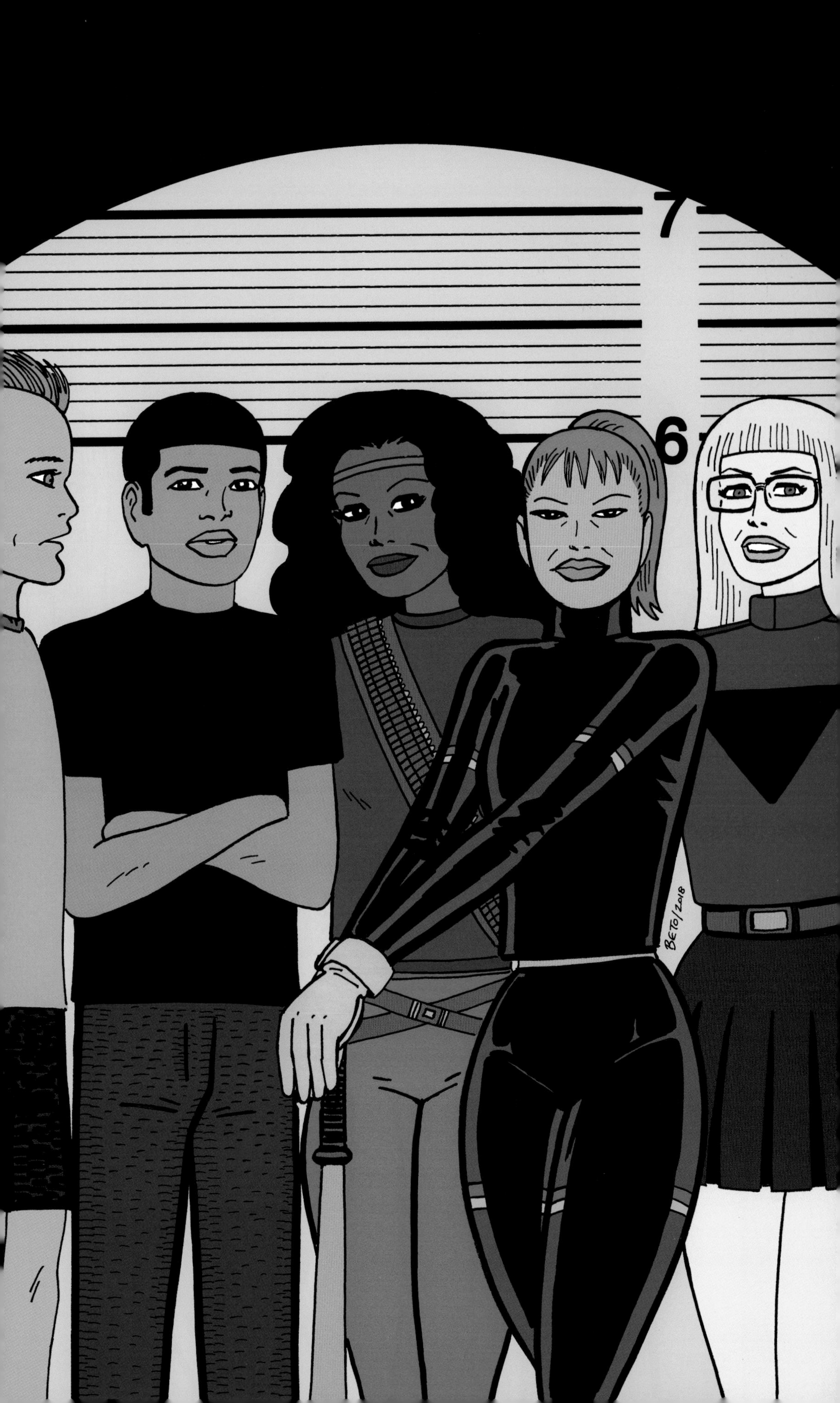
7
6
BETO/2018

“It’s surprising how much you find yourself liking this stuff.”

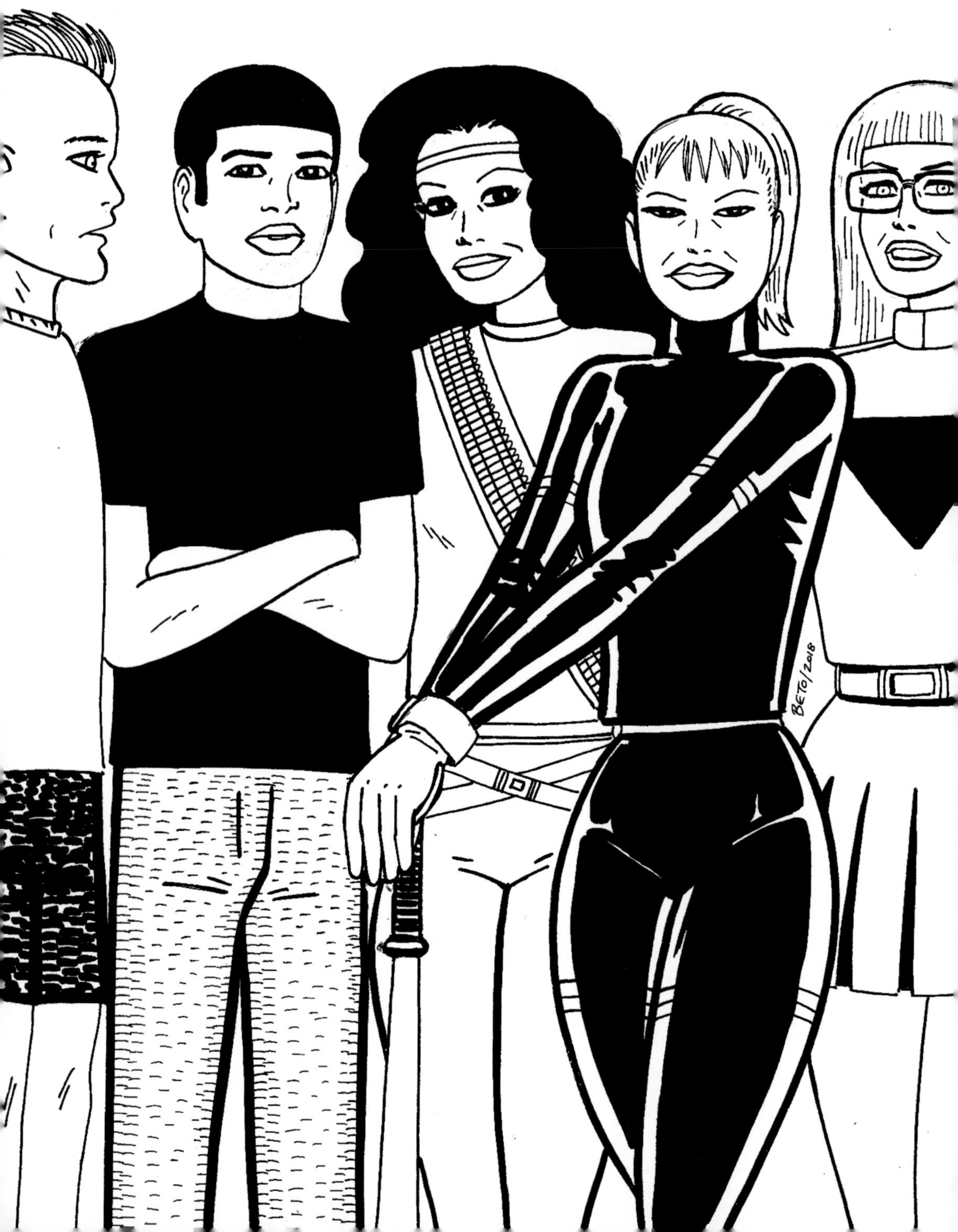
BETO/2018

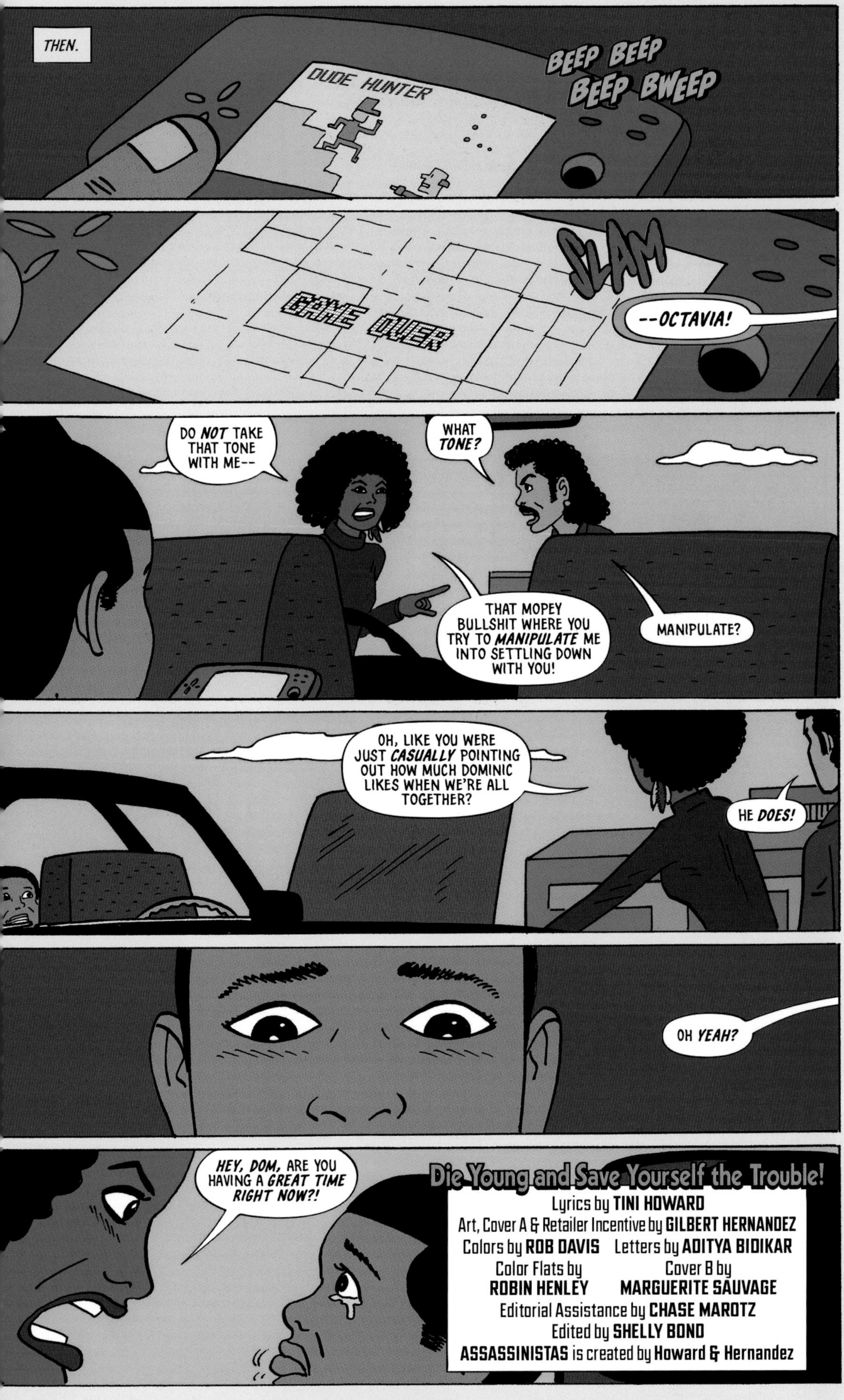

THEN.
DUDE HUNTER
BEEP BEEP BEEP BWEEP
GAME OVER
SLAM
--OCTAVIA!
DO NOT TAKE THAT TONE WITH ME--
WHAT TONE?
THAT MOPEY BULLSHIT WHERE YOU TRY TO MANIPULATE ME INTO SETTLING DOWN WITH YOU!
MANIPULATE?
OH, LIKE YOU WERE JUST CASUALLY POINTING OUT HOW MUCH DOMINIC LIKES WHEN WE'RE ALL TOGETHER?
HE DOES!
OH YEAH?
HEY, DOM, ARE YOU HAVING A GREAT TIME RIGHT NOW?!
Die Young and Save Yourself the Trouble!
Lyrics by TINI HOWARD
Art, Cover A & Retailer Incentive by GILBERT HERNANDEZ
Colors by ROB DAVIS Letters by ADITYA BIDIKAR
Color Flats by ROBIN HENLEY
Cover B by MARGUERITE SAUVAGE
Editorial Assistance by CHASE MAROTZ
Edited by SHELLY BOND
ASSASSINISTAS is created by Howard & Hernandez

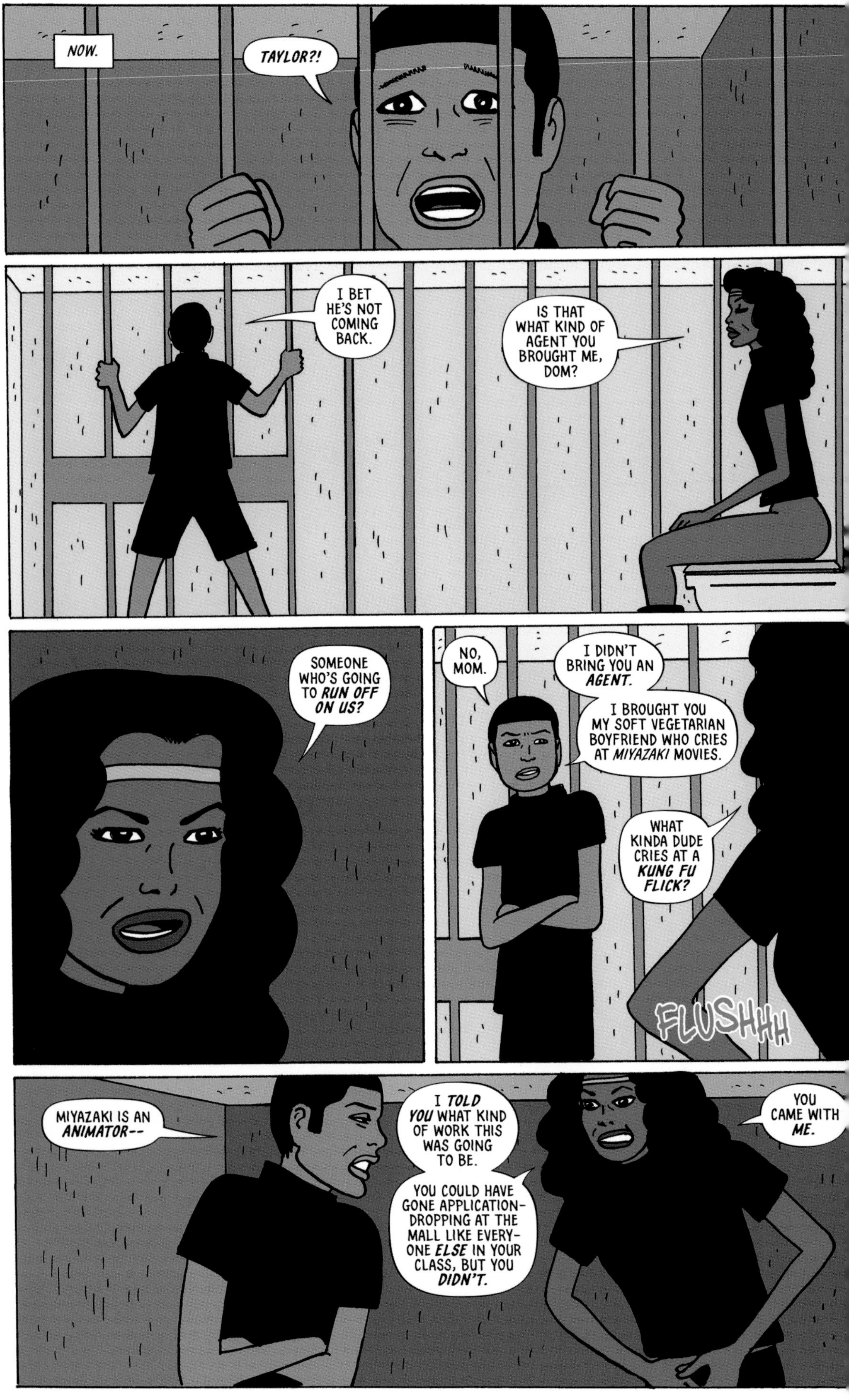
NOW.
TAYLOR?!
I BET HE'S NOT COMING BACK.
IS THAT WHAT KIND OF AGENT YOU BROUGHT ME, DOM?
SOMEONE WHO'S GOING TO RUN OFF ON US?
NO, MOM.
I DIDN'T BRING YOU AN AGENT.
I BROUGHT YOU MY SOFT VEGETARIAN BOYFRIEND WHO CRIES AT MIYAZAKI MOVIES.
WHAT KINDA DUDE CRIES AT A KUNG FU FLICK?
FLUSHHH
MIYAZAKI IS AN ANIMATOR--
I TOLD YOU WHAT KIND OF WORK THIS WAS GOING TO BE.
YOU COULD HAVE GONE APPLICATION-DROPPING AT THE MALL LIKE EVERY-ONE ELSE IN YOUR CLASS, BUT YOU DIDN'T.
YOU CAME WITH ME.

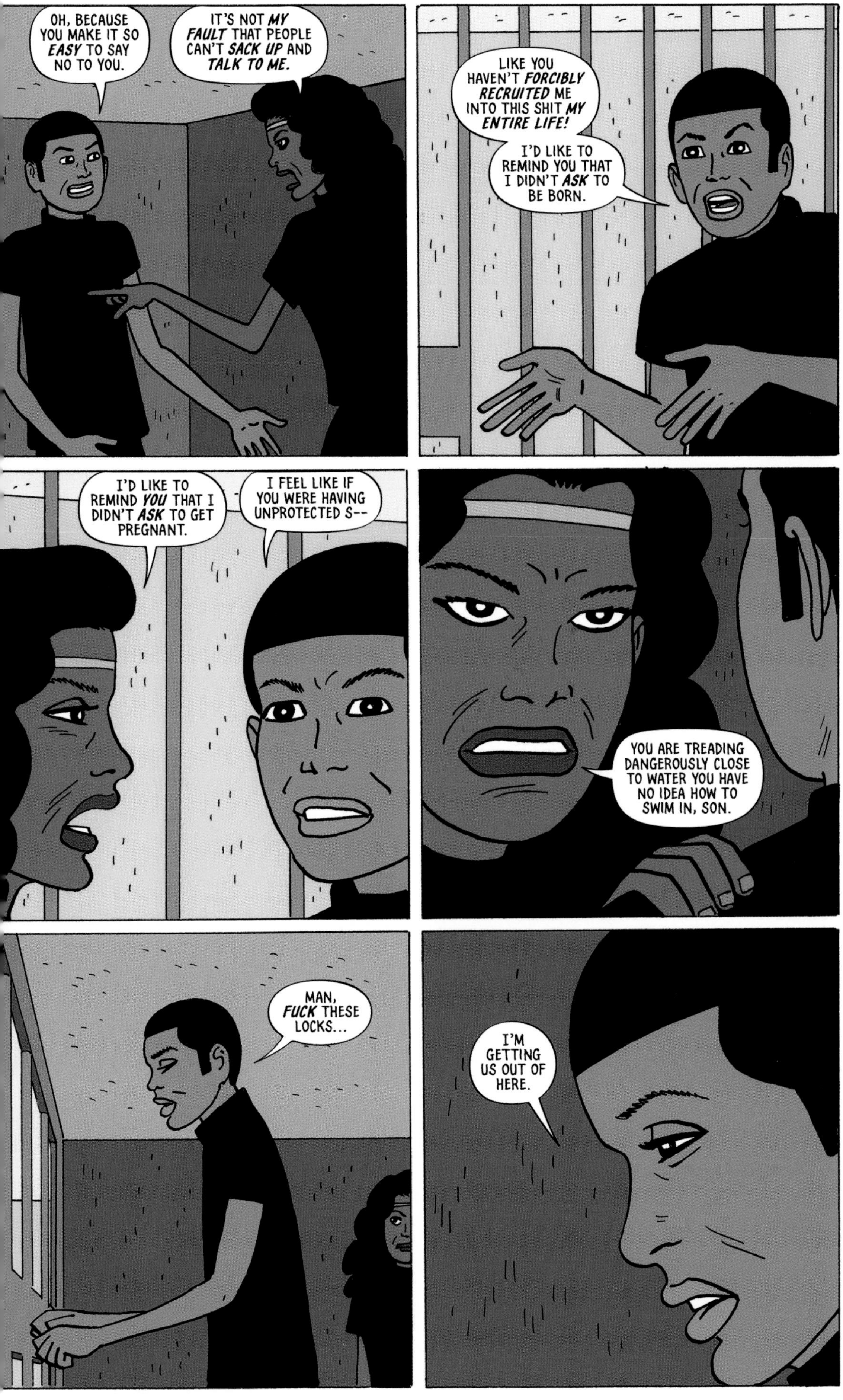
OH, BECAUSE YOU MAKE IT SO EASY TO SAY NO TO YOU.
IT'S NOT MY FAULT THAT PEOPLE CAN'T SACK UP AND TALK TO ME.
LIKE YOU HAVEN'T FORCIBLY RECRUITED ME INTO THIS SHIT MY ENTIRE LIFE!
I'D LIKE TO REMIND YOU THAT I DIDN'T ASK TO BE BORN.
I'D LIKE TO REMIND YOU THAT I DIDN'T ASK TO GET PREGNANT.
I FEEL LIKE IF YOU WERE HAVING UNPROTECTED S--
YOU ARE TREADING DANGEROUSLY CLOSE TO WATER YOU HAVE NO IDEA HOW TO SWIM IN, SON.
MAN, FUCK THESE LOCKS...
I'M GETTING US OUT OF HERE.

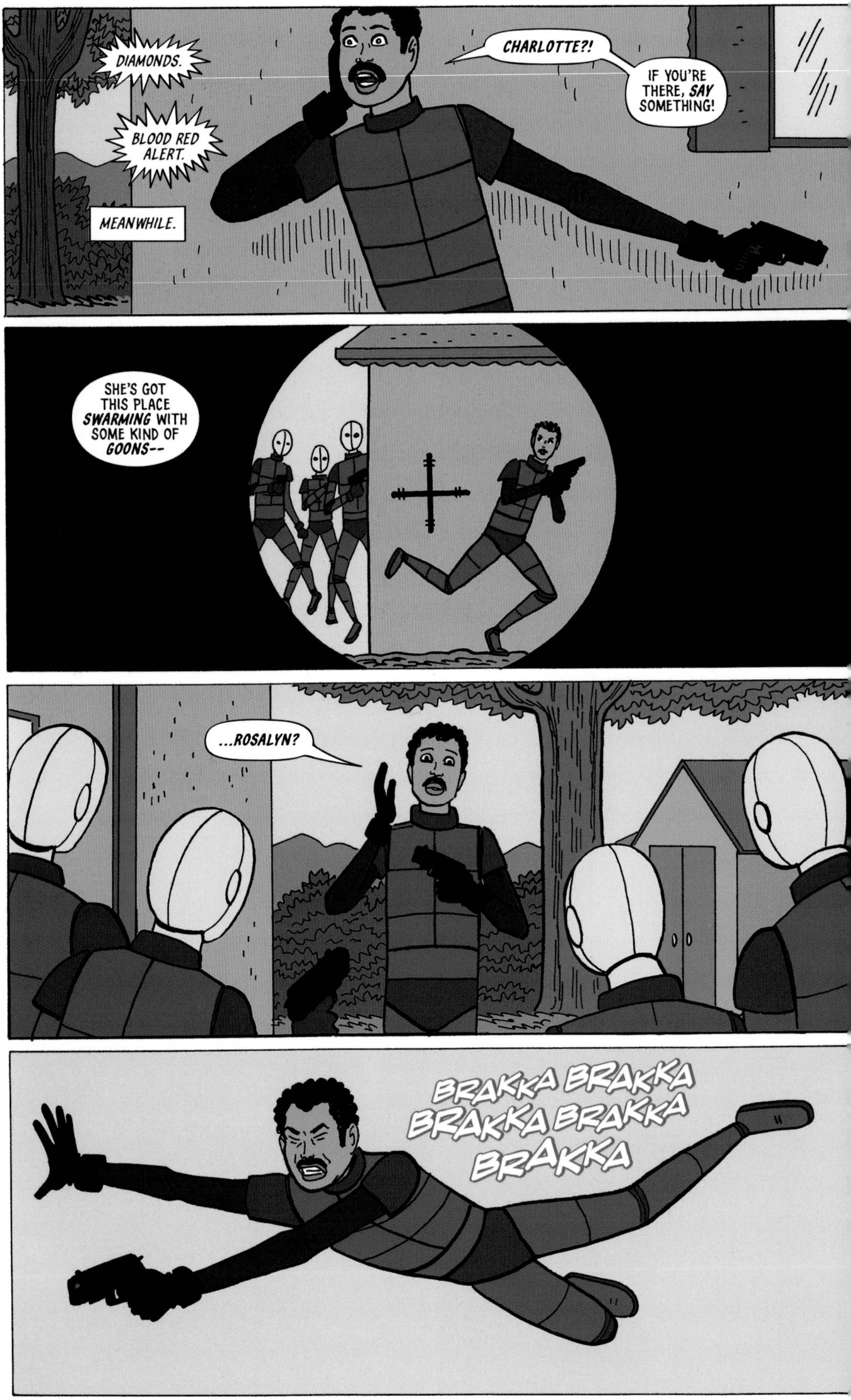
DIAMONDS.
BLOOD RED ALERT.
MEANWHILE.
CHARLOTTE?!
IF YOU'RE THERE, SAY SOMETHING!
SHE'S GOT THIS PLACE SWARMING WITH SOME KIND OF GOONS--
...ROSALYN?
BRAKKA BRAKKA BRAKKA BRAKKA BRAKKA

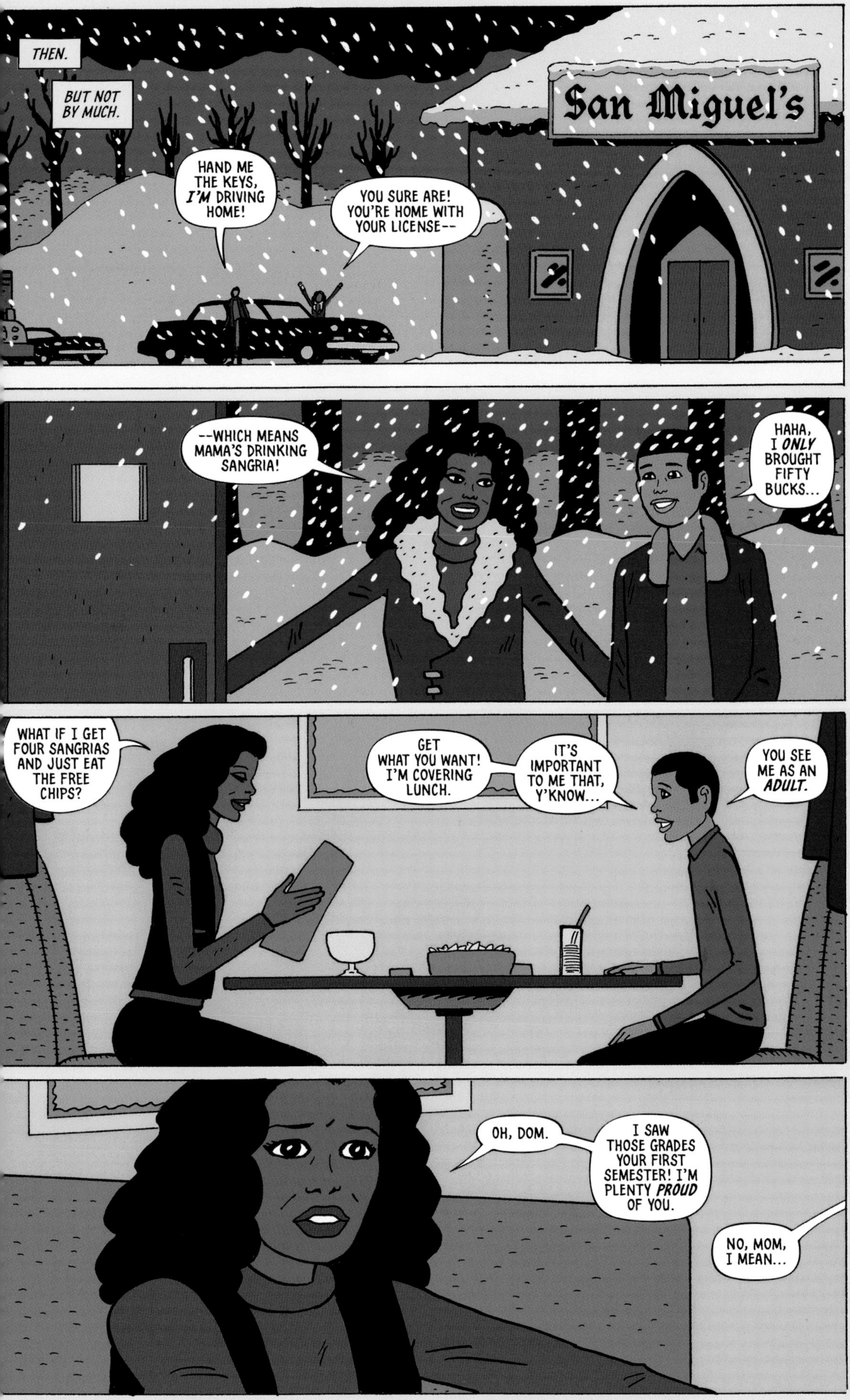
THEN.
BUT NOT BY MUCH.
San Miguel's
HAND ME THE KEYS, *I'M* DRIVING HOME!
YOU SURE ARE! YOU'RE HOME WITH YOUR LICENSE--
--WHICH MEANS MAMA'S DRINKING SANGRIA!
HAHA, I *ONLY* BROUGHT FIFTY BUCKS...
WHAT IF I GET FOUR SANGRIAS AND JUST EAT THE FREE CHIPS?
GET WHAT YOU WANT! I'M COVERING LUNCH.
IT'S IMPORTANT TO ME THAT, Y'KNOW...
YOU SEE ME AS AN *ADULT.*
OH, DOM.
I SAW THOSE GRADES YOUR FIRST SEMESTER! I'M PLENTY *PROUD* OF YOU.
NO, MOM, I MEAN...

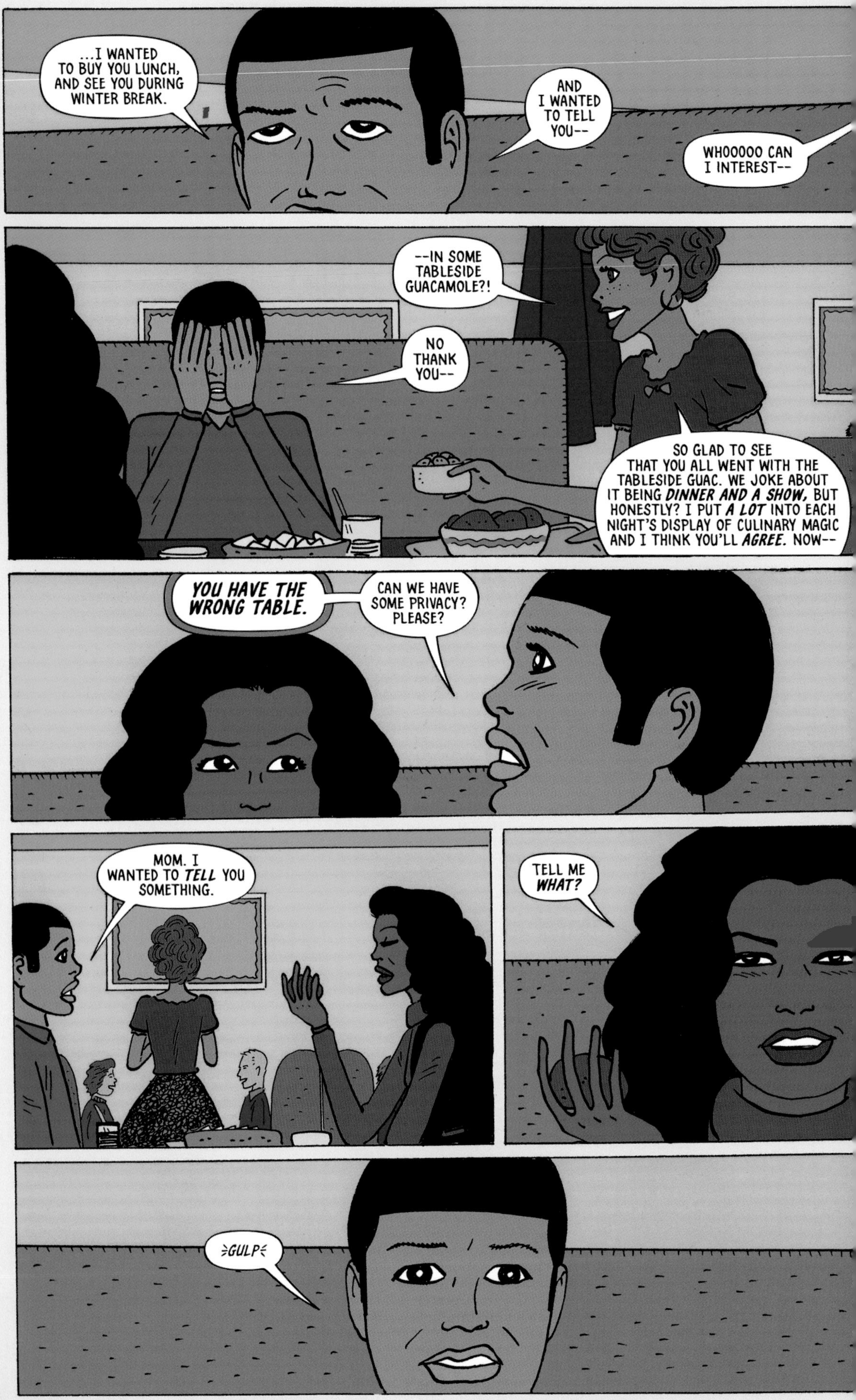
...I WANTED TO BUY YOU LUNCH, AND SEE YOU DURING WINTER BREAK.
AND I WANTED TO TELL YOU--
WHOOOOO CAN I INTEREST--
--IN SOME TABLESIDE GUACAMOLE?!
NO THANK YOU--
SO GLAD TO SEE THAT YOU ALL WENT WITH THE TABLESIDE GUAC. WE JOKE ABOUT IT BEING DINNER AND A SHOW, BUT HONESTLY? I PUT A LOT INTO EACH NIGHT'S DISPLAY OF CULINARY MAGIC AND I THINK YOU'LL AGREE. NOW--
YOU HAVE THE WRONG TABLE.
CAN WE HAVE SOME PRIVACY? PLEASE?
MOM. I WANTED TO TELL YOU SOMETHING.
TELL ME WHAT?
GULP

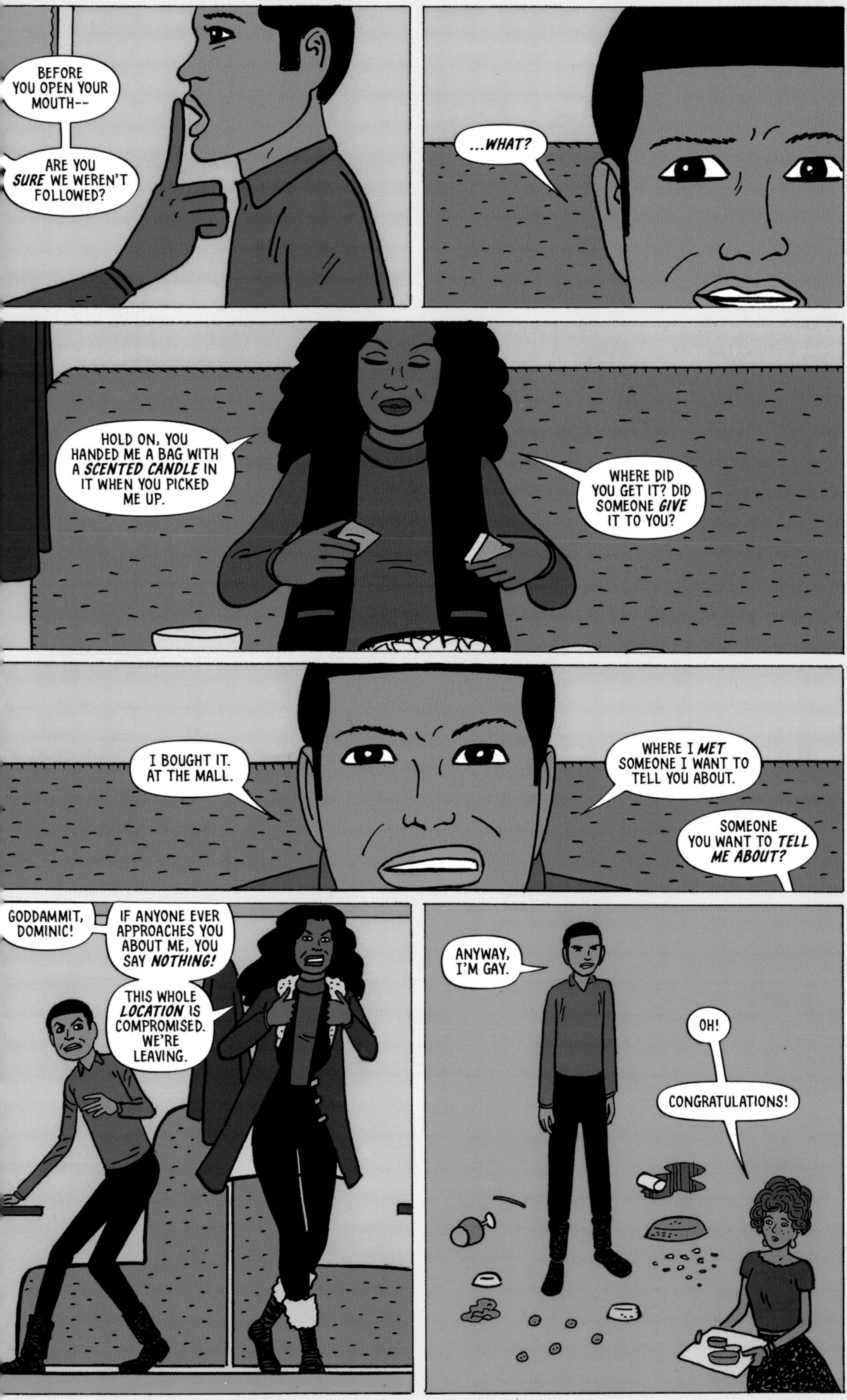
BEFORE YOU OPEN YOUR MOUTH--
ARE YOU SURE WE WEREN'T FOLLOWED?
...WHAT?
HOLD ON, YOU HANDED ME A BAG WITH A SCENTED CANDLE IN IT WHEN YOU PICKED ME UP.
WHERE DID YOU GET IT? DID SOMEONE GIVE IT TO YOU?
I BOUGHT IT. AT THE MALL.
WHERE I MET SOMEONE I WANT TO TELL YOU ABOUT.
SOMEONE YOU WANT TO TELL ME ABOUT?
GODDAMMIT, DOMINIC!
IF ANYONE EVER APPROACHES YOU ABOUT ME, YOU SAY NOTHING!
THIS WHOLE LOCATION IS COMPROMISED. WE'RE LEAVING.
ANYWAY, I'M GAY.
OH!
CONGRATULATIONS!

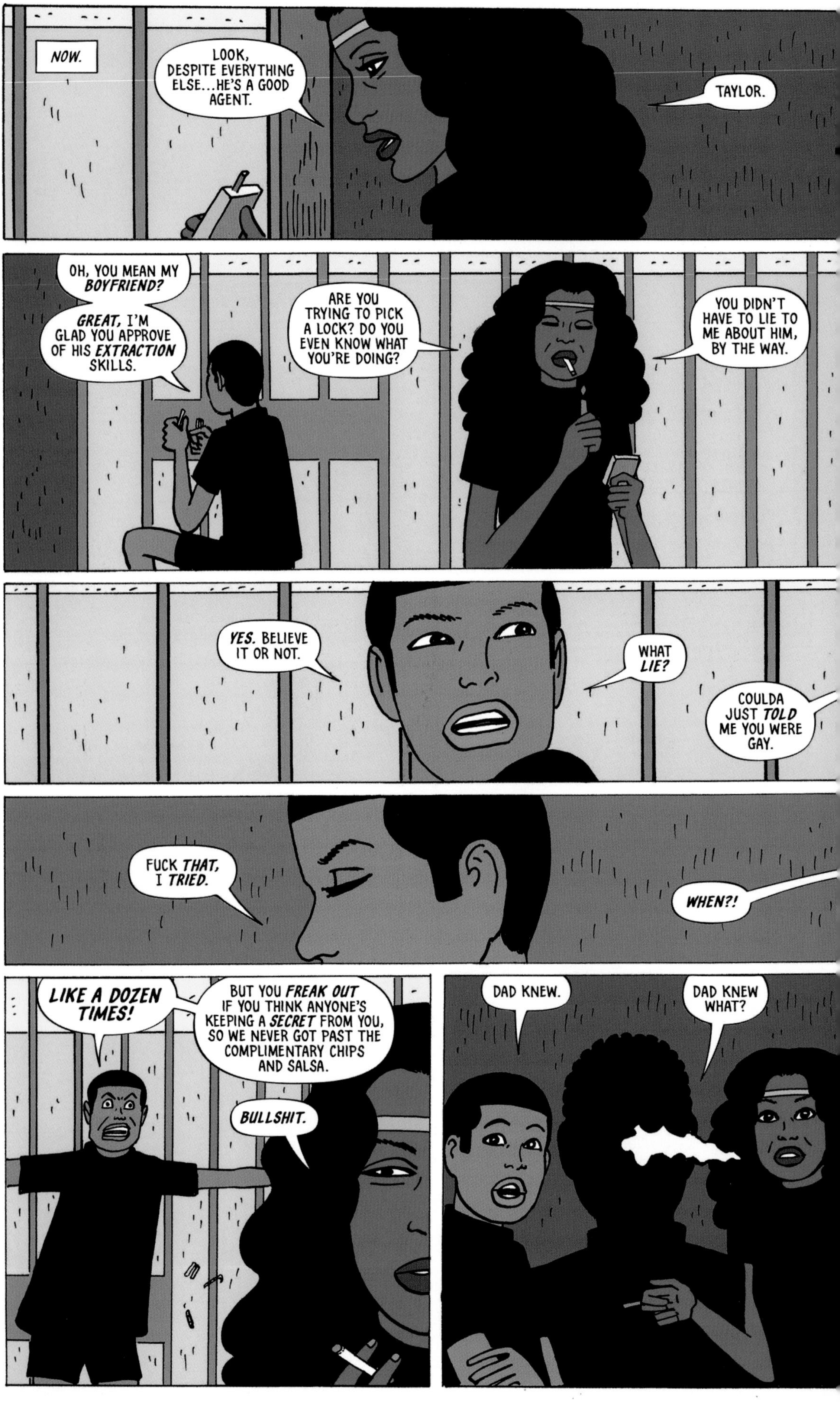
NOW.
LOOK, DESPITE EVERYTHING ELSE...HE'S A GOOD AGENT.
TAYLOR.
OH, YOU MEAN MY *BOYFRIEND?*
GREAT, I'M GLAD YOU APPROVE OF HIS *EXTRACTION* SKILLS.
ARE YOU TRYING TO PICK A LOCK? DO YOU EVEN KNOW WHAT YOU'RE DOING?
YOU DIDN'T HAVE TO LIE TO ME ABOUT HIM, BY THE WAY.
YES. BELIEVE IT OR NOT.
WHAT *LIE?*
COULDA JUST *TOLD* ME YOU WERE GAY.
FUCK *THAT,* I *TRIED.*
WHEN?!
LIKE A DOZEN TIMES!
BUT YOU *FREAK OUT* IF YOU THINK ANYONE'S KEEPING A *SECRET* FROM YOU, SO WE NEVER GOT PAST THE COMPLIMENTARY CHIPS AND SALSA.
BULLSHIT.
DAD KNEW.
DAD KNEW WHAT?

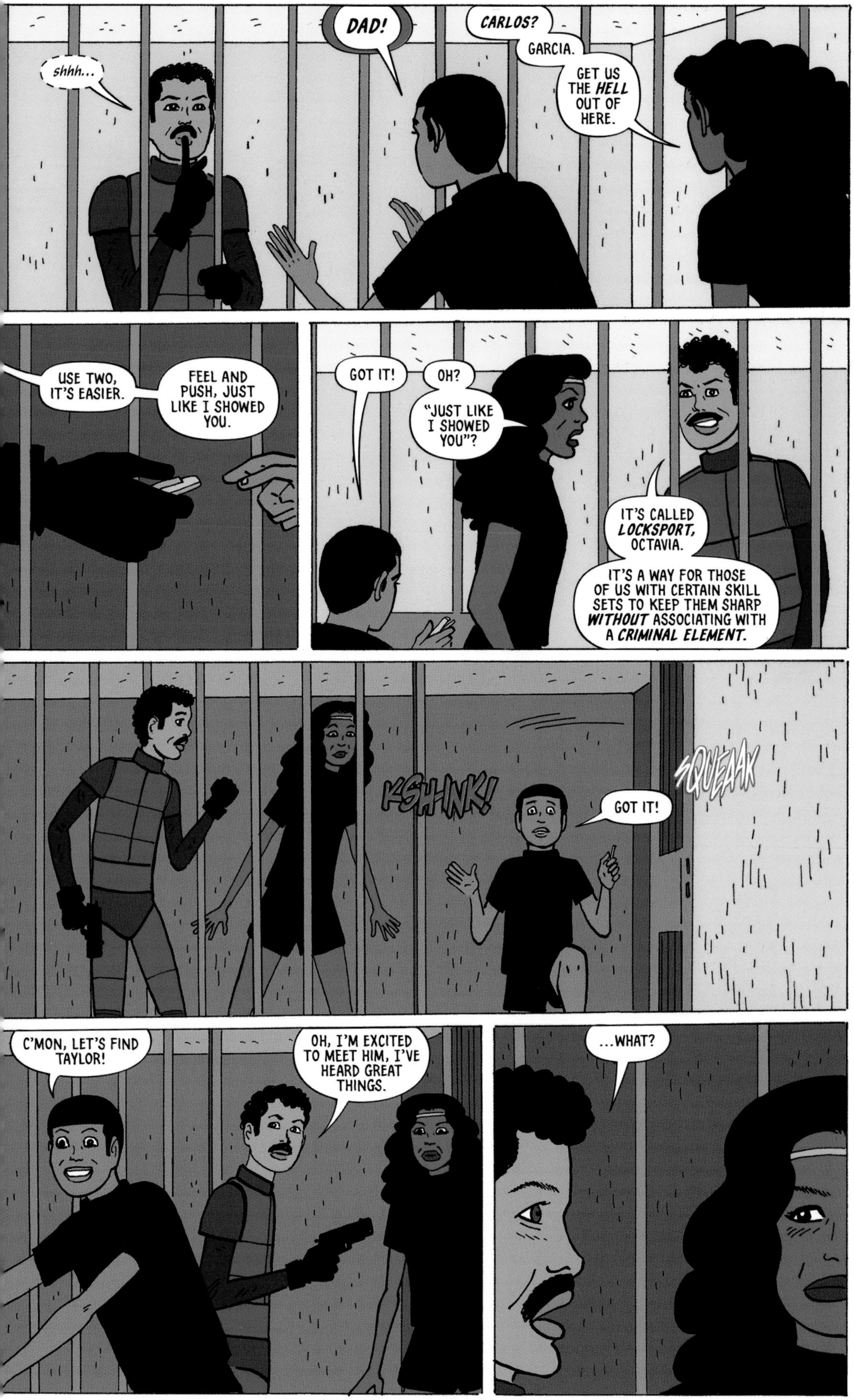
shhh...
DAD!
CARLOS?
GARCIA.
GET US THE HELL OUT OF HERE.
USE TWO, IT'S EASIER.
FEEL AND PUSH, JUST LIKE I SHOWED YOU.
GOT IT!
OH?
"JUST LIKE I SHOWED YOU"?
IT'S CALLED LOCKSPORT, OCTAVIA.
IT'S A WAY FOR THOSE OF US WITH CERTAIN SKILL SETS TO KEEP THEM SHARP WITHOUT ASSOCIATING WITH A CRIMINAL ELEMENT.
KSHHNK!
GOT IT!
SQUEAAK
C'MON, LET'S FIND TAYLOR!
OH, I'M EXCITED TO MEET HIM, I'VE HEARD GREAT THINGS.
...WHAT?

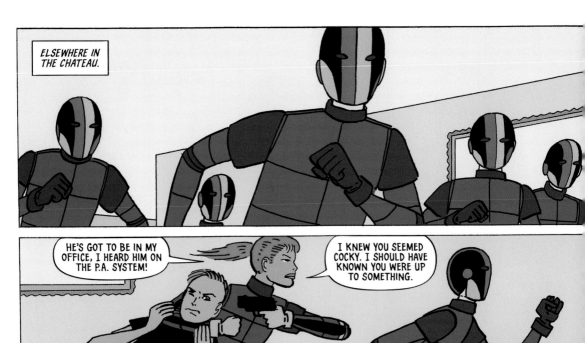

ELSEWHERE IN THE CHATEAU.

HE'S GOT TO BE IN MY OFFICE, I HEARD HIM ON THE P.A. SYSTEM!

I KNEW YOU SEEMED COCKY. I SHOULD HAVE KNOWN YOU WERE UP TO SOMETHING.

DID YOU TRY TO HIDE THAT KID IN MY *OFFICE?*

YEAH, *HEH.*

PREEETTY DUMB OF ME...

HEEWWWWOOOO!!

KEEP OUT

WHAM

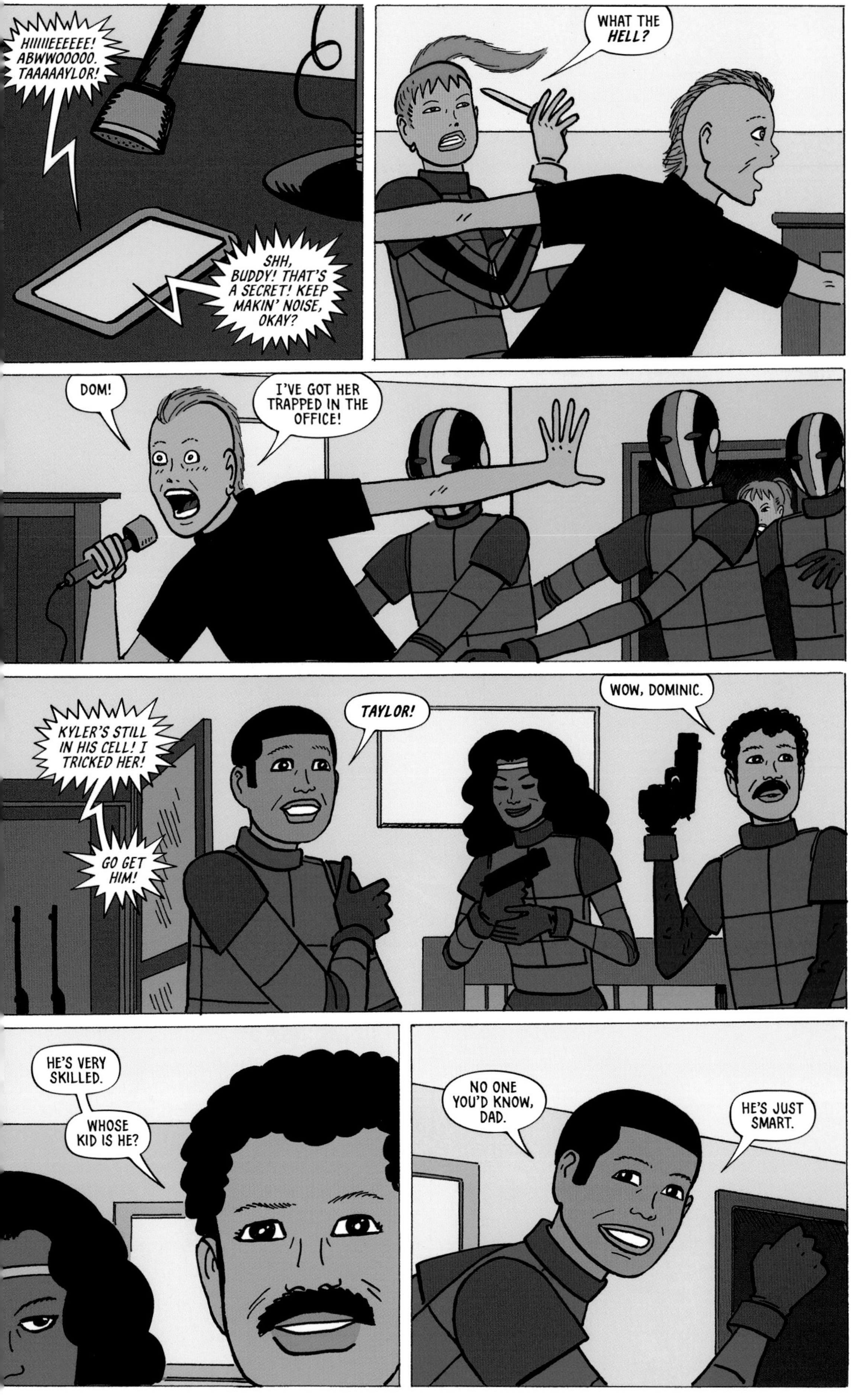
HIIIIIEEEEEE! ABWWOOOOO. TAAAAAYLOR!
SHH, BUDDY! THAT'S A SECRET! KEEP MAKIN' NOISE, OKAY?
WHAT THE HELL?
DOM!
I'VE GOT HER TRAPPED IN THE OFFICE!
KYLER'S STILL IN HIS CELL! I TRICKED HER!
GO GET HIM!
TAYLOR!
WOW, DOMINIC.
HE'S VERY SKILLED.
WHOSE KID IS HE?
NO ONE YOU'D KNOW, DAD.
HE'S JUST SMART.

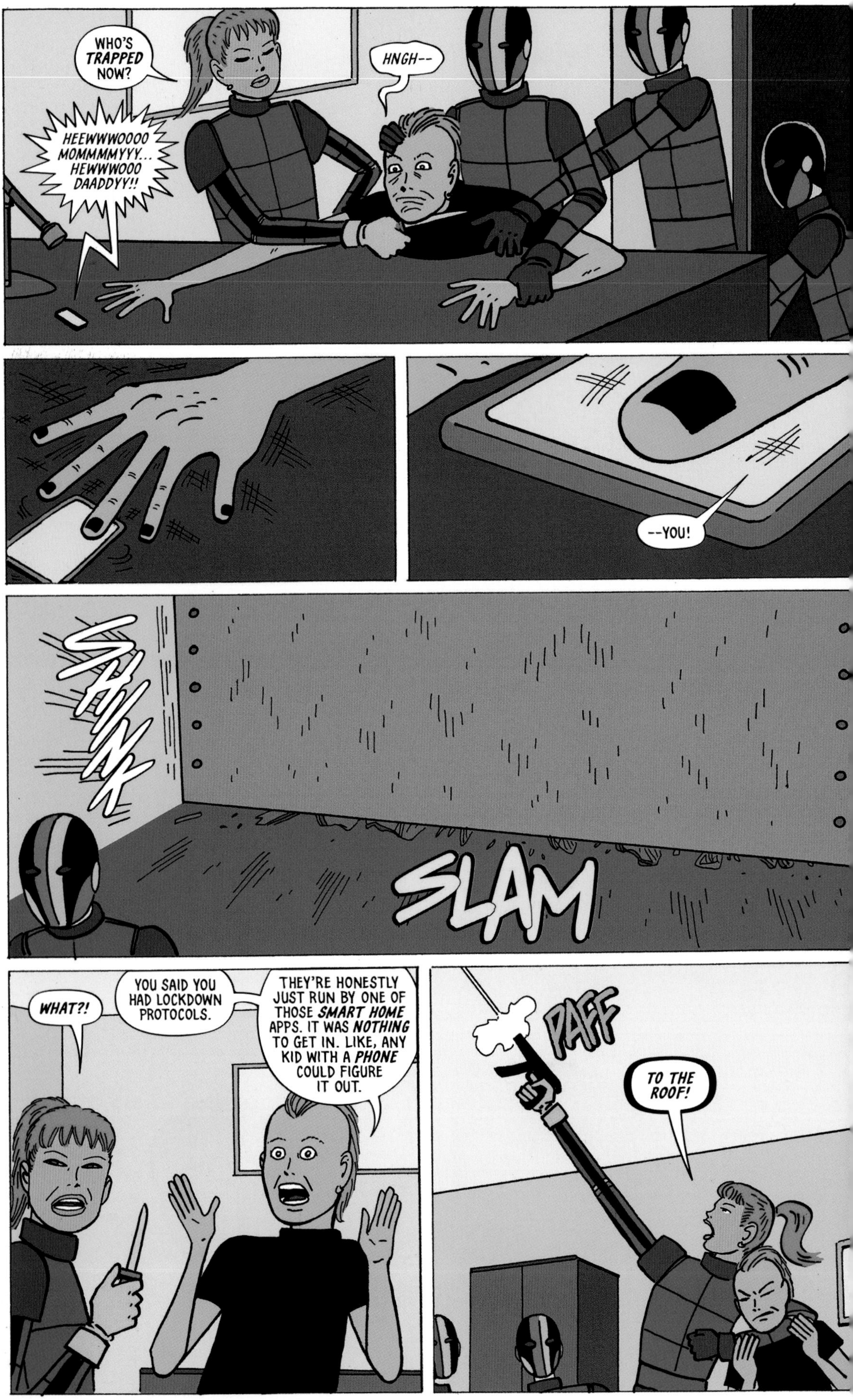
WHO'S *TRAPPED* NOW?
HNGH--
HEEWWWOOOO MOMMMMYYY... HEWWWOOO DAADDYY!!
--YOU!
SHINK
SLAM
WHAT?!
YOU SAID YOU HAD LOCKDOWN PROTOCOLS.
THEY'RE HONESTLY JUST RUN BY ONE OF THOSE *SMART HOME* APPS. IT WAS *NOTHING* TO GET IN. LIKE, ANY KID WITH A *PHONE* COULD FIGURE IT OUT.
PAFF
TO THE ROOF!

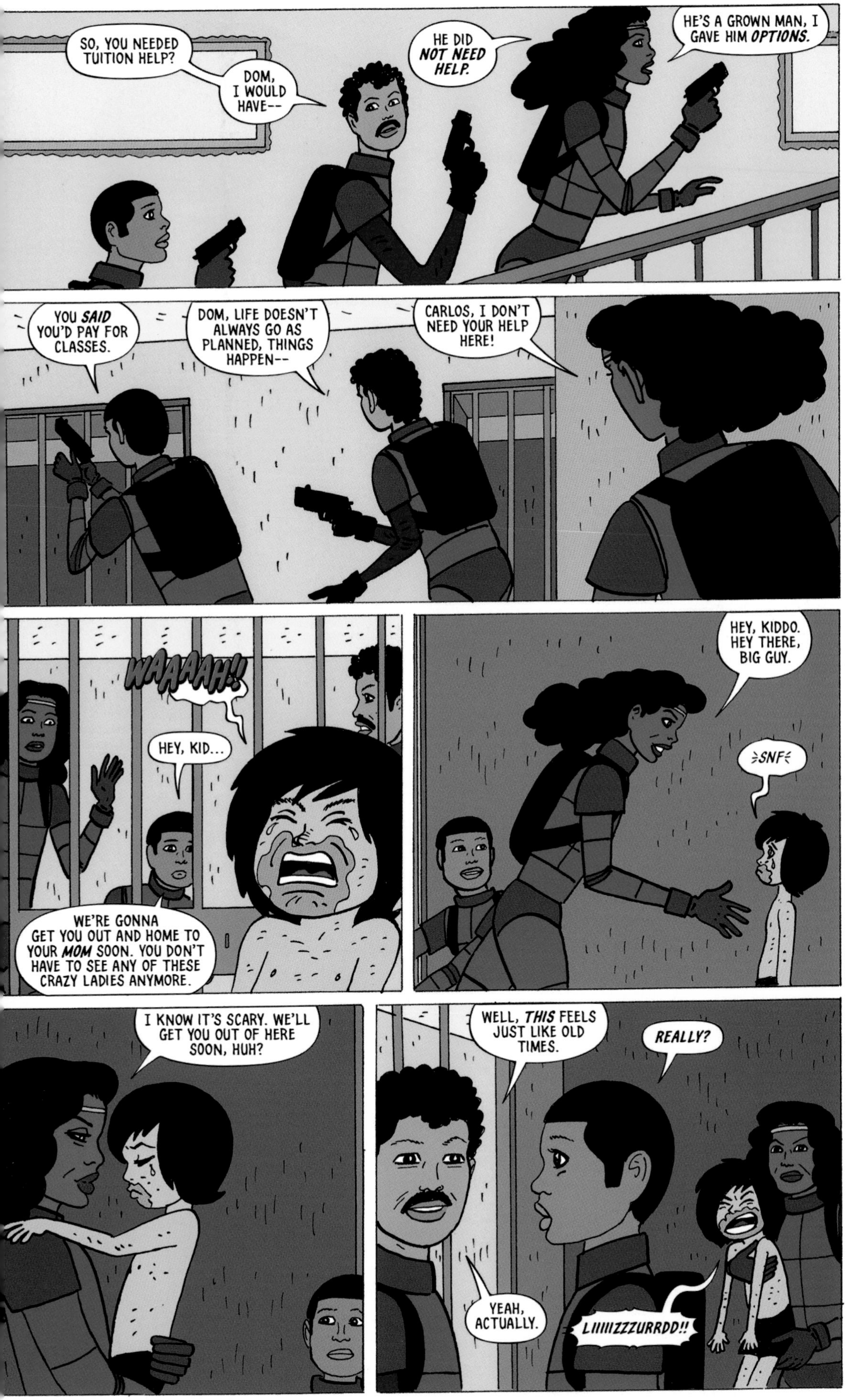
SO, YOU NEEDED TUITION HELP?
DOM, I WOULD HAVE--
HE DID NOT NEED HELP.
HE'S A GROWN MAN, I GAVE HIM OPTIONS.
YOU SAID YOU'D PAY FOR CLASSES.
DOM, LIFE DOESN'T ALWAYS GO AS PLANNED, THINGS HAPPEN--
CARLOS, I DON'T NEED YOUR HELP HERE!
WAAAAH!!
HEY, KID...
WE'RE GONNA GET YOU OUT AND HOME TO YOUR MOM SOON. YOU DON'T HAVE TO SEE ANY OF THESE CRAZY LADIES ANYMORE.
HEY, KIDDO. HEY THERE, BIG GUY.
SNF
I KNOW IT'S SCARY. WE'LL GET YOU OUT OF HERE SOON, HUH?
WELL, THIS FEELS JUST LIKE OLD TIMES.
REALLY?
YEAH, ACTUALLY.
LIIIIIZZZURRDD!!

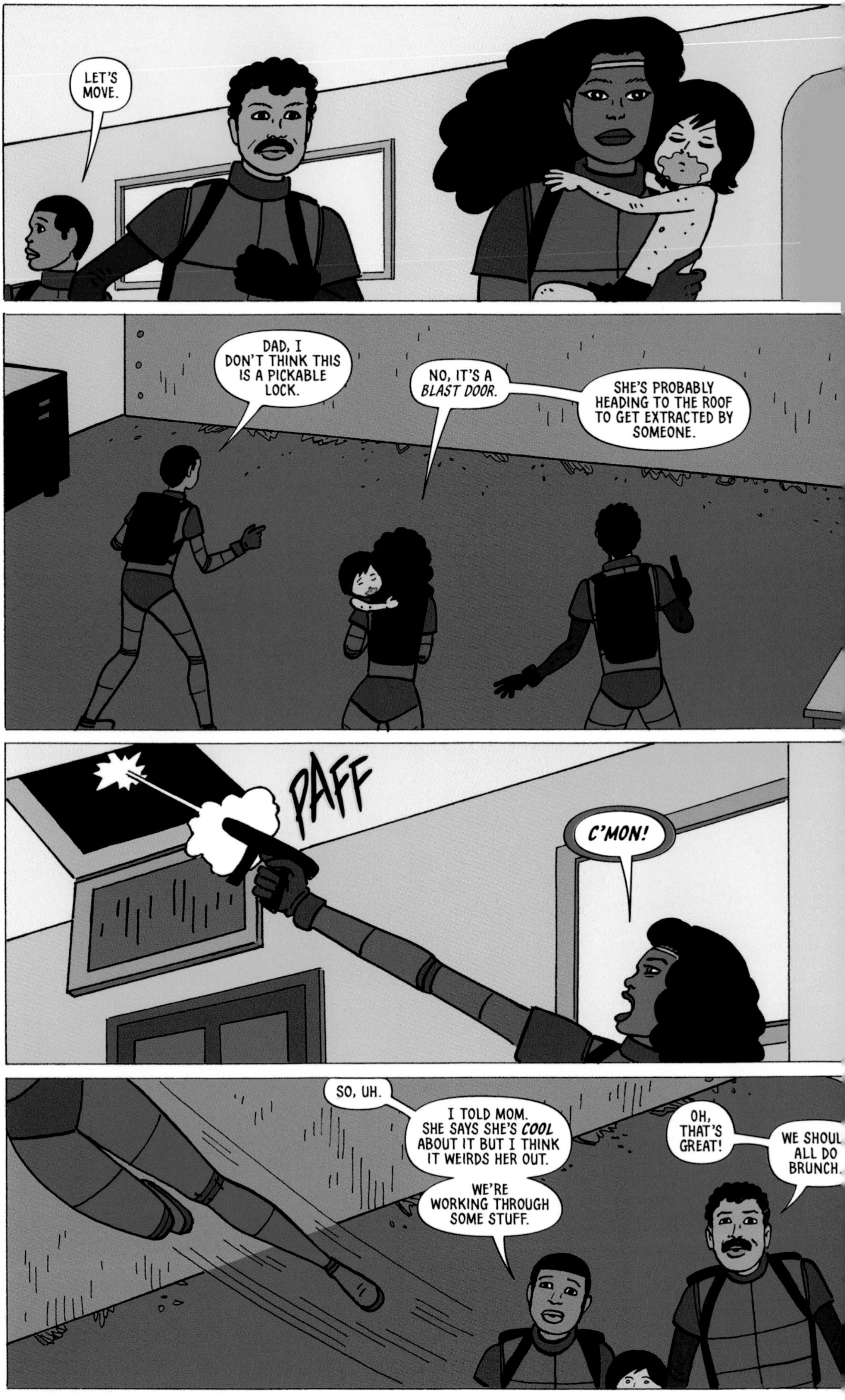
LET'S MOVE.
DAD, I DON'T THINK THIS IS A PICKABLE LOCK.
NO, IT'S A *BLAST DOOR.*
SHE'S PROBABLY HEADING TO THE ROOF TO GET EXTRACTED BY SOMEONE.
PAFF
C'MON!
SO, UH.
I TOLD MOM. SHE SAYS SHE'S *COOL* ABOUT IT BUT I THINK IT WEIRDS HER OUT.
WE'RE WORKING THROUGH SOME STUFF.
OH, THAT'S GREAT!

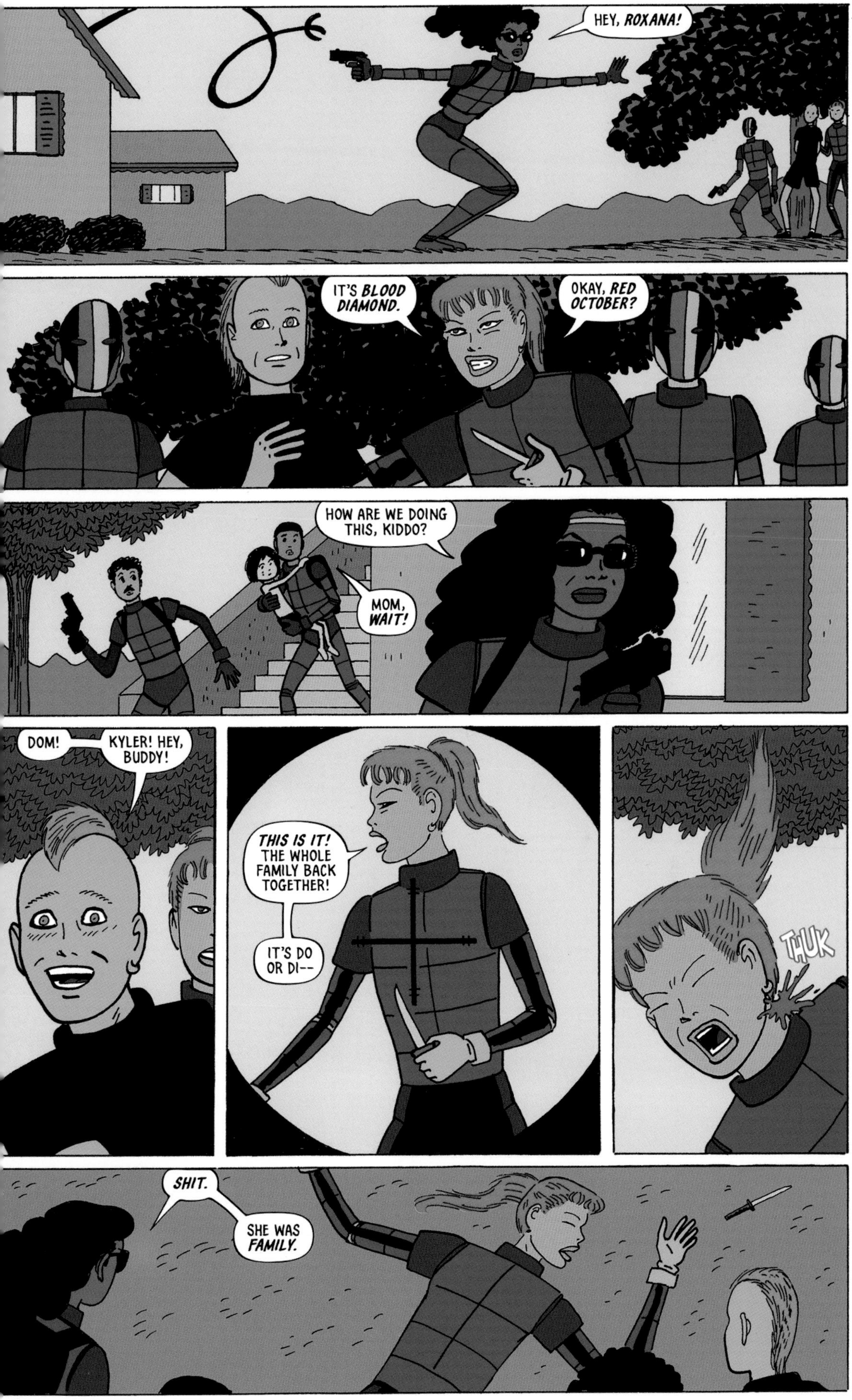
HEY, ROXANA!
IT'S BLOOD DIAMOND.
OKAY, RED OCTOBER?
HOW ARE WE DOING THIS, KIDDO?
MOM, WAIT!
DOM!
KYLER! HEY, BUDDY!
THIS IS IT! THE WHOLE FAMILY BACK TOGETHER!
IT'S DO OR DI--
THUK
SHIT.
SHE WAS FAMILY.

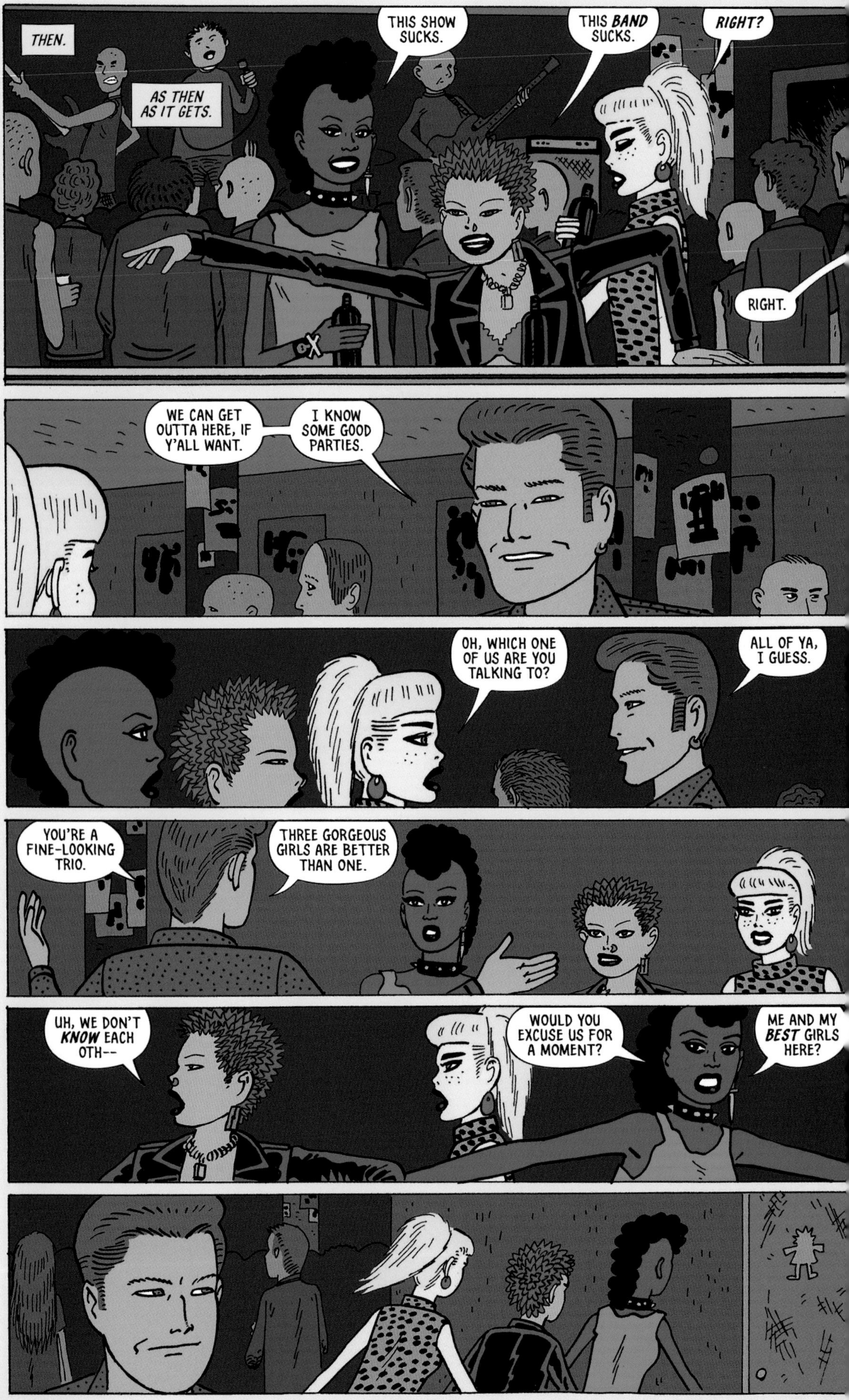

THEN.
AS THEN AS IT GETS.
THIS SHOW SUCKS.
THIS BAND SUCKS.
RIGHT?
RIGHT.
WE CAN GET OUTTA HERE, IF Y'ALL WANT.
I KNOW SOME GOOD PARTIES.
OH, WHICH ONE OF US ARE YOU TALKING TO?
ALL OF YA, I GUESS.
YOU'RE A FINE-LOOKING TRIO.
THREE GORGEOUS GIRLS ARE BETTER THAN ONE.
UH, WE DON'T KNOW EACH OTH--
WOULD YOU EXCUSE US FOR A MOMENT?
ME AND MY BEST GIRLS HERE?

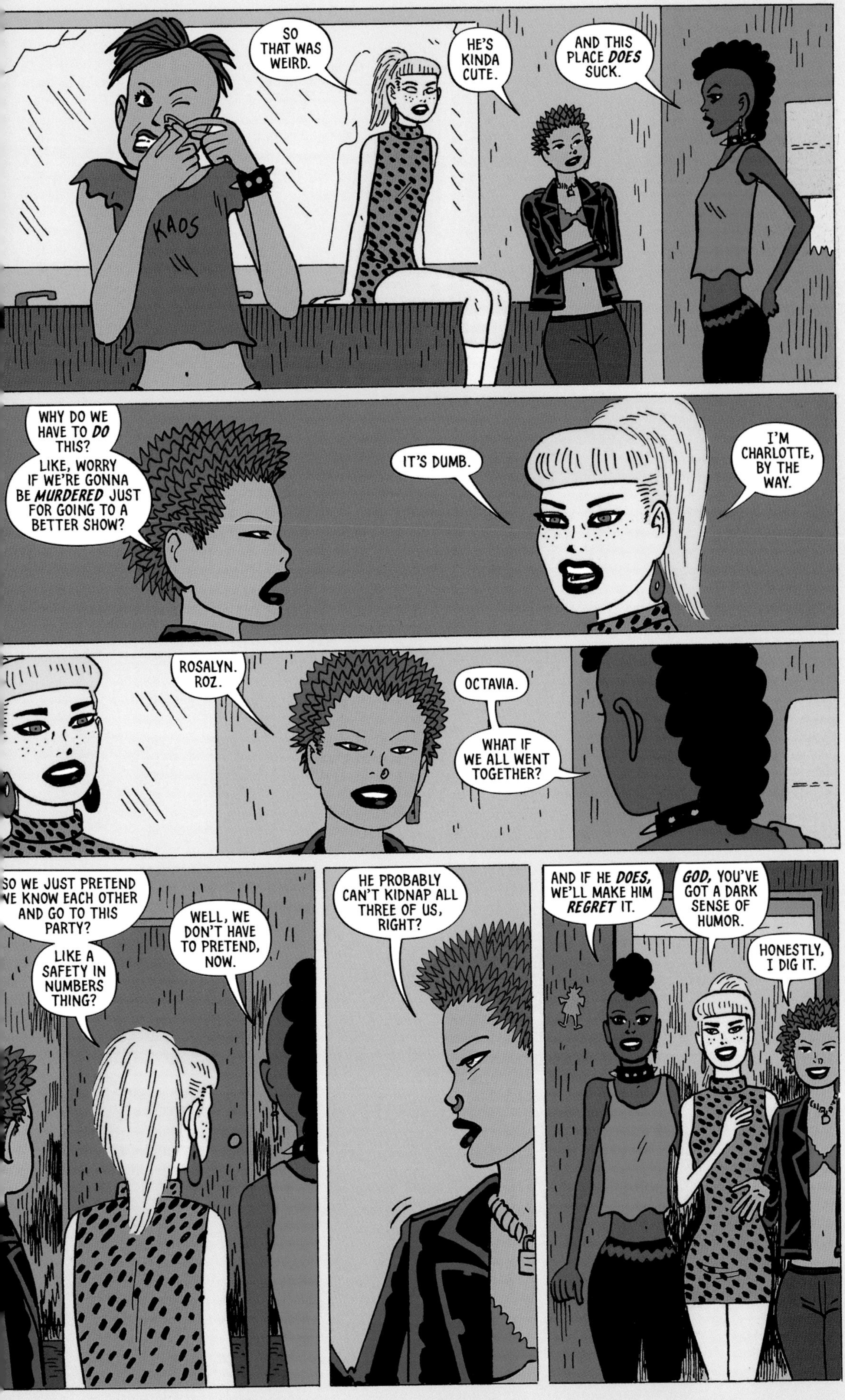
SO THAT WAS WEIRD.
HE'S KINDA CUTE.
AND THIS PLACE DOES SUCK.
KAOS
WHY DO WE HAVE TO DO THIS?
LIKE, WORRY IF WE'RE GONNA BE MURDERED JUST FOR GOING TO A BETTER SHOW?
IT'S DUMB.
I'M CHARLOTTE, BY THE WAY.
ROSALYN. ROZ.
OCTAVIA.
WHAT IF WE ALL WENT TOGETHER?
SO WE JUST PRETEND WE KNOW EACH OTHER AND GO TO THIS PARTY?
LIKE A SAFETY IN NUMBERS THING?
WELL, WE DON'T HAVE TO PRETEND, NOW.
HE PROBABLY CAN'T KIDNAP ALL THREE OF US, RIGHT?
AND IF HE DOES, WE'LL MAKE HIM REGRET IT.
GOD, YOU'VE GOT A DARK SENSE OF HUMOR.
HONESTLY, I DIG IT.

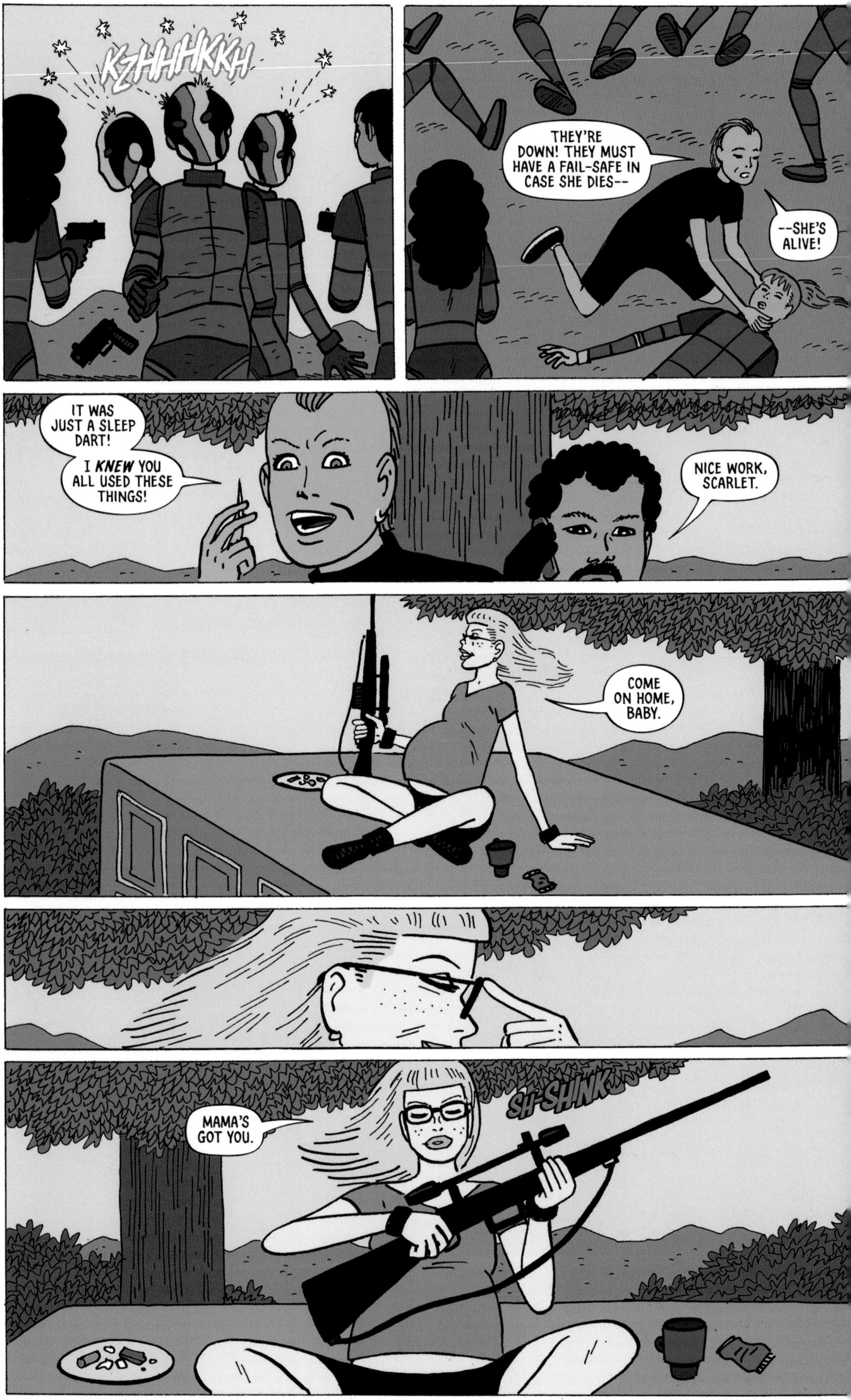
KZHHHKKH
THEY'RE DOWN! THEY MUST HAVE A FAIL-SAFE IN CASE SHE DIES--
--SHE'S ALIVE!
IT WAS JUST A SLEEP DART!
I KNEW YOU ALL USED THESE THINGS!
NICE WORK, SCARLET.
COME ON HOME, BABY.
MAMA'S GOT YOU.
SH-SHINK

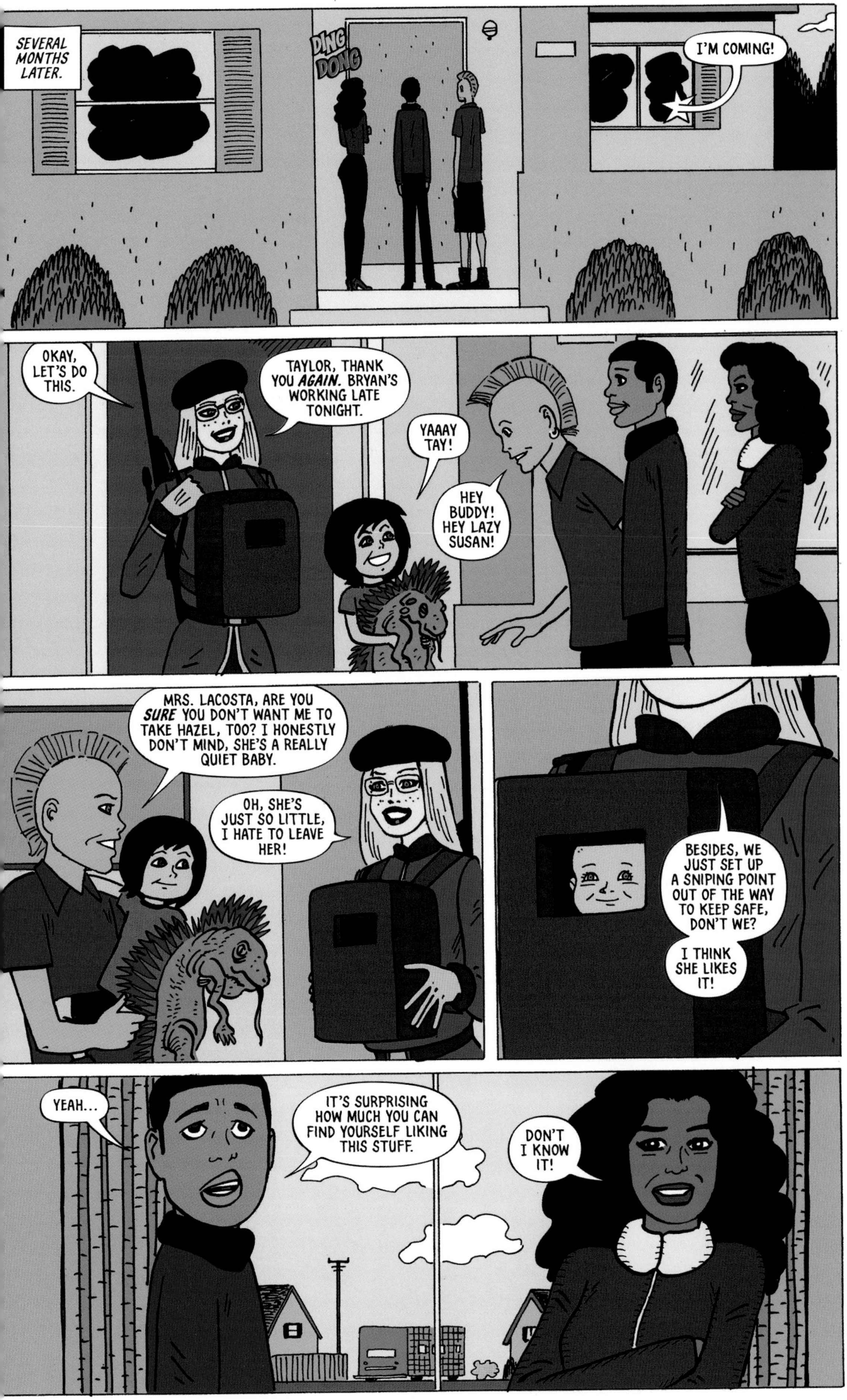
SEVERAL MONTHS LATER.
DING DONG
I'M COMING!
OKAY, LET'S DO THIS.
TAYLOR, THANK YOU AGAIN. BRYAN'S WORKING LATE TONIGHT.
YAAAY TAY!
HEY BUDDY! HEY LAZY SUSAN!
MRS. LACOSTA, ARE YOU SURE YOU DON'T WANT ME TO TAKE HAZEL, TOO? I HONESTLY DON'T MIND, SHE'S A REALLY QUIET BABY.
OH, SHE'S JUST SO LITTLE, I HATE TO LEAVE HER!
BESIDES, WE JUST SET UP A SNIPING POINT OUT OF THE WAY TO KEEP SAFE, DON'T WE?
I THINK SHE LIKES IT!
YEAH...
IT'S SURPRISING HOW MUCH YOU CAN FIND YOURSELF LIKING THIS STUFF.
DON'T I KNOW IT!

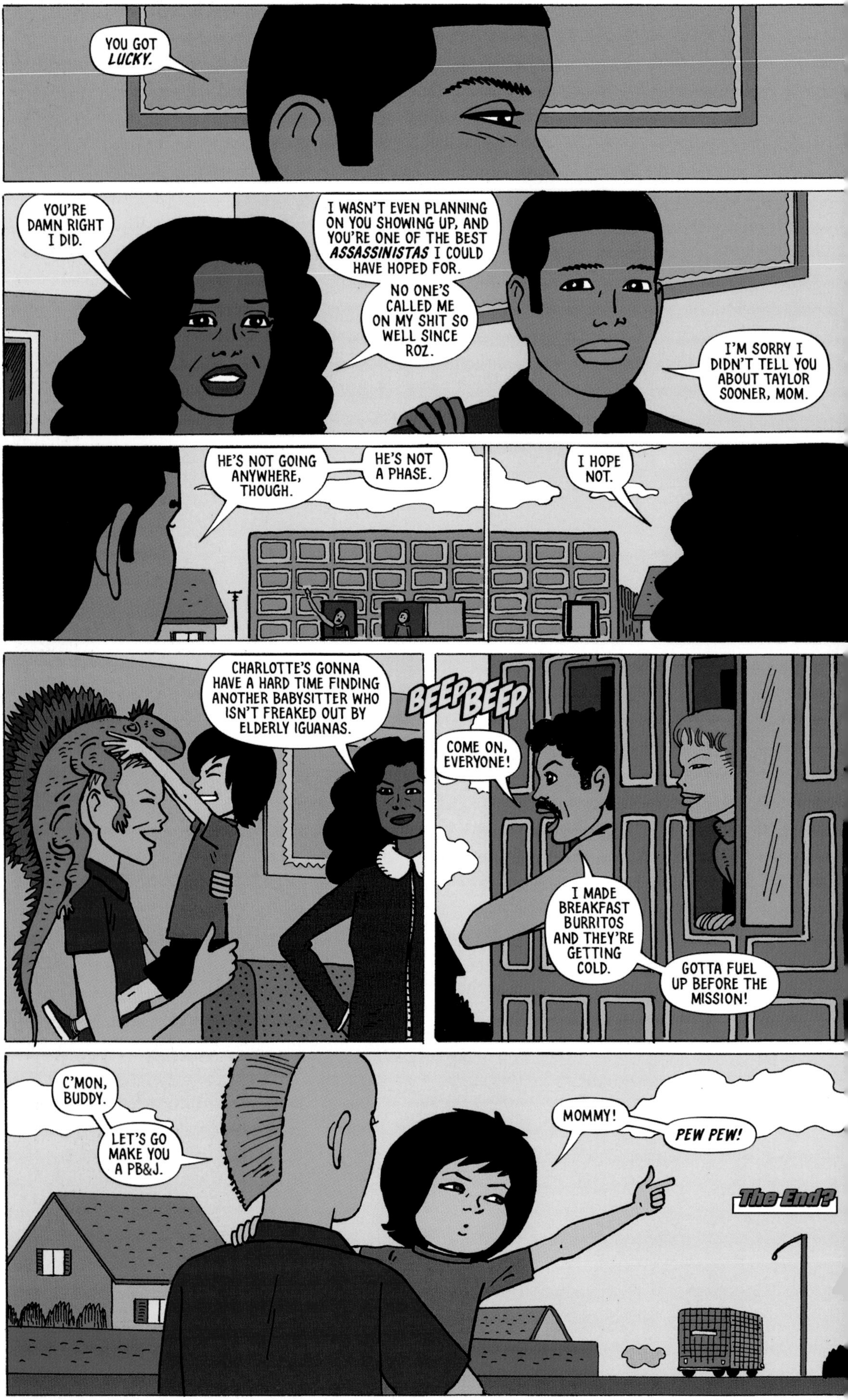

YOU GOT *LUCKY.*
YOU'RE DAMN RIGHT I DID.
I WASN'T EVEN PLANNING ON YOU SHOWING UP, AND YOU'RE ONE OF THE BEST *ASSASSINISTAS* I COULD HAVE HOPED FOR.
NO ONE'S CALLED ME ON MY SHIT SO WELL SINCE ROZ.
I'M SORRY I DIDN'T TELL YOU ABOUT TAYLOR SOONER, MOM.
HE'S NOT GOING ANYWHERE, THOUGH.
HE'S NOT A PHASE.
I HOPE NOT.
CHARLOTTE'S GONNA HAVE A HARD TIME FINDING ANOTHER BABYSITTER WHO ISN'T FREAKED OUT BY ELDERLY IGUANAS.
BEEP BEEP
COME ON, EVERYONE!
I MADE BREAKFAST BURRITOS AND THEY'RE GETTING COLD.
GOTTA FUEL UP BEFORE THE MISSION!
C'MON, BUDDY.
LET'S GO MAKE YOU A PB&J.
MOMMY!
PEW PEW!
The End?

ASSASSINISTAS

SUPPLEMENTARY MATERIAL

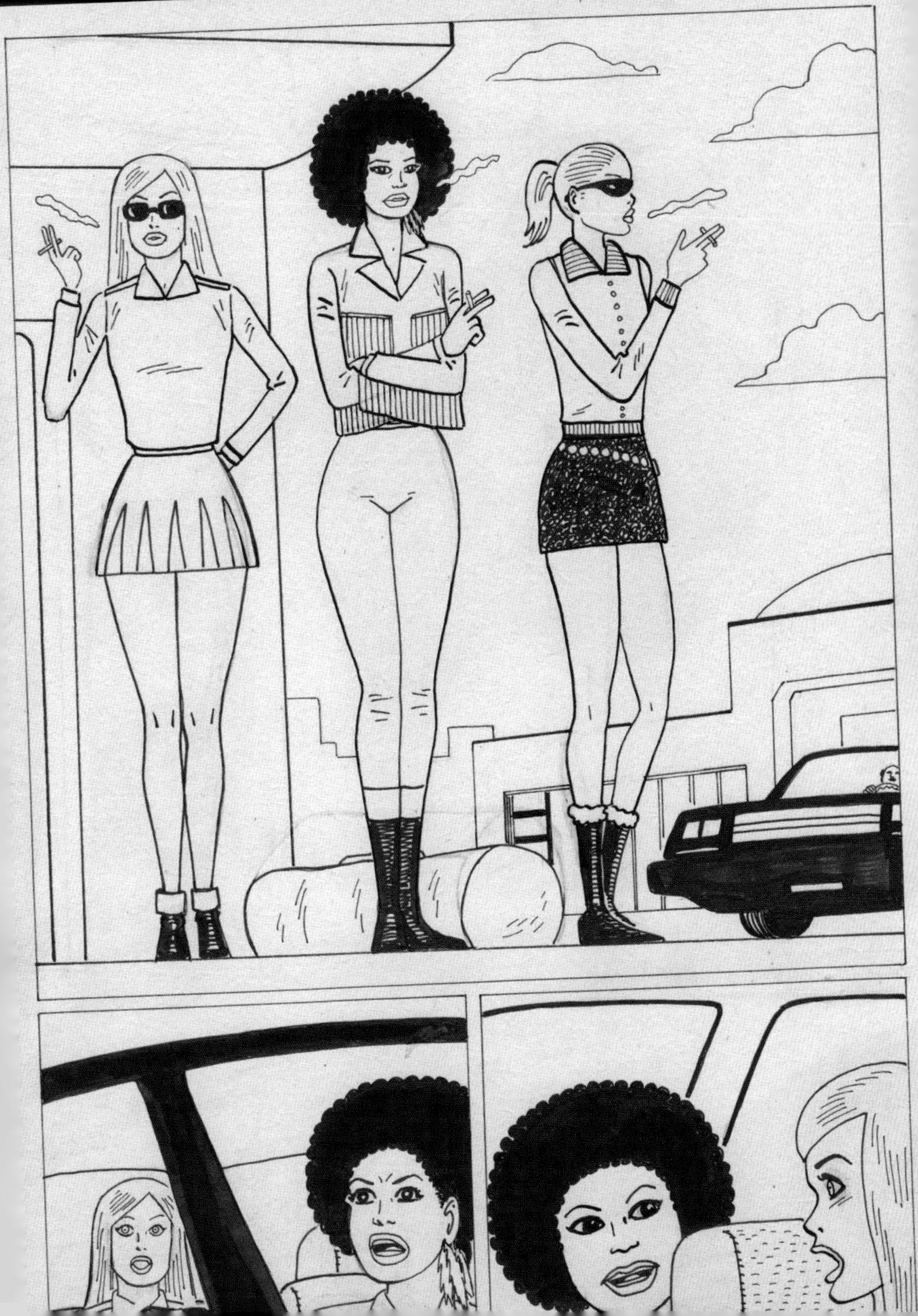

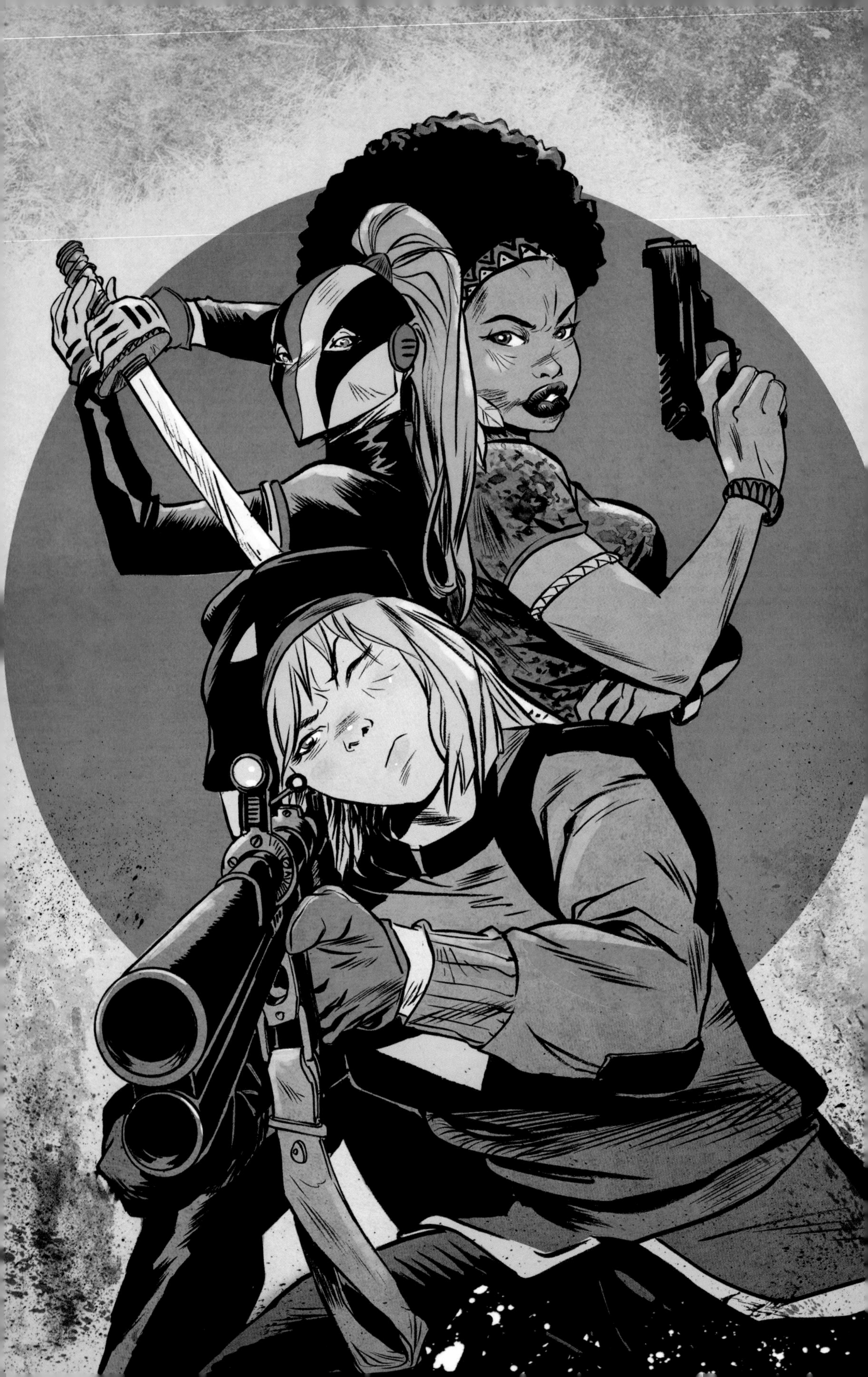

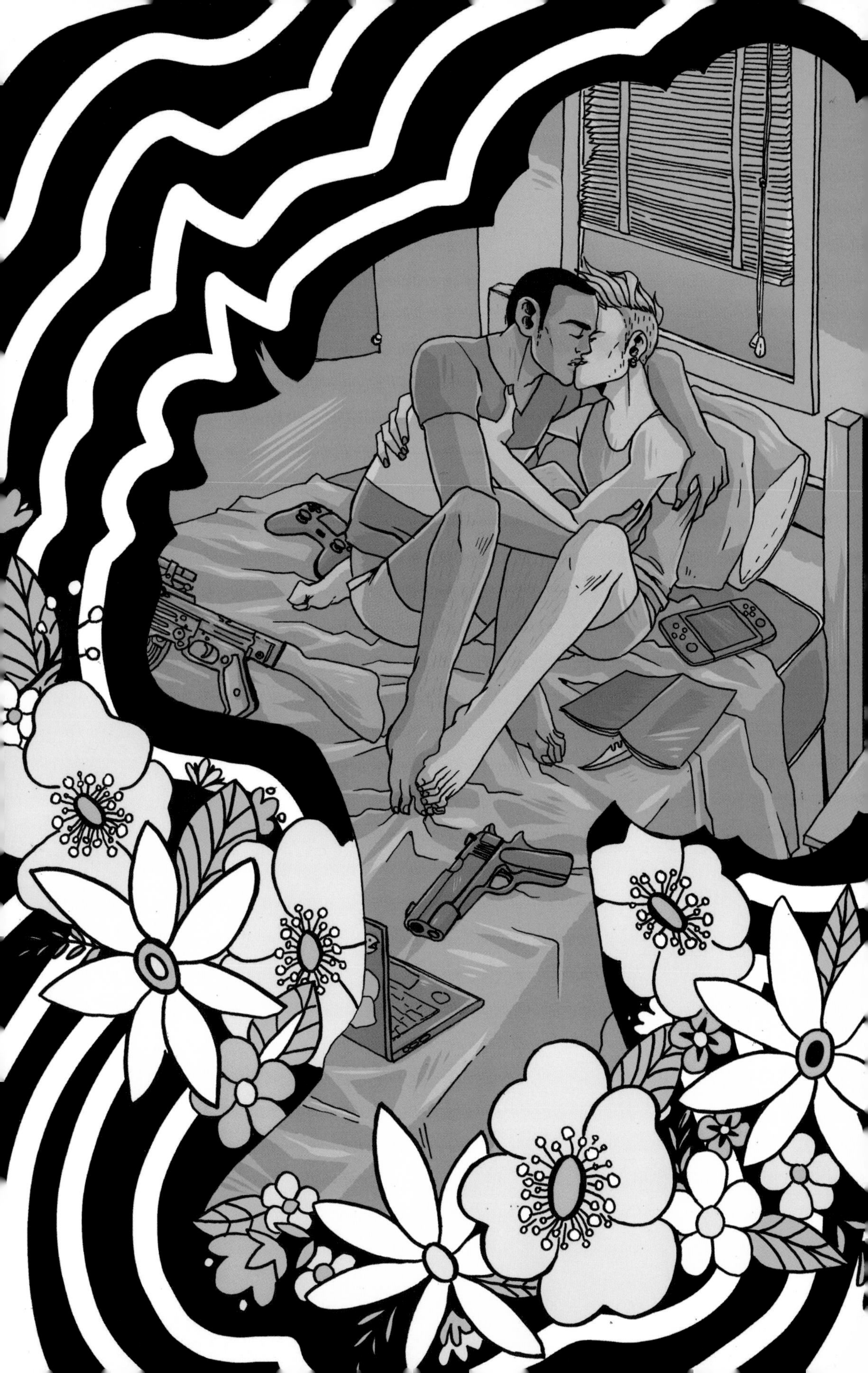

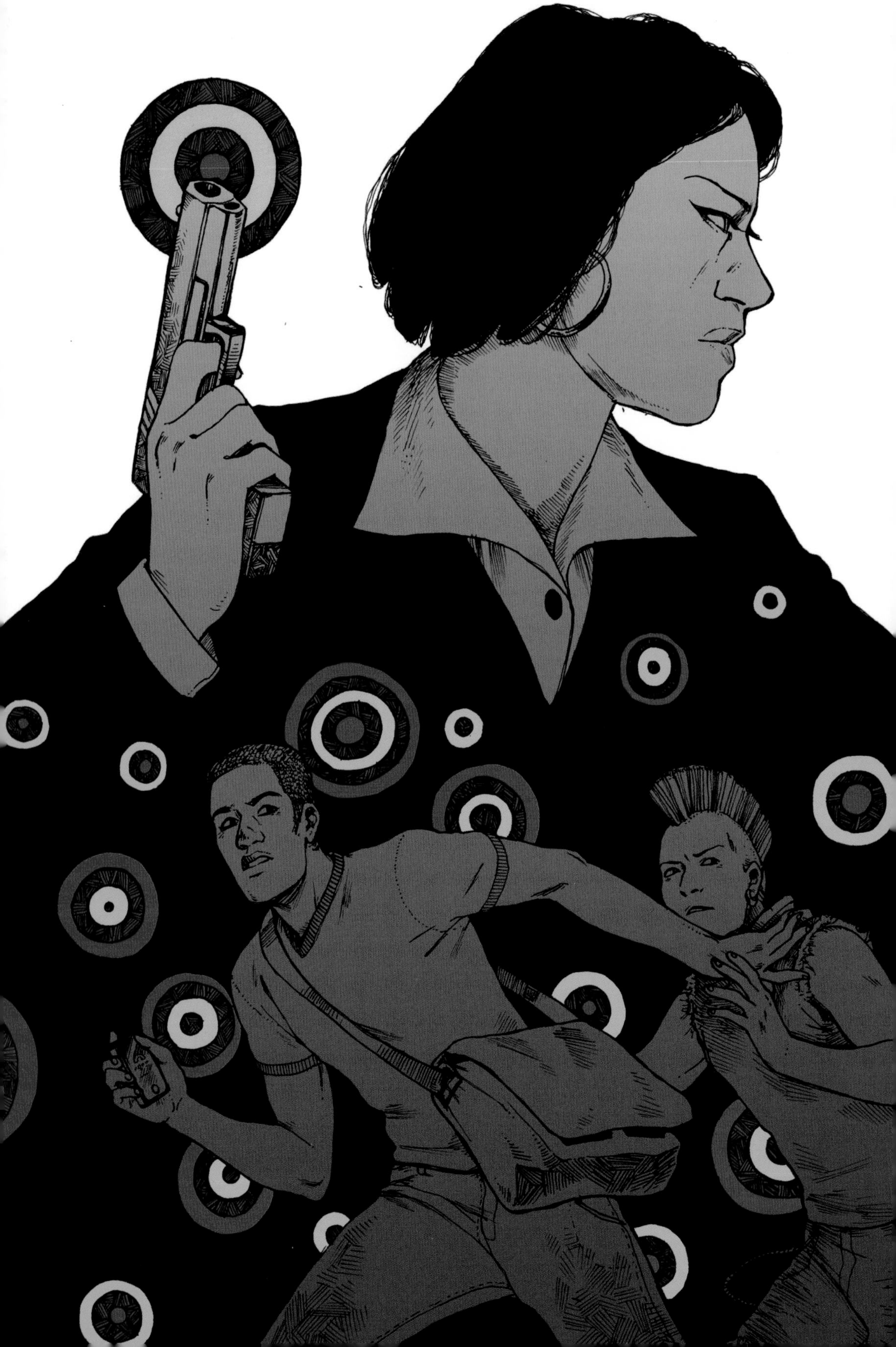

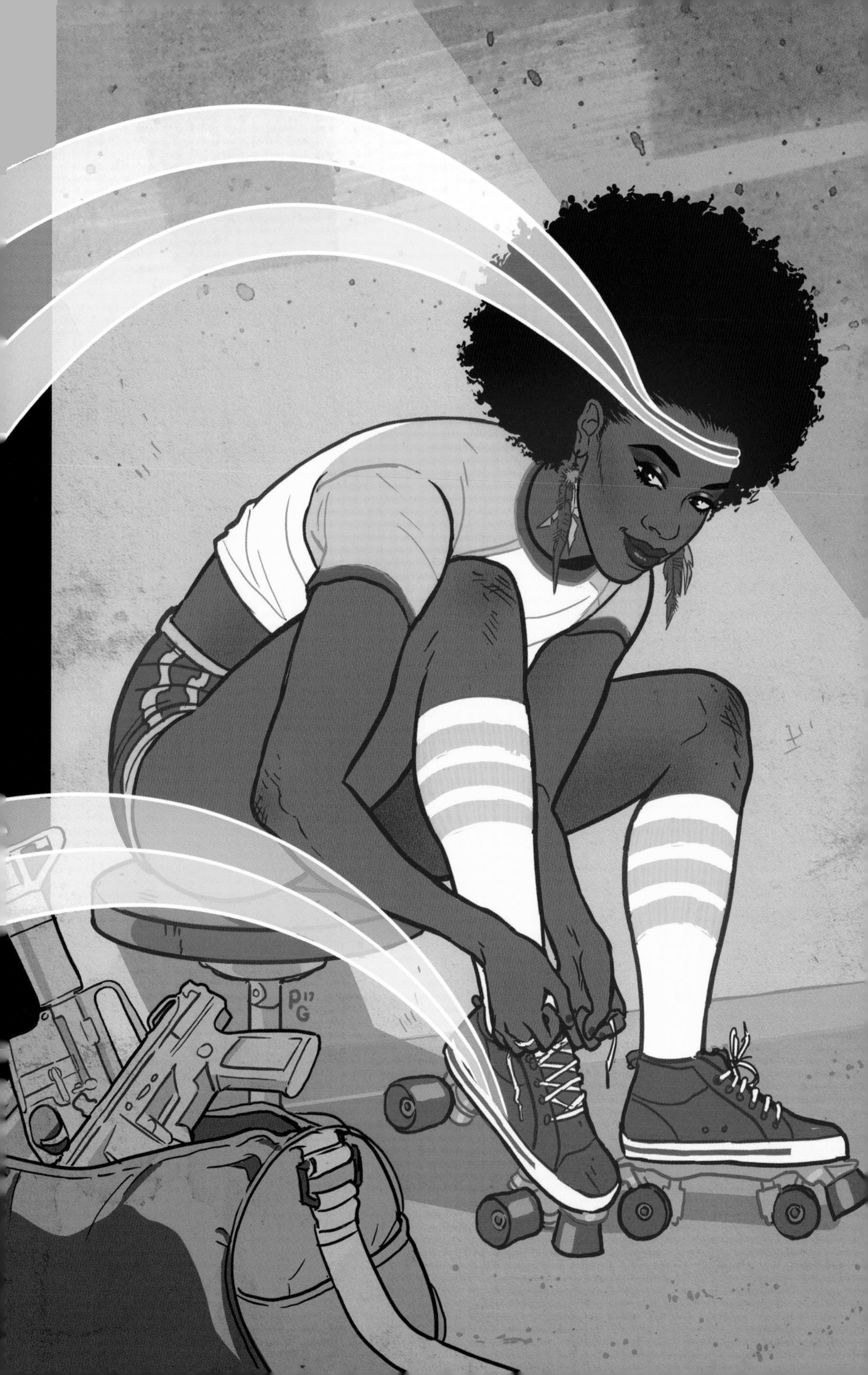

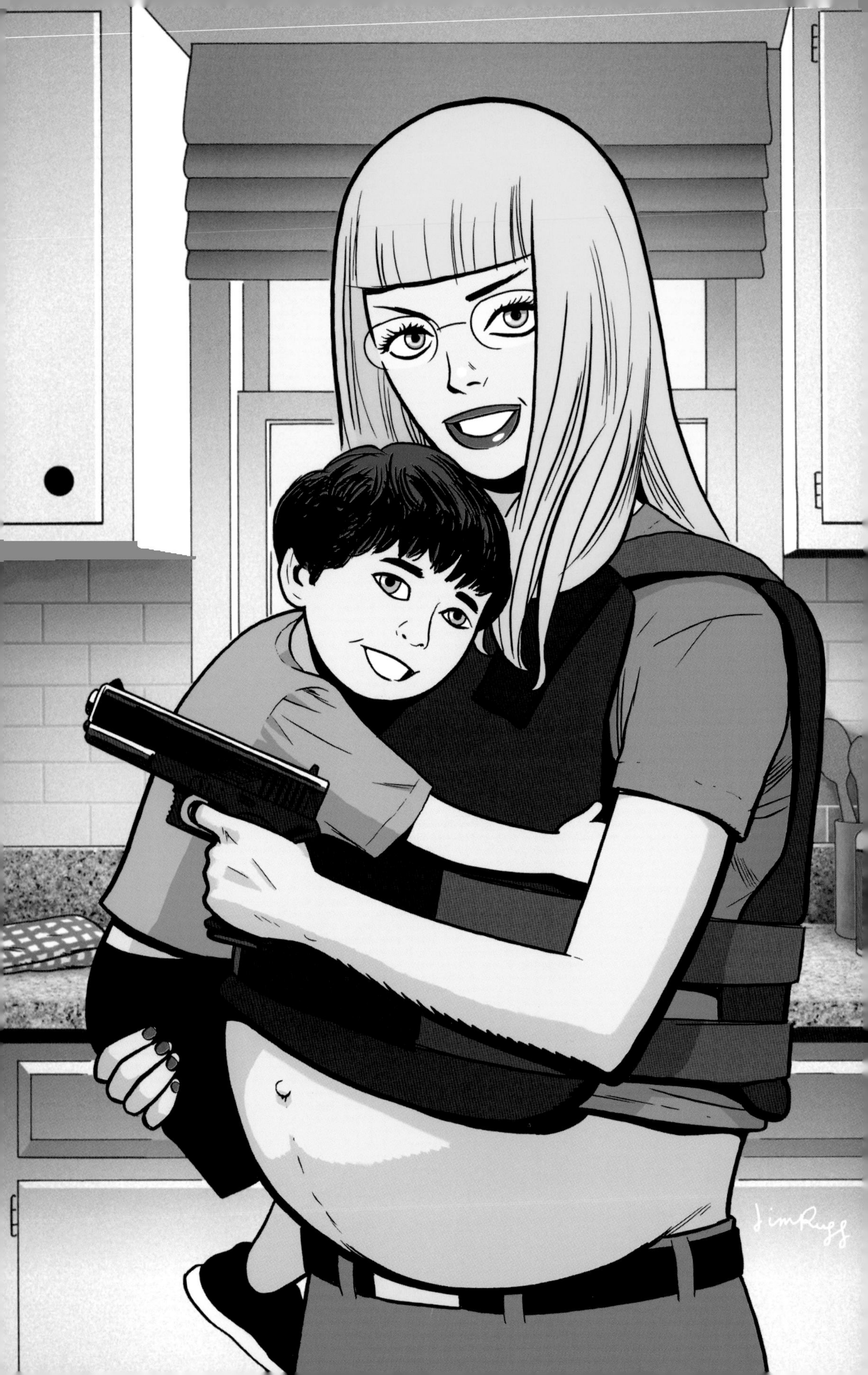
JimRugg

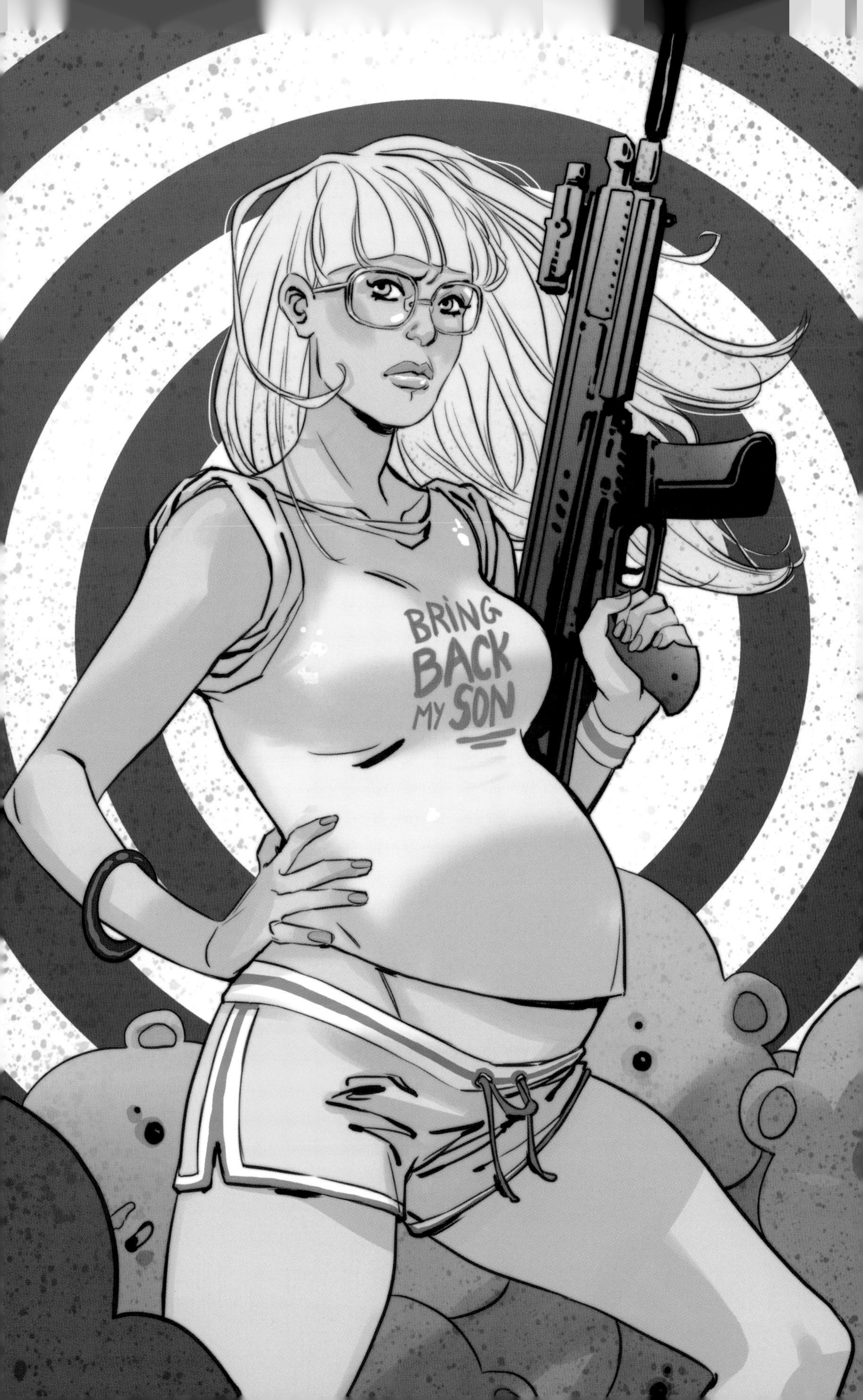
BRING BACK MY SON

ASSASSINISTA

DEAR DOSSIER

4/12/2017

ello, Gilbert!

o, here are some thoughts I've had about the characters. Obviously y genius when it comes to designing amazing characters, and I can't he ready imagine them in your style. Feel free to go weird, go retro, go c Tarantino, go wherever you want with it. Some of these notes are ob t visual but contain notes on personality so you can think about what xpressions you might draw on them.

ank you!
ni

ctavia "Red October" Price:

rican-American, age 43. A morally questionable insurance saleswoman w st as a top-secret super-assassin. Deathstroke, if he was played by Pam d retired. Now, she works a boring insurance job she hates, but the pro her son Dominic's tuition. Vices include smoking, eating fast food meals , and lying to her son to protect him.

ung Octavia: Pam Grier does Deathstroke. Feather earrings, big hair, he nds, and bullet belts. Young Octavia has a little bit of Poly Styrene's loo out her, even.

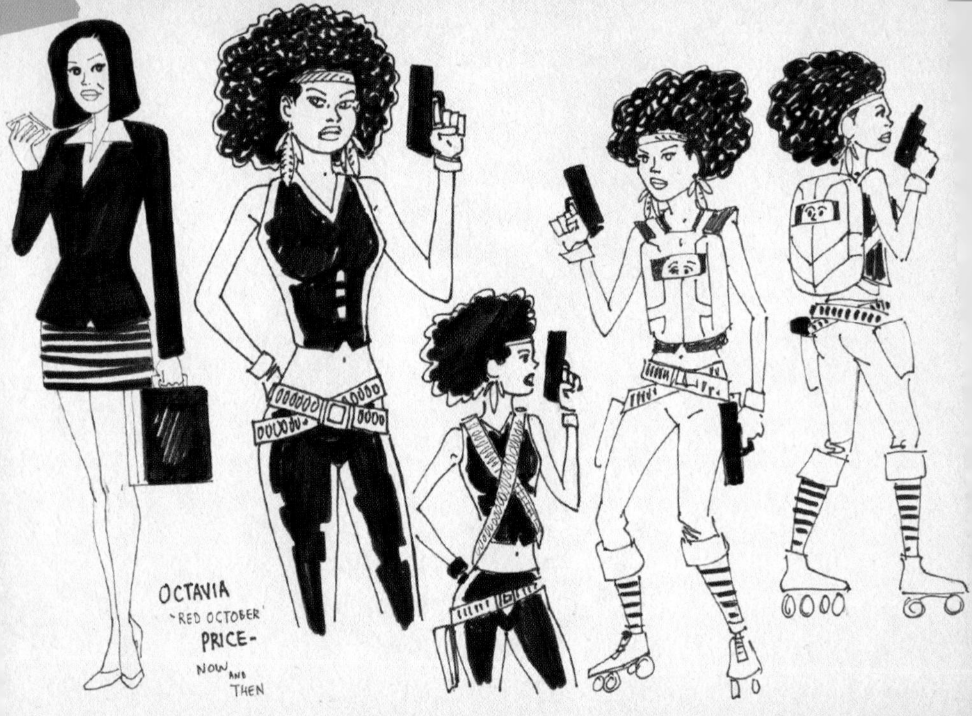
OCTAVIA
"RED OCTOBER"
PRICE-
NOW AND THEN

Rosalyn "Blood" Diamond:

Korean-American. Age: ?? Our villain. Rosalyn was once a part of Octavia's crew, who has returned to the assassin world now that her daughter is grown. Wears, and has always worn, a mask and suit, mech-style that conceals her face. (We see her face in the beginning of issue 1, and in the flashbacks - she has dyed red hair.)

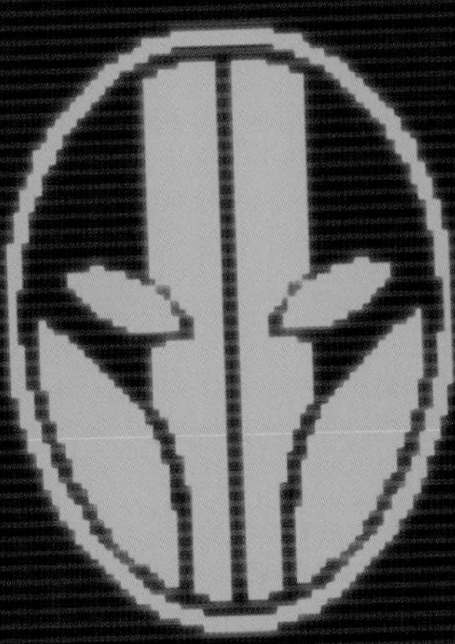

Charlotte "Scarlet" LaCosta:

White, blonde, glasses. 41 years old. Formerly an assassin alongside Octavia and Rosalyn, Charlotte is now one of many former assassins who hung up their guns in the past ten years in order to retire and have children. A helicopter mommy to the Nth degree, assisted by the fact that she's spent much of her life kicking ass from an actual helicopter. Her son, Kyler, is now the center of her world.

Young Charlotte, aka "Scarlet": The freckled "good girl" of the group, she's a sniper who tends toward outfits that look like you could play tennis in them - militaristic berets and epaulets are her murder-aesthetic of choice.

Kyler LaCosta: A chubby, screechy little kid. Dark hair, he's 5 years old, but acts three. It's not his fault. He gets a little cooler as the story goes on. He's most often seen in a T-shirt that reads 'DON'T FEED ME - I HAVE ALLERGIES!'

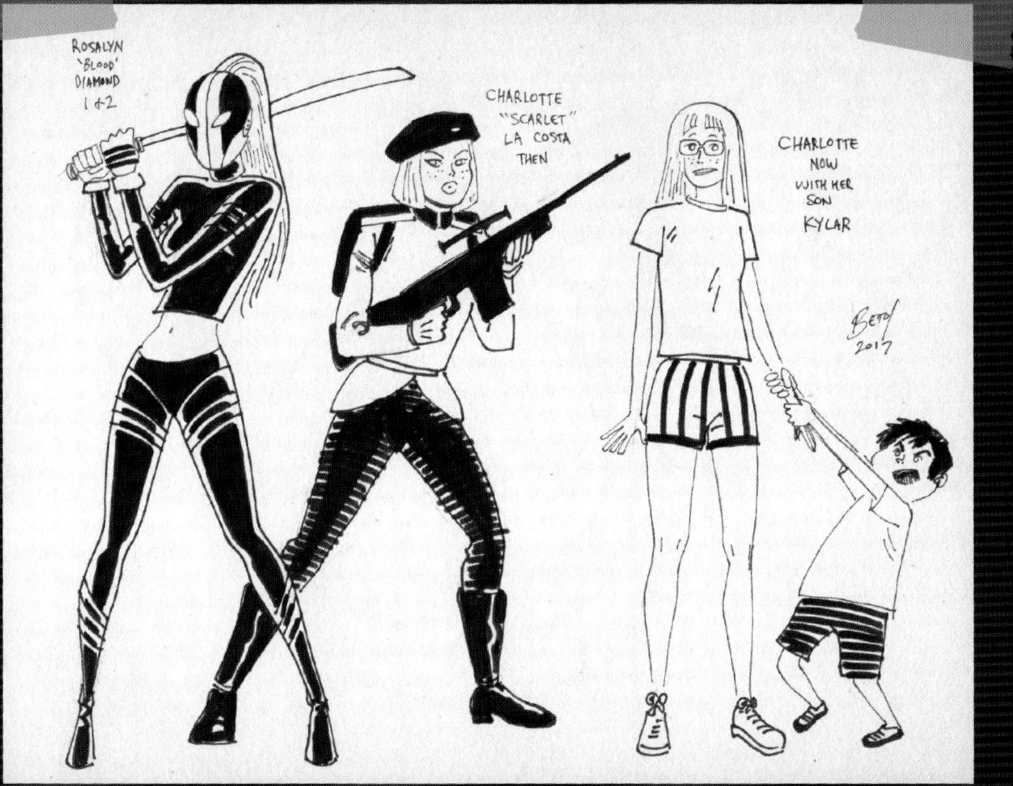
ROSALYN 'BLOOD' DIAMOND 1 & 2
CHARLOTTE "SCARLET" LA COSTA THEN
CHARLOTTE NOW WITH HER SON KYLAR
BETSY 2017

2/27/2017
EDIT* 4/17/2017

4.17.17

Run Tini's note to Gilbert on website + in preview book? Amazing! Every writer should be so warm + inviting. And trés adorbs! ♡ SB

ASSASSINISTAS (#1 of 6)

Dear Gilbert Hernandez -

Honored just to be writing that. <3 Thank you for taking a look at this.

Some notes on the book: I've described *Assassinistas* as a *Kill Bill* story in a *Venture Brothers* world. The perfect fusion of deep themes of revenge, obsolescence, and the fear your parents don't know what they're doing - but depicted with cartoon precision. I can't think of anyone better to be drawing that than you.

A note on the Assassinistas themselves - we see them in two phases in their lives during the comic. The younger version of themselves, when they were mercenaries, which I describe as 'Then' and the older, settled down versions of themselves years later, with kids and jobs, which I refer to as 'Now-ish.' These time frames are nothing specific, somewhat on purpose. The 'Then' shots of the Assassinistas can be as retro or as not as we please - we can make fabulous takes on anything from Emma Peel to Charlie's Angels to Foxy Brown to the Go-Gos. They should be bright, wild, and (something I trust you to do so well) *sexy*. I think with a woman writer and an artist *so amazingly skilled* at rendering women's bodies that are diverse and real, we can make the young Assassinistas sexy in a way that isn't objectifying, and I'd like very much to do that with you.

(A note on the Go-Gos - that first scene is somewhat inspired by stories of those girls misbehaving in hotel rooms on tour. So perhaps they're a good inspiration after all.)

As for 'Now,' it's modern, cool, with bits of that same energy just desperate to sneak back into our characters' lives. Our lead boys, Dominic and Taylor, are college kids, full of passion, emotion, frustration, and a search for purpose. I can't wait to see the expressions you do, their love for each other, their arguments, and their adoration for Octavia (our lead) through your work.

Thank you again.

Tini

Let's add 2 pages for the first issue: A rollerboogie assassins flashback chase scene? Could also let Gilbert choose a scene to extend as the second page. Need another big moment!

★Add more gravitas to the backstory/ glory days. by ways of additional items, Octavia digs up?

Please # pages! → | ← *thanks! SB*

PAGE ONE

Panel 1. Daytime, interior, a mid-range, standard motor hotel room. The room has that day-afte (almost a comic convention) smell of pizza boxes, champagne, makeup, curling irons - but *this* ro has the faint metallic tang of recently-cleaned rifles, boxes of ammunition. It's late afternoon, sur but fading. For now, we see a wide panel, top of page. A splatter of red across a tile floor. Should gory as a plain splash of red can. It's not blood - but it's gotta look like it.

CAPTION
Then

OCTAVIA, OFFPANEL: What have you *done?*

Panel 2. A young woman of Korean descent, around 21, kneeling on a closed toilet with a bunch of red dye in her bleached hair. This is Rosalyn "Blood" Diamond. She's gotten it everywhere, somewhat sloppily, and she's laughing, doesn't really care. The bathroom should be something of a war zone, lipstick and hairspray and bullet belts and magazines - both of the fashion and ammunition sort. A few truly absurd outfit choices - a leopard print crop top, torn up leggings, etc - hang over the towel rack and shower curtain.

Watching this, speaking, leaning in the doorway, is Octavia "Red October" Price. She's got a young Pam Grier thing going on - big hair, feather earrings, but also sort of obviously dressed like a hair metal, cosplay version of an assassin. She's also in her early twenties.

ROSALYN: What?! I don't know why we haven't dyed our hair red *before*, honestly.

OCTAVIA: This is a *hotel room,* they're going to charge us out the *ass* for that stain.

ROSALYN: So *what!* After *this* job we can buy and *sell* this place. C'mon, Octavia, offing stuck-up CEOs comes with a reward *far* beyond the financial...

SFX: (Offpanel, a gun cocking) KA-KLIK!

Panel 3. Another girl, white, blonde, laying in the hotel bed, holding a sniper rifle to her eyes. She's recently woken up, an eyemask pushed up into her hair, her tanktop all rumpled. She's still half under the blankets. She's aiming.

CHARLOTTE: Y'all woke me up.

Panel 4. Octavia and Roz, through the scope. Roz is shocked, laughing. Octavia is raising an eyebrow.

2

OCTAVIA: ...
(beat)
You ready, my *assassinistas?*

Handwritten margin notes (left side): Love the fact that Tim brought up smell on page 1, panel 1. I call that talent

Handwritten note (bottom left): nice!

Handwritten page number (bottom): 3

When my mother was a little girl, she had kidnapping insurance on her.

It's true - my grandfather (rest his soul) was a somewhat high-profile CIA agent, and her being kidnapped was a very real possibility, I suppose. She's going to hate me for saying this. I don't know if I blame her: a childhood spent with things like "kidnapping insurance" hanging over one's head can lead to a sort of craving for normalcy, a life as far from the "badass" and "fantastic" as one can imagine.

Ultimately, that's what ASSASSINISTAS is all about.

Most of us, I think, are pretty mundane. We crave adventure in the great wide somewhere, to paraphrase a French peasant girl and a litigious mouse, because for most of us, it's just a fantasy. Adventure, for most of us, means a carefully planned weekend at a beachside resort, or a backpacking trip through some of the world's most populated cities. An unplanned drive down a planned and maintained highway.

The tradeoff for real adventure is danger, and while most of us are eager to say we'd make the trade any day (*I* sure am), I have the strange privilege of being raised by someone who wouldn't. Perhaps real danger makes us crave normalcy the way normalcy makes us crave adventure.

Dominic and Octavia are the opposite of my mother and me, that way. She's very safe, and always kept me very safe. As a result, I have adopted one of the world's most dangerous lifestyles — freelance writer. Who knows? Maybe I'm the Octavia, out here with my flak jacket on, baring my guts to the world and hoping they pay me for the privilege. Maybe someday I'll have a Dominic of my own, a brilliant, deep, take-no-shit beautiful son who looks at me and says "Mom, let's just be normal."

I can only hope I'll be so lucky.

Tini Howard, co-creator/writer.

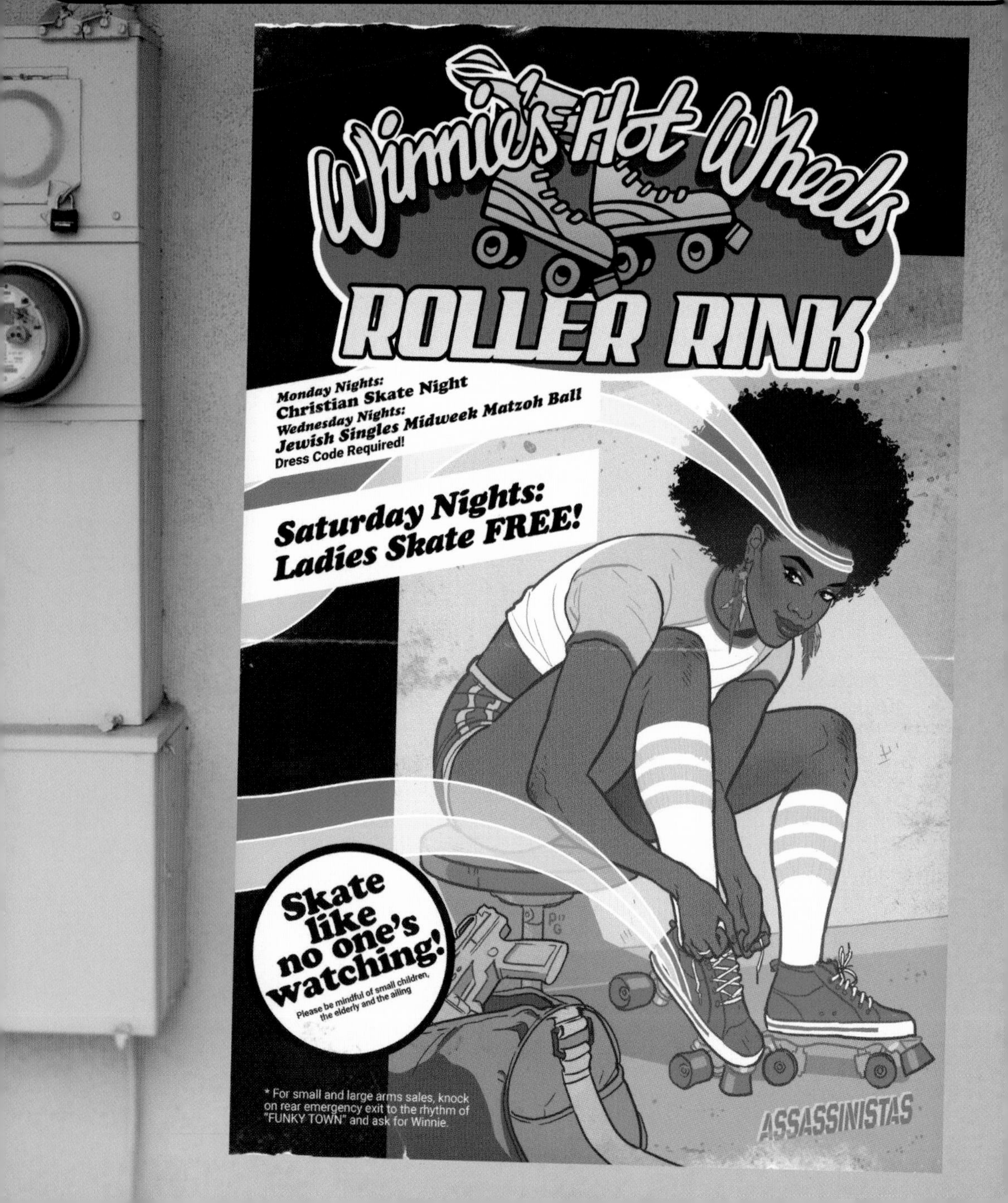

Winnie's Hot Wheels
ROLLER RINK
Monday Nights:
Christian Skate Night
Wednesday Nights:
Jewish Singles Midweek Matzoh Ball
Dress Code Required!
Saturday Nights:
Ladies Skate FREE!
Skate like no one's watching!
Please be mindful of small children, the elderly and the ailing
* For small and large arms sales, knock on rear emergency exit to the rhythm of "FUNKY TOWN" and ask for Winnie.
ASSASSINISTAS

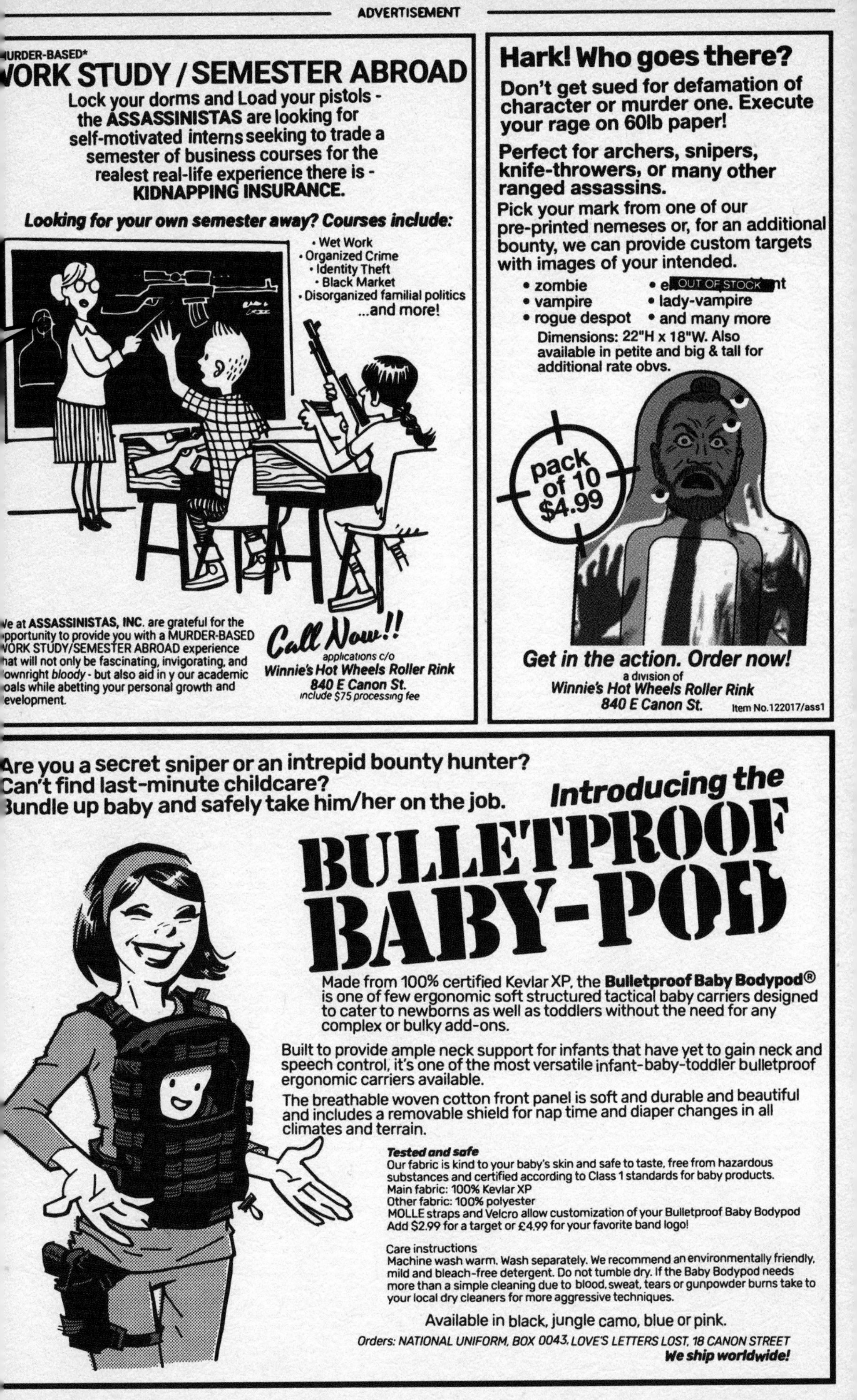
ADVERTISEMENT
URDER-BASED*
ORK STUDY / SEMESTER ABROAD
Lock your dorms and Load your pistols - the ASSASSINISTAS are looking for self-motivated interns seeking to trade a semester of business courses for the realest real-life experience there is - KIDNAPPING INSURANCE.
Looking for your own semester away? Courses include:
• Wet Work
• Organized Crime
• Identity Theft
• Black Market
• Disorganized familial politics
...and more!
/e at ASSASSINISTAS, INC. are grateful for the pportunity to provide you with a MURDER-BASED ORK STUDY/SEMESTER ABROAD experience hat will not only be fascinating, invigorating, and ownright bloody - but also aid in y our academic oals while abetting your personal growth and evelopment.
Call Now!!
applications c/o
Winnie's Hot Wheels Roller Rink
840 E Canon St.
include $75 processing fee
Hark! Who goes there?
Don't get sued for defamation of character or murder one. Execute your rage on 60lb paper!
Perfect for archers, snipers, knife-throwers, or many other ranged assassins.
Pick your mark from one of our pre-printed nemeses or, for an additional bounty, we can provide custom targets with images of your intended.
• zombie
• vampire
• rogue despot
• e OUT OF STOCK nt
• lady-vampire
• and many more
Dimensions: 22"H x 18"W. Also available in petite and big & tall for additional rate obvs.
pack of 10 $4.99
Get in the action. Order now!
a division of
Winnie's Hot Wheels Roller Rink
840 E Canon St.
Item No.122017/ass1
Are you a secret sniper or an intrepid bounty hunter?
Can't find last-minute childcare?
Bundle up baby and safely take him/her on the job.
Introducing the
BULLETPROOF BABY-POD
Made from 100% certified Kevlar XP, the Bulletproof Baby Bodypod® is one of few ergonomic soft structured tactical baby carriers designed to cater to newborns as well as toddlers without the need for any complex or bulky add-ons.
Built to provide ample neck support for infants that have yet to gain neck and speech control, it's one of the most versatile infant-baby-toddler bulletproof ergonomic carriers available.
The breathable woven cotton front panel is soft and durable and beautiful and includes a removable shield for nap time and diaper changes in all climates and terrain.
Tested and safe
Our fabric is kind to your baby's skin and safe to taste, free from hazardous substances and certified according to Class 1 standards for baby products.
Main fabric: 100% Kevlar XP
Other fabric: 100% polyester
MOLLE straps and Velcro allow customization of your Bulletproof Baby Bodypod
Add $2.99 for a target or £4.99 for your favorite band logo!
Care instructions
Machine wash warm. Wash separately. We recommend an environmentally friendly, mild and bleach-free detergent. Do not tumble dry. If the Baby Bodypod needs more than a simple cleaning due to blood, sweat, tears or gunpowder burns take to your local dry cleaners for more aggressive techniques.
Available in black, jungle camo, blue or pink.
Orders: NATIONAL UNIFORM, BOX 0043, LOVE'S LETTERS LOST, 18 CANON STREET
We ship worldwide!

TEAM ASSASSINISTA_

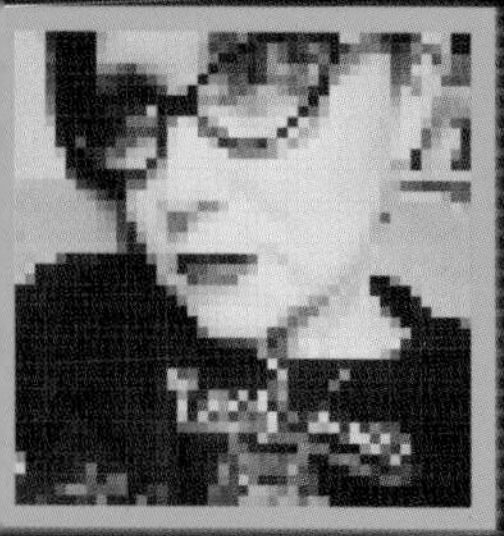

TINI HOWARD

s a writer and swamp witch from the Carolina Wilds. Co-creator/writer of EUTHANAUTS with co-creator/artist Nick Robles, Tini also writes Hack/Slash: Resurrection, with occasional stories for two of her favorite things: Rick and Morty and WWE. Her previous work includes Ghost-Walk with Me from the BLACK CROWN QUARTERLY #3, The Skeptics (Black Mask Studios), and a contribution to FEMME MAGNIFIQUE. @TiniHoward

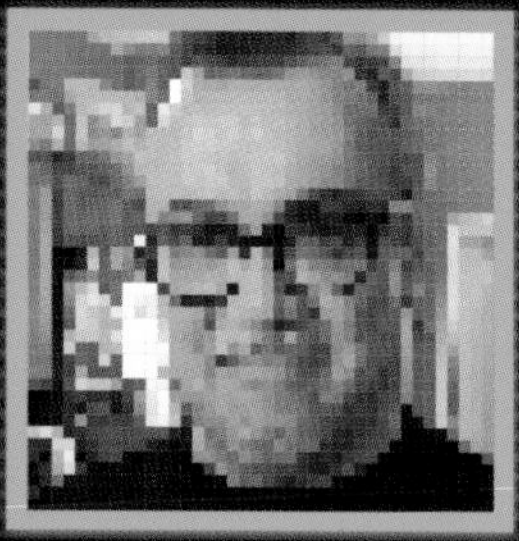

GILBERT HERNA

is the creator, with his brother Love And Rockets, a modern cla debuted in 1981. Gilbert has a with DC, Dark Horse, IDW, and D Quarterly. In 2017, Gilbert and inducted into the Will Eisner Ha Gilbert lives in Las Vegas with h daughter. @BetomessGilbert

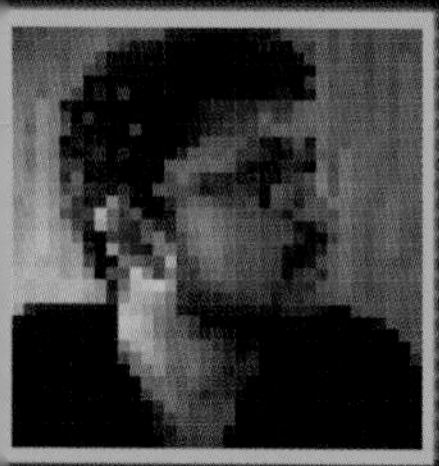

ADITYA BIDIKAR

s BLACK CROWN's esteemed house letterer and the recipient of Broken Frontier's 2017 Best Letterer Award. Based in India, Adi also letters Motor Crush, Grafity's Wall, and TS. Adi often covers the weekly bar tab at blackcrown.pub @adityab and adityab.net.

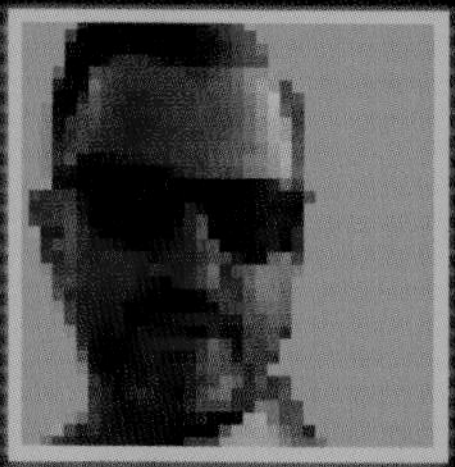

ROB DAVIS

is the ASSASSINISTAS colorist, and writer/artist of Tales from the Black Crown Pub in the BLACK CROWN QUARTERLY. He has been nominated for four Eisner awards for The Motherless Oven, Don Quixote and the anthology Nelson. He won two British Comic Awards and the Lycean prize for The Motherless Oven. @Robgog

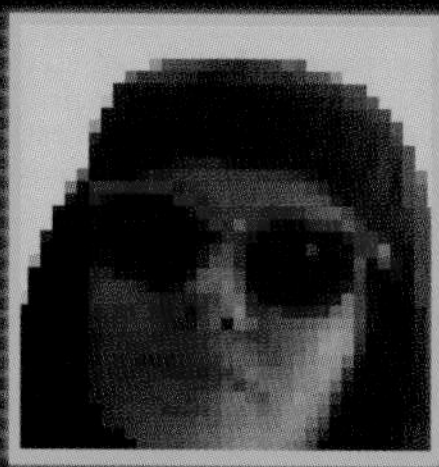

ROBIN HENL

is a freelance illustr designer, with a bur career in comics tha coloring assistance ASSASSINISTAS and color flats for Tales Black Crown. @Robi

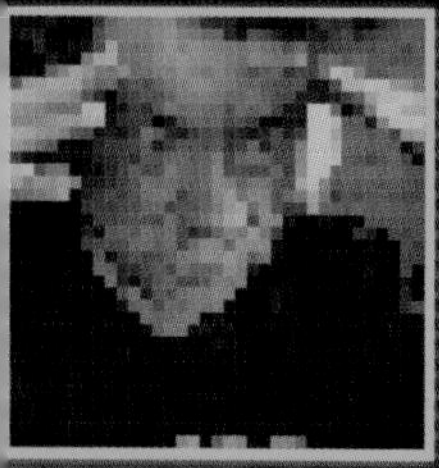

PHILIP BOND

s the logo and publication designer for ASSASSINISTAS and many fine BLACK CROWN titles. He is also the artist on CUD: Rich and Strange, a regular feature in the BLACK CROWN QUARTERLY. <help i am being held hostage at BCHQ and forced to make comics plz

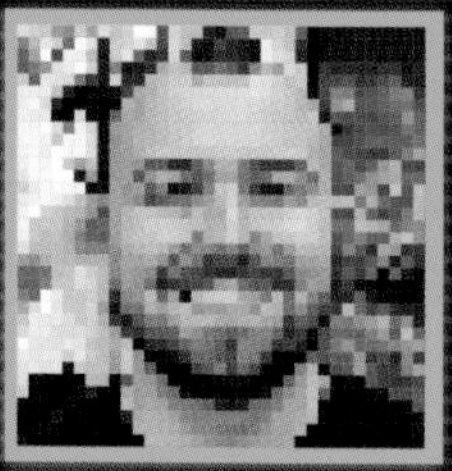

CHASE MAROTZ

started his comics career running the register at Outland Comics in Idaho Falls, Idaho. When not providing editorial assistance to the BLACK CROWN, he likes to go to pizza parties. He lives in San Diego with his wife, Lisa, and their two cats. @thrillothechase

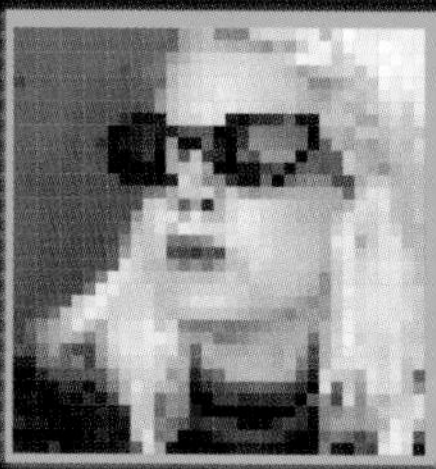

SHELLY BOND

has been driven to c curate comic books, deadlines and innov a quarter century. S Los Angeles with he Philip, their son Spe pair of spectator ta You can follow her e sartorial exploits o

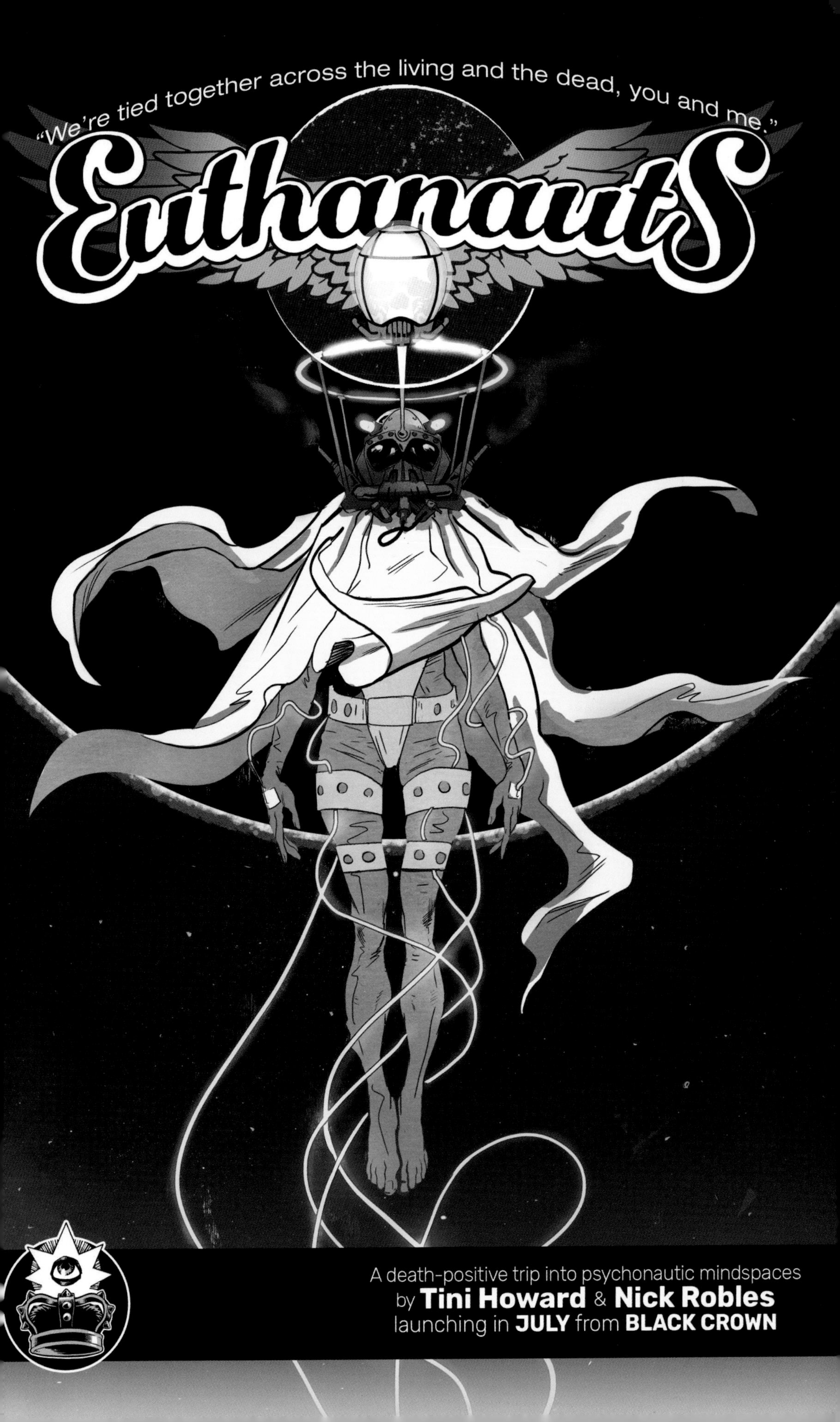

"We're tied together across the living and the dead, you and me."
Euthanauts
A death-positive trip into psychonautic mindspaces
by Tini Howard & Nick Robles
launching in JULY from BLACK CROWN

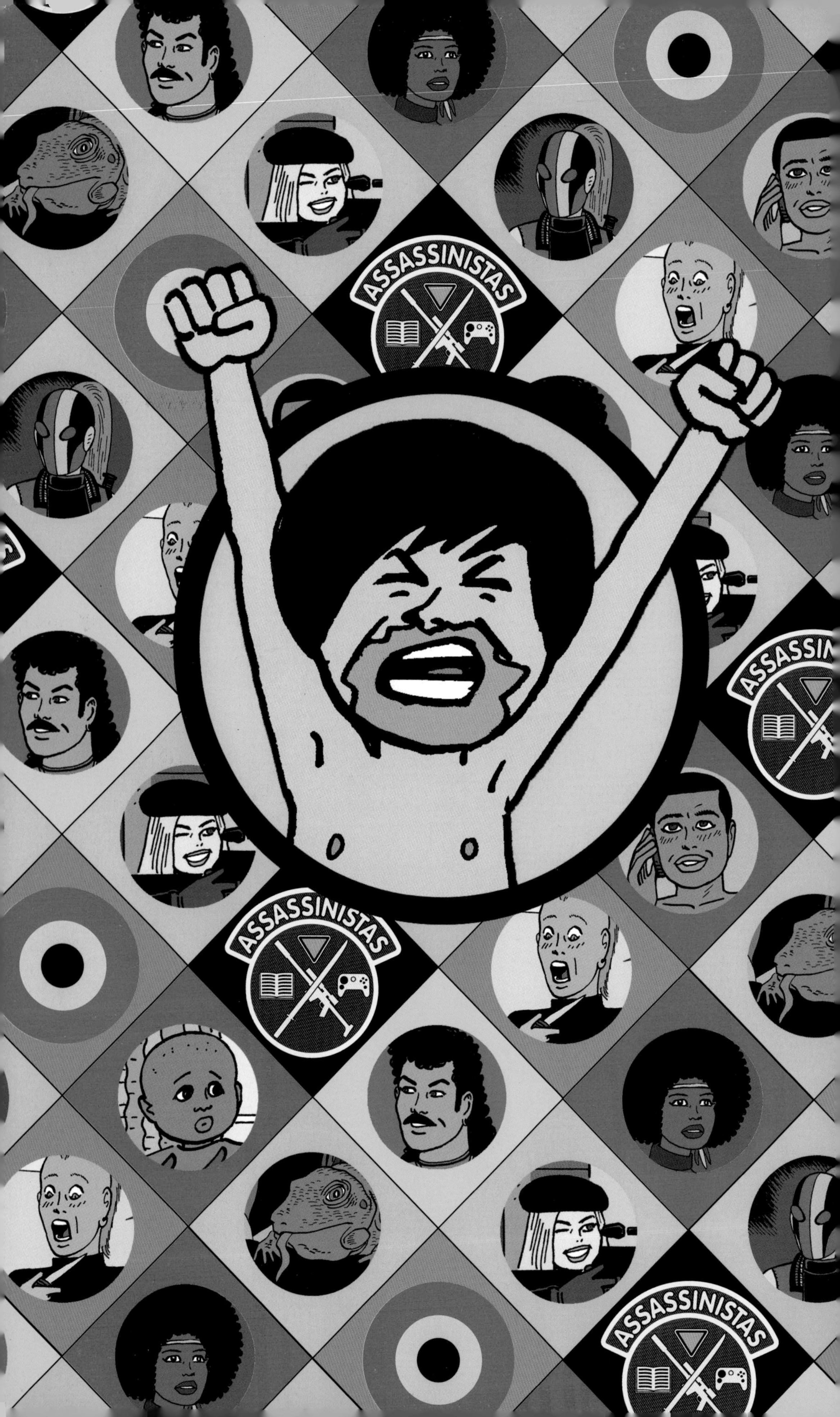
ASSASSINISTAS